Connections after Colonialism

ATLANTIC CROSSINGS
Rafe Blaufarb, Series Editor

Connections after Colonialism

Europe and Latin America in the 1820s

Edited by MATTHEW BROWN
and GABRIEL PAQUETTE

THE UNIVERSITY OF ALABAMA PRESS

Tuscaloosa

Typeface: Granjon

*Desembarque d'el Rei Dom João VI. Acompanhado por uma deputação das cortes, Na
Magnifica Praça do Terreiro do Paço em 4 de Julho d'1821, regressando do Brazil.*
Reproduced with the permission of the John Carter Brown Library, Brown
University, Providence, Rhode Island.

∞

The paper on which this book is printed meets the minimum requirements of
American National Standard for Information Sciences—Permanence of Paper for
Printed Library Materials, ANSI Z39.48-1984.

Library of Congress Cataloging-in-Publication Data

Connections after colonialism : Europe and Latin America in the 1820s / edited by
Matthew Brown and Gabriel Paquette.
p. cm. — (Atlantic crossings)
Includes bibliographical references and index.
ISBN 978-0-8173-1776-8 (trade cloth : alk. paper) — ISBN 978-0-8173-8639-9
(ebook) 1. Latin America—Relations—Europe. 2. Europe—Relations—Latin
America. 3. Latin America—History—Autonomy and independence movements.
4. Latin America—History—19th century. 5. Decolonization—Latin America.
6. Postcolonialism—Latin America. I. Brown, Matthew, 1975– II. Paquette, Gabriel
B., 1977–
F1416.E85C66 2013
327.804009'034—dc23

2012019818

Contents

Acknowledgments

This book is the result of a collaborative research project spanning several years. It would not have been possible without the financial support of the following institutions, which we are glad to acknowledge: Trinity College, Cambridge, particularly the managers of the Raymond and Beverly Sackler Conference Series Fund; the Cambridge Faculty of History, especially the managers of the Trevelyan Fund; Harvard University's Center for History and Economics; the University of Bristol's Institute for Research in the Humanities and Arts (BIRTHA); the Royal Historical Society; the University of Bristol's Centre for the Study of Colonial and Postcolonial Societies; and the Cambridge Centre of Latin American Studies.

We thank the Master and Fellows of Trinity College for hosting the symposium "Re-thinking the 1820s" in May 2009, from which this volume has emerged. We also extend our gratitude to the college's staff for the logistical support provided and hospitality extended during the symposium. The volume was completed thanks to the support of the Department of Hispanic, Portuguese, and Latin American Studies at the University of Bristol and the Department of History at Johns Hopkins University.

We are also glad for the opportunity to acknowledge the support and assistance of individuals who assisted us in various and indispensable ways during the evolution of the project: Chris Bayly, Robert Bickers, Rafe Blaufarb, David Brading, Melissa Calaresu, the late Michael Costeloe, Richard Drayton, Rebecca Earle, John Fisher, Susan Harrow, David Hook, Francis King, Inga Huld Markan, Anthony McFarlane, Phil Morgan, Amy Price,

Lucy Riall, Emma Rothschild, Neil Safier, Rupert Shortt, David Todd, and Alastair Wilson. We have benefited from the constant support and inspiration of Brian Hamnett from the first idea until the final piece of punctuation.

At The University of Alabama Press, we are grateful to the two anonymous reviewers and to Dan Waterman, Dan Ross, Rubye Harrison, Claire Evans, and Joseph Powell for guiding this project toward publication. The ideas and suggestions of Rafe Blaufarb and Christopher Schmidt-Nowara, the academic editors of the Atlantic Crossings series, were both indispensable as we sought to conceptualise the project and realize its ramifications for a wide body of scholarship. Assistance with the bibliography was provided by Arismendi da Silva and Ana Suarez Vidal.

In writing our introduction we were heavily influenced by the discussions that took place at the Cambridge symposium, involving all of the contributors to this book and the *European History Quarterly* special issue (Natalia Sobrevilla Perea, Scott Eastman, and Mónica Ricketts). In addition, we would like to thank David Brading, Chris Bayly, Charles Jones, Tony McFarlane, and Rebecca Earle for their participation in our discussions, which we have drawn on here. We presented a draft of our introduction to the Conversatorio seminar series of the University of Bristol's Latin American Locus in May 2010 and are grateful for the comments of Caroline Williams and Jo Crow there.

We have worked on this project collaboratively since 2008, transnationally (between Cambridge, England, and Asturias, Spain), transcontinentally (between Bogotá, Colombia, and Boston, Massachusetts), and transatlantically (between Bristol, England, and Rio de Janeiro, Brazil, and Baltimore, Maryland). We are grateful to Natasha, Johanna, Calum, Keir, Morag, and Mairi for supporting and inspiring us through these migrations.

Connections after Colonialism

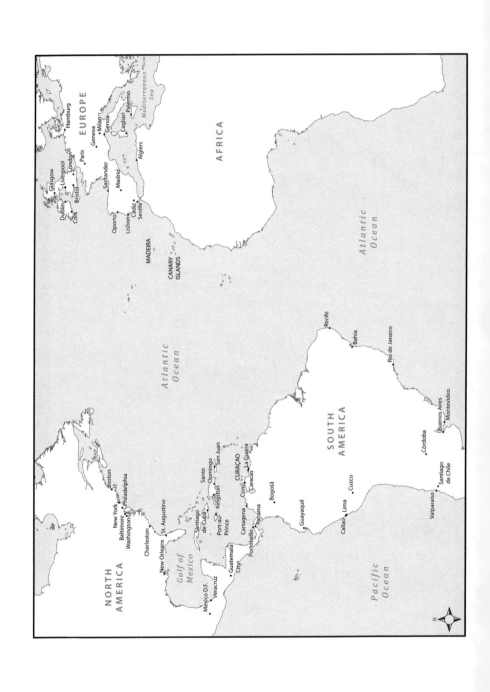

Introduction
Between the Age of Atlantic
Revolutions and the Age of Empire

Europe and Latin America in the Axial Decade of the 1820s

Matthew Brown and Gabriel Paquette

The decade of the 1820s occupies an uneasy place in the imagination of those historians who study the relationship—political, economic, and cultural—between Europe and Latin America.[1] The dominant image is one of rupture: the dramatic disaggregation of the Iberian empires in the crucible of turmoil wrought by two decades of war. With the coming of independence—for Brazil in 1822 and for much of Spanish America by 1825—Europe and Latin America appeared to experience divergent historical evolution, as the bonds that had fastened each to the other were irreparably severed.

New research has demonstrated, however, that the extent of this rupture, of the change wrought by "independence," has been exaggerated, often with a distorting effect. The dissolution of the Iberian empires did not abruptly sever the links between the Old World and the New, but instead dramatically shifted their terms, creating new political imaginaries and unleashing latent dynamics. The persistence of such connections, often overshadowed by the grand discontinuity of independence, is the subject of this book.[2] The volume is a collaborative attempt to assess the tumultuous decade of the 1820s and to examine connections—intellectual, political, cultural, and economic—between Europe and Latin America that were either reconfigured or forged during it.

≈

We brought together the contributors to this volume at a conference held at Trinity College, University of Cambridge, in May 2009 to discuss the extent of the continuity and change that occurred in the 1820s. Even before planes had landed and trains had pulled up, we found that our initial decision to focus attention on the 1820s had reignited long-dormant yet fundamental debates about chronology and periodization. We justified our decision to study this neglected decade because we shared James Dunkerley's conviction that historians should "break with orthodox chronology" in order to question received wisdoms about the past.[3] In most existing works of Atlantic and Latin American history, the 1820s appear either as the *end* of something important (i.e., colonial rule) or as the *beginning* of something else that became important subsequently (i.e., the "republican" or "national" period). In many accounts, "Independence" marks the end of one era and the beginning of another.[4] We wondered how the historiographical picture might appear if we removed the 1820s from these paradigms and identified the shifts and transformations unique to this decade.

During the course of two days of extended presentations and animated conversations, an exciting and unheralded portrait of the 1820s emerged. This was the decade when many nation-states were formed, from the fledgling postcolonial states of Peru and Bolivia to the shaken postimperial polities of metropolitan Spain and Portugal. These were heady years in financial terms too, with the London stock market bubble expanding and then crashing, bringing economic collapse in its wake in the Western Hemisphere. Civil wars rocked both Europe and the Americas while a tidal wave of liberalism crashed, with uneven effects, on both shores of the Atlantic. Amidst this turbulence, pivotal new figures, like British foreign secretary Lord Palmerston, Mexican president Antonio López de Santa Anna, and Portuguese statesman the Duke of Saldanha, rose to prominence while some of the previous generation's defining figures, such as Napoleon Bonaparte, Simón Bolívar, and Lord Castlereagh, faded away. Our discussions in Cambridge were necessarily wide ranging and sought to encompass the entire Atlantic world. In the chapters included in this volume, we concentrate on the relations of Britain, France, Spain, and Portugal with Mexico, Argentina, Colombia, Peru, and Brazil, though the United States and Italy make more than fleeting appearances in our assessment of the decade. Our introduction surveys the four main themes developed by the contributors in their respective chapters. These are the persistence of imperial dynamics in Latin America's external relationships after independence, the rise of new political cultures, the mutual interests—intellectual, cultural, and economic—that bound Europe and Latin America together after the end of formal dominion, and the prevalence (and discernible impact) of colonial legacies in both the Old World and the New.

International Relations in the 1820s

In the 1820s, power in the southern Atlantic passed from Iberian hands into British bottoms, the merchant ships operating out of English, Scottish, Welsh, and Irish ports that benefited from the British Royal Navy's new Atlantic supremacy. New commercial patterns shaped the new geopolitics under the influence of changing Atlantic trading patterns. New national elites in the Americas, however, sought to assert control over their own destinies. When we employ a transnational and comparative lens to analyze the 1820s, the decade acquires a coherence it might lack when studied through solitary national prisms. Amidst the morass of revolutions, coups, and constitutional changes, the prevalence of links between Europe and the Americas after independence affected in crucial ways the political trajectories of the individual states that emerged from the wreckage of the Iberian empires, including the former metropoles of Spain and Portugal.

These links were often denied or ignored at the time. Nineteenth-century intellectuals, including José Manuel Restrepo in Colombia, Lucas Alamán in Mexico, and Bartolomé Mitre in Argentina, who wrote the first histories of their nascent republics, bear partial responsibility for this neglect.[5] The institutional, intellectual, and economic inheritances with which the emergent nations were encumbered, Restrepo contended, hindered the formation of strong and independent nation-states.[6] Yet while disparaging the debilitating legacy of Iberian colonialism, many nineteenth-century historians shared the view that independence had shattered the chains between Europe and America. Many narratives written in the first generations after independence therefore highlighted the birth and maturation of an anticolonial, often anti-peninsular, national consciousness in the last decades of the eighteenth century whose full flowering would topple Spanish rule by 1820.[7] Later writers inherited this focus and depicted Spanish American independence and early national development as largely endogenous processes. They pitted *peninsulares* against Creoles, monarchists against republicans, stodgy defenders of the Old Regime against avant-garde revolutionaries, and enlightenment against tradition.[8] The continued influence of this type of historical writing has meant that, even in the twenty-first century, independence is still depicted as part of a broader severance of Latin America from Europe.[9] In this prevailing interpretation, the decade of the 1820s was marked by a widening chasm, separating Europe and America, that remained for at least half a century. Where international actors were involved, their role was downplayed.[10]

Where Europeans were indelibly present, they were either depicted as "going native" (when they disappeared from view) or as incorrigibly hostile to Latin American interests. From this milieu emerged the obfuscating dualisms of colony-nation, Europe-America, and republic-monarchy, all binaries that became ever more rigid and entrenched with the passage of time. This interpretation has been misleading precisely because, as the essays in this volume collectively argue and demonstrate, these aspects were simultaneously present, complementary, coexistent, and far from exclusive. Older cultures and relationships endured. These were not obviated by the formal transfer of political authority from Old World to New World capitals. Instead, the decade is best characterized by interrupted continuities between Europe and Latin America, not irreparably shattered bonds.

An incomplete understanding of international power relations in the 1820s has left historians struggling to interpret the nature of imperial formations—or, informal empire—in this period.[11] Some have claimed that formal diplomatic recognition of independence did not leave the new states fully autonomous. Brazil remained hamstrung by unfavorable trade treaties with Britain that the transplanted Portuguese monarchy had signed hastily and under duress upon its arrival, courtesy of the Royal Navy, in the New World in 1808.[12] Just as dire economic circumstances compelled impoverished nascent governments to assume considerable loans from European financiers, Spanish American markets, which at least legally had been closed for centuries, were opened up suddenly to foreign penetration.[13] The influx of European capital, in this interpretation, exploited the weakness of Latin American states and secured political and economic conditions that were beneficial to outsiders yet prejudicial to local interests.[14]

Nevertheless, there were no railways, no telegraphs, and few gunboats in the 1820s. For this reason, scholars generally ignored these years in favor of apparently richer pickings in subsequent decades when evidence for imperialism, or at least "informal empire," might more easily be detected or, alternatively, disproved.[15] Later national historians quickly lost interest in the 1820s through 1840s, considering them a period of relative isolation from the wider world during which local elites enjoyed political autonomy and prepared the ground for full integration into the international economy after 1850. D. C. M. Platt described the 1820s as a "blip" caused by a sudden rise in British imports to Latin America at the start of the decade, followed by an equally abrupt fall after the collapse of the British investment bubble in 1826. Tulio Halperín Donghi argued that the 1820s served as the low-water mark for British–Latin American economic relations, signaling the beginning of a long recovery from the devastation caused by the wars of independence.[16]

Historical sources—whether government memoranda, private papers, pamphlets, or political ephemera—produced in the 1820s demonstrate that contemporaries perceived the marked continuity with the colonial period in their new international relations. Indeed, claims that national sovereignty continued to be infringed by foreign powers after independence were rampant and deeply felt. Key and understudied aspects of this phenomenon were the anti-Spanish riots and legislation in Mexico, where half of its ten thousand Spaniards left as a result of the federal expulsion laws of 1827 and 1829, and another is the pervasive Lusophobia that periodically flared up in Brazilian politics until mid-century.[17] An interrogation of the international cultural encounters of the 1820s—what we have labeled "the persistence of mutual influence"—can supply new insights into the meanings of, and limits to, sovereignty across independent Latin America in the nineteenth century.[18] Sovereignty was no longer exercised exclusively by metropolitan elites by the 1820s. Instead, it was fought for by armies, contested by opposing political leaders, clouded by foreign investments, diluted by export-oriented national economies, and hampered by burgeoning public debts.[19] Foreign influence in Latin America was a problem that just would not go away after independence; rather it remained an irremovable feature of the postcolonial landscape.

In the face of this preponderant evidence for the persistence of mutual influence between the Old World and the New, why has the decade of the 1820s received scant attention from historians? The neglect is attributable to the influence of two interrelated paradigms that have structured the study and shrouded the importance of the 1820s. These are, broadly speaking, the age of revolutions and Atlantic history.

The Age of Revolutions and Its Historiographical Discontents

The age of revolutions has a long and distinguished historiographical genealogy that can be but briefly reprised here.[20] This period is generally understood as spanning 1750–1850, but sometimes beginning in 1760 or 1789 or ending around 1840. R. R. Palmer's two-volume *The Age of Democratic Revolutions: A Political History of Europe and America, 1760–1800* (1959–64) was perhaps the most ambitious effort in English to define this age as a coherent entity, marked by political liberation in what he considered to be a unitary "Atlantic Civilization." As Palmer put it, "the main idea seems to have been a demand for self-determination, a sense of autonomy of the personality, a re-fusal to accept norms laid down outside the self."[21] Palmer's conception was of a sustained assault on Old Regime privilege and aristocratic political insti-tutions by those armed with democratic ideas. While claiming universality, Palmer's study is largely one of the North American and French revolutions, stopping before the Haitian and Latin American revolutions. For Palmer, the subsequent revolutions were merely derivative of these North Atlantic prece-dents, another example of the unilateral diffusion of political ideas, ambitions, and institutions from core to periphery, of leader and follower nations in the pursuit of a unitary conception of political modernity. "All revolutions since 1800, in Europe, Latin America, Asia, and Africa," Palmer contended, "have learned from the eighteenth-century Revolution of Western Civilization."[22]

Eric Hobsbawm entertained a more capacious, inclusive view of this epoch, and it is he who contributed perhaps the most to the present understanding of the Age of Revolution in his eponymous landmark 1962 book. Hobsbawm depicted the sixty years between 1789 and 1848 as a coherent entity during which republican and democratic ideas crossed and re-crossed the Atlantic Ocean.[23] For Hobsbawm and those historians working in his wake, it was an epoch in which declarations of independence were made, anticolonial wars for liberation were waged, and new polities came into existence. In short, it comprised a half-century of dramatic change, in which old structures were dismantled and new institutions established.[24]

Historians working after Palmer and Hobsbawm have been aware, none-theless, of the continuities and jagged transitions between the Old and New Regimes. Arno Mayer's influential *The Persistence of the Old Regime* (1981),[25] for example, demonstrated the surprising degree to which Old Regime cul-ture and practices survived the French Revolution across Europe. It was not swept away, but rather metamorphosed in a reinvigorated form that would persist for much of the nineteenth century. Beyond Europe's borders, too, the concept of an age of revolution(s) is not entirely accepted. This reluctant em-brace is attributable to its "strikingly Eurotropic, if not quite Eurocentric" character.[26] It is also due to its failure to "do justice to the complexity of the period."[27] Just as importantly, the age of revolutions stands at odds with the insights proffered by an earlier generation of Latin American intellectuals who perceived that a focus on political independence and revolutionary war-fare often obscured a more profound stasis in the former Ibero-Atlantic em-pires. They recognized the fluidity of the period during which decomposing empires gave way, reluctantly and incompletely, to primordial successor states.

They identified alarming and conveniently overlooked continuities between colonial rule and the postcolonial regimes that supplanted them. The break from the past, they contended, was not as abrupt and decisive as it is often assumed and depicted to have been.[28] Archaic structures proved durable and, in politics as in economics, the old order did not give way fully to a new one. Instead, "no stable or hegemonic model took root."[29]

As Eric Van Young observed in his essay "Was There an Age of Revolution in Spanish America?," it is possible to identify political, social, and economic change during the long "revolutionary" period in Spanish America within the context of even longer-term continuity with regard to resilient colonial legacies.[30] Researchers who have explored Spanish American contexts within an age of revolution paradigm—for example, Marixa Lasso, James Sanders, and Aline Helg for New Granada/Colombia—identify the popular origins of most of that which was revolutionary in this period. Lasso's book on the political engagement of black communities in Cartagena de Indias, following the pioneering work of Alfonso Múnera, and Sanders's research into Afro-Colombian and mestizo political culture in the Cauca region both argue that subaltern political culture has been omitted from conventional studies of the period in Spanish America.[31] This scholarship sits uneasily within an age of revolution perspective because of the local focus; it is less concerned with the transatlantic connections after colonialism, on which this volume focuses. These linkages did not wither away with the achievement of state sovereignty. Examination of these connections reveals myriad neglected continuities and draws overdue attention to the influence of external relations on domestic state-making.

Our skepticism about the extent and rapidity of change is inherited from previous historians and commentators. In Octavio Paz's memorable phrase, liberal and democratic ideologies served merely to "adorn the vestiges of the colonial system" with ornaments of "modernity" without producing significant socioeconomic change.[32] In Brazil, as Maria Odila Silva Dias has observed, many of the leading bureaucrats and families made an almost seamless transition to positions of authority and prestige in the newly established empire, ruled by the Portuguese House of Branganza, which liberally doled out titles of nobility and other honors, a process that she has described convincingly as the "internalization of the metropole."[33] In Central America, as Jordana Dym makes clear, the municipal institutions bequeathed by Spain were not discarded outright as a "limping, unthinking extension of a medieval colonial heritage," but rather embraced as the cornerstone of postcolonial polity-making.[34]

In Mexico, as Brian Hamnett has contended persuasively, monarchism and royalism enjoyed a long afterlife, serving as the precursor to nineteenth-century Mexican conservatism, whose first manifestations were felt during the ascendancy of Anastasio Bustamante and Lucas Alamán in the early 1830s.[35] Many of the nascent republics "dragged the detritus of colonial attitudes, habits and institutions" into the post-independence era.[36] We believe that it is possible to draw attention to the absence and uneven nature of political, social, and economic change without succumbing to out-dated stereotypes of the lethargy, malaise, and stagnation of postcolonial Latin America. Stasis was indeed often the result of agency, self-conscious and self-interested action.

For the vast majority of the population of Latin America, the formal independence achieved from 1810 to 1824 offered only the illusion of change. To varying degrees throughout Spanish America, Spanish law remained in force after independence. In the United Provinces of Argentina, for example, the *Leyes de Indias, Real Ordenanza de Intendentes,* and Spanish corpora like the *Siete Partidas* persisted, except where they might contradict the new government's resolutions, an "inevitable effect of the lack of rules to replace peninsular ones."[37] In Brazil, a great deal of colonial legislation persisted: a criminal code (1830), a commercial code (1850), and a civil code (1916) would come into existence only well after independence.[38] The administrative and military apparatus of the colonial state became, for better or worse, that of the new Brazilian Empire, which crushed provincial efforts to decentralize political authority.[39]

Nor did separation from Europe automatically lead to the dismantling of colonial-era restrictions, including those that stifled international commerce. In Peru from 1820 until 1850, for instance, "free traders were few, far between, foreign, feeble and factionalised."[40] Customs royalties and the export of primary goods remained the mainstay of most of the Latin American states.[41] Other purportedly colonial institutions and attitudes persisted or were resurrected in superficially different form soon after their initial demise. In Mexico, many colonial-era duties on commerce, including the *alcabala,* remained the most important revenue sources for some state governments until the turn of the twentieth century.[42] Indian tribute, too, the abolition of which was declared in the Cádiz Constitution of 1812, was reimposed in Ecuador, Peru, and Bolivia during the 1820s.[43] Land reform meant the expansion of large estates, or *fincas,* and this often prejudiced rather than benefited indigenous cultivators and peasants, as Elizabeth Dore has argued for Nicaragua.[44] For much of the nineteenth century, as Mark Thurner's work on

Peru has shown, the "hierarchical, discontinuous, internal boundaries of ethnic caste, colour, class, gender and corporation persisted" in many places.[45] In Venezuela, slavery survived until 1854, and property and literacy requirements limited male suffrage until 1858.[46] In Brazil, independence facilitated the entrenchment and deepening of the galvanizing force of the colonial economy: slavery. It is no accident that more Africans (621,978 in total) were disembarked as slaves in Brazilian ports in the 1820s than in any other decade.[47] Nor is it surprising that the two peak years of that decade, 1827 and 1829, came after the end of empire.[48] The slave trade continued until 1850, and slavery itself persisted until 1888, a year before the demise of the monarchy.[49]

In short, then, historians have established the tenacious persistence of independent Latin America's colonial heritage. The historical significance long associated with independence now appears diminished, despite the recent wave of bicentenary commemorations. Continuities with the colonial past abounded, and the trope of disjuncture, so fundamental to the age of revolution narrative, now appears to have been exaggerated.[50] A renewed focus on the transatlantic connections that persisted after the end of colonialism may pave the way to unite these increasingly divergent historiographies.

If we accept the curious absence—or, at least, the superficiality, slowness, and incomplete nature—of many types of change during the age of revolution in the Ibero-Atlantic world, we are left to enquire, in C. A. Bayly's formulation, "Was there anything revolutionary about the revolutionary age?"[51] Even for many historians writing within the age of revolution paradigm, where change occurred during the 1820s—if any occurred at all—it moved at a glacial pace, difficult to detect and of far less interest than the more marked change of earlier and later decades.

Significant changes, of course, did occur within an Atlantic or revolutionary paradigm. For example, as monarchical institutions collapsed in Spanish America, the first stirrings of democracy and a culture of rights filled the void across Hispanic America, as Margarita Garrido has argued.[52] Yet, even in this moment of self-emancipation, the influence of the Old World, and the former metropole in particular, proved enduring and decisive. The Constitution of Cádiz remained in force in Mexico until 1824 and in Central America until 1826.[53] Even after independence, the residual influence of the 1812 constitution can be identified in the following national constitutions: Argentina, 1826; Chile, 1828; New Granada, 1830 and 1832; Peru, 1828; Venezuela, 1830; and Uruguay, 1830.[54]

Clearly, however, the end of empire did not mean a moratorium on the engagement with and use of European constitutional ideas in Latin America. Even where change occurred, notable continuities with the pre-independence period remained. In general terms, then, we seek to draw attention to, and analyze the uneven extent, bumpiness, lack of linearity, and spasmodic rhythm of, the reconfiguration of imperial power that occurred in the Atlantic world in the 1820s.[55] We believe that these phenomena have been neglected, in part, because the decade of the 1820s has been lost by being subsumed into paradigms such as the age of revolutions or Atlantic world or artificially divided by the colonial/national–period paradox.[56]

Atlantic History and the Perils of Periodization

We contend that the histories of Europe and Latin America did not diverge abruptly in the 1820s. This view does not coincide with the prevailing consensus in the field of Atlantic history.[57] One of the outstanding achievements of Atlantic history is to have made scholars aware of the interconnected world that was created between circa 1500 and 1800, thus offering an opportunity to overcome national, continental, linguistic, and other parochialisms.[58] Historians of Europe, Africa, and the Americas are increasingly cognizant that their regions of study are "entangled" and that any isolated examination of any one of them is bound to result in distortions or explanatory gaps.[59] Clearly, both European and Latin American history have benefited from "transnational, transoceanic, and hemispheric research."[60] Yet it is not altogether clear what the temporal boundaries of this Atlantic world were. In particular, "its terminus is more fluid and contested."[61] Is its demise found in the fulcrum of the imperial revolutions circa 1776–1825?[62] Or with the end of the slave trade in about 1850? Or with the abolition of slavery in 1888 in its final outpost, Brazil?[63] Most Atlanticists stop somewhere around 1800, though there are new efforts to introduce the category of "late Atlantic history" to encompass the nineteenth century.[64]

Atlantic historians recently have come to identify the 1820s as a crucial period of historical transformation. Nicholas Canny has argued, admittedly only after finding other alternatives implausible, that the transition from a "coherent Atlantic world" to "Global History" probably took place in the 1820s.[65] J. H. Elliott also identifies the 1820s as a watershed between two epochs in Atlantic history, depicting the end of colonial rule as inaugurating a distinct epoch.[66]

Yet even in these interpretations, the 1820s are left strangely orphaned. The decade remains outside the scope of mainstream Atlantic history, and it pre-dates the formal consolidation of the postimperial states whose evolution forms the main plot of "national" history. The decade of the 1820s also sits between the age of revolution, with its master narrative of liberation, and the age of em-pire, with its leitmotiv of domination. C. A. Bayly's account of the birth of the modern world shows the urgent need to reevaluate the persistence in relations between Europe and Latin America in the 1820s from a transnational per-spective. Nineteenth-century changes took place against a backdrop of, and were catalyzed by, global connections of people, ideas, and trade. Bayly con-vincingly presents the 1820s as an "axial" moment in the spread of European domination across the world.[67] Yet it is also the moment when formal Euro-pean dominion over Latin America was shattered. This paradox of the over-lap of an age of resurgent empire with one of emancipation is explored in this book, as it is more generally in a 2009 collection edited by Clément Thibaud, Alejandro Gómez, and Genevieve Verdo.[68] Our approach is to move beyond the recognition of change and continuity within the age of revolution and to explore the untapped possibilities as well as structural limitations of both the age of revolutions and Atlantic history paradigms through analysis of one co-herent and discrete unit of time.

The selection of any unit of time for historical study is bound to be arbi-trary, even apparently obvious periods such as the length of a war (i.e., 1939–45 for the Second World War), a reign (1837–1901, the Victorian age), or a life (1783–1830, that of Simón Bolívar). The purpose of periodization is to pre-sent continuity and change in historical time by noting when key breaks, con-junctures, or disjunctures occurred. A common effect of periodization, un-fortunately, is to leave out long-term causes and consequences that fall outside the chosen delimiting years. All historians are compelled to grapple with this thorny issue. But it is also incumbent upon historians of global interactions and the extra-European world to accept, modify, or subvert conventional pe-riodizations, derived largely from European or North American history and often based on dynasties, political events, legal regimes, forms of sovereignty, and other juridical categories.[69] After all, periodization is made from par-ticular perspectives in space, time, and power.[70] It is therefore "both the prod-uct and begetter of theory" and "exerts formidable, if subliminal, influence on the refinement and elaboration of theory."[71]

The unity of the 1820s heretofore has been apparent only in that it is a period that has been neglected by historians who have seen change or prog-ress as being interrupted around 1821, with the triumph of independence, until the continent's incorporation to the international economy half a century later. Yet we argue that the decade is a coherent unit of study. It has a reasonably clear beginning from 1819 to 1821, marked by the revolutions in Spain, Oporto, Naples, Piedmont, Peterloo, and Greece; the Congress of Angostura and the proclamation of the Republic of Gran Colombia; and George IV taking to the throne in Britain. The rebellions and resistance in Spanish America, Greece, and Italy all speak to the same call for independence from tyranny. These years also witnessed the efflorescence of the congress system and the threat to representative governments both in Europe and overseas.

The period also has a coherent end point: many national historiographical paradigms concur that the year 1830 marks some kind of a watershed, whether it be the advent of the July monarchy in France, which saw a restored Bourbon constitutional monarchy overthrown;[72] Dom Pedro's abdication of the Brazilian throne in 1831, an act which ended the *Primeiro Reinado* and ushered in the turbulence of the Regency period;[73] or Bolívar's death in Colombia, which was a harbinger of new forms of political organization. Many Venezuelan, Colombian, and Ecuadorian national histories begin with the disintegration of Gran Colombia in 1830. This is the same year with which Elliott ends his landmark study of the British and Spanish Atlantic empires, marking the end of a first stage of empire in the Americas and the beginning of something new. Despite the tumult, the decade retains a notable coherence.

The Persistence of Mutual Influence: The Old World and the New after Independence

In 1992 Mary Louise Pratt argued influentially that a "capitalist vanguard" had swept across Latin America in the 1820s, describing how Europe acquired "imperial eyes" toward Latin American resources, landscapes, and peoples, which it then sought to exploit.[74] But the dominant schools of imperial and diplomatic historiography tend to de-emphasize the importance of the Americas in European calculations after independence.[75] For the British Empire, the 1820s have been represented as the culmination of the "swing to the east" (away from North America and toward India) in official imperial strategy.[76] Bayly has argued that the decade was part of an "imperial meridian," where British imperial ideology and its racialist foundations hardened, as well as the moment in which the modes and principles of imperial governance shifted decisively.[77] The Lusophone world is held to follow a similar pattern: Valentim Alexandre's *Os Sentidos do Império* (1993) makes clear how the effective loss of Brazil from 1822 was Portugal's imperial watershed, marking a hiatus between its early modern Indian Ocean and southern Atlantic expansion and its modern African imperial enterprise.[78] In France, the conquest of Algiers in 1830 has been traditionally considered to be the decisive step away from the Western Hemisphere and toward the creation of a Mediterranean-based, territorial empire.[79] In the Spanish case, Michael Costeloe's work on the "response to revolution" in the 1820s argued that Spaniards did not feel the loss of the continental American colonies deeply at all and that events in Peru, Mexico, and New Granada produced scarce impact on general public opinion.[80]

Rather than seeing Latin America as being passed from one European empire to another, as Pratt or others who follow the dependency paradigm would have it, or as being relatively inconsequential to European calculations, which is the prevailing conclusion to be drawn from the lion's share of the existing historiography, the contributors to this volume trace a more nuanced process of structures and relations changing within and between empires. A comparative picture of multi-imperial reconfiguration emerges from the recent historiography, showing how the Americas became ever more important in the European worldview in this period. In his chapter in this volume, Josep M. Fradera identifies a step-change in the 1820s, describing how Spanish imperial administrators in Madrid reluctantly adjusted to the effective loss of the continental American colonies and reconfigured the remaining colonies (primarily Cuba, Puerto Rico, and the Philippines) even while remaining adamant that Peru, Mexico, and the others would eventually return to the fold.[81] Spain even forced the issue by launching a quixotic effort to invade Mexico in 1829, and few of the South American states received official recognition from Spain until Ferdinand VII's death in 1833.[82] Similarly, while the independence of Brazil triggered a major national reassessment in Portugal, the utter dependence of Portugal's African enclaves on the burgeoning Brazilian slave trade meant that Lisbon's imperial designs were hostage to Rio de Janeiro's policy.[83] Similarly, Restoration France could not admit defeat in Haiti: in 1825, the French government dispatched a naval squadron of twelve ships in an effort to force the Haitian government, which three years earlier had begun its occupation of the former Spanish colony of Santo Domingo, to pay an indemnity in exchange for recognition of its independence.[84] Moreover, 137,000 Africans slaves were shipped to the West Indies aboard French ships in the 1820s, while the revival of the plantation system in Martinique, Guadeloupe, and Bourbon meant that in 1826 those three islands exported the same amount of sugar (69 million tons) as Saint-Domingue before the revolution.[85] France, Britain, and the Netherlands clung to sugar-producing islands in the Caribbean and territorial footholds on the northern coast of South America. The British presence was also strengthened in these years: Britain went on to increase its presence in the Malvinas (Falkland) Islands in 1833 and also expanded the frontiers of its colony in Guiana in the 1840s. These episodes reveal that Latin America remained a factor in the political calculations of statesmen. Simply because imperial engagement was not omnipresent or sustained does not mean that we should ignore it or omit it from our calculations.

The 1820s also witnessed a massive reconfiguration of the system of slavery that had underpinned European–Latin American relations for well over a century. These changes have led Dale Tomich to identify the 1820s as the beginning of a period of "second slavery," where the transport of slaves from Africa to the Americas increased in staggering numbers, compared to eighteenth-century levels, and became overwhelmingly directed at the United States and Cuban and Brazilian markets rather than the British and French Caribbean colonies or continental Hispanic America.[86] As Christopher Schmidt-Nowara demonstrates in his contribution to this volume, the numbers of Africans forcibly transported to the Americas also rose exponentially in the 1820s. Reinforcing Tomich's notion of a "second slavery," Carrie Gibson's chapter shows how fear of slave rebellion had a resilient legacy that shaped social relations in the Caribbean and beyond throughout the nineteenth century.[87]

Independence certainly did not sever the intellectual links between Europe and Latin America. The fantastic image of Jeremy Bentham frantically scribbling constitutions for the nascent republics was symptomatic of the continuous, sustained engagement of Spanish American and Brazilian lawmakers with European political thought, jurisprudence, and social policy.[88] Part of this interchange stemmed from direct contact. Between 1808 and 1830, seventy bona fide leaders of Spanish American independence movements lived in London, while many of those who proved instrumental in Brazil's own transition to statehood had studied at the universities of Coimbra, Montpellier, or Edinburgh.[89] Charles-Louis Secondat Montesquieu and Bentham were major references in Latin American debates in the 1820s, and Bernardo O'Higgins, like Bolívar, greatly admired the British system of government in which elections and debates occurred without "tumults, disorders, and insurrections."[90] British political economy, particularly the ideas of

Adam Smith and the conservative liberalism of Edmund Burke, was made available to Brazilian readers through the widely disseminated excerpts translated by José da Silva Lisboa.[91]

More generally, many Spanish Americans politicians were drawn to what they perceived to be, in Karen Racine's phrase, a "British-style aristocratic reformism."[92] At the same time, Swiss-French jurist Benjamin Constant's political thought was the touchstone to which all but the most unrepentant Jacobin or apostolic reactionary paid homage. Some stressed the individual liberties he championed—trial by jury, freedom of the press, and the inviolability of property—whereas others were attracted by his conception of political order achieved through a division of power and the creation of a *pouvoir préservateur* or *pouvoir neutre*.[93] Nowhere in the world was this notion of a "moderating power" enshrined more assiduously than in Brazil's 1824 constitution.[94] Cultural connections with France were similarly robust. As early as the 1820s, Frenchmen moved to Argentina to teach French, direct schools, and open private institutes that taught commercial and scientific skills.[95] Beginning in 1816, the French Artistic Mission to Brazil similarly diffused European culture among Carioca elites while transmitting images of Brazil back to Europe, where they were reproduced and redistributed.[96]

When we arrive at the question of *mutual influence,* the absence of the 1820s from the historiography is even more profound. There has been virtually nothing written on Latin America's influence on Europe in our period. The few studies of Latin Americans in Europe for our decade remain hesitant to claim much for their subjects. Karen Racine's research on the Spanish Americans in London through to 1829 positively recoils at the idea that her subjects might have exerted any influence at all in the British imperial capital, instead arguing persuasively that "in London they became Americans" and focusing on what the exiles learned in Europe and carried back with them to assist in the struggle for independence.[97] Neil Safier argues that travelers were often the "couriers of empire," in whose bags, heads, and wakes change was catalysed.[98] Cultural historians and critics have emphasized the importance of the 1820s in transatlantic knowledge transmission and the wearing away of the mutual ignorance of Europe and Latin America.[99] Travelers like Bolívar, O'Higgins, and others were vectors of change in the 1820s, carrying ideas and contacts with them as they crossed boundaries and oceans, as Scarlett O'Phelan Godoy also shows in her study in this volume.

There is enough evidence for us to discern that these exchanges went both ways across the Atlantic. Latin America continued to impact Europe at various social and political registers after independence. Travel writers—from France, Germany, Britain, and elsewhere—poured into Latin America in the 1820s; and European printing presses churned out travelogues, histories, and plays that brought Old World audiences into contact with the New World. This travel literature boom was part of a genuine "rediscovery" of Latin America by Europe in the 1820s.[100] As Lucy Riall has shown, Giuseppe Garibaldi's adventures in South America in the 1820s were essential to forging his political ideas and to giving him a revolutionary cache in Italy upon his return.[101] Costeloe's pioneering book shows how Mexican financial affairs affected British bondholders, from the commercial elite down to small-town shopkeepers and vicars.[102] Furthermore, South American affairs resonated deeply, perhaps decisively, in political developments and debates in the Iberian peninsula, including Spain's *Trienio Liberal* and the trajectory of the Lisbon Cortes (1821–22). The New World was indeed separating from the Old, but its influence, paradoxically though perhaps not unrelatedly, was expanding in Europe.

Just as India was the clay that English Utilitarians sought to mold in their own image, Latin America offered the European imagination a canvas upon which to paint its aspirations and anxieties.[103] Latin American revolutions and processes of polity-building, like the contemporary struggle in Greece against the Ottoman yoke, fascinated European romantic writers. Latin America beckoned as an uncluttered site for the fulfillment of deferred dreams of liberty. To them, Europe was exhausted by war, corrupted and corroded by commercial society, and lethargically subjected to revivified monarchies.[104] Lord Byron explicitly linked the Greek and Latin American causes in his poem "The Age of Bronze" (1823): "One common cause makes myriads of one breast / Slaves of the East, or Helots of the West; / on Andes' and on Athos' peaks unfurled, / The self-same standard streams o'er either world."[105] The Portuguese poet and politician Almeida Garrett would go so far as to claim that the liberal revolutions in Europe in the early 1820s—in Naples, Greece, Piedmont, and the Iberian peninsula—had received "the example and impulse of liberty from America."[106] As Maurizio Isabella has demonstrated in an original, persuasive monograph, upon which he expands in this volume, Italians brought back ideas and programs from their exile in the 1820s; these provided the bedrock of the Risorgimento at mid-century. For example, the creation of republics in the New World was seen as the first step on the road to the creation of a global federal order. Toward the end of the decade, the "authoritarian turn" of many of the republics, especially those influenced by Bolívar, spawned debates between Abbé de Pradt and Constant.[107] As Paquette's chapter in this volume shows, Dom Pedro's bestowal of a constitution in 1824 on Brazil and in 1826 on Portugal excited similarly heated debates in Europe.

Colonial Legacies and Degrees of Continuity

The contributors to this volume stress the persistence and continuity of old forms that shaped this moment of apparent rupture. Governors—colonial and national alike—were guided by "enlightened reform" both in Europe, its colonies, and their successor states.[108]

However, the reception of European ideas in Latin America was far from passive and imitative. Fernando Coronil and Walter Mignolo have separately traced the multifaceted reception of European currents in Latin America's nineteenth century.[109] In the 1820s, Latin American revolutionaries drew eclectically and unapologetically from both the "heterodox" texts of radical enlightenment and neo-scholastic Iberian jurisprudence.[110] After independence, there was relatively little European control and precious little European pressure, which triggered the adoption of European modes.[111] As a result, Latin American political writers could engage with and borrow from European traditions free from the dictates of orthodoxy. In Chile, for example, Andrés Bello was the leading jurist and educational reformer after independence, and he corresponded regularly with interlocutors in Europe and integrated their political ideas into the curricula of new universities. But he also developed a highly original jurisprudence and adapted the European ideas to which he was exposed to the peculiar conditions of post-independence Latin America.[112]

Influence was reciprocal. Scholars have established that the wars of Spanish American independence and debates over sovereignty captured the British and French popular imaginations, leading to pamphlet wars, extensive newspaper coverage, and fierce parliamentary debates. Simón Bolívar's presence in the European press was as ubiquitous in the 1820s as that of Hugo Chávez in the first decade of the present century.[113] Daniel O'Connell, the protagonist of Catholic emancipation in Ireland, was integrated into this Atlantic world. He encouraged his son and nephew to serve Bolívar in Colombia and was at the center of a political storm in Dublin in 1820 relating to the desirability (or not) of Irish youths setting out to see the world and prove themselves as men on the other side of the ocean. O'Connell later took Bolívar's title, "Liberator," as his own.[114] Scientific exploration, including that undertaken by the

HMS *Beagle,* carrying Charles Darwin, kept Latin America in the European consciousness long after formal dominion was eclipsed. Historians have only recently begun to explore the links between this "Latin American news" and the political groupings it encouraged with national or "home news." In 1819 and 1820, for example, British newspapers such as the *Times* or the *Morning Chronicle* carried hundreds of column inches relating to just two subjects: the Queen Caroline affair and the recruitment (in breach of British neutrality) of mercenary expeditions to fight in Venezuela. The future foreign secretary, George Canning, was a key figure in both scandals. But scholars who have examined his career have neglected the extent to which his support on one matter was conditioned by or linked to animosities created by the other.[115] We hope that our call for the study of *mutual influence* and global connections and consequences will cast new light on these subjects and open up new interpretative possibilities for researchers as they venture outside of the national or area studies frameworks that have often hindered such exploration.

The Difficulties and Advantages of Studying the 1820s as Part of the Revolutionary Atlantic

Analysis of historical change in the 1820s is, it should be clear by now, much more than a case of historical revisionism for its own sake. Approaches to the 1820s that cast the decade as a minor but integral part of the age of revolution, following Palmer's and Hobsbawm's influential work, view the 1820s as offering signs to support a narrative of gradual liberation, whether from colonialism, economic dependence, or ancien régime institutions. Recall that Hobsbawm's age of empire began in 1875, separate from, rather than intermeshed with, his age of revolution.[116] Bayly's approach differs from Hobsbawm's by casting the 1820s as one stage in the strengthening and expansion of European domination of the globe. His is therefore a narrative of interlinked imperialisms rather than revolutionary resistance. The question of whether we see the understudied 1820s as a decade of rupture or of continuity matters profoundly to the respective persuasiveness of these two interpretations.

Several other historical paradigms and explanations also hinge upon the 1820s, the decade that has been most bereft of serious scholarly investigation in nineteenth-century historiography. Indeed, it is as if a heavy body of interpretation has found its strongest support upon a vacuum of evidence and analysis. These different paradigms—not only the age of revolution and the birth of the modern world, but also Latin American nation- and state-building and independence—share assumptions about the interpretive neutrality of the 1820s, which, while drawing on distinct perspectives, share the same (hitherto unstudied) causes. This state of affairs should cause us some anxiety. So little is known about the 1820s, yet so much hangs upon assumptions that are made about the ruptures held to have transpired in those years.

∽

Colonial legacies and continued connections "after" colonialism are quickly apparent to historians of this decade, just as they were to contemporaries. Historians of Latin America have been much more open to considering "foreign" influence than have historians of Europe.[117] The influence of European exile on Latin America's political leaders has long been recognized, for example. The protracted negotiations over the precise conditions of the abolition of the slave trade—nationally and internationally—provide another aspect of the persistence of mutual influence in the 1820s, studied by Latin Americanists but usually ignored by Europeanists. The Brazilian, Portuguese, and British governments established mixed-commission courts, with judges from each country, to try those accused of violating these earlier treaties abolishing the slave trade south of the equator.[118] These are two examples, amongst countless others, of ways that awareness of the connections after colonialism can open up new research vistas.

These commonalities and continuities should be taken with several pinches of salt, however. Our contributors try not to overreach themselves in generalizing, comparing, and tracing links between peoples and places. At the same time, we try to break up collective groups when they lose interpretive value. This means increasing our knowledge of the Catalan, Asturian, and Castilian variants of Spanish imperialism in the 1820s, following the large body of work that has analyzed the divergent Irish, Scottish, Welsh, and English experiences of the British Empire.[119] In Latin America itself, we shy away from a "foreign-local" dichotomy, preferring instead to pick apart the gradations of foreignness that suffused societies in this period.[120] For example, in southern Peru in the aftermath of the Battle of Ayacucho in the middle of the decade, many of the war's protagonists were considered "foreign" by the Peruvians they lived and fought alongside. The Englishman William Miller, the Chilean-Irishman Bernardo O'Higgins, the Venezuelan-Colombian Simón Bolívar, and the Andean-Peruvian Andrés Santa Cruz were all considered as foreigners by inhabitants of the coastal capital, Lima. Each of them was viewed with varying degrees of suspicion and acceptance according to political circumstances that often had precious little to do with ideas of lineage, origin, or ethnicity.[121] A transnational approach to the 1820s, such as that adopted by Reuben Zahler in his essay on heresy, death, and foreignness in this volume, allows us to recognize these differences while assessing their various weights in triggering or shaping historical processes.

The historiographical currents and research questions outlined above explain why we have focused attention on the long-neglected decade of the 1820s. New significance and cohesion can now be brought to disparate phenomena that previously were difficult to integrate into the dominant narratives of Latin American independence. Historians are increasingly aware of the persistence, even deepening and creation, of robust links between Europe and the new nations that emerged from the defunct Iberian empires. Here, too, there were continuities and discontinuities, often interwoven unpredictably. First, of course, imperial dominion did not perish altogether in the 1820s. Spain clung to Cuba and Puerto Rico while the Braganzas held on to the Brazilian throne.[122] Second, older dynamics assumed new prominence. Formerly clandestine commercial relationships flourished in the wake of the dismantling of colonial economic regulations while new waves of investors swooped in, eager for access to sources of long-famed wealth.[123] Cotton from northern Brazil was sent in ever-greater quantities to the mills of rapidly industrializing Britain.[124] Banks extended enormous loans to fledgling South American states, many of which had defaulted by 1830, plunging many small investors—including middle-class lawyers, priests, and salesmen—into debt and destitution.[125] Latin America and Europe were both key actors in the global changes that brought about the birth of the modern world in the first half of the nineteenth century. Well-known historical figures such as Bolívar, O'Higgins, and Rafael del Riego were only a small part of the story. The in-depth studies of the persistence of mutual influence between Europe and Latin America in the 1820s presented here reveal the importance of a wide range of spatial, geographical, and political factors in shaping the birth of the modern world on both sides of the Atlantic.

The 1820s are a coherent unit of study, a period in which many similar problems and opportunities were shared by historical actors across the Atlantic. It was a decade of unrealized plans, of the roads not taken, a decade when cries of freedom fell against the brick wall of Royalist resistance, when the resilience of colonial legacies was tested but not destroyed. But it was also, as contributors to this volume emphasize, a decade of considerable reconfiguration of imperial networks and relationships. The chapters in this volume follow four of those networks and relationships in particular: transatlantic liberalism; Anglo-American involvement in Latin America; transnational linkages of people and ideas; and the transformations of slavery and the slave trade. This was a decade in which the vectors of power that swept across the Atlantic were realigned according to the reach of the British Royal Navy, victorious at Trafalgar in 1805. The revolutions in the New World and the Old may have ended in the 1820s, but the cultural, political, and commercial forces they unleashed influenced the long-term evolutions in the Atlantic World well after independence was recognized.

Notes

1. Earlier versions of this introduction were presented at the University of Cambridge in May 2009 and at the University of Bristol in May 2010. We are grateful to all those who have commented on it, particularly Christopher Schmidt-Nowara, Brian Hamnett, Reuben Zahler, Caroline Williams, and David Rock. We also thank the two expert reviewers for The University of Alabama Press for their useful and edifying critique of an earlier draft of this introduction.

2. A new addition to this literature is a special issue of the *European History Quarterly* 41, no. 3 (2011), featuring essays by Scott Eastman, Brian Hamnett, Gabriel Paquette, Mónica Ricketts, and Natalia Sobrevilla Perea.

3. Dunkerley, *Americana,* 30–33.

4. In John Charles Chasteen's popular textbook, the period 1825–1850 is covered in a chapter entitled "Postcolonial Blues." See Chasteen, *Born in Blood and Fire,* 119–48.

5. See, among others, Adelman, "Colonialism and National History."

6. For an example of how such ideas have influenced contemporary economists and political scientists, see Acemoglu, "The Colonial Origins of Comparative Development," 1369–1401; for an overview and analysis of such views, see Adelman, "Institutions, Property, and Economic Development in Latin America."

7. The best summary of the "Creole Patriotism" phenomenon is Brading, *The First America*; for a reconsideration of the links between colonial dissent and revolution and the role of the enlightenment in bringing about the demise of the Spanish Empire, see McFarlane, "Identity, Enlightenment, and Political Dissent in Late Colonial Spanish America."

8. An approach neatly summarized in Humphreys, *Tradition and Revolt in Latin America and Other Essays.*

9. For insightful comments on such a view, see Schmidt-Nowara, *The Conquest of History.*

10. But now see Blaufarb, "The Western Question," 742–63.

11. On "imperial formations," see Stoler, "On Degrees of Imperial Sovereignty."

12. For an excellent discussion of the background and impact of the opening of Brazil's ports, see Cardoso, "A Abertura dos Portos do Brasil em 1808."

13. Between 1822 and 1825, 20 million pounds in Latin American government bonds were floated on the London capital market, together with the shares of companies capitalized at over 36 million pounds, to operate Latin American mining, commercial, and other ventures. See Dawson, *The First Latin American Debt Crisis,* preface.

14. See Miller, *Britain and Latin America in the Nineteenth and Twentieth Centuries,* 45; and also Smith, "New World Diplomacy," 3–24.

15. Lynn, "British Policy, Trade, and Informal Empire in the Mid-nineteenth Century," 101–121. The literature is reviewed in M. Brown, *Informal Empire in Latin America,* 1–16.

16. See, for example, Abel and Lewis, *Latin America, Economic Imperialism, and the State*; Halperín Donghi, *Reforma y Disolución*; Platt, *Latin America and British Trade.*

17. Sims, *The Expulsion of Mexico's Spaniards*; Mosher, *Political Struggle, Ideology, and State Building,* esp. chapter 7, "Political Parties, Popular Mobilization, and the Portuguese."

18. These points are articulated fluently in Rock, "The British in Argentina"; and Thompson, "Informal Empire."

19. This point is well made in Marichal, *A Century of Debt Crises in Latin America*; and Centeno, *Blood and Debt.*

20. For a more complete, as well as stimulating, survey, see Armitage and Subrahmanyan's introduction in their *The Age of Revolutions in Global Context.*

21. R. R. Palmer, "The World Revolution of the West: 1763–1801," *Political Science Quarterly* 69, no. 1 (1954): 5.

22. Palmer, quoted in Armitage and Subrahmanyan, *The Age of Revolutions in Global Context,* xvii.

23. Hobsbawm, *The Age of Revolution.*

24. While this volume is focused on political, intellectual, and social history, it should be noted that Hobsbawm also was concerned with a second "revolution" of the period: the industrial revolution in Britain and its global diffusion.

25. Mayer, *The Persistence of the Old Regime.*

26. Armitage and Subrahmanyan, *The Age of Revolutions in Global Context,* xviii. Note that in our terminology we are following Armitage and Subrahmanyan's usage of "revolutions," plural, rather than Hobsbawm's "revolution," singular. Given the

many different revolutions discussed in the chapters that follow, not least in the next footnote, the reason should be quite clear.

27. J. Lynch, *Latin American Revolutions*, 27.

28. See Thurner, *From Two Republics to One Divided*, 148–49.

29. Adelman, *Sovereignty and Revolution in the Iberian Atlantic*, 391.

30. Eric Van Young, "Conclusion: Was There an Age of Revolution in Spanish America?," in Victor Uribe-Uran, ed., *State and Society in Spanish America during the Age of Revolution* (Wilmington, DE: Scholarly Resources, 2001), 219–46.

31. Lasso, *Myths of Harmony*; Múnera, *El fracaso de la nación*; James Sanders, *Contentious Republicans: Popular Politics, Race, and Class in Nineteenth-Century Colombia* (Durham: Duke University Press, 2004); Helg, *Liberty and Equality in Caribbean Colombia*.

32. Paz, *El Laberinto de la soledad*, 133. Of course, scholars must be careful to avoid the teleological traps, essentialist formulations, and implication of transhistorical immutabilities when they analyze the legacies of colonialism in the national period. For an excellent discussion, see Jeremy Adelman's preface and "Introduction: The Problem of Persistence in Latin American History," in Adelman, ed., *Colonial Legacies*, x–xi and 12–13, respectively.

33. Silva Dias, "A interiorização da Metrópole."

34. Dym, *From Sovereign Villages to National States*, xxvi.

35. Hamnett, *Revolución y Contrarrevolución en México y el Perú*, 403.

36. Larson, *Trials of Nation Making*, 34.

37. Chiaramonte, "The 'Ancient Constitution' after Independence," 466–71, passim. Of course, institutional-legal stasis must not be exaggerated. As Reuben Zahler has shown for Venezuela, independence "catalyzed significant changes" in political and legal culture, ushering in greater transparency, clearer demarcations among jurisdictions, a modicum of due process, and empirical standards of evidence. See Zahler, "Liberal Justice," 522.

38. Rodrigues, *Independência*, 5:231–32.

39. See, for example, the alternative visions of political union espoused by the short-lived Confederation of the Equator in Brazil's northeast in 1824, described in Evaldo Cabral de Mello, *A Outra Independência: O Federalismo Pernambucano de 1817–1824* (São Paulo: Editora 34, 2004).

40. Gootenberg, *Between Silver and Guano*, 33.

41. Centeno, *Blood and Debt*, 118.

42. Jáuregui and Marichal, "Paradojas Fiscales y Financieras de la Temprana República Mexicana," 128–29.

43. Larson, *Trials of Nation Making*, 34.

44. Dore, *Myths of Modernity,* 70–71.

45. Thurner, *From Two Republics to One Divided,* 3.

46. Zahler, "Complaining Like a Liberal," 357.

47. Andrews, *Afro-Latin America,* 77; statistics for 1820 through 1830 were taken from the Transatlantic Slave Trade Database, www.slavevoyages.org (accessed February 25, 2011).

48. In, 1827, 66,511 African slaves were disembarked in Brazil; in 1829, 78,872 were disembarked. Statistics for 1820 through 1830 were taken from the Transatlantic Slave Trade Database, www.slavevoyages.org (accessed February 25, 2011).

49. Needell, "The Abolition of the Brazilian Slave Trade in 1850"; Bethell, "The Rise and Fall of Slavery in Nineteenth-Century Brazil."

50. Stein and Stein, *The Colonial Heritage of Latin America;* Adelman, *Colonial Legacies.*

51. Bayly, "The Age of Revolutions in Global Context," 212. See also Bayly, "The 'Revolutionary Age' in the Wider World," 21–43.

52. Garrido, "Independencia y bicentenario."

53. M. Rodriguez, *The Cádiz Experiment in Central America.*

54. Safford, "Politics, Ideology, and Society."

55. In making these observations, we draw on Cooper, *Colonialism in Question,* esp. chapter 4, "Globalization."

56. Some influential exceptions are Méndez, *The Plebian Republic;* Schmidt-Nowara, *Empire and Antislavery.*

57. For important overviews, see Bailyn, "The Idea of Atlantic History"; and David Armitage, "Three Concepts of Atlantic History," in *The British Atlantic World, 1500–1800,* edited by David Armitage and Michael Braddick (Basingstoke: Palgrave Macmillan, 2002), 11–27.

58. Morgan and Greene, "Introduction: The Present State of Atlantic History," 8.

59. Gould, "Entangled Histories, Entangled Worlds," 764–86.

60. Thurner, "After Spanish Rule: Writing Another After," in Thurner and Guerrero, *After Spanish Rule,* 46.

61. Games, "Atlantic History." This is updated more recently in Caroline Williams, "Introduction: Bridging the Early Modern Atlantic World," in Williams, *Bridging the Early Modern Atlantic World,* 1–32.

62. There are valid arguments for demarcating Atlantic history at the end of the eighteenth century. As Morgan and Greene note, "the presumption seems to be that the expansion of global imperialism and the spread of commerce after 1800 make a global framework of more utility than an Atlantic one," though they argue that "wherever the Atlantic remains a vital, even privileged area of exchange among the

four continents surrounding it, Atlantic History can be a useful tool of analysis." See Morgan and Greene, "Introduction," 21.

63. Interestingly, one of the first textbooks in Atlantic history made precisely this case. As Alan Karras noted, with reference to the abolition of slavery in Brazil in 1888, "a shift away from one socioeconomic system and toward another had clearly and definitively taken place." See Karras, "The Atlantic World as a Unit of Study," 7; José C. Moya, "Modernization, Modernity, and the Trans/formation of the Atlantic World," 179–97.

64. Rothschild, "Late Atlantic History."

65. Canny, "Atlantic History and Global History," 17–36.

66. Elliott, *Empires of the Atlantic World.*

67. Bayly, *The Birth of the Modern World.* Bayly plays here on Karl Jasper's concept of an "axial age," which he used to describe a very different historical epoch. For a trenchant analysis of Jasper's usage, see Shmuel N. Eisenstadt, "The Axial Age: The Emergence of Transcendental Visions and the Rise of Clerics," *European Journal of Sociology* 23, no. 2 (1982): 294–314.

68. Thibaud, Gómez, and Verdo, *Les empires atlantiques entre Lumières et libéralisme.*

69. For recent analyses (and critiques) of conventional periodization due to its failure to take into account phenomena of interest to world historians, see Goldstone, "The Problem of the 'Early Modern' World." On historical periodization, Peter Hulme has pointed out that "the most resistant categories of Eurocentrism are those which are so deeply embedded that we have come to think of them simply as parts of the natural geohistorical landscape." Quoted in Loomba, "Periodisation, Race, and Global Contact."

70. Paraphrase of a line in McKeown, "Periodizing Globalization," 221; as Kathleen Davis recently has pointed out, periodization ignores the historicity of categories and "requires us retrospectively to collapse the difference between history and theory of history, the basis of what is always a *particular* claim upon 'the now.'" See Kathleen Davis, *Periodization and Sovereignty: How Ideas of Feudalism and Secularization Govern the Politics of Time* (Philadelphia: University of Pennsylvania Press, 2008), 20, 134.

71. Green, "Periodizing World History," 53.

72. We might add the first stage in the colonization of Algeria as well, with the French conquest of Algiers taking place months before the advent of the July monarchy. On the connections between French domestic, Atlantic, and nascent Mediterranean policy in this period, see Todd, "A French Imperial Meridian," 155–86.

73. Barman, *Brazil.*

74. M. Pratt, *Imperial Eyes.*

75. Paul Schroeder points out, "The continental powers accepted Anglo-American domination of the Western Hemisphere. . . . Both the Monroe Doctrine and the Polignac Memorandum really suited Europe's wishes, applying to Latin America the principles of mutual aggrandizement and renunciation of force which Europe was practicing at home." See Schroeder, *The Transformation of European Politics,* 635.

76. Citation from Harlow, *The Founding of the Second British Empire,* who coined the phrase; P. Marshall, *"A Free though Conquering People."* This picture has been revised somewhat through the important book by Joseph E. Inikori, *Africans and the Industrial Revolution in England,* which makes clear the continued significance of the Atlantic.

77. Bayly, *Imperial Meridian.*

78. Fradera, *Gobernar colonias;* Alexandre, *Os Sentidos do Império.*

79. Aldrich, *Greater France.*

80. Costeloe, *Response to Revolution.*

81. See also Fradera, *Colonias para después del imperio.*

82. Anna, *Spain and the Loss of America,* 294.

83. Gabriel Paquette, "After Brazil: Portuguese Debates on Empire, c. 1820–50," *Journal of Colonialism and Colonial History* 11, no. 2 (2010): online only.

84. Klooster, *Revolutions in the Atlantic World,* 113.

85. Todd, "French Imperial Meridian," 167–68. Todd further offers evidence for the continuities in personnel and policy between Saint-Domingue and Algeria.

86. Tomich, *Through the Prism of Slavery,* 56–74.

87. See also Gómez, "Le syndrome de Saint-Domingue."

88. See, among others, Williford, *Jeremy Bentham in Spanish America;* and Harris, "An English Utilitarian Looks at Spanish American Independence."

89. Racine, "'This England and This Now,'" 423; Kenneth Maxwell, "Idea of a Luso-Brazilian Empire," in his *Naked Tropics,* 109–44.

90. O'Higgins, quoted in Collier, *The Ideas and Politics of Chilean Independence,* 201.

91. On this theme see Gabriel Paquette, "José da Silva Lisboa and the Vicissitudes of Enlightened Reform in Brazil, 1798–1824," in Paquette, *Enlightened Reform,* 363–88.

92. Racine, "'This England and This Now,'" 424.

93. On Constant's concept of a preserving/neutral/moderating power, see Fontana, *Benjamin Constant and the Post-revolutionary Mind,* esp. 63–65.

94. Bonavides, "Constitucionalismo Luso-Brasileiro"; Miranda, *O Constitucionalismo Liberal Luso-Brasileiro;* and Peixoto et al., *O Liberalismo no Brasil Imperial.*

95. Daughton, "When Argentina was 'French,'" 839.

96. See, among others, Valéria Lima, *J.-B. Debret, historiador e pintor: A Viagem*

Pintoresca e histórica ao Brasil (1816–39) (Campinas: Editora da Unicamp, 2008); and Lilia Moritz Schwarcz, "Sobre Modelos, Ajustes, e Traduções: O Sol do Brasil e os Trópicos Dificeis nas Telas de Artistas da 'Colônia Lebreton,'" *Revista do Instituto Histórico e Geográfico Brasileiro* 168 (2007): 187–222.

97. Racine, "Imagining Independence," 387.

98. Safier, "A Courier between Empires," 265–93.

99. Roldán Vera, *The British Book Trade and Spanish American Independence.*

100. Desmond Gregory, *Brute New World: The Rediscovery of Latin America in the Early Nineteenth Century* (London: I. B. Tauris, 1993). Iona Macintyre's chapter in this volume uncovers some of the unexpected pathways taken by these cultural encounters.

101. Riall, *Garibaldi.*

102. Costeloe, *Bonds and Bondholders.*

103. Stokes, *The English Utilitarians and India*; for a sampling of British views of postcolonial Spanish America, see Paquette, "The Intellectual Origins of British Diplomatic Recognition of the Spanish American Republics," 75–95.

104. This analysis draws heavily from Nigel Leask, *British Romantic Writers and the East: Anxieties of Empire* (Cambridge: Cambridge University Press, 1992), 10–19, 36–37, passim; and Crane Brinton, *The Political Ideas of the English Romanticists* (New York: Russell & Russell, 1952), 152.

105. Lord Byron, "The Age of Bronze" (1823), stanza vi, lines 272–75, quoted in Rebecca Cole Heinowitz, *Spanish America and British Romanticism, 1777–1826: Rewriting Conquest* (Edinburgh: Edinburgh University Press, 2010), 123; on British philhellenism, see William St. Clair, *That Greece Might Still Be Free: The Philhellenes in the War of Independence* (Oxford: Oxford University Press, 1972).

106. Garrett, "Da Europa e da América e de sua mutual influência na causa da civilisação e da liberdade," 85.

107. Isabella, *Risorgimiento in Exile.*

108. See, for example, the essays contained in Paquette, *Enlightened Reform.*

109. For example, see Mignolo, *The Idea of Latin America*; and Coronil, *The Magical State.*

110. On the latter sources, see O. Carlos Stoetzer, *The Scholastic Roots of the Spanish American Revolution* (New York: Fordham University Press, 1979).

111. Pino Iturrieta, *País Archipiélago,* 68–69.

112. Jaksic, *Andrés Bello.*

113. See the two volumes edited by Filippi, *Bolívar y Europa*; also Graham-Yooll, *La independencia de Venezuela vista por The Times.*

114. M. Brown, "Rebellion at Riohacha," 76–97.

115. For example Rolo, *George Canning: Three Biographical Studies,* which divides Canning's life into "man," "politician," and "statesman."

116. Hobsbawm, *The Age of Revolution*; Hobsbawm, *The Age of Capital*; Hobsbawm, *The Age of Empire.*

117. In making these observations on what we might call the "insularity" of European imperial history with regard to Latin America, it will be obvious that we have been influenced by postcolonial works such as Mignolo, *The Idea of Latin America*; and Chakrabarty, *Provincialising Europe.*

118. Bethell, *Abolition of the Brazilian Slave Trade,* 122–50; Martinez, "Anti-slavery Courts and the Dawn of International Human Rights Law"; and Shaikh, "Judicial Diplomacy." The Spanish and British also set up mixed-commission courts to deal with the consequences of privateering in the 1820s. See McCarthy, "Maritime Predation and British Commercial Policy," chapter 6.

119. This literature is summarized in Thompson, *The Empire Strikes Back,* 179–202; and T. M. Devine, *Scotland's Empire, 1600–1815* (London: Penguin, 2005).

120. As, for example, in Dym, "Citizen of Which Republic?"

121. There are some preliminary remarks on this topic in M. Brown, *Adventuring through Spanish Colonies,* 121–25.

122. On Spain's relationship with its colonies in this period, see Schmidt-Nowara, *Empire and Antislavery*; on Brazil in this period, see Barman, *Brazil.*

123. See Platt, *Latin America and British Trade,* 3, 29.

124. Manchester, *British Preeminence in Brazil.*

125. Dawson, *First Latin American Debt Crisis,* 2, 127; Costeloe, *Bonds and Bondholders.*

I

Themes and Tensions in a Contradictory Decade

Ibero-America as a Multiplicity of States

Brian Hamnett

The 1820s are as alive as tomorrow.
—Neill Macaulay, *Dom Pedro*

The most striking feature of the 1820s is the formation of independent Ibero-American states. This represented a lasting blow to the counter-revolutionary structures put in place at the Congress of Vienna of 1814–1815. Despite counter-revolutionary interventions in Italy and Spain in 1822 and 1823, the continental European monarchies would never be able to reverse this, not least because of British naval supremacy in the Atlantic Ocean. Republican forms of government superseded the Bourbon monarchy in all the newly independent, Spanish American states, despite an early and unsuccessful experiment in monarchy in Mexico in 1822 and 1823. The Braganza monarchy in Brazil was independent of the Portuguese branch of the same dynasty and ruled a separate sovereign state. Issues that would become overridingly important during the rest of the nineteenth century and into the twentieth had their origin in the new political structures of the 1820s. Foremost of these were the questions of the distribution of power within the sovereign states, the fiscal relationship between their component parts, and the distribution of wealth within their territories. Once sovereignty had been asserted as a bastion of defense against the former imperial powers and the European states in general, this doctrine had to be put into practical effect by the assertion of control over territory.

The feasibility and durability of all the great projects of the 1820s—monarchy, republicanism, constitutionalism, federalism, nationalism, continentalism—would be harshly put to the test thereafter. Somehow the Catholic Church, integral part of the Old Regime, defender of the Iberian monarchies, and, at the same time, an international institution, had to come to grips with the new realities and assess its position. Tensions between projects and processes ran continuously through this decade, which combined astonishing transformation of political forms with less ambitious tasks of renovation, innovation, and conservation.

Unitarism or Separatism?

Two key developments defined Iberian relations with Ibero-America in the early years of the 1820s. They made the old unitary monarchies no longer a practicable proposition and opened the way to the assertion of independence and separate sovereign status.

The first of these was the inability of the Cortes of Madrid (1820–23) to transform what survived of the Hispanic monarchy on the American continent into one "Hispanic nation" in any form acceptable to either the American deputies or the power groups within the Americas. The unilateral declaration of self-government by the Mexican elites, tactically aligned with the remnants of the insurgency of the 1810s, under the terms of the Plan of Iguala of February 24, 1821, thwarted any such attempt. Although the plan shied away from outright separatism, maintaining the Bourbon monarch as the ruler of a "Mexican Empire," it repudiated the authority of the Spanish metropolitan government within the territory of New Spain. The Cortes's rejection of this project led to a separate Mexican monarchy in June 1822 under Emperor Agustín I.[1]

The second was the decision of the Cortes Gerais of the United Kingdoms of Portugal, the Algarves, and Brazil in Lisbon to reduce the Kingdom of Brazil, proclaimed by João VI in Rio de Janeiro in 1815, to a series of separate provinces directly dependant on the metropolitan government. This opened the way for the proclamation of a Brazilian Empire as a constitutional state under Pedro I (1822–31) by the provinces governed from Rio de Janeiro and their secession in September 1822 from what had been the Luso-Brazilian monarchy.

The idea of "federalizing" the entire Hispanic monarchy had been since 1810 anathema to Spanish liberals, who were dedicated to the preservation of a unitary, though constitutional, state. They similarly resisted American autonomy within the empire as the slippery slope to separatism. Discussion in the Madrid Cortes on the "American question" continued that of 1810–1814 but in graver circumstances. The liberal regime's intransigence, not even prepared to make concessions on the number of American deputies in the Cortes, confirmed the disintegration of the American sector of old monarchy into a multiplicity of weak sovereign states. The Spanish liberals and their Lisbon counterparts of 1821–1823 failed to understand the dimension of the disputed relationship between the American territories and the home countries.[2]

Within South America, the final achievement of independence produced a more coherent Brazil than the disparate provinces of the Portuguese era and contrasted with an even more divided Spanish America. Nevertheless, the imperial government in Rio discovered that it had to coerce the northern and northeastern provinces, which had closer maritime communications with Lisbon, into the empire in the years 1823–1825. Bahia, center of resistance by Portuguese merchants and army officers loyal to the Portuguese Constitution of September 23, 1822, was occupied by Rio's Pacification Army in July 1823. When Pernambuco and Ceará formed the Confederation of the Equator in July 1824, they, too, had to be reduced and the ringleaders punished. These conflicts in the north and northeast were not resolved in 1823 or 1824, but formed the context for further outbreaks between 1832 and 1848. The Brazilian Empire inherited the expansionist aspirations of its Portuguese past, especially in the far south. The war with Argentina for control of the Banda Oriental (Uruguay) from 1825 to 1828 testified to this. Even so, the origins of *modern* Brazil are less in the Portuguese era than in these events of the 1820s.[3]

The final collapse of any solution based on the integration of American continental and European territories signified the end of the two historic empires, which had joined these two parts of their monarchies since the early sixteenth century. This removed two once powerful units from the international structure of power, leaving an array of weak, divided, successor states in both Europe and America.

The political and military situation, however, had changed radically in Ibero-America in the years 1817–1824). The debt of the viceroyalty of Peru, core of the military counter-revolution, increased from 8 million pesos in 1812 to 20 million pesos in 1820, crippling the royal government's further resistance.[4] The collapse of the Miraflores negotiations between Viceroy Joaquin de la Pezuela's government and the liberator José de San Martín in September 1820 ensured that no solution would be found on the basis of reconciliation under the 1812 Cádiz Constitution and recognition of the dynastic rights of the Bourbon monarchy. San Martín, despite instinctive monarchist sentiments, insisted on the absolute independence of Peru and the elimination of the Bourbon monarchy and the imperial Cortes from its political life. The Cortes's commissioners were sent to Venezuela and the viceroyalty of New

Granada, reached the former only to find that the Royalist commander Pablo Morillo had already arranged an armistice with Simón Bolívar. Those destined for New Granada never arrived.[5]

In effect, the ecclesiastical hierarchy and the greater part of the lower clergy across Spanish America changed sides during the years 1821–1824, abandoning the Spanish monarchy as their principal line of defense and opting, instead, for independent American states. This course resulted not simply from suspicion of the Madrid Cortes's ecclesiastical policies but also from Ferdinand VII's failure, during the period of the restored absolutism (1814–1820), to address the reasons for insurrection in Spanish America. The basic issue among Mexican bishops was the necessity for different laws in America than those applicable in Spain. In other words, they had abandoned, along with leading figures in civil society, their former belief that America and Spain could subsist together within the same state.[6] Clerical support for the 1812 constitution, which still remained in force in Mexico until March 1823, however, was conditional on maintenance of the Catholic establishment under Article 12, regarded as the basis for the construction of a Catholic Mexican nation.[7]

The departure of Primate Pedro Fonte in 1821 left the Mexican Catholic Church weakened at a time when the country was in the process of establishing new institutions. The extinction of the episcopate by 1829 became a matter sufficiently alarming for the papacy to allow the nomination of six new bishops in 1831, although the Holy See did not recognize the existence of the Mexican state until 1838. Even so, clerical influence proved sufficiently strong to ensure that the Federal Constitution of October 1824 preserved the Catholic establishment, as would its successors in 1836 and 1843.[8]

The Spanish constitutionalism of 1812 had a profound impact throughout Spanish America, especially in the older territories, where its application led to far-reaching changes in the structure and distribution of political power. Nevertheless, the gathering together of the forces of provincial opposition to central power in the summer of 1823 ensured the success of federalism and, with it, the demise of the Spanish constitution.[9] Similarly, the 1812 constitution remained in force in the fluctuating territories of Royalist-held Peru between 1820 and 1823.[10]

Interrupted Continuities

The transitional authorities attempted to preserve as much as they could of the territorial extent of the viceroyalties and captaincies general, which they superseded. Despite nationalist *ex post facto* rhetoric and the nineteenth-century tendency to write "national histories" under the assumption that nations existed before history and were the natural goal of human social experience, the independence movements were not the nationalist movements of particular territories. The liberators initially intended to preserve what they could of the territorial structure of Spanish America, while transforming the institutions. They had no intention of sponsoring the formation of more than twenty separate sovereign states. This was clear from the time of Simón Bolívar's Jamaica letter of 1815. There were, however, problems in this. Bolívar's "Republic of Colombia" included three territories, Venezuela, New Granada, and Quito, which had been moving away from one another politically during the eighteenth century. The Spanish Crown had, in fact, established Venezuela as a distinct captaincy general in 1786. After 1819, Bolívar incorporated it into the new state, where power would be centered (at least theoretically) in Bogotá, not Caracas; and in 1822, he forcibly incorporated the autonomy-seeking port of Guayaquil into the same state. He was unable, however, to prevent Antonio Sucre's recognition of a separate Republic of Bolivia in 1825 and 1826, which meant that Buenos Aires, capital of the former viceroyalty of the Río de la Plata, lost control of Upper Peru, which it had ruled since 1776 but effectively lost after 1810.[11]

One might say, then, that Bolívar was a "continental nationalist," if that is not a contradiction in terms. In this sense, his goal, achieved by 1825 and 1826, was independence, that is, the destruction of the Spanish political order in South America. This entailed the formation of sovereign states out of the territories of the Spanish Empire, clearly a distinct process, but one in which twenty-five years of warfare ensured that there would be no necessary continuity between the territorial structure of the old order and the new. Conflict, and the degree of violence involved, brought to the surface the diversity of ethnicities and races within these territories and corresponding disparities of wealth, status, and culture.[12]

These, more than anything else, accounted for the failure of what we may describe as "continentalism" in the period 1822–1826. As a result, no supranational organization, however tenuous, replaced the European empires on the American continent in the 1820s. The inconclusive meeting of Bolívar and San Martín in Guayaquil in July 1822 marked the first discussion of a project of cooperation between liberators. The second stage came with Bolívar's letters to the new governments, proposing a conference in Panama to discuss the future of Spanish America. He envisaged cooperation on foreign policy issues, the promotion of collective security, and the establishment of a permanent body for those objectives. He even suggested that Great Britain might act as the guarantor or informal protector. The liberator of five countries, however, received little support for his proposal from the other governments. Only representatives from Mexico, the Central American Federation, Colombia, and Peru, and a British observer, attended the Panama Congress of 1826. Only Colombia ratified the decisions. Similarly, Bolívar's idea of an Andean federation of Colombia, Peru, and Bolivia came to nothing. With the collapse of Colombia in 1830 and the disintegration of the Central American Federation, fragmentation became the rule of the day. It is best to speak of "successor states" to the two great empires, rather than of new "nation-states," since they came into being after a chain of political and military circumstances rather than as the result of any common national consciousness on the part of their ethnically and culturally diverse peoples.[13]

In geopolitical terms, the problem of the separation of Upper and Lower Peru remained a political issue from 1826 until 1841. The military success of the Army of Upper Peru, created by Viceroy José Fernando Abascal in 1810 and under José Manuel de Goyeneche's command until 1813, had ensured that Buenos Aires would never again rule in Upper Peru. Not even the final defeat of this army at Junín and Ayacucho in 1824 could reverse that. Even so, Upper Peru, formerly the territory of the pre-1825 Audiencia of Charcas, had never functioned as a distinct political entity. Abascal had re-annexed it in 1810 to the viceroyalty of Peru, from which the Bourbon ministers had separated it in 1776. This raised the question of the future reunion of the Perus. The two principal military politicians of both territories, Agustín Gamarra and Andrés Santa Cruz, came from the Andean zone, and each at some stage promoted reunification.[14]

Given New Spain's position as creditor to Old Spain, it is not difficult to build a case for independence based on the principle of keeping metropolitan Spain's hands off Mexican resources. Spanish and international pressure on the mining sector accentuated the imbalance of the Mexican economy. Instead, New Spain's resources might have been devoted not to Spanish imperial needs but to internal needs, such as the defense of the northern frontier from raids by the *indios bárbaros,* the preservation of the far north (within the United States from 1848), and the more effective distribution of power within the viceroyalty. All these issues became urgent from 1821 onward in the early history of the Mexican state, but they were alive before that and insufficiently attended to within the imperial state. The origins of independent Mexico's economic and financial problems lay in the late colonial era: the imbalance of the arable and mining sectors at a time of population recovery in the eighteenth century; international and metropolitan pressure on the silver sector of the economy, which, by the 1780s was buckling under the strain; and metropolitan fiscal pressures, especially after 1795. It could be argued that Spain, in terminal decline as an American continental power, dragged its richest colony and creditor down with it, even before the insurrection of 1810 had begun. The full consequences only became visible during the 1820s, when the Mexicans undertook the construction of a sovereign state of their own.[15]

Independence in the 1820s exposed the precarious nature of the finances of the new American states. Mexico, the former creditor of imperial Spain, faced independence with enormous debts. In September 1822, the debt inherited from the viceroyalty was estimated at 76.0 million pesos, in contrast to 31.1 million pesos in 1810 and 3.0 million in 1770. In November 1824, the republican government recognized a debt of 44.7 million. Mexico rapidly acquired an external debt, as well as an internal debt, as a result of the two British loans of 1824, but by 1827 it had defaulted on payments to British bondholders. Although payments would be sporadically resumed afterwards, the country would no longer be eligible for credit on the European financial markets; and few capital owners would want to invest in the economy, as the seven joint-venture mining companies, established in 1824 and 1825, ran into difficulties one after the other as the decade ended. Deprived of internal sources of credit, the Mexican state fell into the hands of domestic creditors, known as *agiotistas*.[16]

Inherent Tensions within the New States of Iberian America

In contrast to the "ominous decade," 1823–1833, in Spain, when for a second time Ferdinand VII ruled as absolute monarch, Spanish America presented a different picture of incipient constitutional republics, of elections with varying degrees of franchise, and of experiments in federalism. Under the constitution of 1824, Brazil's moderate constitutional monarchy lasted until the removal of Pedro II in 1889. Few Spanish American constitutions were in force that long.

In several respects, the new Spanish American states drew back from the radicalism of the 1812 constitution, establishing bicameralism and a more restrictive franchise or reducing the number of deputies in relation to population. The division within liberalism between "moderates" and "radicals" (*exaltados* or *puros*), which would become such a characteristic feature of, for instance, Mexican liberalism from the 1820s to the 1870s, owed its origin to the conflicts over the pace and nature of reform, the structure of the new institutions, and the extent of the franchise, which had been evident in the Madrid Cortes of 1820–1823. In Mexico, this would involve two distinctive aspects: the ongoing debate concerning the nature of federalism, and the distribution of powers that this entailed, and the recruitment of popular support from the socio-ethnic majority of the population.[17]

As an established system of government, Mexican federalism, established in 1823 and 1824, was one of the most distinctive results of the ideas and pressures at play in the former New Spain during the 1820s. Its origins lay in earlier issues in Mexican political life, and, as such, it was distinct from the type of federalism established in the United States in 1787. The federal experience in Mexico, with all its internal tensions, variants, and oppositions, would provide a vital source for comparative study of federal systems established thereafter. Mexican federalism contained a radical wing favoring an extended franchise and municipal liberties. In practice, the Federal Constitution of 1824 represented a compromise between the center and regions, giving state governors broad powers and enabling state governments to deny the federal government sufficient revenues for effective administration.[18]

Formal Incorporation into the International Economy

Direct incorporation of Spanish America into the international economy only rarely fulfilled the promise of its initial advocates, whether European or American. Contact with the world market had always existed, despite formal restrictions in the colonial era, since Spain had never been able to transform its claim to be the economic metropolis of its empire into a reality. In that sense, the legalization of this trade at independence simply confirmed preexisting conditions and eliminated the taxing, former metropolis. New Granada, for example, had long been a gold exporter, as much through the "contraband" trade as through the Spanish colonial system, and remained so after independence. Not until after 1850 did landowners and exporters commit themselves to the development of tropical produce as a key element in the economy. The separatist elite of the 1820s attributed backwardness to Spanish rule and used their control of the state to open the economy to the world market, encouraging the import of foreign capital and applying for loans in the years 1822–1825. Foreign interest, however, quickly dropped off, and in 1826 the government defaulted on payments to foreign bondholders, as Peru had already done in the previous year. By the early 1830s, British and other foreign pre-eminence in the external trade began to wane at a time of general economic contraction.[19]

The situation in the River Plate was radically different. Tulio Halperín Donghi argues that British merchants, during the 1820s, installed a commercial relationship similar to the Spanish system, which they had helped to destroy. Even so, the greatest impact of the import of British manufactures, which principally consisted of textiles, was in the city of Buenos Aires and its countryside, where as much as two-thirds were absorbed. The decline of the domestic textile industry, then, was not due to competition in the interior, but to the loss of the urban and littoral market. In the interior, a low-wage zone, local textiles, woven mainly by women, continued to find a market.[20] British merchants, in effect, superseded the Buenos Aires home merchants, who had been instrumental in pressing for the opening of the external trade in 1809 and 1810. Local merchants, after the achievement of independence, redeployed their capital into livestock farming, which had not hitherto been a prime attraction for them. The objective conditions facilitating such a development became available when Bernardino Rivadavia in 1822 authorized the renting of public land for period of twenty years at fixed rent. Juan Manuel de Rosas's rise to power in 1829 led to the abandonment of restraints and to the sale of land in freehold. The basis for the establishment of large-scale cattle estates, geared toward the export market in Europe and North America, was laid in the 1820s, despite the Brazilian blockade of Buenos Aires in 1827 and 1828, and radically extended from the 1830s. Sons of colonial merchant families were among the new *estancia* owners.[21]

In the River Plate provinces, the capital-city liberal project collapsed in 1829, leaving these dispersed territories exposed to extemporary rule under local chieftains, who would be obliged to establish some kind of arrangement with Rosas, who until 1852 became, in effect, the "national caudillo." Rosas, in alliance with the cattle barons of the expanding pampas, enforced his rule with ruthless indifference to legal processes and urban sensibilities. In such a way, the turmoil of the 1820s prepared the way for the ongoing dialectic of Argentine politics through the rest of the century and for much of the twentieth as well: authoritarian rule or constitutional legality.[22]

In several Spanish American countries, for instance, Mexico, Peru, and New Granada, the debate on free trade versus protectionism began in earnest in the 1820s. The broader context pointed to the future role of these newly independent states in the international market as primary producers and metal or mineral exporters rather than producers of manufactures. Only low purchasing power in the domestic market and poor communications inland saved what was left of artisan manufacturing. After 1824, Great Britain became the principal importer into Mexico—up to 64 percent of the total by 1840, with textiles as the main commodity. The essential problem continued to be the technological lag of Mexican home producers in relation to factory production in northwestern Europe. Puebla cotton went into crisis, while the cotton industry of Guadalajara collapsed by the mid-1820s, and Querétaro woolens went into terminal decline and the city's population fell from around seventy thousand in 1810 to twenty-five thousand by 1826.[23]

The Search for a New Order

The search for a new order following the breakdown of Spanish power was accompanied by the spread of military satrapies, chieftain networks, and guerrilla or brigand bands. Often rough leaders arose from below, alongside educated proponents of representative government. Spanish American liberals and conservatives made tactical alliances with military chieftains like Antonio López de Santa Anna, Gamarra, or Santa Cruz or caudillos such as José Antonio Páez in Venezuela or *cacique* rulers of localities if they wished to gain or retain power in the new states. In most states, the ties between constitutionalism and private power were interwoven, which explained the nature of the political system for some fifty years.

The 1820s was the decade in which the real poverty of Latin America, rather than its fabled riches, was revealed to the outside world for the first time. Investors and bondholders discovered instability and then, from as early as 1825 to 1827, default on debt payment, unresolved and unforeseen technological problems in the mining sector (dating from the colonial era), the absence of effective communications across country, and inadequate port facilities on the coasts. They were dismayed to find a largely unskilled labor force, mainly illiterate; and in large parts of Mexico, Guatemala, and the Andean countries, the potential consumers did not understand the Spanish language.

During the latter part of the 1820s, several colonial taxes were restored and attempts to establish new forms of direct taxation were made in order to address the fiscal problems of these struggling states with their uncertain futures. Independent Mexico made its first moves in the direction of direct taxation on June 23, 1823, based on the Cádiz model of 1813, but it would prove to be an inflammatory issue during subsequent decades, especially in the Centralist period from 1836 to 1846. In Peru, agricultural production collapsed in the period 1820–1824, particularly in the coastal valleys, largely as a consequence of war. During the decade, silver production declined at Cerro de Pasco from 312,931 marks to 95,261 marks, after a long period of expansion up to 1800. Inevitably, this led to contraction of the ancillary arable and livestock sectors. Government revenue fell 50 percent from the 1800s to the early 1820s. After independence, the Peruvian government proved incapable of raising revenue in proportion to the growth of population. Paper currency was issued in 1822 and 1823. The loss of tribute revenue, abolished by the Cortes in 1811 and by the colonial *alcabala* by 1826, made it necessary to reestablish the tobacco monopoly in the same year and reconstitute the tribute. This *contribución de indígenas* in 1826 and 1827 would supply three-quarters of government revenue, which at the same time remained heavily dependent on customs revenues. In Bolivia, silver production had collapsed and shortage of money hampered trade and government: silver introduced into the National Mint declined from 457,537 marks in 1800 to 181,142 in 1829. Bolívar and Sucre reasserted state control over unexploited mines in Potosí and hoped for foreign capital to revive them and rescue government finance. Only after 1829 was the National Mint able to increase production sufficiently to respond to the needs of the internal economy. Although silver production declined between 1830 and 1860, regional commerce did not substantially suffer in proportion to the share of silver traditionally used to pay for imports from abroad through Arica and Buenos Aires—around 60 percent in the later colonial era. The greater part of the silver coined—an annual average of 1.49 million pesos between 1825 and 1830—went abroad. Even so, Bolivia remained only loosely connected to the international economy until the mid-1870s. As in Peru, the Bolivian government depended upon the *capitación de indios* for 40 percent of its revenue. In such a way, the greatest burden of sustaining the Andean states fell on the poorest sectors of the population.[24]

Plantation owners, oriented toward the export trade, dominated the processes of government in imperial Brazil, rather than the emperor, who was unsympathetic to slavery, and his ministers. While the northeastern sugar sector, faced with competition from Spanish Cuba, declined in relative importance, world demand for coffee stimulated the opening of the Paraíba Valley in the province of Rio de Janeiro from the 1820s, and the port overtook Salvador de Bahia as the principal entry point for African slaves bound for the interior. An annual average of thirty-seven thousand slaves entered Brazil between 1811 and 1850. Great Britain persuaded Portugal to recognize Brazilian independence in 1825, partly to sever Brazil's traditional ties with Angola and Dahomey, principal sources of slaves. Britain hoped to tie recognition to the abolition of slavery, at least after 1830. This led to lasting conflict between Britain and Brazil for the following two decades.[25]

Both Brazil and Mexico wrestled with the question of what to do about their Portuguese and Spanish minorities. The Portuguese issue resurfaced in imperial politics in the late 1820s and contributed to the abdication of the emperor in 1831. In Mexico, the question of expulsion tore apart the First Federal Republic in the years 1825–1830. Although the two Federal Expulsion Laws of December 20, 1827, and March 20, 1829, were unevenly applied, allowed many exceptions, and left 52 percent of the estimated ten thousand peninsular Spaniards still in the country, they caused hardship and mortality for those expelled and further impoverished the country in the process, draining the country of perhaps 12 million pesos in silver. Spanish merchants' links with European trade explained the resulting decline in customs revenues, a principal source of governmental income.[26] The expulsion question led to a regrouping of conservative forces as the *hombres de bien,* opponents of the "popular party," liberal, moderate, radical, or federalist, during the period 1830 to 1867.[27]

The 1820s saw the emergence of a new factor in international politics, the independent Ibero-American sovereign states. Without supranational support and frequently at conflict either with one another or within their own territories, these states were vulnerable to outside intervention. We observe in the 1820s the beginnings of the exchange of claims and counter-claims between regions and centers in most of the newly independent states. Although it is true that provincial pressures for a greater say in decision making can be discerned at least as far back as the 1790s, only during the 1820s do they become clearly articulated as political projects. Mexican federalism, established under the 1824 constitution, was a striking example of this. It sought to maintain the cohesion of a new national polity not remarkably different in territory from the former viceroyalty of New Spain. Federalism and regionalism reflected the internal dimension of independence, viewed no longer in relation to the European metropolis but in terms of emancipation from dominant capital-city elites within the Americas. The external debt question also became a major issue during the 1820s, affecting Latin America's relations with the wider world through the rest of the century and well into the twentieth. The problem accompanied and exacerbated the outstanding internal debt question, inherited from the late colonial era, which contributed substantially to the destabilizing of the new states. The weakening of artisan industries through foreign competition in manufactures made it necessary to think of Ibero-America in terms of primary exportation as a means of economic recovery. Coffee exportation from Brazil and Costa Rica would provide early examples of this, with Colombia following from mid-century. Similarly, Cuban sugar proved vital to the island's survival and to its continued Spanish metropolis. The inherent danger, evident as the century advanced, was monoculture and dependency on fluctuating external markets. However, inadequate infrastructures of transportation, communication, and banking held back recovery. From the 1820s the weak purchasing power of the majority of the population of the subcontinent became evident to outsiders for the first time.

The quotation from Neill Macaulay at the opening of this chapter points to the contemporary relevance of the 1820s. We may see this in the issue of Latin American integration or, stated less intensely, coordination. I have drawn attention here to a spectacular failure in this respect during the 1820s and highlighted the consequences. Contemporary international alignments already suggest increased weight for several leading Latin American countries, the consequence of a diminished US hegemony and the collapse of the ideological politics that dominated most of the twentieth century. Some Latin American commentators stress the urgency of union during the period 2010–2035, with individual states becoming the *patria chica* and Latin America viewed as the *patria mayor*.[28] Outstanding issues, familiar to most students of the region, threaten to frustrate such a goal. Furthermore, the two overriding issues of the practical nature of supranational integration and its moral basis remain to be defined. What, for example, might be the existing models? What would be the purpose of such a union—to overcome existing impotence on a continental scale, to prevent a lapse into a worse scale of poverty, to counterbalance other unions or alliances? Viewing Latin American history from its origins, what might be the role of Christianity in defining the moral basis of integration? Finally, the anticolonial breach with Europe was determined during the 1820s: what example might Latin America provide as the earliest region to cast aside tutelage to the old monarchies?

Independence in the 1820s should always be viewed within the context of the great power rivalries of the later eighteenth and early nineteenth centuries. Great Britain's decision to move toward recognition, for example, was motivated less by commercial interests than by the French intervention in Spain in 1823, which revived fears of Franco-Spanish cooperation dating from the time of Louis XIV. Even so, the unresolved conflicts within Ibero-America provided the overriding explanations for the triumph of separatism in the 1820s. The armed conflicts across the subcontinent had exacerbated these and also provided new issues, which independent states would have to resolve, if they could. Weak as the new states were, they owed their formation to armed struggle and rejection of European tutelage. Any concept of informal empire by European powers needs to take this history into consideration. Ibero-American responses to the French intervention in Mexico from 1862 to 1867 revealed this strikingly.

The emergence of new states on the American continent during the 1820s did not prove to be an isolated event. In Europe, the Greek struggle for independence broke out in 1821 and continued right through the decade, weakening the Ottoman Empire in the Balkans and Eastern Mediterranean. Further fissures occurred in the cases of Romania and Bulgaria and, finally, Crete, Epirus, and Macedonia between the 1870s and early 1910s. After the 1820s, however, the next two periods of imperial collapse came, first, with the fall of the Romanov, Habsburg, and Turkish Empires and the collapse of the Second German Empire and the Hohenzollern monarchy between 1917 and 1923 and, second, with the dissolution of the overseas empires of Great Britain, France, the Netherlands, and Belgium between 1942 and the 1960s and the loss of the Portuguese Empire in Asia and Africa between 1963 and 1975. The difference between the collapse of the Iberian empires on the American continent in the 1820s and the first of these later periods was that in the latter nationalism had already become the predominant mode of political consciousness and behavior. The monarchies of Spain and Portugal, furthermore, both survived imperial collapse on the American continent. The Ibero-American states in the 1820s fell prematurely into statehood before the emergence of national consciousness in their territories. Even so, the sovereign states of Venezuela and Chile, for example, existed a century before the creation of entities such as Austria or Hungary and half a century before the creation of unified Italy or Germany. Although the second phase of state creation, mainly after 1947, represented the rejection by overseas possessions of their former metropoles, this, too, differed from the experience of the 1820s, in that Spanish and Portuguese America retained a primary linguistic and cultural connection to their former metropoles.

This connection remained vital. Although linguistic usage and forms differed in the two continents and between areas, literary and artistic developments remained mutually influential after the 1820s. Nevertheless, Ibero-America opened to other outside influences, literary, political, or economic, in so far as literacy, book publication, receptivity, and economic trends permitted. Fascinating as they are, we do not have space here to discuss the many examples of this. Immigration patterns from Iberia to America after independence further strengthened cultural and family ties.

The principal commercial relationship had been and continued to be across the Atlantic, both because of and in spite of the Iberian colonial systems. Internal developments, however, provided a significant determinant of the pattern of this connection during the nineteenth century. This relationship continued to be mainly with the Western European seaboard, while the Brazilian connection to Africa became a subject of intense dispute with Great Britain because of the slave trade from the 1820s onward. The Pacific and Asiatic dimensions of Ibero-America's external relations by and large lapsed for most of the nineteenth century but would be reconstructed on different bases from the late twentieth century.

Ibero-America's Atlantic world consisted predominantly of enclaves. While it is correct to argue that enclaves had hinterlands related to them, that is not the completed picture. Again, internal developments, the distinct ethno-social characteristics, and the economic activities involved all contributed to wide differentiation between coastal, plantation, or mining enclaves and the rest of the interior. Whenever commercial relations with the external world passed into recession, the economic activities and political pressures from the interior rose once more to prominence. The construction of federal systems reflected such pressures.

In the 1820s, the final outcome of political conflicts between European metropoles and Ibero-American dependencies confirmed the latter's place as the third component in the phenomenon often described as the Atlantic revolutions. Its periodization should stretch, therefore, from 1776 to 1826. Different in origin, composition, and character, these movements were in no way dependent on or subsidiary to the two earlier revolutionary movements in the thirteen colonies or in France, which the originators of the Atlantic thesis short-sightedly took to be its sole components.

Notes

1. Felipe Tena Ramírez, *Leyes fundamentales de México, 1808–1864,* 6th ed. (Mexico City: Editorial Porrúa, 1975), 113–16; Anna, *The Mexican Empire of Iturbide,* 61–86.

2. Macaulay, *Dom Pedro,* 45, 81, 104; Anna, *The Mexican Empire of Iturbide,* 27–60; Chust, "Federalismo *avant la lettre* en las Cortes hispanas," 77–114.

3. Rodrigues, *Independência,* 1:111, 3:31; Sérgio Buarque de Holanda (director),

História Geral da Civilização Brasileira, II O Brasil monárquico, 2 Dispersão e Unidade (Sao Paulo: Difel, 1968), 244–67; Barman, *Brazil,* 65–126; Reis, *Rebelião escrava no Brasil,* 143–82; Souza, *A Sabinada,* 10–11, 15, 19–23; Slemian, "Instituciones, legitimidad y [des]orden," 89–108; Macaulay, *Dom Pedro,* 138–39, 165–66.

4. Anna, *The Fall of the Royal Government in Peru,* 150.

5. Hamnett, *Revolución y contrarrevolución en México y el Perú,* 303–4 (the second edition is currently in press); Anna, *Spain and the Loss of America,* 221–57; Earle, *Spain and the Independence of Colombia,* 154–56; Thibaud, *Repúblicas en Armas,* 469–507.

6. Connaughton, *Dimensiones de la identidad patriótica,* 46–47.

7. Ibid., 13–23.

8. *Constitución de los Estados Unidos Mexicanos,* Article 3, in Ramírez, *Leyes fundamentales de México,* 167–95.

9. Frasquet, *Las caras del águila,* 121, 228, 266–67, 297, 307; Ortiz Escamilla and Serrano Ortega, *Ayuntamientos y liberalismo gaditano en México.*

10. Hamnett, *Revolución y contrarrevolución en México y el Perú,* 300–304, 323–40, 349, 353.

11. Dated Kingston, September 6, 1815, the letter was not published in Spanish until 1833, although its ideas ran through Bolívar's thought on colonialism. He differentiated the South American from the US experience and moved toward a centralist, authoritarian liberalism. John Lynch, *Simón Bolívar, A Life,* 92–95, 198–99.

12. J. Lynch, *Simón Bolívar,* 212.

13. Ibid., 171–75, 213–15. San Martín secured Bolívar's aid for the final liberation of Peru but held no support for his idea of a European monarchy in Peru.

14. Glave, *Vida, símbolos y batallas;* Glave, "Una perspectiva histórico-cultural de la revolución del Cuzco de 1814," 11–38; Walker, *Smouldering Ashes,* 97–151; Aldana Rivera, "Un norte diferente para la Independencia peruana," 142–64. For Santa Cruz, see Sobrevilla Perea, *Caudillo of the Andes.*

15. Marichal, "Beneficios y costos fiscales del colonialism," 475–505. These arguments are further developed in Carlos Marichal, *Bankruptcy of Empire: Mexican Silver and the Wars between Spain, Britain, and France, 1760–1810* (Cambridge: Cambridge University Press, 2007); Tenebaum, *The Politics of Penury,* 11–36.

16. Marichal and Marino, *De Colonia a Nación,* 37–58; Villegas Revueltas, *Deuda y diplomacia,* 10–11, 21–48; Pi-Suñer, *La deuda española en México,* 32–46, using John TePaske's figures (1998); Tenenbaum, "Mexico's Money Market and the Internal Debt," 257–92.

17. Comellas, *El Trienio constitucional,* 130–73; Thomson, "Popular Aspects of Liberalism," 265–92; Guardino, *Peasants, Politics, and the Formation of Mexico's National State,* 81–98.

18. Anna, *Forging Mexico,* 98–175; Serrano Ortega and Jáuregui, *Hacienda y política.*

19. Frank Safford, "Commercial Crisis and Economic Ideology in New Granada," 184, 186–89, 192–93.

20. Halperín Donghi, "La apertura mercantil en el Río de la Plata," 122, 134.

21. J. Brown, *A Socioeconomic History of Argentina,* 34, 48–49, 90–91, 116, 147. The population of the city of Buenos Aires rose from 24,205 inhabitants in 1777 to 42,252 in 1810 and stood at 55,416 in 1822, climbing rapidly thereafter. J. Lynch, "Foreign Trade and Economic Interests in Argentina," 140–41.

22. John Lynch, *Juan Manuel de Rosas (1829–1852): Argentine Dictator* (Oxford: Oxford University Press 1981), 23–91; J. Lynch, *Caudillos in Spanish America.*

23. Gootenberg, *Between Silver and Guano,* 34–67; Thomson, "Traditional and Modern Manufacturing in Mexico," 56, 67–70; Bernecker, "Comercio y comerciantes extranjeros en las primeras décadas de la independencia mexicana," 88, 90, 92, 108–9.

24. T. Platt, *Estado tributario y librecambismo en Potosí,* 16–23, 31–32; Mitre, *El monedero de los Andes,* 28–33, 116, 118; Burga, "El Perú central," 250–61, 279–80; Jacobsen, "Taxation in Early Republican Peru," 311–39; Contreras, "Las contribuciones directas en la formación del Perú republicano," 123–48.

25. Rodrigues, *Brazil and Africa,* 139–44; P. A. Curtin, *The Rise and Fall of the Plantation Complex,* 191; S. Stein, *Vassouras;* Macaulay, *Dom Pedro,* 88–92, 215–22.

26. Sims, *Descolonización en México,* 9–13, 16, 21–23, 33, 36, 38–40, 44, 48, 51, 54–59, 223, 229–30, 244–46, 252–53; Macaulay, *Dom Pedro,* 246–53.

27. Sims, *Descolonización en México,* 62–68, 73–74, 79–80, 84, 88, 120–23, 127, 136–37, 164, 203, 206–8, 217, 227. See also Vincent, *The Legacy of Vicente Guerrero,* 158–207.

28. See, for example, "Entrevista: Porfirio Muñoz Ledo: Unificación latinoamericana, vieja utopía hoy factible," *La Jornada* (Mexico City), March 7, 2010, 5; and Alberto Caturelli, "Génesis y Naturaleza de la Integración Iberoamericana," magistral conference, *XI Encuentro Internacional de Centros de Cultura: "Memoria e Identidad Nacional,"* Universidad Popular Autónoma del Estado de Puebla, March 9–11, 2010.

2

Rafael del Riego and the Spanish Origins of the Nineteenth-Century Mexican *Pronunciamiento*

Will Fowler

Spanish Liberalism and Revolution in the Atlantic World

In James Dunkerley's unorthodox study of the Americas around 1850, he decided to include Ireland's history alongside that of Spanish America, Brazil, and the United States in what he termed the "Atlantic Space." For Dunkerley there was nothing arbitrary about this decision: "My support . . . for the idea that Ireland is really an American country located in the wrong continent is by no means original—the diasporas of the eighteenth and nineteenth centuries ensured its continuous displacement."[1] Dunkerley's Atlanticism was, in part, inspired by his teacher, Professor Gwyn A. Williams, who had argued, "Politics in Wales begin with the American Revolution."[2] However, it was also representative of a historiographical shift that started in the 1950s, when Robert Palmer and Jacques Godechot had the audacity to suggest that the "French Revolution was part of a wider Atlantic movement against the western old regimes."[3] This Atlanticist view has been ultimately responsible for a major change in the way historians like Dunkerley (and the contributors to this volume) have come to understand the "national" histories of a range of Western European and American countries, especially within the given, albeit contested, time frame of the so-called age of democratic revolutions (1750–1850). While issues of national or regional exceptionality paired with conceptual problems posed by notions of race and ethnicity cannot be underestimated or overlooked,[4] the Atlanticists' research of the last four decades has forced us to reflect on the extent to which local conditions merit consideration in a broader context, what Eric Van Young termed "the relationship between the tempest (imperial crisis) and the teapot (local conflict and violence),"[5] and on how far it is possible to trace and distinguish the imitation, influence, rejection, adoption, and transformation of specific trans-national ideas in countries on both sides of the Atlantic. More specifically, Atlanticism has inspired a move to interpret the close political, economic, and cultural bonds that linked the respective histories of Europe and the Americas (with Africa coerced into providing the slaves) within the concrete historical period that Peggy Liss originally defined as having been one of "trade and revolution" and which she viewed as stretching from the Treaty of Utrecht in 1713 to the first pan-American congress in Panama in 1826.[6]

From the perspective of the Hispanic world, numerous studies have since highlighted the shared mental constructs and ideas that flowed across the Atlantic, alongside the slaving ships, disseminating constitutional and revolutionary beliefs that went on to influence and inform political developments on both sides of the ocean. Although this is not the place to engage in an in-depth critical review of the recent historiography on the subject, worthy of note is the extent to which growing numbers of monographs, edited volumes, book chapters, and journal articles have, indeed, tackled the age of democratic revolutions (1750–1850) from a trans-national, inter-American, and trans-Atlantic perspective.[7] The "thaw in nationalistic historiography," which Palmer and Godechot started, has resulted, as Anne Pérotin-Dumon predicted back in 1984, in historians thinking "beyond their nationalistic fortresses."[8] The Seven Years' War (1756–1763), the subsequent reordering of the American possessions of the British and Spanish Crowns, the American war of independence (the Revolutionary War, 1775–1783), the French Revolution (1789), the Haitian Revolution (1791), the French invasion of the Iberian Peninsula (1808), and the subsequent Spanish and Spanish American wars of independence (1808–1826) are events that are, by now, commonly viewed as having been closely related. Although the 2010 celebrations, marking the bicentenary of the eruption of the wars of independence in Venezuela, Argentina, and Mexico, continued to endorse a patriotic, nationalistic vision of their countries' respective revolutionary movements,[9] Jaime E. Rodríguez O.'s Atlanticist interpretation has become the standard view in scholarly circles: "The independence of Spanish America can best be understood as part of the larger process of change that occurred in the Atlantic world in the second half of the eighteenth and the early nineteenth centuries."[10]

Bearing in mind this relatively recent historiographic tradition, Matthew

Brown and Gabriel Paquette rightly stress, in the introduction to this volume, that historians have become "increasingly aware of the persistence, even deepening and creation, of robust links between Europe and the new nations that emerged from the defunct Iberian empires."[11] That there was a constant flow of people and ideas from one end of the Atlantic to the other and in between the emergent independent nations and their former colonial powers during the age of revolutions is by now taken for granted. Revolutionaries like Francisco de Miranda, called the "Precursor of Spanish American Independence," to take one example, as Karen Racine reminds us, "lived and fought on four continents, [and] schemed with the Atlantic world's most powerful leaders."[12] Although Miranda may strike us as having been exceptional in that his travels took him from his native Venezuela to the United States, North Africa, Europe, Russia, and Asia, and he was "at various times a Spanish military officer, an informant of the British in the Caribbean, a colonel in the Russian army, a commander of French Revolutionary forces in the Netherlands,"[13] as well as generalissimo of the Venezuelan First Republic, his globetrotting circumstances were not entirely unique. A glance at the lives of a significant number of leading figures in the Spanish American wars of independence shows that many of them, like Miranda, whether they fought for the patriots or the Royalists, came and went from one side of the Atlantic to the other, acquiring experiences and ideas that would result in their actions paralleling those of their counterparts *and* antagonists in other parts of the Atlantic world, before, during, and after the wars of independence.[14]

From the perspective of the Hispanic world, if there was one political movement that spread like wild fire on both sides of the Atlantic, this was Spanish liberalism with its ardent faith in representative government and constitutionalism, its defiant anti-absolutism, its emphasis on liberty (free trade, freedom of the press, freedom of movement, freedom of religious belief), equality before the law (calling for an end to ecclesiastic and military privileges, i.e., the *fueros*), and its defense and romantic glorification of the individual vis-à-vis the collective and corporate practices of the ancien régime (e.g., Catholic Church properties, communal lands, etc.).[15] As Roberto Breña states in no uncertain terms: "The magnitude of this influence . . . went well beyond the Cádiz constitutional years."[16] The extremely progressive 1812 Constitution of Cádiz, together with the experience of its application from 1812 to 1814 and from 1820 to 1823, provided a constitutional framework that was subsequently emulated in a range of Spanish American countries, most notably, in Mexico, where the war of independence (1810–21) did not prevent the constitution from being implemented from 1812 to 1814 *and* from 1820 to 1821, with the subsequent creation of provincial deputations, town councils *(ayuntamientos),* and the organization of local and trans-Atlantic elections.[17] The 1814 insurgent Constitution of Apatzingán and the 1824 Federal Constitution were visibly influenced and inspired by the Cádiz charter.[18]

The liberal Masonic gatherings, brotherhoods, and secret societies that became, at the same time, the think tanks and social networks of anti-absolutism and organized clandestine political activity (especially after Ferdinand VII revoked the 1812 constitution in 1814) likewise spread across the Hispanic world as liberal army officers posted in the expeditionary armies that were dispatched to crush the independence movements in the colonies found themselves recruiting sympathetic *criollos* who would thereafter, following independence, engross the renamed lodges that were to become the incipient political parties of the 1820s.[19] In brief, constitutionalism and the use of Masonic gatherings to conspire against absolutism were two obvious exports that liberalism disseminated throughout Spain and Spanish America. However, a slightly more problematic liberal practice, which originated during the so-called dark years of Ferdinand VII's return to absolutism (1814–20) and proved equally successful in crossing the Atlantic, but which has not merited as much attention as liberal constitutionalism, was the pronunciamiento.

This chapter is specifically concerned with how what was initially a subversive liberal political practice originating in Spain, that is the pronunciamiento, became the way of "doing politics" on both sides of the Atlantic and, in particular, in Spain and Mexico, following the success of Rafael del Riego's *grito* of Cabezas de San Juan of January 1, 1820. In order to do this, after briefly outlining what is meant here by a pronunciamiento, this chapter traces the manner in which this "typically Spanish" practice crossed the Atlantic,[20] from Spain to Mexico, and became a common feature of the political landscape in both countries for the following fifty-odd years (i.e., until 1874 in Spain, when Arsenio Martínez Campos's pronunciamiento of Sagunto, of December 29, ushered in the comparatively stable years of the Restoration and the *turno pacífico,* and until 1876 in Mexico, when Porfirio Díaz's pronunciamiento of Tuxtepec, of January 10, gave way to his thirty-five-year-long stint in power). On the one hand, its aim is to show why the pronunciamiento proved so attractive and addictive to liberal politicians and army officers on both sides of the Atlantic. On the other hand, it is concerned with the manner in which Rafael del Riego's first successful and trend-setting pronunciamiento of January 1, 1820, consecrated a practice that was subsequently emulated and developed in Mexico, paying attention to how news of what Riego's pronunciamiento actually achieved reached and impacted upon Mexican society on the eve its independence from Spain.

The *Pronunciamiento* and a Shared Atlantic Context of Contested Authority

As was noted by Carlos Banus, with a certain degree of pride, in his 1881 *Tratado de historia y arte militar,* "The word *pronunciamiento* indicates that with regards to this matter the privilege of its invention is ours [i.e., Spain's]."[21] The view that this was a Spanish practice is, in part, a question of nomenclature. Initially, its "Spanishness" stemmed from the fact that the term itself, *pronunciamiento* (literally, pronouncement),[22] was coined by Riego in his address to the battalions of Asturias, Guías, Sevilla, and Aragón on January 3, 1820. In his address he stated: "Soldiers: The Glory you have acquired with your heroic pronunciamiento will not be erased from the Spaniards' hearts as long as the sweet voice of the Patria is not devoid of meaning."[23] Thereafter, the term was used until the mid-twentieth century in Spain, Mexico, and a number of Central American countries, even though it was rarely employed in the insurrectionary vocabulary of other Spanish-speaking countries.[24] This gives further credence to the view that this was, to quote the *Diccionario de Historia de España,* "a typical Spanish phenomenon from a very determined period of our history."[25] Following on from this, the most common definition of pronunciamiento, found in popular encyclopedias such as Wikipedia, is that it was a Spanish variant of the Napoleonic coup d'état.[26] For the sake of clarity, and before we focus on the extraordinary influence Riego's pronunciamiento had on both sides of the Atlantic, it is important to offer a succinct definition of what is meant here by a pronunciamiento.

Unlike a coup d'état or a revolution, a pronunciamiento did not openly set out to overthrow the government or to mobilize a mass following. Invariably supported by a written text (manifesto, address, petition), it was what Miguel Alonso Baquer defined as "a gesture of rebellion":[27] an act of insubordination that included a threat of violence that was staged in a particular community in the hope that other towns and garrisons would follow suit, forcing the government to listen to the rebels' demands. The successful pronunciamiento, as would be seen for the first time in 1820, was one that initiated a cycle of copycat pronunciamientos that spread across the country, from the periphery to the center, ultimately forcing the government, in this case the king, to implement the *pronunciados'* demands, which, in Riego's case, entailed bringing back the 1812 constitution without this resulting in a change of ruler (Ferdinand VII did not abdicate and remained on the Spanish throne). The numerous pronunciamientos that surfaced thereafter in Spain and Mexico, accepting that there were variations and exceptions, generally attempted to emulate this pattern of forceful lobbying/mobilization. A town was taken over by a given garrison or military unit in collusion with the local civilian authorities; a petition was somewhat theatrically "pronounced," claiming the aggrieved pronunciados were responding to and acting on behalf of the ignored and trampled "general will" of the *patria*; its text was then circulated to the neighboring towns, garrisons, and key political players; and, if sufficient and powerful cities and regiments supported it with their own pronunciamientos of allegiance (*de adhesión*), the government, without being overthrown, addressed the insurrectionists' demands. On paper it was, to quote Josep Fontana, "a new political formula that facilitated a controlled revolutionary process."[28] In Mexico, the 1834 "religión y fueros" corpus, the 1835 pro-centralist constellation, and the 1842 San Luis Potosí and Huejotzingo series could be considered textbook examples of how a successful pronunciamiento cycle was meant to unfold. In all three cases, without the president or his cabinet being overthrown, they resulted in the pronunciados' demands being met, for example: the closure of Congress and the reversal of its unpopular radical reforms in 1834, the end of the 1824 constitution and the change to a centralist political system in 1835, and the closure of Congress and tearing up of its proposed federalist constitution in 1842.[29] The fact that a significant number of pronunciamiento cycles did end in a change of government (even though these did not explicitly set out to do so) may account for the reason why scholars such as Edward Luttwak have viewed the pronunciamiento as a Hispanic variant of the coup d'état.[30]

The Spanish context of 1814–1820 certainly lent itself to the development of this practice. To begin with, there were the ongoing reverberations of the constitutional crisis unleashed by the Napoleonic occupation of the Iberian peninsula in 1808. Although Ferdinand VII had been restored to the throne, the experience of the usurpation of the Spanish Crown, with Ferdinand VII's capture and the imposition of Joseph Bonaparte, paired with its consequent context of upheaval and disputed authority, had raised fundamental questions about the ruling bodies' legitimacy, which, once asked, were not easily forgotten.[31] The armed imposition of a new monarch, together with Napoleon Bonaparte's forceful activities in Europe, had made it perfectly clear that authority was actually an incredibly fragile construct. It could be questioned, challenged, overcome, and ultimately appropriated. The juntas that surfaced in Spain and later in Spanish America, claiming to represent their country's sovereignty and the will of the people, in opposition to the usurper Bonaparte (and later the tyrant Ferdinand), similarly set a precedent whereby any group of people could claim, through the use of pseudo-legal proclamations, minutes, and, eventually, constitutions, to be the true and legitimate source of authority. With hindsight, it is tempting to say that the events of 1808 unleashed a century-long constitutional crisis in which all governments and constitutions were questioned, contested, and challenged. Once it became apparent that no institution, monarchical or republican, was sacred, and that anybody anywhere could claim to represent the national will and set up a government with a constitution and a new set of rules, there was no looking back. It was going to take at least five decades for any government or constitution in Spain and Mexico to acquire a sufficient degree of authority and recognized legitimacy not to be repeatedly and forcefully challenged.

Ferdinand VII's abolition of the 1812 constitution certainly fueled the liberals' development of insurrectionary politics. Faced with the impossibility of giving Spain a representative government using constitutional means, Spain's ousted and persecuted liberals opted to explore extra-constitutional ways of doing so, namely, by conspiring to *force* the monarch to bring back the Cádiz charter. They did so by developing the pronunciamiento, which was, after all, a curiously liberal form of instigating forceful change in the way that it advocated a liberal constitutionalist agenda (once the extra-constitutional sequence of intimidating pronouncements had been carried out), was perpetrated by notorious Spanish liberals, and, because of the manner in which the pronunciamiento appealed to the "general will," was seeking in the expected chain of pronunciamientos of allegiance a certain kind of popular/representative legitimacy. The fact that Spain was also seething at the time with popular war heroes from the Peninsular War, who had neither been promoted nor rewarded by Ferdinand VII following his return to Spain, also meant that there was a significant number of disgruntled officers willing to take up arms against the monarch and support the liberals' conspiracies. As was noted by Karl Marx in his particularly perceptive 1854 analysis of revolutionary Spain, "the army and guerrilleros . . . like Porlier, Lacy, Eroles, and Villacampa, . . . Mina, Empecinado, etc—were the most revolutionized portion of Spanish society, recruited as they were from all ranks, including the whole of the fiery, aspiring and patriotic youth . . . ; part of them, like Riego, returning after some years' captivity in France. We are, then, not to be surprised at the influence exercised by the Spanish army in subsequent commotions . . . when taking the revolutionary initiative."[32]

Bearing all of this in mind, Spanish historian José Luis Comellas came to the conclusion that all the pronunciamientos in Spain between 1814 and 1820 were characterized by their liberal agenda,[33] a view that Raymond Carr endorsed, arguing: "The pronunciamiento was the instrument of liberal revolution in the nineteenth century."[34] This was certainly the case during the subsequent so-called *década ominosa* (1823–33), after Ferdinand VII abolished the 1812 constitution for a second and final time. As explored in Irene Castells's study on the period, the pronunciamiento became the "subversive formula of liberalism . . . to recover that constitutional power which had been sequestered by absolutism."[35]

Having said this, it could be argued that the first proto-pronunciamiento was, in fact, instigated and played out by absolutists. The 1814 *Manifiesto de los Persas,* in legitimizing Francisco Javier Elío's "pronunciamiento-cum-*golpe de estado,*" whereby the 1812 constitution was abolished and absolutism was restored in Spain, set the precedent wherein a text, countersigned by a representative number of individuals (in this case sixty-nine *diputados*), served to justify the use of intimidating politics. Elío's intervention, moreover, typically arose following a lengthy conspiratorial stage, involving an array of influential political actors, and was launched from the periphery (i.e., Valencia), preparing the ground for the bloodless coup that was executed by Francisco de Eguía in Madrid.[36] Whether Elío's intervention was a pronunciamiento or not is still a matter of controversy.[37] What is unquestionable is that the forceful return of Ferdinand VII, together with the liberal attempts that were made thereafter to bring back the constitution, adopting this ritualized and bureaucratic revolutionary repertoire, served to set the precedent of this Hispanic practice. The failed pronunciamientos of Francisco Espoz y Mina in Pamplona (1814), Juan Díaz Porlier in La Coruña (1815), Vicente Richart in Madrid (1816), Luis de Lacy in Caldetas, Barcelona (1817), and Joaquín Vidal in Valencia (1819) set out to employ similar strategies to enforce change, aiming to force the monarch to listen to the conspirators' demands by seizing a peripheral town (Pamplona, La Coruña, Barcelona, or Valencia). Richart's plan was the exception in that his aim was to murder the king in a brothel. In a context of ongoing constitutional crisis brought about by the restored monarch's abolition of the 1812 constitution, these failed Spanish *cuartelazos, levantamientos, conjuras,* and *conspiraciones* of 1814–1819 ultimately provided

Riego with a model of action that he then went on to consecrate and name in January 1820.

The Importance of Rafael del Riego's
Pronunciamiento of January 1, 1820

On January 1, 1820, Riego, at the head of the Asturias battalion, launched his pronunciamiento of Cabezas de San Juan, demanding the reinstatement of the 1812 constitution; and, in so doing, he put a stop to his troops' projected departure to the Americas. As in so many subsequent pronunciamientos, he combined the sublime with the grotesque, providing a stirring call for the re-introduction of "the just and liberal Spanish Constitution . . . drafted in Cádiz in the midst of blood and suffering" alongside a barely disguised unwilling-ness to cross the Atlantic to fight in the Spanish American wars of indepen-dence: "I could not consent, as your leader, for you to leave your patria in rot-ten ships, to take you to fight an unjust war in the New World."[38]

Having launched his *grito* and ensured the men under his command sup-ported him, Riego gave himself powers that were not, in theory, his to give and created a constitutional town council in Cabezas de San Juan. Again, set-ting an extremely influential precedent for future pronunciados, the actions Riego took, which accompanied his written *proclamas* (addresses), demon-strated that anybody could ostensibly pass laws and enact them and, for ex-ample, constitute an *ayuntamiento*. Riego's pronunciamiento and its conse-quences were soon to be endorsed, justified, and celebrated by the radical liberal press of the time, giving it both crucial coverage and an evident de-gree of resonance. The *Gaceta patriótica del egército nacional* of January 25, 1820, actually stated, "The time had come in which everything had to be in-vented: whatever means was legitimate as long as the salvation of the patria was its end."[39] This would be, of course, the justification that would be given to all subsequent pronunciamientos: they were unlawful, but they were legiti-mate on the basis that, faced with tyranny and despotism, it was the obliga-tion of well-meaning citizens, initially soldiers, but later civilians, to resort to their so-called right to insurrection and take up arms, if needs be, to save the patria.[40]

Riego mobilized his troops to the nearby village of Arcos de la Frontera and awaited news from his commander, Antonio Quiroga. Like so many sub-sequent pronunciamientos, Riego's move was not a spontaneous revolution-ary eruption but part of a conspiracy that, albeit kick-started by his *grito,* was meant to be seconded by parallel actions elsewhere in the region.[41] However, the following stage of the pronunciamiento did not go according to plan. Riego's co-pronunciado Quiroga failed to stage a revolt in Cádiz (because of "rain and inefficiency," according to Raymond Carr).[42] Over the next few weeks, Riego found himself pursued by the government troops that were dispatched to quell the pronunciamiento. Having failed to take Cádiz, and desperately needing to muster support, Riego set off on what one historian described as a "romantic journey . . . through Andalusian lands," discovering along the way that only one village, the pueblo of Grazalema, thought him worthy of being welcomed as a hero.[43] From the perspective of Riego and his men, the pronunciamiento had not been successful, and Riego went as far as calling an end to the uprising on March 11, except that by the time he reached this decision, his call for the restoration of the 1812 charter had found favor in other parts of the country and a domino effect ensued, which would later be seen as typical of a successful pronunciamiento. A pronunciamiento in support of Riego's revolt was launched in La Coruña on February 21, which, in turn, was backed by El Ferrol, Vigo, and other garrisons in Galicia. Oviedo and Murcia followed, and by the beginning of March, Zaragoza, Barcelona, Pamplona, and even Cádiz had come out in support of Riego's *grito*. Faced with an angry crowd that converged before the palace in Madrid, on March 7, 1820, Ferdinand VII capitulated to the pronunciados' demands and on March 10, 1820, formally swore that he would abide by the 1812 constitution and accepted the creation of a *Junta provisional consultiva* while the Cortes was assembled again.[44] According to Roberto L. Blanco Valdés, Riego's 1820 pronunciamiento was the result of a lengthy and elaborate nationwide conspiracy involving multiple actors, both civilian and military, which explains why it triumphed "in spite of the failure of Riego's pronunciamiento at the head of the expeditionary army."[45]

The lesson drawn from the extraordinary series of events that unfolded as a result of Riego's pronunciamiento of January 1, 1820, was that it opened the possibility of bringing about significant political change. It also showed how participating in a pronunciamiento could bring fame and recognition. In the words of Comellas, "Riego, commander of one of the battalions that participated in the pronunciamiento, following Quiroga's orders, and whose involvement in the conspiracy had been relatively unimportant, will become the leading hero of the venture, the incarnation and symbol of the entire period of Spanish liberalism. Riego will be the author of liberty, his person will be glorified in petitions, disseminated in illustrations, immortalized in poems; his name will become engraved in streets, and an anthem composed in his honor by one of his regiment's musicians will mark a period of Spanish history."[46] It is evident that in a context of contested authority, Riego's example would serve as an inspiration to liberal army officers both in Spain and in its kingdoms: "it did not take long to become a tempting example for New Spain's criollos."[47] According to Castells, after 1823 liberals remained fascinated "by the experience of 1820, given further prominence by the mythification of Riego following his execution in the Plaza de la Cebada in Madrid on 7 November 1823," and would concur "in putting in practice the general scheme of the insurrectionary pronunciamiento."[48]

News of Riego's extraordinary feat reached Veracruz on April 26, 1820. The copies of the *Gaceta de Madrid* that were unloaded in the harbor that day came with news, as well, of how the king had wisely listened to the pronunciados and sworn his oath to restore and abide by the 1812 constitution. Although a number of Spanish authorities in Mexico dragged their feet over swearing their allegiance to the Cádiz charter, restoring the constitutional institutions, and organizing the respective local and trans-Atlantic elections— leading one future serial Mexican *pronunciado* to state, "The Mandarins of America swore only with their mouths what their intentions abhorred"— the constitution was implemented nonetheless.[49] Riego's achievement would be duly recorded in one Mexican pamphlet in the following resonant terms: "Europe admires the noble audacity of the commanders and soldiers who . . . proclaimed on 1 January 1820 the august code of 1812. The provinces went on to imitate the example of these brave men . . . and became the champions of liberty throughout the entire Peninsula. . . . The King finally adhered to the will of the nation . . . and thus swore before the eyes of the people his willingness to make them happy."[50] The lesson had already been learned: (1) a group of officers and soldiers could challenge the government with a pronunciamiento; (2) if their example and strategy were emulated by the provinces, liberty could triumph; and, (3) it was possible this way to instigate significant political change (ensure the "will of the nation" was respected) without bloodshed. The impact Riego's pronunciamiento had on the Spanish and Mexican imaginary cannot be overstated. As subsequent events would show, with the proliferation and popularization of the pronunciamiento in both countries, Riego's successful 1820 gesture of rebellion provided the template of what was to become the legitimate yet unlawful practice that would be used thereafter, time and again, to effect meaningful political change at local and national levels for the next five decades. The question of the pronunciamiento's legitimacy would also prove crucial. This can be evidenced in an article that appeared in the Puebla-based newspaper *La Abeja Poblana* on April 5, 1821, defending Agustín de Iturbide's pronunciamiento of Iguala (February 24, 1821): "Who authorized Quiroga in Spain to impose laws on Ferdinand VII? He demanded these with bayonets and triumphed: he is a hero; now an American [Iturbide] proclaims [Ferdinand] king [of independent Mexico] and he is a traitor. . . . How absurd! [¡*Qué inconsecuencias*!]."[51]

That Riego's pronunciamiento had a major impact in Mexican politics at the time is unquestionable. In part this was due to the fact that the insurgency in Mexico, consisting of not more the eight thousand poorly armed guerrillas, did not control any of the main cities in New Spain. The entire country was thus mobilized into swearing in the constitution, holding elections, sending representatives to the Spanish Cortes, and reconstituting its provincial deputations and local authorities as stipulated in the Cádiz magna carta. As can be evidenced in a letter insurgent leader Vicente Guerrero wrote to Colonel Carlos Moya on August 17, 1820, even guerrilla fighters who were reduced to carrying out hit-and-run operations in the remote sierras of the Tierra Caliente were knowledgeable of events in Spain and perfectly aware of what a pronunciamiento could do: "Since I consider your Excellency well instructed in the liberal revolution in the Peninsula, those disciples of the great Porlier, Quiroga, Arco-Agüero, Riego and their comrades, I will not waste time going over this [their exploits] and instead go on to state to you that this is the most precious time for the sons of this Mexican land . . . to adopt that model to become independent."[52]

In other words, Spaniards and Mexicans alike experienced at firsthand the consequences of a successful pronunciamiento. Their everyday lives were noticeably affected with the re-introduction of the 1812 charter in a way that, in a sense, those of their contemporary Gran Colombians, Argentines, and Chileans were not. Riego's pronunciamiento of January 1, 1820, extra-constitutionally yet legitimately brought back the liberal constitution of 1812 without removing the king or overthrowing the powers that be and, in so doing, established the model that would be subsequently taken up by anybody who was somebody in Spanish and Mexican politics.[53]

The prestige of this practice would undoubtedly become further consolidated in Mexico thanks to the Plan of Iguala of February 24, 1821. Evidently inspired by the success of Riego's pronunciamiento of Cabezas de San Juan, Agustín de Iturbide, in collusion with conspirators on both sides of the Atlantic, set in motion a replica cycle of pronunciamientos, calling for independence while asking King Ferdinand or a member of his dynasty to be crowned emperor of Mexico. In a matter of seven months and, again, with comparatively little bloodshed, a pronunciamiento, this time that of Iguala, succeeded in bringing about meaningful political change: the independence of Mexico.[54] From the Mexican perspective, and in a matter of two years, the pronunciamiento, as a practice, had become the obvious way of influencing politics. First it had restored the 1812 constitution, and then it had brought about their country's independence. Furthermore, with Riego having become a living legend and with Iturbide having gone from Royalist colonel to Emperor Agustín I (following the subsequent pronunciamiento of May 19, 1822), the pronunciamiento had also shown ambitious army officers how it was possible to significantly improve their career prospects overnight. Until a respected constitutional order was fully established (i.e., one that was considered legitimate by the majority, whose norms and procedures were abided by, and which had unquestionable authority) the pronunciamiento would remain the way of doing politics for Mexicans and Spaniards alike.

Conclusion

Stanley Payne defined the first half of the Spanish nineteenth century as the "era of *pronunciamientos.*"[55] In Mexico, as may be seen in the Pronunciamientos Database (http://arts.st-andrews.ac.uk/pronunciamientos/), there were over fifteen hundred pronunciamientos between the 1821 Plan of Iguala and the 1876 Plan of Tuxtepec. The frequency with which Spaniards and Mexicans "pronounced" to promote political change confirms in itself François-Xavier Guerra's verdict: "Because of its recurrence it must be considered one of the most important practices of the nineteenth century."[56] It also clearly points to both countries having shared a context of constitutional disarray, weak government, and contested legitimacies. However, given that this context was not one that only Spain and Mexico confronted during the age of democratic revolutions, the manner in which the pronunciamiento became a hallmark of these countries' political landscapes must, in great measure, be attributed to the extraordinary impact that Riego's original successful pronunciamiento had in both nations in 1820. The process that Riego's pronunciamiento started, whereby clusters of plans of allegiance forced the king to listen to "the popular will," clearly resonated in the collective imagination of all those people who suddenly discovered that it was actually possible to restore a constitution and put a stop to absolutism by staging a series of defiant forceful representations. If there was a practice that would have a lasting influence on both Spanish and Mexican politics, for better or for worse, for the greater part of the nineteenth century, it would be, undoubtedly, the one Riego developed successfully for the first time on January 1, 1820: the pronunciamiento. The reason is because it worked, and did so, moreover, without bloodshed. Although few subsequent pronunciamientos would succeed in achieving their aims, the memory of Riego's extraordinary feat would remain a source of inspiration for the hundreds of pronunciados that were to follow his example for the next fifty-odd years because, to quote the famous *"Himno"* that was composed in his honor, "His voice was followed."[57]

Notes

1. Dunkerley, *Americana,* xxii.

2. Gwyn A. Williams, quoted in Dunkerley, *Americana,* 49.

3. Hobsbawm, *Echoes of the Marsellaise,* 95. Given that this Atlanticist vision was propounded at the beginning of the Cold War, Palmer and Godechot's suggestion was initially met with fierce criticism by left-wing intellectuals since it was deemed to "reinforce the western contention that the United States and western Europe belonged together against Eastern Europe (as in North American Free Trade Organization)" (ibid., 95).

4. As an example, Laughlin's *Beware the Great Horned Serpent! Chiapas under the Threat of Napoleon* explores how Cádiz liberalism was interpreted and understood in the context of a remote indigenous community in Chamula, Chiapas, by analyzing the Tzotzil-Tzeltal translation of the Duque del Infantado's decree of August 30, 1812, in which Napoleon became "a horned serpent wearing a false mark on his face" (133).

5. Van Young, "Of Tempests and Teapots," 31.

6. See Liss, *Altantic Empires.* She subsequently extended this periodization to have it originate in 1650, "when the patterns of the European empires in America were already solidly established," and end in 1850, when "the success of the Industrial Revolution in England . . . plus a series of technological revolutions diffused the center of gravity in this Atlantic-focused world." See Knight and Liss, *Atlantic Port Cities,* 3, 5.

7. See the bibliography for a sample of seminal relevant texts by José Antonio Aguilar, Timothy E. Anna, Alfredo Ávila, David A. Brading, Roberto Breña, Matthew Brown, Manuel Chust, Michael P. Costeloe, Rebecca A. Earle, Ivana Frasquet, Virginia Guedea, François-Xavier Guerra, Brian R. Hamnett, R. A. Humphreys, John Lynch,

Kenneth R. Maxwell, Juan Ortiz Escamilla, Gabriel Paquette, Karen Racine, Jaime E. Rodríguez O., Rafael Rojas, and José Antonio Serrano Ortega.

8. Pérotin-Dumon, "French America," 551.

9. As an example of the tension that still exists between the outdated patriotic official discourses on independence and the views held by professional historians on the subject, the contrast between the politicians' and "official historian" José Manuel Villalpando's opening words in the "Acto de Inauguración" (at the "V Congreso Internacional. Los procesos de independencia en la América española," Veracruz, Mexico, November 25–28, 2008) and the revisionist papers that were then given could not have been more striking. For a succinct historiographical survey of the "emotional, political, and ideological" strands to this ongoing debate, see Manuel Chust and José Antonio Serrano Ortega, "Un debate actual, una revisión necesaria," in Manuel Chust and José Antonio Serrano Ortega, eds., *Debates sobre las independencias iberoamericanas* (Madrid: AHILA/Iberoamericana/Vevuert, 2007), 9–25.

10. Rodríguez O., *The Independence of Spanish America*, 1.

11. See the introduction to this book.

12. Racine, *Francisco de Miranda*, 258.

13. Ibid., xiii.

14. To name but a few, Lucas Alamán (1792–1853), Carlos de Alvear (1789–1852), Simón Bolívar (1783–1830), José Tomás Boves (1770–1814), José de Canterac (1787–1836), Thomas Cochrane (1775–1860), Manuel Dorrego (1787–1828), Francisco Xavier de Elío (1766–1822), José de la Mar (1778–1830), José de la Serna (1770–1831), Santiago Liniers (1753–1810), William Miller (1795–1861), Juan Domingo Monteverde (1772–1823), Pablo Morillo (1778–1838), Bernardo O'Higgins (1778–1842), Pedro Antonio de Olañeta (died in 1825), Daniel O'Leary (1801–1854), Joaquín de la Pezuela (1790–1873), and José de San Martín (1778–1850). Matthew Brown has recently examined the political and cultural impact that seven thousand European adventurers and the independence of Gran Colombia had on each other between 1816 and 1825. See M. Brown, *Adventuring through Spanish Colonies*.

15. For Mexican nineteenth-century liberalism see Reyes Heroles, *El liberalismo mexicano*, 3 vols.; Hale, *Mexican Liberalism in the Age of Mora*; Fowler, *Mexico in the Age of Proposals*, 129–217; Hamnett, *Juárez*, 9–12, 49–70; Thomson, "Popular Aspects of Liberalism"; and Thomson with LaFrance, *Patriotism, Politics, and Popular Liberalism*.

16. Breña, *El primer liberalismo español*, 548.

17. See Benson, *La diputación provincial y el federalismo mexicano*; Guedea, "Las primeras elecciones populares"; and Ortiz Escamilla and Serrano Ortega, *Ayuntamientos y liberalismo gaditano en México*. In 1813 Mexico elected and sent twenty-

one deputies to the Spanish Cortes. In 1820 Mexico elected and sent seven. For names and figures see Suárez, *Las Cortes de Cádiz,* 43–44; and Rubio Mañé, "Los diputados mexicanos a las cortes españolas," 347–95.

18. See Rodríguez O., "The Constitution of 1824"; and Rodríguez O., "Una cultura política compartida"; see also Frasquet, *Las caras del águila.*

19. Hamnett, "Liberal Politics and Spanish Freemasonry."

20. Castells, *La utopia insurreccional del liberalismo,* 17.

21. Banus, *Tratado de historia y arte militar,* 2:23.

22. *The Concise Oxford Dictionary,* interestingly, highlights the fact that a pronunciamiento entailed the production of a written document and that it belonged to an insurrectionary political tradition. It correctly does not equate a pronunciamiento with a coup d'état, but it fails to note that the term has only been used in Spain, Mexico, and Central America, rather than in all Spanish-speaking countries: "pronunciamiento n. (pl.—s). proclamation, manifesto, esp. (in Spanish-speaking countries) one issued by insurrectionists; pronouncement." *The Concise Oxford Dictionary* (Oxford: Oxford University Press, 1999), 824.

23. Gil Novales, *Rafael del Riego,* 37.

24. It remains to be seen whether there were pronunciamientos (as understood here) in the rest of Spanish America even if these parallel movements were given a different name.

25. Bleiberg, *Diccionario de Historia de España,* 353.

26. See http://en.wikipedia.org/wiki/Coup_d'%C3%A9tat (accessed March 30, 2012).

27. Baquer, *El modelo español de pronunciamiento,* 40.

28. J. Fontana, "Prólogo," ix.

29. For a collection of essays that argues that the pronunciamiento was a practice aimed at forcing negotiation rather than overthrowing the powers that be, see Fowler, *Forceful Negotiations;* for a study that argues that the pronunciamiento was not an exclusively military practice but one that involved significant civilian participation, see Fowler, "El pronunciamiento mexicano del siglo XIX"; and for an essay that explores the pronunciamiento's multiple, versatile, and dynamic functions and purposes, see Fowler, "'I Pronounce Thus I Exist.'"

30. Luttwak, *Coup d'état,* 22–23.

31. For a recent interpretation of these events and their consequences, see Breña, *El primer liberalismo,* in particular, 73–83.

32. Marx, "Revolutionary Spain," 423.

33. Comellas, *Los primeros pronunciamientos,* 24.

34. Carr, *Spain, 1808–1939,* 124.

35. Castells, *La utopia insurreccional del liberalismo,* 5. Castells demonstrates this by studying the failed pronunciamientos of Francisco Valdés, Marconchini, and Pablo Iglesias in 1824 (Tarifa, Almería, Marbella, and Cartagena), the Bazán brothers in 1826 (Guardamar), Milans del Bosch in 1829 (the Catalan Pyrenees), and José María Torrijos in 1830 and 1831 (southern coast of Andalucía and Málaga).

36. See Fontana Lázaro, *La quiebra de la monarquía absoluta,* 75–81.

37. Julio Busquets ranks Elío's intervention as the first pronunciamiento in Spanish history in his *Pronunciamientos y golpes de estado,* 204. However, he is alone in doing so. The fact that this was not a liberal intervention and that it did not elicit the expected wave of *pronunciamientos de adhesión* has resulted in most specialists not considering it as an early pronunciamiento.

38. "Cabezas de San Juan, 1 de enero de 1820. Proclama a las tropas" and "Cabezas de San Juan, 1 de enero de 1820. Proclama a los oficiales y al pueblo," in Gil Novales, *Rafael del Riego,* 34–35. I thank both Professor Andrew Ginger and Dr. Guy P. C. Thomson for giving me useful bibliographical suggestions with regards Riego's revolt. Also see Artola, *La España de Fernando VII,* 507.

39. *Gaceta patriótica del egército nacional,* January 25, 1820, 4. For a study of this liberal newspaper, see Saiz, "Liberalismo y ejército," 127–46.

40. The "derecho de insurrección" is one of those extraordinary aspects of nineteenth-century political culture that still needs to be researched in depth. Suffice it to say that following its inclusion in the 1812 constitution (Art. 373: "Todo español tiene derecho de representar a las Cortes o al Rey para reclamar la observancia de la Constitución.") a whole range of otherwise peaceful and law-abiding citizens believed that, faced with oppression, it was every citizen's legitimate right to actively resist and, if need be, revolt.

41. See Rodríguez O., "Los caudillos y los historiadores," 309–35; and Blanco Valdés, "Paisanos y soldados en los orígenes de la España liberal," 273–92, for two studies that demonstrate that Riego did not act alone and that his actions were part of a large movement that included a wealth of civilian actors.

42. Carr, *Spain, 1808–1939,* 128.

43. Comellas, *Los primeros pronunciamientos en España,* 335.

44. Buldain Jaca, *Régimen politico y preparación de Cortes en 1820,* 22–33.

45. Blanco Valdés, "Paisanos y soldados en los orígenes de la España liberal," 284.

46. Comellas, *Los primeros pronunciamientos en España,* 324.

47. Vázquez, "El modelo del pronunciamiento mexicano," 34.

48. Castells, *La utopia insurreccional del liberalismo,* 28.

49. Tornel, *Manifiesto del origen,* 10.

50. Ibid., 8.

51. *La Abeja Poblana,* April 5, 1821.

52. Vicente Guerrero, quoted in Torre, *La independencia de México,* 127.

53. Although I am loath to make anachronistic comparisons, I think it is possible to argue that the pronunciamiento model became a source of inspiration for nineteenth-century Spanish and Mexican officers much in the same way the Cuban Revolution (1956–59) and Ernesto Guevara's theory of the *foco revolucionario* became a source of inspiration for twentieth-century revolutionaries throughout Latin America.

54. For studies on how the Plan of Iguala consecrated and developed the pronunciamiento as a practice in Mexico, see Vázquez, "El modelo de pronunciamiento mexicano"; Anna, "Iguala: The Prototype"; Frasquet and Chust, "Agustín de Iturbide"; and Will Fowler, "The Nineteenth-Century Practice of the Pronunciamiento and Its Origins," in Fowler, *Forceful Negotiations,* xv–xxxix.

55. Payne, *Politics and the Military in Modern Spain,* 18.

56. Guerra, "El pronunciamiento en México," 15.

57. The complete words of the original song can be found at the following website, where a sung version can be downloaded: http://www.eroj.org/fonoteca/Riego .htm (accessed March 30, 2012).

3
Include and Rule

The Limits of Liberal Colonial Policy, 1810–1837

Josep M. Fradera

The central aim of these pages is to understand the meaning and the limits of the efforts, made by Spanish liberals in the years 1810–1814 and 1820–1823, to give new life to an exhausted empire. Although in the end it was incapable of this, Spanish liberalism attempted to halt the unstoppable progress of the third great decolonization process in the Atlantic space after the separation of the thirteen British colonies and French Saint Domingue. In less than two decades, between 1808 and 1824, two of the largest and oldest European empires entered a profound crisis that they came through weakened, reduced, and with a position clearly subordinate to the reconstructed British and French Empires.[1] Nonetheless, the Portuguese Empire retained important positions in Asia and a presence in the form of enclaves on the Indian subcontinent, Southeast Asia, and China; meanwhile, the Spanish took refuge in three insular possessions: Cuba and Puerto Rico in the Caribbean and the Philippine archipelago in the South China Sea, as well as a tenuous position on the west coast of Africa. For this reason, because the imperial crisis did not lead to the elimination of the Iberian presence from the colonial world, what happened between the ancien régime empire and the colonialism characteristic of the nineteenth century needs to be read in two ways: as the time when the old empire was liquidated and as the moment of the beginning of new realities that, in the Spanish case, would last until 1898 and, in Portugal's case, until 1974.

The Spanish Empire's crisis cannot be understood exclusively as the breakdown of the colonial system, of the link between colony and metropolis. The disintegration of the empire constitutes part of a greater crisis, that of the entire monarchy on both sides of the Atlantic. For this reason, a consideration exclusively from the American world's perspective will always be a partial one. The French invasion inevitably caused the downfall of the monarchical state, a crisis whose foundations had already been revealed in previous events in the metropolitan space itself. The Aranjuez Uprising with the fall of the royal favorite, Minister Manuel Godoy, and Ferdinand VII's coup d'état against his father in March 1808 were indications of the ancien régime's political breakdown within the framework of significant social violence.[2] As had happened in France in 1789, the system's failure began in the metropolis itself and its consequences extended throughout the vast imperial space later on. While the Spanish army collapsed and the Junta Central, the state's highest representation, sought refuge in the south of the country, the municipal authorities and representatives in the Americas rose up to defend Ferdinand VII's rights and decisively reject Napoleonic efforts to construct a new imperial legitimacy embodied in the Constitution of Bayonne.[3] In this context, faced with the Spanish internal crisis and the growing political autonomy of the Americans, the Junta Central, after much vacillation, convoked the Cortes and published the first rules for the election of representatives to the constituent assembly. Only with the dissolution of the Junta Central—which had emphatically promised the Americans treatment in accordance with the principles of political equality—and the constitution of the Regency at the end of January 1810 did the Americans begin to be suspicious of the Spanish leaders' aims. They organized juntas (between April and July 1810) and some of them gently moved down the path of political secession. With the opening of the Cortes, in September 1810, the dissensions between Spaniards and Americans were resolved through both a merciless struggle throughout the vast imperial space and the ideological debate in the legislative assembly that was to prepare the new constitution.[4] With its approval, in March 1812, the hereditary monarchy of the ancien régime was transformed into a liberal nation, without renouncing its sovereignty over the American and Philippine dominions.

The first liberal Spanish constitution was, in fact, a genuinely imperial constitution built on the idea of equality among the territories and former subjects, now also elevated to the position of citizens of the new political entity reborn from the ashes of a crisis of transatlantic proportions. However, both in the process of discussing the constitution and later on, the Americans could see for themselves that the mandate of equality promised in 1808 and 1810 by the Junta Central, taken on by the Regency, and expressed by the constitution with extraordinary emphasis, sat uneasily with certain aspects of the architecture structuring the approved text and, even worse, with the political behavior of the peninsular Spaniards. These contradictions, which divided the American world between those who argued for participating in the Spanish liberal experiment and secessionists, remained present throughout the years dealt with here, until the time of the second period of liberal predominance in the metropolis, between March 1820 and October 1823.[5]

I

Liberalism's imperial policy was founded from the beginning upon the imperative of political equality, the principle that is stated in the manifestos of the Junta Central, the Regency, and the constituent Cortes. The motto that was emphatically codified in the first article of the first chapter of the 1812 constitution is this: "The Spanish nation is the union of all Spaniards of both hemispheres." This policy of equality arose from an idea common to the whole of Hispanic liberalism: the empire's extra-European territories formed part of the same political body and were therefore deserving of the same rights as those enjoyed by people living in the monarchy's European territories. For this reason, the Americans were called on to form part of the monarchy's governing bodies and to participate in the constituent Cortes.[6] This explains why liberals maintained at all costs their conviction to secure an understanding among peoples who shared the same creed once the unhealthy practices of restored absolutism had been eradicated. It was in the name of this conviction that Francisco Javier Mina traveled from London to Mexico to sacrifice himself alongside the Mexican insurgents.[7] It was this way of seeing things that forced the liberals of the Triennium to pin their hopes on negotiation with the Americans who had not yet completely opted for secession and to accept, in 1822–1823, a desperate negotiation on foreign soil (England or the Netherlands) with those parts of the continent that had separated but were still ready to accept integration into a kind of Hispanic commonwealth. All these attempts ended in failure, but Hispanic liberalism's profound conviction explains many of those moments and many of the indecisions within the politics carried out by the liberals of the time. However, this does not explain the limits and the ending of a historical process in which other variables intervened. But we cannot confuse a policy with an inclusive slant with benevolence. The empire that the Spanish liberals proposed to defend by political and military means was not a view of unconditional friendship or a mere constitutional arrangement between liberals on both sides of the Atlantic. On the contrary, it implied control and the affirmation of sovereignty. It is on this point where the texts give way to the actions, to the historical process where interests, social coalitions, and specific factors arranged the dreams of the generations who lived through the 1820s.

It would be useful to take a broader look at the way in which the liberals' imperial project was structured in order to understand better the reasons why it suffered a foreseeable collapse. The starting point consists of the affirmation of its holistic ideological character. That is why the two crucial years of 1808 and 1809 saw the complete revision of the national perspective.[8] Unlike the reformists of the preceding period, the Spanish liberals faced the task of completely transforming the Hispanic world.[9] The very meaning of the connection between Spain and its territories in the Americas and the Philippines was called into question. We need to take into consideration two elements of the Spanish decision: the first is the fact that the liberals argued that Spain did not possess *colonies* but rather *territories* on the other side of the ocean, as emphatically stated in the Junta Suprema's famous decree of October 1809 (an overt plagiaristic reaction to the Napoleon's constitution of Bayonne). For this reason, Hispanic liberalism carefully avoided referring to empire or to colonies (a French and British word that was somewhat randomly used in the second half of the eighteenth century). For the same reason, the Cortes would correct the problematic manifestations of practical inequality in the Americans' representation in February 1811, in this way re-establishing relations between "peninsular Spaniards" and "American Spaniards" in conditions of theoretical equality, in the liberal terminology. It is for this reason that a famous exile, the ultra-liberal politician and economist Álvaro Flórez Estrada, would dare to say that the Spanish had been the first Europeans to accept the "colonials" on an equal basis, forgetting much of what happened in France since 1791.[10] It is this sense that they formed an inseparable part of the same political body that impelled the Spanish liberals to transfer all the blame for oppressing the Americans onto the absolute monarchy. From this ideological perspective, this oppression had weighed equally heavily on Spaniards in Europe, who were offered, on a par with the Americans, a new constitution in very classical terms that referred to the restoration of ancient liberties, an élan to which Lord Holland was no stranger.[11]

The second element refers to the complexities deriving from the multi-ethnic nature of the empire, which the Spanish liberals proposed to reform and reinvigorate. In other words, for whom were the liberal institutions and the right of representation, which were so generously conceded to the Americans and Filipinos, intended? The liberty that lit up what the Spanish liberals defined as the "Spanish Revolution" was obviously designed for educated people who were able to act "politically" to make use of their personal liberty. Contemporaries had few doubts about who met those qualifications: in short, an educated male adult, without economic ties of servitude, since other kinds of personal dependency did not exist in Spain. However, given that the 1812 constitution was approved within the context of collective mobilization against Napoleon, it did not seem prudent to reject any social group from the sphere of citizenship either for reasons of income or ethnicity. In principle, only women and servants were explicitly excluded.[12]

What could the effect be, in the American world, of a strongly inclusive project like that of the first liberal constitution? How would it be possible to create a common project involving the three great ethnic groups making up the empire's social landscape, that is to say, white Creoles and peninsular Spaniards, Indians, and the so-called *castas pardas* (the descendents of slaves: *libres de color* [freemen of color] or *pardos y morenos libres* [free blacks and other coloreds]), categories very different from those used by these groups to refer to themselves?[13] This was not in any way a purely theoretical matter, but a practical and immediate one. It was the problem that Jeremy Bentham considered to be insoluble, the one that led to his publication "*Get Rid of Ultramaria.*"[14] The metropolitan view of the empire's "ethnic" complexity would nonetheless be a continual thorn in the flesh of Spanish liberals.

The most eloquent testimony of the Spanish view on American diversity was left for posterity by the aforementioned Álvaro Flórez Estrada.[15] It contains an implicit but clearly defined idea of how that first generation of liberals intended to rule the American societies: the Spaniards would govern the Creoles and these in turn would hold the weight of American representation on their shoulders.[16] This was to be done in the name of an equality in which Indian minority status, the denial of political rights to the free blacks and mulattos because of their closeness to the black slaves (the pariahs of the social pyramid), granted Creoles all the prominence.[17] This political hierarchy, structured on the ethnic reality of the late empire, proved to be nothing more than a fantasy almost from the moment when it was announced. The Spanish juggling of the censuses, on one hand, and the complex and diverse movements of the groups granted inclusion as "passive citizens" or excluded unreservedly, on the other, contributed to tipping an imperial transition, agreed on between the peninsular and Creole elites, into open war, a war in which the uncertain course of the political alliances determined the direction taken by events.

In reality, the Spanish idea of leading the old colonial order by means of a political hierarchy with the blessing of universal indirect male suffrage and the mandate of equality was not viable in practice. If the equal representation for Americans established in February 1811—the only means for halting the separation processes underway—was to be applied, the Spanish liberals understood that the overseas subjects would have a majority in the Cortes. If this was so, the destiny of the empire of equality would be in their hands. To avoid this nightmare, which was impossible to assimilate from their viewpoint, they would resort to the Pandora's Box of excluding the *castas pardas* from active citizenship, which practice meant excluding them from the electoral censuses.[18] (This was something, by the way, that in 1820 the Portuguese would wisely avoid in their explicit copy of the Spanish constitution.)[19] Some Spaniards would even hint at the convenience of extending exclusion to the Indians, although such a possibility was rejected since it would have meant questioning the very right to possession of American soil.[20] In short, with the separation of the *libres de color,* the decrease in American representation was assured. This decision could not be imposed upon a blank sheet, however, and had to be adjusted to the conflicts that were already underway across the empire. I mention here only the most obvious: the popular Mexican revolt of 1810, with a harsh background of racial war against the viceroyalty's whites, both *gachupines* (Europeans) and *de la tierra* (Creoles); the ethnic alignments in the Andes; the conflicts between whites and free coloreds in part of New Granada; and the conflict introduced into a turbulent Caribbean by the Aponte Rebellion in Cuba.[21] The interminable discussions in the Cortes regarding the exclusion of the *castas pardas* gave a clear idea of those tensions: while the majority of New Spaniards and Peruvians were against exclusion, the Cubans strongly supported it. Furthermore, the weight of the Antilleans did nothing but increase at the same pace as the financial difficulties of the Spaniards fighting against the French armies. Despite the many conflicts involved in the matter of the *castas pardas,* exclusion was maintained when the Cádiz constitution was re-established in March 1820.

II

The Spanish liberals' political project reached its inevitable collapse between 1820 and 1823, the period that also saw the failure of the military attempts to recover Peru and the idea of a pact between equals in New Spain/Mexico as well as the military and political collapse of the restoration operation in Venezuela and New Granada. It was in those years of forced withdrawal from the American continent, however, when a limited version of the plan to breathe life into the empire took shape in the three insular enclaves of the Antilles and the Philippines. One of the situation's paradoxes is that the new colonial cycle that began in those enclaves was forged with the materials accumulated within the ideological framework designed for the empire as a whole in the previous stage. This happened similarly to how the characteristics of the Republican projects for the continent were affirmed, retaining many of the pieces that made up the old imperial framework. In this section, I would like to reflect on three main lines that marked the transformation of the Spanish liberals' initial ideological perspective into something quite different, indeed, almost opposing.

The first of these lines relates to the modification of the Spanish liberals' economic project, a matter that has warranted little attention until now. During the years of the Napoleonic Wars, the peninsular liberals' effort consisted of imposing a project of imperial political economy based on three pillars. The first involved reforming the traditional institutions that weighed on the inhabitants of the Spanish dominions, those that could not be assimilated within the framework of genuine liberal reform. I am referring to the work obligations imposed on the Indians (for example, the Potosí mining *mita* and the coerced labor of the *repartimientos*) or the ancien régime's tax concepts, such as the tax monopolies, one of the fundamental pieces of the so-called Bourbon reforms.[22] In both cases, the demands of social order in the colonies, as well as the financial needs resulting from the war, blocked any consistent effort to reform the old system and replace it with a new one.

The second pillar consisted of the reform of the trade regime that governed relations between the European metropolis and its overseas colonies, the central aim of liberal political economy throughout Europe. The main British demand in return for its military and financial support for Spanish resistance against Napoleon was the dismantlement of the Spanish monopoly system, and this same measure determined the level of collaboration with the American secessionists.[23] The contradictions involved for the Spanish reformists were nonetheless clear: the empire, in its twilight years, would continue to be a reserved empire, the sole preserve of the Spanish merchant navy. The reforms of the period of Charles III—the 1776 decree in favor of "*comercio libre*," in particular—were mainly internal reforms, aimed at increasing the number of peninsular ports able to handle American commerce but not permitting direct trade between Europe and Spanish possessions.[24] In these conditions, the Spanish rulers were forced to choose between bending to the wishes of those who profited so greatly from the oligopoly or sacrificing these and benefiting those areas of the empire that demanded greater freedom of trade, accepting the presence of European and North American fleets in the American ports. It was a false dilemma, given that the Cortes survived isolated in Cádiz, the most important port and perennial opponent of any reform in that direction and the place where the funds that would feed the Regency's coffers and finance the military effort against the American secessionists were collected.[25] In those conditions, liberalizing trade would have been political suicide. What happened with the famous apocryphal order of 1810—a decree in favor of free trade obtained thanks to the bribery of bureaucrats by important Havana interests and revoked before being approved when the operation was uncovered—is indicative of what was happening in those years.[26]

The third pillar consisted of the matter of slavery and the trade in Africans. The Spanish Empire came late to the plantation economy model. Only toward 1770 to 1780 did slaving units of a certain size take shape in some places in the Americas, such as in the Cauca Valley and the Caribbean coast of New Granada, in the area around Caracas, and in Cuba and little more.[27] As a result of this, the rise of the plantation gave the slave trade an extraordinary dynamism and, in the end, made its liberalization unstoppable at the end of the 1780s.[28] The transformation of slavery meant, in turn, a substantial change in the position of the population of *libres de color,* of great importance in the empire's social life and military structure. Mobilization in the areas with a greater African presence became intense. The instability of the world of plantations and diffuse slavery is evident if we look at the frequency of slave revolts. For example, the revolt led by José Leonardo Chirino in Coro (Venezuela) in 1796, the uprisings of Bayamo and the Havana area in Cuba in the years 1795 and 1806, respectively, and the very intense mobilization of the *libres de color* in New Granada and Cuba from 1810 deserve to be mentioned, for these spaces received the immediate echoes of what was happening in the French Caribbean.[29] The example of the great Haitian slave revolt was received by the *pardos y morenos libres* as a viable model for emancipation from below throughout the Spanish imperial space, and it did so in parallel with the political transformation that we are studying.[30] These expectations would remain in the unfounded hope that the political change in Spain might mean the end of slavery in the Spanish Empire.[31]

In these multiple contexts, international and local at the same time, a section of the liberal spectrum toyed with the idea of an abolitionist solution along British lines. Agustín de Argüelles himself, the president of the Constitutional Commission in Cádiz, in his fierce defense of the exclusion of the *castas pardas,* stated his sympathies for British abolitionism. In his own words, the arguments against the full citizenship of free colored people was pure and simple realpolitik aimed at nothing other than forging a peninsular majority in the legislative assembly. At the same time, he publicly declared his admiration for the British abolitionist policy. This was not simply rhetoric: Argüelles had attended the Westminster Parliament debates over the abolition of the slave trade in 1806 and 1807, at which time the Grenville-Fox government's initiative to force foreign powers into abolition was being discussed.[32] This was not the only case. Sympathy for what was happening in the British Empire was common within a circle of high-profile liberals grouped around the *Semanario Patriótico.* One of its founders, Manuel José Quintana, was the writer of the famous proclamation by the Junta Central in which political equality for the Americans was promised for the first time.[33] Some of the members of that group were prominent and explicit abolitionists. This was the case, for example, of Isidoro de Antillón, the first Spaniard to declare himself publicly against slavery and the slave trade. His pioneering speech of 1802 in the Real Academia Matritense de Derecho Español y Público was published later on, during the Cortes debates, in which he actively participated.[34] Also pioneering is the work by the much better known José Maria Blanco White, an Andalusian expatriate on British soil. In 1814 he published an eloquent pamphlet against the slave trade that was a collection of his contributions to the newspaper *El Español,* which he had founded in 1810 in the London exile in which he would finally die.[35] Blanco was very critical of Spanish liberalism's weaknesses and limitations with regard to the rights of slaves and *libres de color.*[36]

Nonetheless, the idea of abolition from above quickly sank, leaving little trace. During the years of the Junta Central and the Regency, British policy cautiously and discreetly pressed in that direction. The British aim was to impose the same direction as that expressed in the tenth article of the treaty of alliance signed by Great Britain and Portugal in 1810.[37] In the end, the conjunction of the spirit identifying liberal reform with abolitionism, and discreet pressure by British ambassador Henry Wellesley, convinced some representatives to take the initiative. In March 1811, the New Spanish deputy, José Miguel Guridi Alcocer, identified slavery as the target to aim for, while Argüelles referred exclusively to the slave trade, in line with the gradualist approach of official British policy. In agreement with the goals set out, a parliamentary commission, including the Cuban Andrés Arango, was created. When the news of what was happening in Cádiz reached Havana, the effect was considerable, and not only among the major planter interests. For the important estate owners, the proposal of abolition constituted a *casus belli*. On July 7, a letter from the captain general of Cuba, the Marquis of Someruelos, was read out in the Cortes, behind closed doors, warning of the risks that proposing abolition entailed.[38] The joint action of the main Cuban institutions and their able representative on the commission soon brought that body's activities to a halt.[39] The pressure of the Cuban lobby in Cádiz, the possibilities that its financial aid opened up for the Cortes, and the strategic importance of the port of Havana ended any consideration of an "empire without slaves," in Christopher Brown's expression regarding the British Empire.[40] The matter of abolition would not be raised or discussed again, despite the efforts of Isidoro de Antillón to reopen the debate in the Cortes in 1813.[41]

With the opening of a new liberal period in 1820, which witnessed the definitive collapse of the empire on the continent, Spanish liberalism's perspectives changed completely. The liberal governments of the period no longer proposed overall reform of the empire's institutions, something that made little sense given the situation. As is well known, the only measure of real interest for the overseas subjects was the reform of the number and the powers of the *diputaciones provinciales* (provincial councils). Meanwhile, the delicate matter of slavery was displaced from the center of attention due to the supposed effects arising from the abolition treaty of 1817 entering into force.[42] However, everybody in Spain, Cuba, and Great Britain was aware that the treaty was meaningless since the Spanish government had no interest in applying it in practice. For this reason, Wellesley and British diplomacy continued to strive for a truly effective, agreeable solution for two and a half years. The time for abolition had passed in Spain, despite the liberal governments' promises.[43] Everything ended with the creation of a parliamentary commission in March 1821, a pale imitation of what had happened a decade previously.[44] In their campaign, the Cuban representatives in Madrid referred to this episode; in accordance with the most influential Cuban institutions, they even nurtured the dream of revoking the treaty signed, unwillingly, by Ferdinand VII in 1817. Only the inclusion of Article 273 of the penal code, approved by the Cortes in June 1822 against those Spaniards involved in the slave trade, suggests that the embers of prior abolitionist sympathy were still glowing.[45]

What the Spanish liberals who returned to power in 1820 intended had a much more modest and realistic scope: the reform of the bases of the Spanish economy and its relationship with a waning colonial area. There were two essential instruments of that policy: the prohibition of the import of foreign wheat and flour on August 5, 1820, and the imposition of a general tariff that same year for the whole monarchy, both the peninsula and the dominions under Spanish control.[46] The intention was to give shape to a system of interrelationships among different sections of the Spanish economy and between this and the colonial economy.[47] On the peninsula, the challenge consisted of opening wider avenues for the integration of cereal agriculture in the inland regions of Castile and Andalusia and the market of the coastal regions, those that had previously consumed imported wheat and flour.[48] Some of those regions, for example, Catalonia, were also undertaking a rapid process of industrial development.[49] On this point, the tariff measures were designed to set up a more sophisticated framework of interdependence with the agricultural Spain of the interior, used to receiving a continuous flow of manufactured products from certain European countries.[50]

The approach of the liberals of the Triennium was a true novelty in terms of the state's goals and, as such, marked a clean break with the past. That model of integrated development, after the complete collapse of the imperial system and the demonetization of the Spanish economy, was established on the commercial relations that were still conducted with the Americas.[51] However, in 1820, this last possibility was practically reduced to the absorption capacity of the Cuban market and the exchanges with the continent that passed through the port of Havana. This new importance of Cuba's place in the economy of an empire in ruins in turn revalued the slaving foundations that sustained it. Perhaps for this reason the spectacular development of slavery on the island was no longer a subject for debate in the parliamentary discussions.[52] There was only silence on the matter. This was, in any case, a dispute among Cubans, as the divergent positions of its representatives in Madrid, Juan Bernardo O'Gavan and Father Félix Varela, make clear on more than one occasion. In these conditions, the liberals of the peninsula faced a grave dilemma: what to do if the Cuban exporters did not show the least predisposition to integrate into a model that vetoed their exchanges with Europe and the United States, their liberty to relate to the international economy, which they had achieved a short time previously in 1818, the moment of the *habaneros'* greatest influence at the Spanish court.[53] The Cubans' declared goal was to maintain Spanish protection for the world of the slave plantation while importing flour and foodstuffs from North America and exporting sugars and molasses to the United States and European markets. If it depended on them, the October 1820 tariff was condemned and, with it, any notion of recovering the imperial rhythm in terms of colony-metropolis interdependence. Therefore, rectification became indispensable and occurred in 1822, almost at the end of that second liberal period. The third period of colony-metropolis economic relations took shape after the failure of the colonial policy of 1820, first with restored absolutism in 1823 and later on with liberalism once again in power from 1836 onward. It was to be composed of easily identifiable general characteristics: complete free trade for the Cubans, tariff advantages for some export sectors and for the Spanish merchant navy (the platform for a significant migratory diaspora), tolerance regarding the slave trade, and a system of tax exploitation wisely administered by future Spanish governments.[54]

The development of the liberals' colonial policy was largely conditioned by their failure to stabilize a system of alliances in the possessions maintained during the Triennium. In other words, it was impossible to decide which system of political alliances would enable a certain minimum of political stability to be forged in the possessions under its effective control. In the conditions established by the imperial collapse, which was symbolized by the 1824 Battle of Ayacucho, the control of local policy in those places that remained within the metropolitan orbit proved to be an enterprise beyond the capabilities of the Spanish governments. The re-establishment of the 1812 constitution involved orienting colonial political life along lines identical to those in the peninsula, except with regard to the exclusion of *pardos* and *morenos* from active citizenship, an exclusion that was maintained without reservations in the 1820s. This policy meant giving political visibility to the dissensions and conflicts inherent in each of those societies. Some derived from matters that could only be explained in terms of local politics; other derived from liberalism's attempt to guide an ideological program inherited from that of 1810.

On this point it is important to look at the particular contexts. In the most important possessions, like Cuba, Puerto Rico, and the Philippines, it proved impossible to ensure municipal elections or freedom of the press and of association or to guarantee representation in the Cortes without dealing with serious conflicts and opening up deep divisions between the peninsular Spaniards and the overseas subjects.[55] In Cuba, for example, the opening of a new liberal period triggered an acute political conflict between peninsulars and Creoles, a conflict in which both proclaimed their Spanish patriotism. The Spanish party, known as *piñerista* from the name of the cleric that gave it its ideological orientation, Tomás Gutiérrez de Piñeres, was principally made up of Spanish traders and seamen as well as soldiers from the local Havana garrison. Its most important representative, the Canarian liberal Diego Correa, defined it as a political current made up of "honest citizens, industrious craftsmen, rich property owners and affluent merchants," in short, an urban world that excluded the landed aristocracy and the new sugar plantation owners.[56] Its program was the Cuban reproduction of what the Spanish liberals were attempting to introduce from the Cortes and the metropolitan executive. Its main objective was to guarantee the unity of the Spanish nation, still understood in terms of a transatlantic political body, the sum of the peninsula and the American territories. It was within this unitary framework that the set of reforms created by the Spanish governments from the time of the reopening of the Cortes, from spring 1820 onward, would be imposed. Among them, and of the first importance, was their vision of the space under Spanish sovereignty as a potential economic unit. This was a program of economic nationalism, complementing the aforementioned one being affirmed at that time in the peninsula through the reform of the tax system, presented by José Canga Argüelles on July 13 and 14, 1820, and of the tariffs on foreign trade, presented by Guillem Oliver in October the same year.[57]

The key figure in the drive to halt the imposition of the peninsular liberals' economic program was the head of the Cuban treasury.[58] Alejandro Ramírez opposed the application of the new tariff when it reached the island, at the cost of creating enormous tension in Havana. He died in suspicious circumstances shortly afterwards.[59] Undoubtedly, Spanish interests in the city were behind the commotion. The only possibility for those groups to impose metropolitan liberalism's economic and political program lay in dominating municipal politics and, as part of this, the national militia. For the Creole party, on the other hand, the essential space in terms of power was the *diputación provincial,* a space that was free of *piñeristas,* given their rarity on the rest of the island, away from Havana. For this reason, the Spanish party did not settle for control of politics in the city of Havana. Anticipating future developments in colonial politics, it made an effort to block the Creoles' access to that most important of representative bodies, the Cortes. This is what happened on the occasion of the first Triennium elections, in August 1820, when the dean of Havana Cathedral, Juan Bernardo O'Gavan, was elected. He was the author of a vigorous defense of slavery at the precise moment when the Count of Toreno made an offer to reconsider the British abolitionist position. Accused of falsifying the censuses, the representative-elect was removed from his position. The conflict would re-occur during the November 1821 elections, with the pro-Spanish party succeeding once more, thanks to the providential sinking of the brig *Sorpresa,* in which the electoral documents showing the results were traveling. After a tense discussion, the Cortes decided not to authorize those elected. Responding to accusations of a lack of patriotism, José Arango replied with a spirited defense of Cuban loyalty. Arango argued for the possibility of defending the island's interests within the framework of national unity, against the concealed secessionism of those he called *"liberales guapetones"* or *"independientes a la venezolana."*[60] The same was done two years later by his cousin Francisco Arango y Parreño, the great theoretician of the sugar interests, in a text replying to the Abbé de Pradt, in which he asked rhetorically about the meaning of independence in order to then discredit it.[61] In the third elections of December 1822, clear representatives of the Creole world were elected. This time, the representatives-elect were able to take their seats. What happened on that third occasion was that the highest authority on the island, Nicolás Mahy, chose to support the Cuban Creoles, shifting policy toward an alliance between this group and Spanish power on the island.[62] For the *piñeristas,* the behavior of this authority represented the creation of a dangerous independent power, away from the national representation embodied by the Cortes.[63] In fact, the support received from the highest Spanish authority seemed to be fully justified. Only an alliance with the Creoles guaranteed political stability on the island. Had Mahy not done this, the political and military commander would have lost his most important support at a time of great external risk, as made clear by the secessionist conspiracy of the Soles y Rayos de Bolívar in 1823, clearly backed from the secessionist Venezuela.[64]

Although what was happening in Havana was unquestionably important, this was not the only place where, without there being a secessionist movement of any significance, it proved impossible to stabilize the re-establishment of the liberal institutions. On the Spanish part of Santo Domingo, for example, the proclamation in 1820 of the Cádiz Constitution meant the removal of the very precarious Spanish presence, the end of the period known as the *España boba.* At such a critical moment, the capital's merchants were divided between those loyal to Spain and those loyal to France, which had not yet renounced its claims over the island. However, the factor that triggered the breakdown of the authority of the last Spanish governors, Sebastián Kindelán and Pascual Real, was the re-establishment of the limitations on the *castas pardas.* In fact, the refusal to grant the *libres de color* active citizenship broke the precarious alliance between metropolitan power and the only social group with the strength to sustain it. In 1821, the battalions of *pardos y morenos,* led by Pablo Alí, broke with the Spanish governor in protest at their exclusion. They facilitated the island's occupation by Jean-Pierre Boyer's Haitian troops in January 1822.[65]

It is possible to point to examples of greater importance. During the Triennium, the Philippines was the setting for radical ideas similar to those in Cuba, except for the great difference between the two situations and contexts. The similarity even takes on a dramatic look if we confine ourselves to the surface of political events. If in Cuba it was treasury head Ramírez who died in unusual circumstances, in the remote Asian possession it was Mariano Fernández de Folgueras, the highest military and political authority, who perished tragically.[66] Folgueras, who had already been acting captain general between 1806 and 1809 and would be so from 1816 to the time of his death, was the *bête noire* of Manila's Creole party because of his declared preference for giving administrative posts to peninsular Spaniards and even foreigners. From the point of view of those divisions, the 1820–1823 period was the culmination of a long chain of high-intensity conflicts from the end of the eighteenth century onward, in particular, on the island of Luzon.[67] Indeed, while in Cuba the imperial power completely withdrew from production (in the most noticeable instance of this, the abolition of the tobacco monopoly in 1817) to limit itself to tax collection, in the Philippines the imperial administration's economic functions lasted beyond the breaking of the Pacific trade link thanks to tax monopolies and a more effective ethnic-based tax policy.[68]

The combination of more or less latent rural conflict with the perception that change was underway lasted until the 1820s. For this reason, the years of the liberal Triennium were a time when a set of tensions converged in Manila and the world connected to it. Conflicts occurred among the different sections of the local Spanish or native Philippine (of Tagalog or Chinese origin) elite and foreign traders (given that Manila was the only port in the empire open to foreign trade), or between these and the native population of Tagalogs, Pampangans, and other groups. And there were tensions, in the end, between the metropolitan power and the Creole groups that felt the impact of the American revolutions. This all had a direct and intense impact, since the islands were frequently the destination for deported American insurgents. The visible manifestation of these tensions was the popular uprising of September 1820 against foreigners (with more than a hundred people killed) due to the cholera epidemic, a popular exasperation probably encouraged by the religious orders and other elements of the old imperial apparatus that were against political change on the peninsula.[69] In that context, crucial to political stability in the Asian possession, the election of representatives for the colony at the Spanish Cortes afforded a number of surprises. The first of these was the election of a majority made up of representatives from the country, with a significant presence of *chino-mestizos* (mixed-race European-Chinese), among others. Although, on occasions, the *chino-mestizos* were described as *castas* by the Spanish administration, census restrictions were not applied to *castas pardas,* something that would be senseless in the archipelago for obvious reasons. Their important numerical presence and social weight, as well as the lack of peninsular Spaniards, made Manila a very special case.[70] Everything seems to indicate that the Spanish authorities, alarmed by the loss of control of politics in the capital port, decided to take extreme measures with Creole conspiracies against Spanish control.[71] When they were preparing to deport a large number of Philippine notables to Spain, the self-proclaimed Hijos del País (sons of the country)—among them the trader and financier Domingo de Roxas—the situation was exacerbated by the uprising of both soldiers and civilians previously deported from New Spain and led by the Bayot brothers and Captain Andrés Novales.[72] It was in the fight against the rebels that above-mentioned Captain General Folgueras lost his life. The uprising was put down and its most important leaders were executed without ceremony. These dramatic events occurred in the first few months of 1823, as the second liberal cycle in Spain was gradually expiring.

III

It is necessary to take these questions to their logical conclusion, to their inevitable epilogue of 1837. After the death of Ferdinand VII, liberalism returned to power as the result of a twofold process of an agreement at court and conflict in the streets of the peninsula's main cities. Given this situation, the regent queen and her councilors opted for a quick deal with the moderate sectors of liberalism in exile. The aim was to prepare a political solution following the example set by the French restoration, with the effective exclusion of liberalism's radical, democratically inclined factions. This gentlemen's agreement found its *raison d'être* as a result of the dynastic conflict and the revolt of Don Carlos (Ferdinand VII's brother) and his followers throughout the country, who united under the flag of the old order. In this context of extraordinary political fluidity, the governmental initiative of creating the *Estamento de próceres* in the summer of 1834, in the middle of the changes caused in Madrid by the cholera epidemic, was an attempt to find an ordered solution to the ever greater division that the country was experiencing. The representatives of the overseas possessions were called once again to take their places in that rather undemocratic chamber. Meanwhile, in Havana, an aging Francisco de Arango y Parreño was preparing an undercover project for an autonomous Cuban government, in agreement with Javier de Burgos, the Spanish minister of Fomento (public works and local administration), who was very soon to be removed from his post.[73] For the authoritarian Spanish officers who oversaw the overseas dominions, that initiative represented nothing other than a weary repetition of what had happened in 1808, 1810, and 1822–1823. The inclusive experiment, whether in Madrid or in Havana, could not be maintained for much longer. Consequently, Spanish colonial policy moved forward in a different direction.

The popular uprisings of summer 1835 forced the regent queen to call on the liberals who had until then been the central government's opposition. A new cycle of revolts in summer 1836, after unsatisfactory progress in the war against the Carlist legitimists, forced the proclamation of the 1812 constitution.[74] In September 1836, Santiago de Cuba joined the metropolitan clamor. The insurrectional movement in that Cuban city was a demand for the Creole elites' participation in the general political process, a demand made before receiving the express authorization of the captain general of Havana, at that time the despotic *ayacucho* Miguel Tacón.[75] The chain of events was now unstoppable. The Spanish liberals' intention was to reform the venerable political code of Cádiz in a more conservative direction, in other words, to build a politically stable situation. New elections to constituent Cortes were convoked in order to proceed with constitutional reform. All the Spanish provinces, including the overseas ones, took part in these elections. When the representatives elected in the three insular possessions attempted to take their seats, they were prevented from doing so by the majority of the chamber, despite their objections and the press's protest campaign, amply bribed with money coming from Cuba. The reason for the exclusion became quite clear during the constituent Cortes sessions. During these, a small majority backed the proposal to stop the colonials from being represented in the legislature and a large majority favored the proposal to govern the colonies, from then on, by means of a specific legislation to be approved. This promise to create what were called "special laws" (clearly taken from the Napoleonic constitution of the year VIII [1799]), different from those that prevailed in the rest of the monarchy, was incorporated into the 1837 constitution as an additional provision.[76] It would appear again in the 1845 constitution, the unborn one of 1855, and those of 1869 and 1876.[77] Its real meaning was transparent: the overseas provinces were separated from the Spanish constitutional framework, set aside in a political limbo whose form was uncertain.[78] The same would happen, in a very interesting way, with the Portuguese colonies in the constitution of March 1838.[79] The first article of the tenth heading established that "the Overseas Provinces can be governed by special laws that the necessities of each of them require."[80] However, unlike what happened with the Spanish policy of total exclusion, the Portuguese liberals still allowed a modest representation from the overseas colonies in the Cortes in Lisbon, a more liberal attitude that can be qualified by noting how that representation went always to Portuguese-born citizens loyal to the metropolis.[81]

This form was uncertain, but not inexistent. The move from an inclusive policy, based on political equality, to one of exclusion, separating colonials from the liberal institutions prevailing on the peninsula, was a clear indication that political life overseas would have other foundations. To begin with, one of its features would be the unrestricted military and political power of the foremost authority in the colonies, the governor–captain general.[82] Not by coincidence, many of those asked to fill those posts were former *ayacuchos,* the young officers who had fought and lost the American wars. With their exclusive command and authority, regardless of the division of powers prevailing on the peninsula, with the capacity to guide colonial policy (which did not, of course, exclude conflicts with the metropolitan ministries), governing in a space without elections or political press, with exceptional functions as regards repression and with no oversight whatsoever, the intention was to avoid the repetition of the moments of crisis undergone during the years of the liberal Triennium. It is not a coincidence that this policy consisted of taking, once again, the path of strengthening military authority, started in the Triennium years as a response to the political crisis in the metropolis and in the imperial space.[83] It was hardly surprising then, that restored absolutism would take this to an extreme with the 1825 decree of "absolute powers" for the captain general in Cuba. Later on, liberals would follow the same path with few hesitations. Furthermore, the faculty of command derived not only from the concentration of authority, but also from the manipulation of the ubiquitous ethnic and racial boundaries that pervaded the colonial societies that were heir to the empire. In Cuba, the colonial laboratory par excellence, the military high command called that form of governing "racial balance" politics.[84] In other words, it was the administration of the fear of slave revolt and the manipulation of the boundaries between the population of European origin, the *libres de color,* and the slaves. Something of this spirit was transmitted to the neighboring colony, the island of Puerto Rico, in the crucial years of 1830–1850, when plantation slavery was strongly developed in part of the island.[85] The same happened in the Philippines, the most complete model of a colonialism built on innumerable ethnic lines, whether among the native population or those created by the continuous influx of Chinese and the presence of white minorities of European or American origin. In short, the Spaniards of the nineteenth century were the conspicuous heirs to a long tradition of government over a multiethnic empire since this was the world constructed by them since 1492. Worthy heirs to that so-recent past, they prepared to translate that old wisdom to the new conditions resulting from their insertion into the area of the European liberal countries. They extracted the opportune lessons on the meaning of the expansion of the liberal gospel in the world and in their world, and they acted in consequence.

Notes

1. Excellent general summaries of the period can be consulted, for example, Lynch, *The Spanish American Revolutions*; Anna, *España y la independencia de América*; Hamnett, *La política española en una época de revolución*; and a very intelligent approach to general problems in Hamnett, "Process and Pattern."

2. For the political history of these years, see Artola, *Los orígenes de la España contemporánea*; J. Fontana, *La época del liberalismo.*

3. Moreno Alonso, *La Junta Suprema de Sevilla.* Regarding the resistance movements in Spain and the Americas, see Chust, *1808: La eclosión juntera en el mundo hispano.* On the constitutional text backed by Napoleon, see Martiré, *La Constitución de Bayona entre España y América.*

4. Lorente, "América en Cádiz," 21–66.

5. Rodríguez O., *La independencia de la América española*; and, particularly for New Spain, Rodriguez, "La transición de colonia a nación."

6. On the constitutional culture that sustained the first liberal experiment, see Tomás y Valiente, "Génesis de la Constitución de 1812," 13–125; Petit, "Una Constitución europea para América: Cádiz 1812," 57–71.

7. Ortuño Martínez, *Expedición a Nueva España de Xavier Mina.*

8. I take the expression from Guerra, *Modernidad e Independencias,* 116 and ff. Also see Portillo Valdés, *Crisis atlántica.*

9. Paquette, *Enlightenment, Governance, and Reform in Spain and Its Empire.* The limits of imperial reform are explored in depth in Stein and Stein, *Apogee of Empire.*

10. Flórez Estrada, *Examen imparcial de las disensiones de América con España,* 2:12.

11. Moreno Alonso, *La forja del liberalismo en España.*

12. Pérez Ledesma, "Las Cortes de Cádiz y la sociedad española," 175–81; Pérez Ledesma, "Ciudadanos y ciudadanía," 1–35; Pérez Ledesma, "Ciudadanía y revolución liberal," 103–28.

13. Regarding this matter for the Indians, see Rodríguez O., "Ciudadanos de la nación española," 41–64; Irurozqui, *La ciudadanía en debate en América Latina.*

14. Clavero, "Libraos de Ultramaria," 109–38.

15. Varela Suanzes-Carpegna, *Álvaro Flórez Estrada.*

16. As expressed by the radical Álvaro Flórez Estrada in his *Examen imparcial de las disensiones de América con España,* 31–32.

17. I covered this matter in Josep María Fradera, "Raza y ciudadanía: El factor racial en la delimitación de los derechos políticos de los americanos," in Fradera, *Gobernar colonias,* 51–70.

18. King tackled this question for the first time in an early article, "The Colored Castes and the American Representation in the Cortes of Cádiz," 33–64.

19. Article 21 of the Portuguese Constitution of September 23, 1822, made no reference to the African origins of Portuguese citizens. Furthermore, freed slaves were explicitly recognized as citizens.

20. Pagden, *Lords of All the World,* 51 and ff.

21. Van Young, *The Other Rebellion*; Helg, *Liberty and Equality in Caribbean Colombia*; the last chapter of Múnera, *El fracaso de la nación.* For the Cuban case, see Childs, *The 1812 Aponte Rebellion in Cuba.*

22. Tandeter, *Coacción y mercado.* Regarding the importance of tax monopolies, see Marichal, *La bancarrota del virreinato.*

23. Adelman, *Sovereignty and Revolution in the Iberian Atlantic.*

24. On this point, see Delgado Ribas, *Dinámicas imperiales.*

25. García Baquero, *Comercio colonial y guerras revolucionarias.*

26. Lucena Giraldo, "La orden apócrifa de 1810 sobre la 'libertad de comercio' en América"; Fradera, *Colonias para después de un imperio,* 350–53.

27. For the Cuban case in the second half of the eighteenth century, it is important to mention the classic book by Moreno Fraginals, *El ingenio: Complejo económico social cubano del azúcar.* Also see García Rodríguez, *Entre haciendas y plantaciones.*

28. Delgado Ribas, *Dinámicas imperiales,* 521–68.

29. Geggus, *The Impact of the Haitian Revolution in the Atlantic World.*

30. Ferrer, "Cuba en la sombra de Haití," 179–231; and Ferrer, "Temor, poder y esclavitud en Cuba en la época de la revolución haitiana," 67–84.

31. Referring to the Cuban case for 1809–1810, see García, "Vertebrando la resistencia," 269–71.

32. D. Murray, *Odious Commerce*, 27.

33. Dérozier, *Manuel José Quintana y el nacimiento del liberalismo en España*. More specifically about the group, see Duran López, *Crónicas de Cortes del Semanario Patriótico*; Francisco Duran Lopez, ed., *Manuel José Quintana, Memoria del Cádiz de las Cortes* (Cádiz: Universidad de Cádiz, 1996); Moreno Alonso, *La generación española de 1808*.

34. Antillón, *Disertación sobre el origen de la esclavitud de los negros*. On Antillón's text, see Benavides, "Isidoro de Antillon y la abolición de la esclavitud."

35. Blanco White, *Bosquejo del comercio de esclavos*. Regarding his London publication, see Portillo and Viejo, *José Blanco White*, xxxvii–xciv.

36. On the exclusion of the *castas pardas,* Blanco White published a brilliant article under the pseudonym Juan Sintierra, "Carta VI: Sobre un artículo de la Nueva Constitución de España," 96–108.

37. D. Murray, *Odious Commerce*, 28–29, 31.

38. Corwin, *Spain and the Abolition of Slavery in Cuba*, 23–24.

39. Piqueras, "Leales en época de insurrección," 183–206.

40. C. Brown, *Moral Capital,* C. Brown, "Empire without Slaves," 273–306.

41. Corwin, *Spain and the Abolition of Slavery in Cuba*, 25–26.

42. D. Murray, *Odious Commerce*, 50–71.

43. Ibid., 82 and ff. Also see Fladeland, "Abolitionist Pressures on the Concert of Europe," 355–73.

44. D. Murray, *Odious Commerce*, 82.

45. Ibid., 83–84.

46. Fradera, *Indústria i mercat*, 137–45.

47. This was shown clearly in the report presented in the Cortes by the president of the tariff commission, the Catalan Guillem Oliver on August 31, 1820. See Oliver, *Discusión que hubo en las Cortes españolas del año de 1820*.

48. J. Fontana, *La quiebra de la monarquía absoluta,* 249 and ff.

49. Maluquer de Motes, "La revolución industrial en Cataluña," 199–226; Carreras, "Cataluña, primera región industrial de España," 259–95.

50. On the transformation of Spanish foreign trade, see Prados de la Escosura, "Comercio internacional y modernización económica en la España del siglo XIX," 97–111.

51. Prados de la Escosura, *De imperio a nación*.

52. In terms of total product (1,520,000 cwt.), it represented half of the entire British West Indies' total production.

53. For these questions, see Moreno Fraginals, *El ingenio,* 2:120–25, 130–43.

54. Regarding the model that was introduced in the 1830s, see Fradera, *Colonias para después de un imperio,* 327–438, 538–69; Saiz Pastor, "Imperio de Ultramar y fiscalidad colonial," 77–95; Saiz Pastor, "Las finanzas públicas en Cuba," 69–109.

55. For the case of Puerto Rico, see Navarro García, *Control social y actitudes políticas en Puerto Rico*; Castro, "La lealtad anticolonial," 277–300.

56. Hernández González, "El liberalismo exaltado en el trienio liberal cubano," 68; Hernández González, *Diego Correa, un liberal canario ante la emancipación americana.*

57. Canga Argüelles, *Memoria sobre los presupuestos de los gastos.*

58. I looked into this matter at length in Fradera, *Colonias para después de un imperio,* 378–88.

59. On this dark episode see Franco, *Política continental americana de España en Cuba,* 309–10.

60. The text by Arango can be read in the appendix of Rosario Sevilla Soler, *Las Antillas y la independencia de la América española* (Seville: CSIC, 1986), 140–49. See also González-Ripoll Navarro, "Vínculos y redes de poder entre Madrid y La Habana, 304–5.

61. Arango y Parreño, "Reflexiones de un habanero sobre la isla de Cuba," 2:343–44, 376.

62. The recovery of the Creole party around Count O'Reilly is well documented in José Antonio Piqueras, "El mundo reducido a una isla: La unión cubana a la metrópoli en tiempos de tribulaciones," in *Las Antillas en la era de las Luces y la Revolución,* edited by Piqueras, 323–29.

63. Hernández González, "El liberalismo exaltado en el trienio liberal cubano," 75.

64. It is still worth consulting the old 1929 book by Garrigó, *Historia documentada de la conspiración de los Soles y Rayos de Bolívar.*

65. For this period in Dominican history, see Moya Pons, *La dominación haitiana,* 63–70.

66. There is a succinct biography of him in Capel et al., *Los ingenieros militares en España,* 179.

67. An overview is in Sturtevant, *Popular Uprisings in the Philippines*; for the case of one of the most mobilized regions, see Mendoza, *Pangasinan, 1572–1800.*

68. The comparison between the two models is set out extensively in Fradera, *Colonias para después del imperio,* 327–438, 439–534. For the Philippine case, see Fradera, *Filipinas, la colonia más peculiar.*

69. An anonymous Englishman, witnessing the events, attributed the massacre to the conjunction of two factors that he considered to be equally deplorable: first, the Spanish authorities' tolerance of the assault on the neighborhood of Binondo, second, the propaganda that spread the idea that "the land belongs to the Indians," clearly inspired by liberal terminology. Anonymous, *Remarks on the Philippines Islands and Their Capital.*

70. On this matter, see Fradera, *Colonias para después de un imperio,* 237–38.

71. I owe some of the information contained here to the historian Ruth de Llobet (Universitat Pompeu Fabra–Wisconsin University, Madison), whose current doctoral thesis deals with this turbulent period of Philippine history.

72. Regarding the long tradition of deportation to the Philippines, see García de los Arcos, *Forzados y reclutas.* References to the case of the Hijos del País are in Lahiri, "Rhetorical *Indios*," 251.

73. Arango, "Indicaciones sobre el gobierno civil de Cuba," in *Obras de Don Francisco Arango y Parreño* (Havana: Ministerio de Educación, 1952), 2:620–29.

74. There is a narrative of the events in J. Fontana, *La Revolución Liberal,* 175–215.

75. Navarro García, *Entre esclavos y revoluciones.*

76. For the French debates, see Benot, *La Révolution française et la fin des colonies.*

77. Fradera, "Why Were Spain's Overseas Laws Never Enacted?," 334–49.

78. Alonso Romero, *Cuba en la España liberal.*

79. Regarding the Portuguese colonial world, an important work is Alexandre, *Os Sentidos do Império.*

80. Miranda, *As Constituiçoes Portuguesas,* 201.

81. Alexandre, *A Questâo Colonial no Parlamento,* 1:110–12.

82. Fradera, *Colonias para después de un imperio,* 183–326.

83. Blanco Valdés, *Rey, Cortes y fuerza armada en los orígenes de la España liberal,* 496–504.

84. For an attempt to relate the political options to the social background in a comparative context see J. M. Fradera, "L'esclavage et la logique constitutionelle des empires," 533–63.

85. Scarano, *Sugar and Slavery in Puerto Rico.*

4
Entangled Patriotisms

Italian Liberals and Spanish America in the 1820s

Maurizio Isabella

The 1820s represented a period of defeat and setbacks for the Italian revolutionary movement. The failure of the 1820–1821 revolutions in Turin, Milan, and Naples, in the face of international intervention and repression, marked the end of a whole generation's dreams of introducing constitutional charters and their frustrated (though vague) designs to build loose federations among the Italian states. These revolutions have traditionally been considered to represent the tail end of the Napoleonic era, led as they were by former Napoleonic civil servants and army officers nostalgic for the achievements of Napoleon Bonaparte's rule, or by aristocrats anxious to regain the roles they had enjoyed in the pre-revolutionary period: in short, a generation linked to the past, that produced either a backward or a nostalgic liberalism.[1] Recently, however, work on Italian nationalism has highlighted the importance of the 1820s, and of the pre-1848 period more generally, in the development of a cultural definition of the nation through literary and visual representations. Such studies tend to dismiss the political dimension of 1820s patriotism in order to highlight instead the emotional dimension of a patriotism whose appeal was heavily indebted to the growing dissemination of romantic culture in these years.[2] However, even after the end of the Italian revolutions and the restoration of absolute monarchies, Italian patriotism continued to be shaped in political terms. With the collapse of revolution at home, international events and revolution abroad became the source of inspiration and discussion for Italian political culture. This is why Italian liberals' attention was caught by events taking place across the Atlantic. In order to understand how Italian liberalism and patriotism evolved after 1821, we need to look beyond Italy to find both sources of intellectual and political debate and places where Italian patriots could freely discuss these matters. It is precisely in this context of displacement that Latin America became so relevant to Italian patriotism.

Revolutionary movements in different territories were linked by the international, spontaneous mobilization of individuals who volunteered to join foreign uprisings and fought wars of independence against existing states and empires elsewhere, even when, as in the case of Italy in 1821 and Spain in 1823, their domestic struggles appeared to have been defeated.[3] This global movement of individuals who did not belong to regular armies and were motivated by ethical as well as personal reasons to fight for freedom included hundreds of people who left the Italian peninsula to join wars in Greece and Spain, as well as volunteers from other European countries. Admittedly, this phenomenon had a strong Mediterranean dimension, and the volunteers led by Giuseppe Pacchiarotti in Catalonia or by Pietro Tarella in Greece in the 1820s inaugurated a tradition of engagement for the emancipation of the region that lasted until the end of the century. However, in the same years the international fight for freedom went beyond the Mediterranean and into the Americas. Besides the hundreds of British and Irish soldiers and officers enlisting in Simón Bolívar's army, there were also many Italian volunteers, mostly former Napoleonic soldiers or officers who joined Bolívar, as the forces of independence in Mexico.[4] Among the most famous of them was, for instance, the Piedmontese Carlo Castelli, who joined Bolívar in Haiti in 1816, was involved in all his campaigns, and was promoted to general in 1830. Another Piedmontese volunteer was Giuseppe Avezzana, who in 1826 defended Tampico against Spanish aggression and later fought in the Mexican civil war against Anastasio Bustamante.[5] Finally, while still in Europe, several of these Italian volunteers became involved in plots that linked the emancipation of the Spanish colonies to revolution in Italy. Similar acts of informal foreign policy represented a key dimension of the process leading to the recognition of the new republics.[6]

These careers in themselves provide evidence of the profoundly international nature of patriotism and liberalism across the Atlantic, based as they were on notions of international solidarity and on the profound conviction that the fight for freedom was a collective endeavor that transcended the boundaries of existing states. Although the sheer number of Italian volunteers going to the Americas is unknown and the size of the phenomenon requires further investigation, the group did contain an elite whose leading role is at least partly known. While in the case of volunteering in Greece or Spain, the notion of a common Mediterranean culture and a deep historical bond between bordering countries (especially in the case of Greece) might serve as a rallying cry, in the case of the fight against Spanish colonial rule in the Americas, the mobilizing myth was the association with the idea, rooted in Enlightenment culture, of civilization and freedom abandoning old and corrupt Europe in order to move West.

After the revolutions, an Italian diaspora abroad was thus composed of military volunteers, along with other individuals who had been members of secret societies, like the Carboneria, and were at the same time political exiles and volunteers, economic migrants, and travelers, often sharing, to use Matthew Brown's expression, a "culture of adventure."[7] The most politicized segment of this world joined groups of liberals and revolutionaries across the Atlantic, whose ideals and activities transcended national boundaries. As I have argued elsewhere, these Italian exiles and volunteers were part of trans-Atlantic and pan-European networks of liberals and democrats that included revolutionaries from Mexico, Spain, Portugal, and Greece, whether exiled or temporarily traveling to the major European political centers, and prominently French, Swiss, or British intellectuals and politicians sympathetic to their causes. Thanks to their constant exchanges these networks constituted a "liberal international" community of individuals who, in spite of their different national backgrounds, formed a transnational civil society of people fighting for the same ideals, sharing a similar vision for a revised international order based on the principles of self-determination and popular sovereignty, and debating and engaging in discussions across the Atlantic. In the 1820s this transnational world was responsible not only for the dissemination, but also for the negotiation and creation of a new and original liberal culture. This meant that Italian liberalism was able to thrive and develop mainly outside Italy in the 1820s.[8]

Admittedly, echoes of the events unfolding in Latin America did also reach the Italian peninsula, in spite of the constraints imposed by censorship and the limitations upon free discussion of revolutionary episodes. In some cases Italian journalism did report—with great interest and frequency—on the economic and political conditions of Latin America, often employing information gleaned from the French press. The Milanese review *Annali Universali di Statistica* is a case in point. Conceived and printed in the then intellectual capital of the peninsula, Milan, the *Annali,* whose editorial staff was made up of former Napoleonic civil servants, reflected the political culture of the school of the philosopher Giandomenico Romagnosi, being democratic and patriotic in nature.[9] In spite of the censorship, in many articles the reviewers did not hide their support for the new republics. Indeed, they generally rated their chances of political success very highly, convinced as they were that the new republican institutions and free commercial exchanges with European countries, and especially with Britain, would do much to overcome the former colonies' current poverty, blaming colonial rule for their backwardness.[10]

Nevertheless, the most important and direct intellectual exchanges took place outside Italy, in the metropolitan centers of Europe, like Paris and London, or even in Brussels or directly in Spanish America. In addition, it must be stressed that ideas traveled in both directions of the Atlantic and affected both Italian and Spanish American patriots. Liberal and patriotic values first and foremost circulated thanks to the personal contacts established in the two continents. Italian exiles in England, France, and Belgium had direct contact with Spanish American liberals and, in particular, with the diplomatic representatives of the new republics in Europe, like Emanuel de Gorostiza, Vicente Rocafuerte, and José Mariano Michelena. In London, Giuseppe Pecchio and Fortunato Prandi were directly involved in the exchanges between Jeremy Bentham's circle and the Guatemalan patriots and regularly met with the Guatemalan diplomat Marcial Zebadua.[11] Furthermore, a substantial number of exiles moved to Latin America not only to join the armies, but also simply to travel or to participate in the political life of the republics. Claudio Linati, Orazio Santangelo, and Fiorenzo Galli, for instance, went to Mexico and became directly involved in the clashes between Yorkinos and Escoceses before returning to Europe. Others put down roots in Latin America. Among them was the Neapolitan Pietro de Angelis, who, after living for a few years in Paris, in 1827 settled in Buenos Aires, where he became the staunchest supporter of the president of the United Provinces of the Rio de la Plata; and Juan Manuel de Rosas sided with him in the clashes between Federalists and Unitarians. As the case of Pecchio's exchanges with José Cecilio del Valle, which I will discuss in the next section, suggests, the circulation of ideas among Italians and Spanish Americans was further encouraged by epistolary exchanges.

In addition, the intellectual connections between the Italian diaspora and Latin America were enhanced by the circulation of printed material. The involvement of these exiles in the politics of the new republics often took the form of a number of more or less successful journalistic enterprises designed to educate a new republican public opinion and to influence contemporary political debates. Linati and Galli published the review *El Iris* in Mexico City, while de Angelis was the editor of a number of different periodicals, from *El Conciliador* to the *Crónica política y literaria de Buenos Aires*. They also set up educational institutions both in Mexico and in the River Plate. At the same time, the Italian exiles in Europe not only were informed about the events taking place on the other side of the Atlantic through the European press, but also were well aware of the debates going on among Spanish American liberals about the nature of the new republics and read many of the political tracts published by them on both sides of the Atlantic. For instance, they knew Vicente Rocafuerte's publications on the political system were attributed to the former colonies. In turn, many of the exiles wrote about Latin American events in Europe, whether on the basis of their direct experience in the new republics or thanks to documents they had received from their overseas contacts. These documents, which I shall discuss in the third section of this chapter, demonstrate the impact of Latin American democratic federalism among the Italian patriots and the influence over their political imagination.

It should be noted that such contacts and exchanges and mutual understanding and sympathy between Italian and Latin American patriots were facilitated by the striking commonalities existing between their political cultures and liberal values. In the Italian peninsula, as well as in Latin America, the Constitution of Cádiz had an enormous influence. Having started to circulate in Italy soon after its declaration in 1812, it became the banner of the majority of the revolutionaries in Naples and Turin in 1820 and 1821 and the very symbol of their liberalism. Likewise, the discussions of the constitutional assemblies as well as the charters of the newly founded republics, from the River Plate to Brazil and Mexico, were greatly indebted to the 1812 constitution for their definitions of citizenship, sovereignty, and nationhood.[12] As Mónica Quijada has argued for the case of Latin America, the constitution "was an ideological as well as a political movement whose projection (influence) well exceeded the scope of application of its constitutional text," but this statement could likewise be applied to Italian liberalism in the same period.[13]

The connections, commonalities, and entanglements between Italian and Spanish American patriotism that I shall discuss in the following sections undoubtedly marked the creation of a new political culture in the 1820s that on both sides of the Atlantic was labeled as "liberal." At another level, however, the liberalism developing in the Mediterranean as well as in Latin America in this period was characterized by strong continuities with the past. In fact, the shared culture of the Enlightenment, existing between Italy and Spanish

America since the previous century, when the ideas of the Neapolitan Enlightenment had circulated widely in the Ibero-American world, continued to exert its influence in the 1820s. In particular, Ibero-American patriots resorted to the authority of Gaetano Filangieri's constitutional ideas during the period leading to independence, and these ideas re-emerged in the debates around the drafting of the new republican constitutions. Likewise, the revolutionary wave of 1820–1821 in the Italian states renewed Filangieri's popularity among Italian democrats and led to the publication of several editions of his work. Filangieri's enduring popularity appears even more striking if one considers the attacks waged by Benjamin Constant on his reputation as a constitutional theorist in his edition of the *Scienza della Legislazione* in Paris between 1822 and 1824. Here, the French liberal took the opportunity to highlight the inadequacy of Filangieri's theories, arguing that they relied too much on government's reforming role for them to meet the standards of modern liberal constitutionalism. In Constant's words, Filangieri "conferred upon the legislator an empire almost without limits over human existence."[14] On the other hand, Italian and Latin American liberals alike continued to refer to Filangieri because, while he was part of their own local cultural tradition, his admiration for the Constitution of the United States of America, as against the British one, and his belief in the need to base legislation on natural rights made it possible for them to view him as a democratic, anti-despotic writer. Among the revolutionaries of the newly created republics, equal importance was attributed to Filangieri's belief in the role of legislation in creating a public spirit and to his advocacy of legal uniformity to attack corporations, privileges, and the Catholic Church.

For instance, Vicente Rocafuerte, like Filangieri, saw in the US Constitution a model to adopt and, at the same time, agreed with him that a constitution should respect the peculiarities of each country. Thus, in his *Ensayo Político* (1823), a eulogy to US federalism, he wrote, "Almost all of what I will say can be found in the first volume of the *Scienza della Legislazione*."[15] In these same years the Calabrese exile Francesco Saverio Salfi, who in Paris regularly contributed to the *Revue Encyclopédique,* published an *Eloge de Filangieri* along with Constant's edition of the *Scienza,* in which he portrayed the Neapolitan philosopher as a republican and an anticolonialist and attributed to his salutary influence the recent development of public spirit in Naples and Italy, implicitly attributing the revolutionary wave of 1820–1821 to his ideas. Some Italian exiles explicitly endorsed Filangieri's idea of a "College of the Censors," an institution modeled on the example of the Roman Republic and designed, through the preservation and fostering of public morality, to turn the people into citizens.[16]

The existing commonalities in the political culture of Ibero-American and Italian patriots were further reinforced by the direct exchanges taking place during the 1820s in Europe and the Americas. In the following pages, I shall discuss three case studies that cast some light on the exchanges that took place between the two communities of patriots. In the first section I demonstrate how the new republic of Guatemala was imagined in the correspondence between the "father of its independence" and an Italian liberal in exile. In the second, I explore how the presence of Italian exiles in Mexico influenced the conceptualization of nationhood among both Mexican and Italian patriots. Finally, I briefly discuss some aspects of the debate, conducted on both sides of the Atlantic, that points to the existence of transatlantic liberal currents in the 1820s. I have confined my research to those people who were engaged in journalistic activities in the European and Spanish American press, to published travel accounts and memoirs, and to some correspondence that has survived. While I include individuals of various social backgrounds, many of them were among the leaders of the 1820–1821 revolutions in Italy, had held high administrative or military office under Napoleon (the Neapolitan Orazio Santangelo de Attellis), and were of aristocratic background (like the Milanese patrician Giuseppe Pecchio, who was a former Napoleonic civil servant, an economist, and writer, or Count Claudio Linati, an army officer). Indeed, these case studies demonstrate that ideas traveled between both communities and in both directions, to the extent that it is sometimes difficult to ascertain their precise trajectory. What is certain is that, by the end of the decade, a common intellectual humus had been created, and new transatlantic connections had been forged.

Giuseppe Pecchio, José Cecilio del Valle, and the Invention of Guatemala

In the 1820s the leaders of the new Latin American republics maintained close contacts with European intellectuals.[17] Their exchanges demonstrate the importance attributed by Latin American patriots to European liberal and democratic culture at a time when their republics needed legitimization from the elites of the old continent, advice on constitutional and political matters, and authoritative political alliances. It also points to the importance and impact of transatlantic exchanges in the definition of the new national communities. José Cecilio del Valle, widely known as the father of Guatemalan independence, numbered among his most faithful correspondents an Italian exile in England, Giuseppe Pecchio. Formerly the leader of the anti-Austrian plot in Milan in 1820, Pecchio had been a civil servant working for the Napoleonic kingdom of Italy and, after the Restoration, a leading figure in Milan's romantic and liberal circles. During his exile he had a hand in all revolutionary events in Europe, from Spain to Greece, and was at the center of a vast network of liberals across Europe, including other exiles and some of the most prominent intellectuals of the time.

Del Valle never left Guatemala, but he had a wide range of international correspondents, including Álvaro Flórez Estrada, the famous exiled Spanish economist, Jeremy Bentham, Alexander von Humboldt, Dominique de Pradt, and several Latin American diplomats stationed in Europe, as well as Pecchio.[18] When in 1821 some provinces announced their desire to free themselves from the Spanish yoke, del Valle joined the movement for emancipation and found himself entrusted with the task of writing its declaration of independence.[19] In 1823 he was chosen as a member of the triumvirate that led the country until the general election and the preparation of a constitutional charter. In 1825 del Valle lost the presidential elections but was elected to the Federal Congress a few months later as a liberal.[20]

The relationship between the two correspondents, Pecchio and del Valle, presupposed the superiority of European culture and experience and the notion that American intellectuals were pupils of their European counterparts. Del Valle sought the guidance of his European peers in order to realize a vision that he felt was his own, but which was also indebted to their intellectual tradition. Since he perceived his nation to be at the periphery of civilization, and Europe as the center of progress and culture, he sought a formal recognition of his intellectual credibility by corresponding with European elites.[21] Pecchio sent him his own publications, along with the collection of the Italian eighteenth-century economists and the writings of Cesare Beccaria, which del Valle prided himself upon having quoted in his speeches in the congress. Del Valle wrote to Pecchio:

> I would like to ask you and the most enlightened men of Europe, turning your attention to America, to declare with all the energy of reason and the beauties of eloquence, that every type of task demands a special education that gives the aptitude for carrying it out; and that if the states do not follow this undeniable principle, they will sink forever into

the chaos of anarchy, or they will eventually be governed by an absolute power. . . . The wise men of Europe must be the masters or directors of America.[22]

At the same time the correspondence reveals that the two patriots felt themselves to be part of a single intellectual community and shared the same faith
in the role that intellectuals like themselves had to play in the construction of
a liberal society (for which the expertise and culture of Europe was needed)
and also a belief that after independence an almost unlimited progress awaited
Guatemala, one undoubtedly facilitated by its unlimited natural resources,
which made it appear almost like a paradise on earth. Both of them recognized the gap between a small middle class of enlightened men and an Indian
population afflicted with poverty and ignorance. Pecchio bluntly informed
del Valle that he must have been an exception and that America needed more
men of culture. However, he perceived the same intellectual distance between
educated elites and uneducated masses in Europe too, using this to explain
the lack of progress made by liberalism in the Old World, as the people would
not "support a revolution for the ideas."[23] The conditions for the success of
the liberal revolution were even less favorable in Guatemala, where, as del
Valle admitted, "In each province there is a small number of families which
represent a veritable municipal aristocracy . . . [and] they abhor constitutions
founded on equal rights."[24]

In imagining Guatemala's future as a fully fledged, independent, and thriving community, what prevailed in the exchanges between the two men was
the advice Pecchio gave del Valle about the policies needed to reinforce the
state. This was in turn based on liberal principles indebted both to the Napoleonic experience in Italy and to the example of contemporary Britain. It was
with the economic and educational policies of Britain and with the financial
measures and legal tools of Napoleonic Italy that Guatemala would stabilize
and thrive. For Pecchio, universal education was the primary tool to bridge
the gap between the different social classes.[25] There were two goals: one was
to adapt the population to the civilizing program the liberals had in mind;
the other was to improve the masses' ability to work hard and contribute to
the development of a fully realized commercial society. With these ends in
mind, Pecchio described the workings of the Lancasterian and infant schools
to del Valle, advised him of the principles of adult education provided by the
Society for the Diffusion of Useful Knowledge, and informed him of the existence of new methods of gymnastics that would help combat the "natural"

laziness of the Indians.[26] Opening up trade with Britain and building an appropriate network of communications would in turn guarantee the economic development of the country. At the end of a civil war in 1830, when del Valle stood in the presidential election in order to prevent further civil strife and tackle the financial weakness of the state, Pecchio recommended the creation of a national guard, based on the French model introduced in Italy by Napoleon, and suggested that Catholic Church properties be sold off in small lots, arguing that this was necessary as a way of "increasing the number of the government's supporters" contributing the taxes to the exchequer.[27]

Their correspondence had begun with an almost utopian faith in the progress of Guatemala. In later years their letters became more pessimistic, reflecting the widespread disappointment among European liberals at the news of apparently continuous civil strife in Latin America. The disillusioned transatlantic liberals had come to believe that neither an adequate ruling class nor a sufficiently educated and disciplined population existed to ensure the success of liberal revolution and stable republics in Latin America. Their correspondence does demonstrate, however, precisely the importance, in the eye of European observers, of the new republics as laboratories where liberalism could at least be applied without the historical and political impediments existing in Europe, as well as the influence that Europeans had on the political imaginations of the American patriots. It was in the 1820s that a new era of mutual exchanges and influence was inaugurated, serving to bind the two regions together for decades to come.

Are Foreigners Part of the Republic? The Case of the Exiles and Latin American Politics

In the 1820s, the encounters between Italian émigrés and American patriots had an impact both on Italian and on Hispanic American patriotism. The presence of Italian exiles and volunteers in Hispanic America stimulated a discussion about the nature of the newly established republics.

Indeed, these debates confirm the observations of Claudio Lomnitz, Matthew Brown, and Jordana Dym regarding the importance of foreigners in defining new concepts of nationhood and patriotism in Spanish America. Sometimes nationalism, as Lomnitz suggests for the case of Mexico, was "an excluding ideology (even [as] a xenophobic ideology)"; sometimes the patria and the nation were sufficiently open and flexible constructions to accommodate foreigners and welcome their contribution. In all cases, the debate over the status of foreigners was relevant to the definition of citizenship, nationality, and sovereignty.[28] While at first foreigners were almost unquestionably welcomed for the contribution they could make to the new republics, in some cases, as with the presence of the Spanish community in Mexico, they could also be seen as a potential threat to the very existence of the republic.[29] This controversy was also part of a broader European debate over the rights of refugees to seek asylum and over the duties of free countries toward exiled revolutionaries. In Paris, Benjamin Constant was adamant that while emigration from one country to another should be left free, as individuals had a right to choose where to live and pursue their activities, any attempt to limit the rights of foreigners who were resident and seeking refugee status in a country had to be condemned.[30]

The dispute occasioned by the expulsion of Orazio Santangelo from Mexico following his involvement in national politics and choices about foreign policy in 1826 provides further evidence for the importance of "the other" in shaping national identities in the period. Given their militant support for one or the other of the political factions of the new republic, the federalist Escoceses and the democratic Yorkinos, the presence of the exiles in Mexico had been controversial since the outset.[31] In particular, the departure of Santangelo became a cause célèbre and triggered a heated debate among Mexican publicists, whose bone of contention was precisely the attitude that the new Mexican nation should have toward "foreigners." Beyond the specific case of Santangelo, what was at stake was the very nature of Mexican patriotism. In some cases, what was defended was an exclusive idea of the republic, based on the rights and duties granted by the constitution to its citizens, who were in turn bound to it by a sacred oath. Thus, the constitutional protection of the citizens' liberties could not be applied to foreigners, who could well be, after all, a potential threat to the stability and security of the patria, and thus legitimate targets for extreme measures.[32] However, Mexican patriots advanced a rather different notion of republic or nation, which they saw to be coterminous with the principles of philanthropy and hospitality ("this virtue necessary to humankind that is naturally cosmopolitan") and which they believed should be open to those who recognized the same principles of freedom against despotism.[33] "*El solitario,*" the anonymous author of *Juicio Imparcial sobre la espulsion de Santángelo,* argued in favor of recognizing the rights of all foreigners who were de facto part of Mexican society, advocating the introduction of "more liberal laws" in Mexico. To this end, he made reference to the authority of European liberals to support his case, quoting Benjamin Constant's *Eloge de Sir*

Samuel Romilly to advocate a distinction in the legal treatment of those who were just visiting the country and those foreigners who were resident and contributed to its life and the Abbé de Pradt to condemn the religious intolerance of the Mexican constitution. Mexico, argued *El solitario,* should have legislation less cruel than the English Alien Bill.[34] Others likened the Mexican government's behavior in Santagelo's affair to that of the Turks, explicitly associating the expulsion of foreigners to an act of despotism.[35]

But the presence of the exiles in Spanish America did not only affect the nature of Creole patriotism. The example of Spanish American independence also exerted considerable influence on Italian patriotism in the 1820s. The exiles' involvement in the new republics' politics served to vindicate a model of nationhood that was open to external cultural influences, porous and inclusive, permitting and encouraging their own involvement in the political and economic life of the host countries. As Santangelo recalled after being expelled from Mexico, nation-building and civilization were processes arising out of cross-national exchanges, and neither the United States of America nor the older European countries could have achieved political stability and prosperity without the contribution of foreigners.[36] In addition, the example of the new republic encouraged among Italian observers a notion of nationhood that was based not on race or ethnicity, but on granting citizenship to the whole population of the new countries. As a consequence, they all unreservedly supported the Creoles in the "Dispute of the New World" and dismissed the Buffon-De Pauwian view of the Indians as biologically inferior, while supporting their ability to become part of the nation. Thus Italian observers' position in the "Dispute of the New World" was uncompromisingly supportive of the Latin American patriots, in defense of the natural qualities and talents of the indigenous populations. Once back in Europe and engaged in the task of writing about the history of Mexico, Linati rejected the notion of Aztec barbarity and likened the cruelty of Aztec priests to that of the Catholic Holy Inquisition, thus condemning any form of superstition and reaffirming the universality of human progress and civilization.[37] Pecchio forcefully argued, "It is by no means true . . . that the Indians are inferior to Europeans in physical force or in intellectual faculties."[38]

In turn, the exiles endorsed and disseminated in Europe the Creoles' historical *indigenismo,* which conceived of fully fledged national identities on the basis of a reinterpretation of America's precolonial history and defended local civilizations against their detractors.[39] Giacomo Costantino Beltrami, who after traveling in Mexico published (in London) an extensive account of the country, defined Mexico under the rule of Moctezuma as "a nation," likened the emperor to Napoleon, and extensively described his discovery of a precious "Evangeliarium epistolarum et lectionarium Aztecum," an ancient translation of the Aztec language into Latin, as a symbol of the country's cultural identity.[40]

The combination of the advancement of such an open idea of patriotism with the support for Creole political and cultural patriotism is strikingly illustrated by Linati in his famous collection of engravings describing the new Mexican nation, published in Brussels in 1828. The opening image of the collection was a portrait of Moctezuma, which implicitly hinted at the existence of a Mexico before the conquest. Linati praised the ethnic variety of the country but warned that the *Indios* would have to abandon some of their customs and their language to become citizens and be educated toward citizenship through schools and military service under the supervision of Creole elites.[41] These latter were Linati's heroes, praised for their role in the revolution. The most striking element in his representation of the nation, however, was the presence of foreign volunteers. Through a number of engravings he celebrated the contribution of Italian volunteers to the establishment of the republic of Mexico, arguing that foreign volunteers like Count Giuseppe Stavoli and General Vicente Filisola were indeed part of the nation since they had linked its emancipation to the worldwide struggle for emancipation:

France can be proud of Lafayette, and England of Byron, who have offered the tribute of their arms and their lives to the cause of freedom of the New World and to peace, Italy too can claim its share of glory in these honourable battles. Her sons leave for different countries in the globe as they do not dare contemplate the fate of their unlucky country, always disappointed in their hope of regaining the national sceptre, they have looked under the banner of the foreigner for glory or death; some of these pupils of Napoleon's military century have offered their services to despotism, but the majority has found under the flags of Bolivar the end of their stormy career.[42]

While keen on stressing the historical origins of the American nations and the need for some internal cultural homogeneity, on the basis of the example of the Spanish American republics, other Italian exiles went as far as to question the need for cultural uniqueness as a precondition for a successful national identity, thus emphasizing the pre-eminence of the political over the cultural element in the concept of nationhood. In his *Dei futuri destini dell'Europa* (1828), Vitale Albera claimed that, in an age of proliferating contacts between nations and increasing cultural exchanges, linguistic divisions as a source of identity and as barriers to communication were, in fact, losing importance. For Albera, "the principle of keeping one language to the exclusion of all the others belongs to the times of hostility and political intolerance," convinced as he was that "each and every national spirit stems from the people's governments, and from their institutions."[43] Finally, they all unquestionably viewed the creation of the republics as a step toward the creation of a new global order based on democracy, constitutionalism, the free exchange of goods and ideas, and the establishment of a new international legal system to prevent war. In this respect, they praised the Congress of Panama as an important step toward the creation of American and European federations.[44] Thus the confirmation of the independence of Latin America in the 1820s reinforced and expanded the exiles' cosmopolitan patriotism, based on a non-racial, open, tolerant idea of nationhood indebted to republican patriotism, in which national emancipation and universal freedom were different sides of the same coin.

The New Republics and the Birth of a
Transatlantic Democratic Federalism

The rise of Bolívar and the increasingly authoritarian nature of his constitutions and political proposals during the 1820s were at the center of a transnational debate about the nature of the executive power in a republic, the compatibility of military leadership with liberal values and democracy, and the qualities attributed to democratic heroism. This debate involved not only Creole patriots but also European intellectuals. As is well known, the compatibility of Bolívar's 1826 Bolivian Constitution with liberal values was at the center of a dispute between Constant and Abbé de Pradt.[45] The Italian exiles' contribution to this debate reflected their own experience and assessment of Napoleonic rule. After 1815, the former Napoleonists continued to believe that military leadership and heroism were crucial for the accomplishment of their programs. At the same time, however, they looked for models and figures that would overcome Napoleon's dictatorial tendencies. In the 1820s, Spanish America seemed to provide plenty of opportunities to celebrate these alternative models of democratic leadership. The exiles, however, gave a clear indication that the authoritarian model embodied by Napoleon, in the form it had taken, could not be replicated in history as his rule had been incompatible with truly representative institutions and political freedom. Admittedly, they all conceded that exceptional times required exceptional measures and that a recently emancipated country threatened externally and internally demanded a strong executive power. In Mexico, for instance, Santangelo viewed the weakness of the executive, rather than federalism, as the real cause of the republic's instability.[46] The exiles condoned temporary censorship and control over freedom of the press during or immediately after a revolution. More importantly, they went as far as to conceive the introduction of military dictatorship in exceptional circumstances. At the same time, their model of dictatorship was the ancient Roman one, that of the military leaders who, after fighting for their country, relinquished their power and returned to the frugality of private life. Thus, the majority of them, while first displaying a high degree of admiration for the "Libertador," ended up criticizing his constitution as illiberal.[47]

While the impact of Bolívar's career on European political thought in the 1820s is quite well known, the importance of the debate between federalists and centralists has surprisingly received much less attention. A key element in the makeup of the new republic that met with the approval of most European liberals and, in turn, exerted some influence over Italian and, more generally, European liberalism was the frequent appearance of federal structures. The disputes between federalists and centralists reverberated in Spanish émigré journals in London and in the publications of prominent Spanish American liberals in Europe, like Vicente Rocafuerte, author, along with José Canga Arguellas, of a passionate defense of Mexican, Guatemalan, and American federalism against Bolívar's authoritarian constitution.[48] In London, the Italian exiles were fully aware of the conflicts that divided Spanish American liberals about the desirability of federalism or centralism to consolidate the new republics, and most of them sided with the federalists. One of the main reasons for castigating Bolívar was precisely his hostility to federalism.

What emerges from the Italian exiles' own publications is a strong commitment to federal forms of government, the only kind deemed to be genuinely "liberal." In particular, the Italian exiles in Mexico made an important contribution to the political debates of the mid- and late 1820s between Yorkinos and Escoceses. Siding with the Yorkinos—and, in particular, with politicians like Lorenzo de Zavala—Linati, Galli, and Santangelo, in the pages of El Iris or in later articles and publications, supported the view that sovereignty lay in the people and that federalism alone could consolidate the nation and defend individual rights against the privileges of the Catholic Church and the military hierarchies. For Santangelo, the instability of Mexican politics between 1828 and 1832 was not due to the inherent weakness of federalism, but rather to the permanence of laws and institutions incompatible with it and to constitutional flaws. For Linati, it would not be a stronger central authority, but rather education in citizenship and military service that would reinforce the new Mexican nation.

In Europe the Italian exiles continued to celebrate the liberal nature and federal institutions of the "independent, industrial and commercial republics" of the Americas, deeming them to be the only ones compatible with the spirit of modern civilization, and they advocated federalism also for a future independent Italy.[49] In Paris, the ideas of the exiles were shared by a number of influential French liberals—such as General Lafayette, Armand Carrel, and Voyer D'Argenson, who between 1826 and 1827 celebrated North and Spanish American federal republicanism in the pages of the *Revue Americaine*— and also by the Spanish exiles who had left their country with the end of the constitutional experiment in 1823.[50] Thus, the emancipation of the Spanish American colonies was crucial to the strengthening of a transatlantic federalist current and to an American moment of European liberalism that was democratic, compatible with ideas of popular sovereignty, wary of excessive centralization, and supportive of individual rights through local government (and thus committed to a revision of the Napoleonic administrative legacy). Italian exiles and French liberals saw in the birth of the republics an opportunity to extend North American federal republicanism in both hemispheres.

Conclusions

The intellectual contacts between Italian and Spanish American patriots reveal the importance of networks and exchanges between peripheral communities at work constructing new national identities. Diasporic liberalism, republicanism, and patriotism served not only to mediate culturally between different communities, but also to foster the development of these currents on both sides of the Atlantic. Thus the exchanges between Latin American and Italian patriots are important at two levels. First, they point to the need to cultivate a new brand of transatlantic history that goes beyond the long-lasting historiographical obsession with the Anglo-American world and takes into account the contacts and entanglements not only between European metropolitan centers and American peripheries, or between Spain and Latin

America, but also with the Mediterranean. Paris and London were, of course, very important hubs of cultural exchange and mediation, not least because they hosted several diasporic communities coming from other parts of Europe. Second, it also suggests that the circulation of ideas between Europe and Latin America was not unidirectional. While European patriots had a considerable impact on Latin American political cultures, the opposite was true as well. The interest in the birth of the new republics among European liberals reflected and at the same time reinforced a European liberalism that was democratic and federalist without being radical. This is because, at least at the beginning, the emancipation and republican nature of the new states was uncontroversial, and people of different political beliefs converged in their support of it. Moderate liberals praised American republicanism for its moderation, arguing that it could not be transferred to Europe for historical and social reasons. Democratic liberals likewise thought that events in Latin America confirmed the value of republican institutions. At the same time, the permanent independence of the former Spanish American colonies was perceived as an event that was bound to change irremediably the balance of the world and inaugurate a new era for humankind. The Latin American emancipation was important at two levels for the Italian Risorgimento. First, it seemed to confirm that regime change and the defeat of reaction were both possible and achievable at the global level. This was important because it was believed that events in South or Central America were bound to also influence European developments. Second, it demonstrated that political transformations could be achieved and freedom could be attained without the radicalism and the violence of the French Revolution. To the contrary, Spanish American emancipation represented a benign, respectable revolution, evidence of the global advancement of civilization, one that combined the spreading of freedom, constitutional rights, cosmopolitan patriotism, and commerce.

True, the disappointment that greeted the internecine conflicts and the instability of the republics, as well as Giuseppe Mazzini's hostility to federalism, greatly affected the Italian observers admiration for Latin America in the 1830s. However, the impact of this transatlantic connection continued beyond the 1820s. The heroic qualities of the Spanish American caudillos were not forgotten, but rather remembered in a positive light and mythologized in the name of the international brotherhood for freedom. Likewise, Italian diasporic patriotism continued to have a profound impact upon Latin American political culture after the 1820s, and volunteers continued to flock to Latin America. Giambattista Vico's political thought was imported by exiles and had much influence in the River Plate. Mazzini's brand of nationalism had much success among Latin American liberals, and Giuseppe Garibaldi was personally involved in the wars of Rio Grande do Sul. It was precisely Garibaldi's involvement in the wars of South America that enabled Mazzini to turn the general into a symbol of the international patriotism of the Risorgimento.[51] Garibaldi himself was not immune to the myth of the Libertador. As late as 1851, when traveling to Central America, he met Manuela de Saenz, Bolívar's last partner, who delighted him with tales of the general's life. Garibaldi, who remembered the time spent with her with great fondness, was impressed with Bolívar's "entire devotion to the work of his country's deliverance" and his "lofty virtues."[52] Indeed, the relationship between Italian and Latin American political culture was built on older intellectual connections and rooted in the culture of Enlightenment, which continued to exert influence in the 1820s. However, it was also greatly reinforced at the time of the emancipation, when Ibero-American events provided new opportunities to connect the political project of the Risorgimento with international changes, and continued and deepened well into the age of nationalism. The 1820s were the crucial decade in which these post-imperial links were forged and the idea of a mutual connection and a transatlantic solidarity between liberal and republican patriotisms was invented.

Notes

I am grateful to Matthew Brown, Gabriel Paquette, and Martin Thom for their useful comments on earlier versions of this chapter.

1. Candeloro, *Dalla Restaurazione alla Rivoluzione Nazionale.* For a discussion of the historiography and a recent reassessment, see Davis, *Naples and Napoleon.*

2. Banti, *La Nazione del Risorgimento.*

3. Pécout, "The International Armed Volunteers," 413–26; also all the other articles in the same issue of the *Journal of Modern Italian Studies* 14, no. 4 (2009). According to Bistarelli, at least eight hundred left Piedmont and Lombardy between 1815 and the 1820s for Europe and the Americas. Bistarelli, "Cittadini del mondo?"

4. Candido, "Combattenti italiani per la rivoluzione bolivariana," 1–35; Candido, "Appunti all'apporto italiano alla storia delle emigrazioni politiche dall'Italia ai paesi iberoAmericani durante il Risorgimento," 187–202.

5. Mendoza Aleman, *Un soldado de Simon Bolivar.*

6. Blaufarb, "The Western Question," 742–63. On the attempts to link support

for the revolution in Colombia with uprisings in the Kingdom of the Two Sicilies, see Pepe, *Epistolario,* 105–7; Pepe, *Memoirs,* 3:238.

7. M. Brown, *Adventuring through Spanish Colonies,* 7.

8. See Isabella, *Risorgimento in Exile.*

9. On the interest shown by Italian patriots in Latin America in the Risorgimento, see Albonico, "La Gran Colombia in una rivista milanese coeva," 61–72; Albonico, "Tra padri della patria italiana e 'próceres' locali," 400–436.

10. See, for instance, Anonymous, "Viaggio nell'interno della Colombia del Colonnello Hamilton," 203–5.

11. Pecchio to del Valle, May 6, 1830, in *Cartas Autògrafas de y para José Cecilio del Valle,* by del Valle, 496–98; P. Herrera to J. Bentham (1826?), in British Library, London, Add. Mss. 33546, Fos. 108–9; S. Austin to Bentham, December 18, 1826, in Williford, *Jeremy Bentham in Spanish America,* 11.

12. Quijada, "Una constitución singular," 32.

13. Ibid., 32.

14. Quotation from Benjamin Constant, *Commentaire sur l'ouvrage de Filangieri* (Paris, 1822), 37. On Constant's view on Filangieri and on his reception in Italy in the 1820s, see Vincenzo Ferrone, *La società giusta ed equa,* 284–314. On the Neapolitan Enlightenment in Latin America, see José Carlos Chiaromonte, "Gli illuministi napoletani nel Rio de la Plata," 114–32; Federica Morelli, "Filangieri e l'altra America: storia di una ricezione," 88–111; Gonzaléz, "La recepción de Gaetano Filangieri," 29; see also Juan Camino Escobar Villegas and Adolfo Léon Maya Salazar, "Las ideas ilustradas en Colombia: Nuevas rutas, múltiples direcciones. Gaetano Filangieri y su Ciencia de la legislación," in *Nuevo Mundo—Mundos Nuevos,* "Coloquios" (2006), at http//nuevomundo.revues.org/index2651.html (accessed March 31, 2012).

15. Rocafuerte, *Ensayo Politico,* 8.

16. Salfi, *Eloge de Filangieri,* in *Oeuvres de G. Filangieri, accompagné d'un commentaire par Benjamin Constant Constant* (Paris, 1822), 1:i–xcv, esp. xciii. On the impact of Filangieri's ideas on the constitutionalism of the exiles in the 1820s, see also Isabella, *Risorgimento in Exile,* 144–46.

17. Williford, *Jeremy Bentham in Spanish America.*

18. See del Valle, *Cartas Autògrafas.*

19. Gómez, "José del Valle," 1–37; Parker, "Josè Cecilio del Valle Scholar and Patriot," 524–25; Bumgartner, *José del Valle of Central America.* A detailed account of the period of the independence is in M. Rodriguez, *The Cadiz Experiment in Central America, 1808 to 1826;* also see J. Dym, *From Sovereign Villages to Nation-States.*

20. Parker, "Josè Cecilio del Valle Scholar and Patriot," 527–35.

21. Bumgartner, *José del Valle of Central America*, 258, 180, 198.

22. Del Valle to Pecchio, Guatemala, October 21, 1829, in *Cartas Autògrafas*, by del Valle, 137.

23. Pecchio to del Valle, Londres, July 25, 1827, in *Cartas Autògrafas*, by del Valle, 147–48.

24. Del Valle to Pecchio, Guatemala, May 23, 1828, in *Cartas Autògrafas*, by del Valle, 156.

25. See del Valle to Pecchio, Guatemala, March 3, 1828, in *Cartas Autògrafas*, by del Valle, 152.

26. Pecchio to del Valle, York, September 22, 1827, 150; del Valle to Pecchio, Guatemala, March 3, 1828, 152; Pecchio to del Valle, Londres, July 13, 1828, 127, all in *Cartas Autògrafas*, by del Valle. See Pecchio's description of the method, letter, July 13, 1828, in *Cartas Autògrafas*, by del Valle, 127. On adult education, see Pecchio to del Valle, London, July 13, 1828, in *Cartas Autògrafas*, by del Valle, 128.

27. Pecchio to del Valle, London, May 6, 1830, in *Cartas Autògrafas*, by del Valle, 138.

28. M. Brown, "Not Forging Nations but Foraging for Them," 223–40. On the xenophobic nature of early Mexican patriotism, see Lomnitz, "Nationalism as a Practical System," esp. 348–51; Dym, "Citizen of Which Republic?," 477–510.

29. Sims, *The Expulsion of Mexico's Spaniards*.

30. Constant, *Commentaire sur l'ouvrage de Filangieri*, part 2, 60–61; *Eloge de Sir Samuel Romilly* (Paris, 1819), 35–38.

31. On the involvement of the exiles in Mexican politics, see Isabella, *Risorgimento in Exile*, 51–60; see also Tella, *National Popular Politics in Early Independent Mexico*, 165.

32. "El ignorante," *Caprichos de la fortuna* (Mexico, 1826), 14; see also *Justicia de la espulsion de Santangelo* (Mexico, 1826).

33. *Satisfaccion del Senador Alpuche* (Mexico, 1826), 5; quotation from *Reflecsiones imparciales sobre los gritos des Sr. Alpuche* (Mexico, 1826), 9.

34. "El solitario," *Juicio Imparcial sobre la espulsion de Santángelo* (Mexico, 1826), 5–7.

35. *En donde estamos? En Megico, ò en Constantinola?* (Mexico, 1826). The author refers to Benjamin Constant and *Eloge de Sir Samuel Romilly* (Paris, 1819), 36–37.

36. "Elections Mexicaines," *L'Abeille*, February 19, 1833, 1.

37. Linati, "Ruines de Mictal," *L'Industriel*, September 1828, 5, in *Claudio Linati (1790–1832)* (Parma, 1935), 17–19.

38. Giuseppe Pecchio, "Guatemala," *New Monthly Magazine* 14 (1825): 591.

39. Ibid., part 1, 578–93. The article was republished as Giuseppe Pecchio, *Bosquejo de la Repùblica de Centro America: Escrito en inglès por el Conde de Pechio; i tra-*

ducido al espanol por M.S.-Guatemala. Imprenta de la Union (1829). On "historical indigenismo," see Brading, *The Origins of Mexican Nationalism,* 48–55. See also the historical dissertations included in Costantino Beltrami, *Le Mexique,* 2 vols. (Paris, 1830).

40. Beltrami, *Le Mexique,* 2:141, 86–87, 171–72.

41. Claudio Linati, *Costumes Civiles, militaires et religieux du Mexique dessinées d'après nature* (Bruxelles, 1828), plate nos. 8 and 40.

42. Linati, *Costumes Civils,* plate no. 14.

43. Vitale Albera, *Dei futuri destini dell'Europa* (1828), 123–24.

44. Pecchio, "Guatemala," part 2, 74; Orazio Santangelo, *Las cuatro primeras discusiones del Congreso de Panamá: Tales como debieran ser* (Mexico City: Oficina de la testamentaria de Ontiveros, 1826), 138–39, http://openlibrary.org/publishers/Oficina _de_la_testamentaria_de_Ontiveros (accessed March 30, 2012); Fiorenzo Galli, "America y Europa," *El Iris* 2 (1826): 65.

45. Filippi, *Bolivar y Europa,* vol. 1.

46. Orazio Santangelo, "Elections Mexicaines," *L'Abeille,* February 19, 1833.

47. Isabella, *Risorgimento in Exile,* 56–60.

48. Vicente Rocafuerte and Josè Canga Arguellas, *Cartas de un Americano sobre las ventajas de los gobiernos repúblicanos federativos* (London, 1826), 100–101. On this debate see Rodríguez O., *The Independence of Spanish America,* 184–88.

49. For a full account of the exiles' federalism and their involvement in debates in Mexico and Europe, see Isabella, *Risorgimento in Exile,* 42–64; Claudio Linati, "Etat de l'Instruction en Amérique," in *L'Industriel: Revue des Revues* (1829), quoted in "Claudio Linati (1790–1832)," *Memorie parmensi per la storia del Risorgimento* 4 (1935): 24–28, 25.

50. On Constant's federalism, see Oliver Meuwly, *Liberté et Société: Constant et Tocqueville face aux limites du libéralisme* (Geneva: Librairie Droz, 2002), 81–84; Higonnet, "Le fédéralisme américain et le fédéralisme de Benjamin Constant," 51–62.

51. Klaus Gallo, "Esteban Echeverria's Critique of Universal Suffrage"; Jorge Myers, "Giuseppe Mazzini and the Emergence of Liberal Nationalism in the River Plate and Chile, 1835–60"; Peter Burke, "Mazzini and Brazil," all in Bayly and Biagini, *Giuseppe Mazzini and the Globalisation of Democratic Nationalism,* 299–310, 323–54. On Vico in Spanish America, see Albonico, "Tra padri della patria italiana e 'próceres' locali," 407. On Garibaldi, see Riall, *Garibaldi,* chapter 2.

52. Giuseppe Garibaldi, *Autobiography of Giuseppe Garibaldi,* 3 vols. (London, 1889), 2:59.

5

The Brazilian Origins of the 1826 Portuguese Constitution

Gabriel Paquette

The present station of Portugal is so anomalous, and the recent years of her history are crowded with events so unusual, that the House will perhaps not think that I am unprofitably wasting its time.

—George Canning to Parliament, December 12, 1826.

The decade of the 1820s witnessed an explosion of constitution-making. Many constitutions proliferated, but few were implemented, and a miniscule number survived for long before being toppled or significantly amended. In the extended improvisation that accompanied the transition from Old Regime to new regimes throughout the Atlantic world, constitutional forms were disseminated, debated, adapted, adopted, and discarded. The most important of these models were the Constitution of Cádiz of 1812 (itself partly inspired by the French Constitution of 1791), the French Chartre of 1814, and the loose set of institutions collectively referred to as "the British Constitution." Other models percolated as well, including those derived from Benthamism, the US Constitution of 1787, and even its long-discarded forerunner, the Articles of Confederation. To these examples might be added the praetorian consular system bequeathed by Napoleon Bonaparte's empire, itself an heir as well as an antagonist to the centralizing, enlightened, reform-orientated monarchies of the late eighteenth century. The influence of most of these constitutional systems has been well documented.[1] Many of the studies share the assumption that ideas passed from the core to the periphery, whether from Britain and France to the rest of Europe and then onward to the Americas, or from the United States to Hispanic Meso- and South America. Once on American soil, the reverberations of these constitutional doctrines are ignored.[2] Furthermore, the impact of American constitutionalism on Europe is rarely studied.[3] The prevailing assumption is that the intellectual and political history of Europe and the Americas diverged after independence and that the interplay and mutual influence so often pointed out by practitioners of Atlantic history abruptly ceases to exist. Where America's influence in Europe after 1825 is recognized, it is mainly for the inspiration its example offered to frustrated, exiled revolutionaries, as a beacon of liberty, a depiction which dovetailed neatly with the flattering self-perception of postimperial elites in both Americas.[4]

But the Americas were more than a symbol for disgruntled aspirants to political change. The New World also furnished at least one European state with a constitution. The Portuguese Constitution of 1826, also known as the Carta Constitucional, remained in force, except for brief periods (1828–34, 1836–42) and with only slight modification through revisions and "additional acts" (1852, 1865, 1896, 1907), until the fall of the monarchy in 1910.[5] Written by Dom Pedro, emperor of Brazil from 1822 and generally acknowledged heir to the Portuguese throne, and his coterie of advisors, the Carta was a superficial retouching of the constitution he had promulgated and imposed on Brazil in 1824.[6] This 1824 constitution was itself the culmination of a political process sparked by Dom Pedro's rejection of a draft constitution for Brazil modeled closely on the 1822 Portuguese Constitution, which was, in turn, an adaptation of the Spanish Constitution of 1812. As shall be described in greater detail, the 1824 Brazilian and 1826 Portuguese Constitutions established a hereditary constitutional monarchy, with a bicameral legislature, but featuring a robust executive power. Dom Pedro's Carta, then, was an explicit repudiation of representative institutions endowed with significant legislative power and an attempt to re-outfit absolutism with the political language of moderate constitutionalism. The Carta emanated from the throne, not from the elected representative institutions, which, while more than consultative bodies, operated under the constant threat of dissolution by the monarch.

This chapter explores how a hastily prepared constitution drawn up in Rio de Janeiro that embodied the spirit of an anti-popular, revivified monarchy in America, designed largely to mollify the Holy Alliance and appease Brazilians wary of their emperor's continued connection to the ex-metropole Portugal, came to be viewed in Europe both as a threat to royal legitimacy and as the rallying cry of Portuguese liberals and their sympathizers abroad. That Dom Pedro, upon abdicating his Brazilian throne in 1831, came to be depicted as a champion of constitutionalism in Europe confounded those Brazilians who considered him an inveterate enemy of constitutional government as well as arch-conservatives who held out hope for an absolutist *restauração,* until Pedro's premature death in Portugal in 1834.[7] The New World indeed influenced the Old, but not as is commonly supposed, as the fount and paragon of liberty. Instead, I seek to demonstrate, as the reception of the 1826 Carta suggests, that it offered new forms of legitimacy, a reinvigorated moderate conservatism designed to avoid the perceived excesses of popular politics. Latin America launched as well as received political ideas in the aftermath of independence, and Latin Americans were of a monarchical as well as a republican-liberal cast. In general terms, this chapter argues for the persistence of mutual influence between Portugal and Brazil after independence. Tropes of disjuncture, which are fundamental to the historiography of the age of revolutions as well as to nationalist historiography's obsession with the "birth" of the nation-state, tend to obscure pivotal episodes like the one analyzed in this chapter.

Constitutionalism and the End of the Luso-Brazilian Empire

The fracturing of the Luso-Brazilian Empire in the early 1820s was the culmination of a process that dated from at least 1807, when the French invasion of the Iberian peninsula forced the evacuation of the royal court from Lisbon to Rio de Janeiro.[8] But the liberal revolution, which erupted in 1820 in Porto and compelled Dom João VI to return to Portugal in order to reign from the Iberian peninsula as a constitutional monarch, triggered an overt movement for independence.[9] The Cortes that framed the 1822 constitution sought not only to turn Portugal into a constitutional monarchy with robust representative institutions, but also to return the Portuguese Empire to the *status quo ex ante,* to strip Brazil of both the de facto and de jure autonomy it had acquired since 1808, a state of affairs acknowledged by the elevation of the former colony to a status of a kingdom co-equal with the metropole in 1815. "Revolutionary ideas were widespread," the Marquis of Fronteira recalled in his memoirs; "everyone wanted the court to return to Lisbon, and they loathed the idea of becoming a colony of a colony."[10] The Lisbon Cortes' purported recolonization scheme greatly angered the Brazilian deputies to the Cortes and alienated political elites in Brazil.[11] As a leading Rio de Janeiro newspaper wrote, "our reunion with Portugal can only be achieved on the basis of perfect equality."[12] The Cortes' high-handed tactics, including its recall of Dom Pedro to Lisbon, helped to instigate Brazil's declaration of independence, an act that was as much a preemptive "counter-revolution" as an assertion of national sovereignty. Dom Pedro capitalized on the dramatic separation from Europe in order to rally support for his beleaguered monarchy against more radical political projects that were percolating, including those that aimed to implant strong representative institutions in Brazil, akin to those emerging in republican Spanish America.

Dom Pedro rejected outright the notion of a Cortes, whether in Portugal or Brazil, empowered to frame a constitution and legislate on the basis of it. He recoiled at the prospect of governing within the limits defined by such a body. The earliest glimmerings of his hostility toward representative government may be gleaned from his well-known letters to his father in the months preceding the grandiloquent declaration of "Independence or Death!" in September 1822. The main idea conveyed in these letters is a rejection of the Cortes' claimed right to draft a constitution and to legislate on the basis of it. "The Brazilians and I are in favour of a constitution, but we seek to honour the sovereign by having the subjects obey him."[13] By July 1822, he informed Dom João that "circumstances oblige me to convoke an Assembly," but reassured him that such a move was "merely a formality, for I am the one who executes your decrees and none which emanate from there [i.e., the Assembly]."[14] By September 1822, his disaffection was complete as he railed against the "Machiavellian, factious, chaos-causing, and pest-like Cortes."[15]

This spiteful attitude would soon be directed at the Brazilian Constituent Assembly, which "circumstances" had compelled him to convene before independence had been declared.[16] In opening the Assembly in May 1823, Dom Pedro offered perhaps the clearest public statement of his constitutional thought. Demanding a "wise, just, appropriate and executable constitution," which "harmonized" legislative, executive, and judicial power, Pedro warned the Assembly not to frame a constitution that resembled that of "France in 1791 and 1792, whose bases were utterly theoretical, and metaphysical, as the experiences of France, Spain and, lately, Portugal have proven." These constitutions, Pedro asserted, did not promote "general happiness," but rather "licentious liberty," exposing its people to the "horrors of anarchy."[17]

When the debates in the Assembly appeared unlikely to produce a constitution that differed significantly from that framed by the Lisbon Cortes of 1822, Pedro abruptly dissolved that body. When he did so, on November 12, 1823, he acted from a position of bolstered strength. Just three days earlier, on November 9, Lord Cochrane's fleet re-entered Rio de Janeiro, having vanquished military opposition to Brazilian independence in the northern provinces.[18] Dom Pedro promised to issue a constitution that would be "twice as liberal as that written by the Assembly," attributing his decision to the rising "spirit of disunion" purveyed by the "chaos-causing faction."[19] According to one of the emperor's stalwart apologists, José da Silva Lisboa, the Assembly's draft constitution had been imbued with the spirit of "Spanish American republicanism." The principles favored by this "revolutionary hydra" were "opposed to those adopted by the Great Powers of Europe, which had elevated humanity to its present level of civilization."[20] Putting this vitriol aside, it is crucial to recall Pedro's promise to rule as a constitutional monarch, only not in a political system in which the constitution was imposed, instead of freely given (*outorgada*), by the monarch. Pedro's enthusiasm for constitutions that met such criteria therefore must not be shrouded by his actions. As late as February 1824, his enthusiasm for constitutional monarchy remained undimmed. "If I were obliged to govern without a constitution, I would sooner give up my throne, for I want to govern hearts filled with dignity and honor, marked by freedom instead of slavery."[21] At this stage, then, the question for Dom Pedro became which sort of constitution was most appropriate for Brazil.

The 1824 Brazilian Constitution: Influences and Impact

In the Luso-Brazilian world, the influence of the political thought of the French Restoration was pronounced, particularly in the model of the 1814 French Charte. For those critical of radical constitutions based on the 1791 French Constitution, including the 1812 Spanish Constitution, the Charte offered a plausible alternative.[22] Pierre Paul Royer-Collard remarked that the Charte was "nothing else than the indissoluble alliance of the legitimate power from whence it emanates with the natural liberties it recognizes and consecrates."[23] François Guizot called it a "victory of the partisans of the English constitution . . . over the republicans as well as the supporters of the ancient monarchy."[24] Although some scholars would dismiss Guizot's claim as dubious,[25] it was at least superficially accurate and suggested how the "English" constitution could be adapted to circumstances found on the continent. As early as 1820, the notion of Crown-issued Carta on the French 1814 model had been floated by the Marquis of Palmela to Dom João as a way to circumvent radical revolution without resorting to the pure, unadulterated reaction of the sort Ferdinand VII of Spain had indulged in upon his restoration in 1814. Palmela recommended the Charte as a means to "maintain tranquility, placate the rival parties, conciliate diverse spirits, and to satisfy at the same time the interests of the revolutionaries and the nobility."[26]

Dom Pedro was undoubtedly aware of these earlier proposals and received corroborating advice from various quarters, including from a small rump of the now-dissolved Constituent Assembly, whose members he trusted. He also received counsel from Lord Cochrane, who advised him that it was exigent to "declare the type of government he planned to adopt" in order to allay suspicion in Brazil's provinces as well as quell the anxiety of the Holy Alliance. Cochrane suggested that it would be strategically prudent to declare the English constitution as the model after which Brazil's constitution would be fashioned. It would be difficult, Cochrane mused, for critics of Dom Pedro's actions to find fault with a "limited monarchy, surrounded by a free people, enriched by industry which the security of property, by means of just laws, never fails to produce."[27] Nevertheless, Pedro and many of his advisors were aware that it would be impossible to imitate other constitutional models slavishly; the task was to adopt them to Brazil's circumstances.[28]

The origins of the 1824 constitution, issued on March 25 by Dom Pedro, are made murky by misleading, self-aggrandizing claims made decades later by some of the key political figures involved. In 1840, Antônio Carlos Andrada boasted to the Brazilian Chamber of Deputies that he had taken the lead in the commission's work: "And what did I do? After establishing the fundamental bases, I took the best from all other existing constitutions, picking and modifying that which seemed to me the most applicable to our current state. . . . [T]he present constitution is an exact copy of the one I wrote."[29] But this boast is largely inaccurate for archival sources reveal that the emperor was influenced more decisively by two further *projectos* that he received, sources whose imprint on the 1824 Brazilian Constitution are more pronounced. The authors of these *projectos* were Frei Francisco de Santa Teresa de Jesus Sampaio, a trusted advisor and also the editor of the *Diário do Governo,* and Francisco Gomes da Silva, nicknamed "O Chalaça," his close friend.

Frei Sampaio's "Projecto de uma Constituição Monárquica" (1823) is notable for its insistence that constitutions were useful only to the extent that they ensured "internal security" and protected the state from "formidable convulsions." Its preamble is a celebration of "true mixed monarchy," of the "harmony" achieved through the "division of powers."[30] This harmony is described as the "fundamental key" to the system, one capable of "tranquilizing the spirit of the people, so commonly deluded by the false promises of their leaders." Besides endowing the monarch with a role in initiating legislation, Frei Sampaio's "Projecto" praised the virtues of bicameralism, particularly the merits of a senate, which he described as an "asylum for the aristocracy." It also called for the monarch's absolute veto power over legislation. Without it, Frei Sampaio argued, the emperor would be "denied the capacity to conserve mixed monarchy and it would degenerate, becoming a monarchy in name only."[31]

Gomes da Silva's "Bases para um Projeto de Constituição" (1823) is notable for having made the first reference to the "Poder Moderador," though incompletely articulated, an institution that would figure prominently in the 1824 constitution as well as the Carta. As in Frei Sampaio's "Projecto," harmonious balance was key to the "conservation of political liberty," though the "Bases" indicates four instead of three powers. A senate with life-term appointments was advocated, with the selection of senators remaining the exclusive prerogative of the monarch. The guarantees of the "Bases" were clearly enumerated and relatively expansive, including property rights, limited freedom of press, right to petition, and "free public instruction for all classes of citizens."[32] This attempt to learn from, and avert, the excesses of revolution encouraged an explicit engagement with Benjamin Constant's constitutional thought, particularly as expressed in his 1814 *Cours de Politique Consitutionnelle*. Constant was convinced that legislative and executive powers were bound to encroach upon each other unless they were kept apart by a third power, which Constant termed the *pouvoir préservateur* or *pouvoir neutre*. This third power would not so much limit the scope of political authority (a condition that Constant assumed), but by "protecting the different branches of government from mutual interference it contributes to the happiness and improvement of the governed."[33]

The 1824 constitution clearly differed from the Assembly's draft in its emphasis on the emperor's function as guarantor of harmonious interaction among the different branches of government. This goal prompted the creation of a robust executive and also the insinuation of the emperor in almost all branches of government. Legislation emanating from the General Assembly required the emperor's "sanction" (Article 13). But the most obvious break was the creation of the "moderating power," which was described as "the key (*chave*) of the entire political system, and is the private attribute of the Emperor, as the Supreme chief of the Nation, its First Representative, so that he can work tirelessly for the maintenance of independence, and equilibrium and harmony between the other political powers" (Article 98). The moderating power did not overlap with the executive powers also enjoyed by the emperor, but rather made them more expansive, thus encroaching on the powers that the Assembly's *Projecto* attributed to the legislative branch. Among the attributes of the moderating power were the dissolution of the Chamber of Deputies in cases where the "nation's salvation depended on it"; the power to nominate and dismiss ministers; and the nomination of senators (Article 101).[34]

The dissolution of the Assembly and the promulgation of the 1824 constitution were met with rebellion, most remarkably in the attempt by several of the northeastern provinces to secede from Brazil and form an autonomous federation based on republican principles.[35] The emperor's arrogant, arbitrary actions and the centralizing tenor of his 1824 constitution, which severely diminished provincial autonomy, were crucial factors in this revolutionary outbreak. While this Confederation of the Equator was suppressed, without mercy, it clearly affected Dom Pedro. It deepened his suspicion of constitutions and left him exasperated with the impotence of paper. In an 1825 letter, he complained, "What arguments can win over these malcontents? What arguments can there possibly be? Gunpowder and bullets, perhaps, and nothing else."[36] Such sentiments would inform Dom Pedro when he framed Portugal's 1826 Carta, leading him to strengthen the nobility's role and to bolster the power of the executive.

The Portuguese Restoration, the Death of Dom João VI, and the Making of the Carta (1823–26)

Events in Brazil were not the only influences, for Dom Pedro remained privy to information regarding the political situation in Portugal, where the Cortes he loathed was dissolved in June 1823, in the aftermath of the anti-constitutional uprising that took his younger brother Dom Miguel as its symbol, the so-called Vilafrancada, in late May. Dom João's termination of the 1822 constitutional experiment did not proceed smoothly. On June 18, 1823, he promised to promulgate a constitution, or Lei Fundamental, and established a junta for this purpose. The following day, a second decree was issued establishing a junta to review all existing legislation, particularly that which had been passed by the liberal Cortes.

These moves were undoubtedly conciliatory gestures, since they did not abolish *vintismo* legislation outright.[37] Dom João's decree entrusted the seven members of the junta to decide, after "mature reflection," which laws "conform to the true principles of universal public law, with the principles of the monarchy, with the rights and just liberties of citizens, and with the uses, customs and opinions of the Portuguese people (*povo*)," indicating that he would "affirm those which [met this requirement] while revoking the rest."[38] The constitutional junta was composed of an array of ultra-Royalists as well as moderate constitutionalists. Palmela dominated the group and, in a speech delivered at the junta's first meeting, blasted the 1822 constitution for having introduced "innovations contrary to the customs and will of the nation." He argued that the junta's task was to "produce a document not imbued with vague and abstract theses, but rather one that provided practical guarantees for the most essential rights (*direitos*) and secured the most solid basis for public prosperity."[39]

Yet the likelihood of a constitution that could satisfy all parties was remote. The intransigence of the ultra-royalists of the junta foreclosed such a possibility. For the Archbishop of Évora, for example, "to concede to the Cortes anything more than consultative authority is to divide sovereignty between it and the King, and to overthrow the most essential principal of our ancient institutions, to throw to the ground the greatness and consideration of the throne."[40] In spite of several conciliatory voices, who urged moderate or mixed government, the junta failed to produce a new Lei Fundamental. As Dom João pondered his options, he received a great deal of unsolicited advice, including from his Madrid-based daughter, Maria Thereza, who begged her father to recall the "terrible memory" of the seventeenth-century Cortes, which had "diminished royal authority." The present situation, she warned, was even less propitious, with "too many heads filled with radical ideas," and the prospect of being "subjugated under the yoke of the Cortes" even more likely.[41]

A second absolutist reaction, again with Dom Miguel as its figurehead, occurred in April (the so-called Abrilada), and this put an end to the viability of a constitutional solution. Unlike the Vilafrancada, which was welcomed by Dom João, the Infante's latest actions did not earn similar approbation. In a proclamation issued from aboard the English ship *Windsor Castle,* where he had sought refuge from the political chaos unleashed by his son, Dom João castigated the "sinister inspiration" and "treacherous counselors" who impelled Miguel to take actions that were neither "just nor necessary" and that constituted an "attack on [his] royal authority, which is indivisible." By June 4, 1824, a new law declared that the traditional laws of the monarchy were back in effect. Appearances notwithstanding, it was not an entirely reactionary measure: in a message circulated to foreign powers, Dom João indicated that the Antigas Cortes would be called in due course and reassured foreign emissaries that a new Lei Fundamental would be issued "founded, to the extent possible, on the basis of the ancient laws of the kingdom, perfected as demanded by the century in which we live, with a view toward the institutions existing in other constitutional monarchies." Of course, he had made an equivalent promise just a year earlier, one which he had broken in flagrant fashion.[42]

Dom João's dissolution of the two juntas was accompanied by a proliferation of pamphlets. Several endorsed his decision and queried the necessity of a new Lei Fundamental. "The Republicans of Holland," one publicist argued, "were never as free as the Portuguese were in their political state before the era of the *Regeneração*," for "our ancient Cortes is the best example of a political constitution in a independent and hereditary monarchy."[43] Moderates were disappointed by the king's empty promise. Though they acknowledged Dom João's "naturally and insuperably timid nature," they blamed the radical liberals, whom they invariably designated "free masons (*pedreiros livres*)," for having "perverted the cause of liberty" by giving a "partisan posture or character to a cause that was national." Yet the ultra-royalists were not absolved, for their "oppressive" tactics, "destroying the present government and threatening any one that happens to succeed it," had "convinced all Portuguese of the insecurity of the state." It gave rise to a "miserable existence" in which "one faction takes over for another, administration is weakened, and the public coffers are emptied."[44]

As Portuguese legal historians have demonstrated, several of the defunct juntas' constitutional projects appear to have been forerunners of the Carta, a fact that undermines the "*Cartista* myth of rupture." There are unmistakable resemblances, if not continuities, between the proposals discussed by the junta and the institutions established by the Carta,[45] though documentary evidence has not come to light that suggests Dom Pedro or his advisors had perused copies of these constitutional projects, whether before the promulgation of the 1824 Brazilian Constitution or during the revision of that document as they fashioned the 1826 Carta. But unpublished manuscript sources can shed light on two matters relevant to the Carta's origins: first, whether Dom Pedro and Dom João had broached the topic of a Carta for Portugal after 1824 and, second, whether Dom João truly had intended to issue a constitution of some sort after the dissolution of the junta convened to frame one. With regard to the first matter, in an 1824 letter written in the aftermath of the Abrilada, urging his father to recognize Brazil's independence, Dom Pedro made plain that Portugal needed Brazilian commerce to survive. Recognition, by renewing old mercantile links, would spur Portugal's flagging economy and ensure its viability as a sovereign state. This measure, Dom Pedro suggested, should be accompanied by the granting of a constitution. By "giving [Portugal] a constitution," Dom Pedro reasoned, Dom João would secure his position and rescue himself from the "daggers of the assassins who surround [him]," including those wielded by his estranged wife, Dona Carlota Joaquina, and his son Dom Miguel.[46] With regard to the second matter, Palmela's private correspondence from 1825 with his long-time colleague, the Count of Porto Santo, reveals that Dom João "anxiously desired" to convoke the Cortes in order to "fulfill his promise," but that "the views of our continental allies" prevented him from acting. The king, Palmela suggested, was merely waiting for the "fear of revolution to subside, so that [he] could act freely without the exercise of his sovereignty being impeded or misinterpreted," especially in Spain.[47] In light of these documents, it is reasonable to conclude that the possibility of a constitutional charter for Portugal had been raised by Dom Pedro, that Dom João was receptive to this prospect, and that it was the international as well as domestic political climate that bore as much responsibility for inaction as Dom João's penchant for dithering.

Part of the reason why this transatlantic dialogue concerning constitutionalism has been neglected in the historiography of the period is that its importance was eclipsed by Brazil's independence, recognized officially by Portugal in 1825. But this formal recognition did not signify that the affairs of Portugal and Brazil would be entirely disentangled and that the two countries would undergo divergent historical evolution. In one of his final letters to his son, Dom João beseeched him to care for Portugal's welfare. Though somewhat veiled, his meaning is not obscure: the separation of Brazil and Portugal should not be regarded as permanent. Since the juntas convened in 1823 had failed to produce a new constitution and the "ancient" constitution had been restored by Dom João, the rules governing royal succession remained unmodified.[48] Due to calculated inaction, Dom Pedro's status as heir to the Portuguese throne was uncontested, though his claim was muddied by the 1824 Brazilian Constitution's unequivocal stipulation that Portugal and Brazil were never to be unified under a single crown. In addition, there was the non-juridical, but perhaps more important fact that Dom Pedro had been the figurehead, if not the architect, of the dismemberment of the Portuguese Empire just three years before, a role that made him anathema to both Portuguese liberals and conservatives.

News of Dom João's death reached Rio de Janeiro on April 25, 1826. In Portugal, Dom Pedro already had been acclaimed as Dom Pedro IV, king of Portugal. There is some evidence that he had planned for this contingency, even entertaining the idea of granting Portugal a Carta as early as October

1825, something he had encouraged his father to do a year earlier. According to the British emissary (who served simultaneously as Portuguese plenipotentiary), Sir Charles Stuart, "[Dom Pedro] is tenacious of every right which contributes to secure his succession to the throne of [Portugal]. . . . [A]mong the projects he entertains for the future regeneration of the government, [one is] the establishment of a charter, and other schemes of which it is not easy to trace the source."[49] Upon being informed of his father's death, Dom Pedro sent a circular to his closest advisors, informing them that a regency had been formed in Portugal until he "decided what is permitted to him as heir to the kingdom." He acknowledged the "delicate" state of public opinion in Brazil, "zealous of its independence," and asked whether its sovereignty would be deemed threatened were its emperor simultaneously to become king of Portugal, so long as "the two nations remain completely separate." He further queried whether such a situation would violate Brazil's constitution and, crucially, whether it would be possible for a European nation to be governed from the New World. Were such a transatlantic polity deemed impossible to sustain, he asked for advice concerning the best method of abdicating the Portuguese Crown and asked to whom the scepter should pass.[50]

The emperor received several replies between April 26 and 28, 1826.[51] The Viscount of Barbacena reminded the emperor that the 1824 constitution forbade the emperor from leaving Brazilian territory without the Assembly's explicit consent and further prohibited the union of the crowns. But Barbacena did not perceive any obstacle to the acceptance and simultaneous wearing of the two crowns that "belonged to Pedro by the right of birth." Frei Antônio de Rabida informed the emperor that he had three mutually exclusive choices: first, to reign in Portugal; second, "to give them a Carta extracted from the English and French constitutions"; and third, to abdicate in favor of his daughter Dona Maria. Ultimately, Pedro pursued all three options simultaneously, even though Rabida had presented them as incompatible. The Viscount of Vilareal cautioned the emperor against abdication, which he believed would be "eminently disagreeable" to Brazilians, who would "become fearful that future events would be hostile to their independence." The Baron of Alcântara likewise maintained that a revived Luso-Brazilian union was impracticable, noting that the acrid separation of Brazil from Portugal portended even greater obstacles to their reunification. He warned of potential popular disturbances by Brazilians unable to appreciate the subtle differences between the recently overthrown colonial condition and the new form of union contemplated by Dom Pedro in his circular. Much more desirable was a course of action designed to reserve the right of succession for his heirs and, in a single stroke, incorporate Portugal's colonies in Africa, particularly Angola, into the Brazilian Empire.[52]

With this advice in mind, Dom Pedro and Gomes da Silva commenced their revision of the 1824 Brazilian Constitution in order to accommodate it to Portuguese soil.[53] In the course of fewer than three days, they rearranged the order of the articles, eliminated references specific to Brazil, modified language, and made obvious substitutions. Using two copies of the 1824 constitution, they repeatedly swapped annotated texts and attached short explanatory notes to justify the amendments each had made. Dom Pedro objected to Gomes da Silva's crossing out of the word *constitutional* (*constitucional*) to describe the government of Portugal. As he explained, "if a king gives a constitution, the government is constitutional, and it does not seem advisable to remove a word to which at the present time the people have taken such a fancy."[54] At the end of three days, the 1824 Brazilian Constitution had been adapted into the Carta. The most salient differences between Brazil's 1824 constitution and the Carta were these: first, the religious basis of the Carta was muted, as the invocation of the Holy Trinity was excised; second, religious freedom in Portugal was confined to foreigners, whereas in Brazil it was more extensive; third, the 1826 Carta guaranteed the existence of the hereditary nobility, whereas the Brazilian constitution did not provide for a hereditary peerage; and, fourth, the Portuguese Carta gave the king an absolute veto over legislation, whereas in Brazil the emperor could merely suspend its taking effect. But the most striking feature was the retention, even amplification, of the "moderating power" in the Carta.[55]

Though he was keen to assert his right to the Portuguese throne, Dom Pedro realized that the short-term restoration of a union between Brazil and Portugal was a chimera. He therefore pursued a course of action to secure the Portuguese throne for his daughter, Dona Maria, which entailed promulgating the Carta, forcing his brother—still in exile in Vienna—to swear allegiance to it while also arranging for his eventual marriage to Maria, and abdicating the Portuguese throne. The prospect of Dom Miguel as regent during Dona Maria's minority was imperfect, but palatable, certainly better than the unsavory alternatives.[56] Yet to be certain that this state of affairs would transpire, he declared that the regency headed by his sister, Dona Isabel Maria, would last until Dom Miguel publicly swore his allegiance to the constitution and agreed to marry his daughter. Still, the similarity between the two constitutions indicates not only the Carta's hasty completion, but also Dom Pedro's aspiration to reunite Portugal and Brazil at some future stage, as constitutional uniformity would facilitate the realization of that goal.

The Reaction to the Carta in Portugal and the Road to Civil War

The Carta was entrusted to Sir Charles Stuart, who arrived with it in Lisbon in early July.[57] Although it was not published immediately, it was greeted with public celebrations. Laudatory poems were composed and recited in public, praising the "Liberal Constitution" as a "gift from God" that promised to usher in an era of "peace," "union," and "stability." This "divine" constitution, widely understood to have been composed solely by Dom Pedro, was lauded as a "model for other nations" covetous of similar liberties. Very quickly, however, the initial euphoria dissipated and the Portuguese political class splintered into groups in favor and opposed to the Carta. Portugal stood on the brink of political chaos, if not civil war. The supporters of the Carta believed it under attack by "two groups that sought its destruction: the first want to replace it with a pure and abominable despotism; the second seek to re-establish a constitution of illegitimate origin, which but a short time ago led Portugal to disgrace."[58]

Those attracted to the Carta formed a heterogeneous group, but of a pronounced moderate cast. To moderate liberals, the allowance for a representative chamber, elections, and a reasonable guarantee of (limited) individual rights was an improvement over the status quo. To moderate conservatives, the Carta's retention of the royal prerogative, the creation of a hereditary, life-term, Crown-nominated upper chamber (*Pares*), limited suffrage, robust property rights, and the confirmation of Catholicism as the religion of the state were enticing features.[59] For monarchist-leaning conservative liberals, who considered Miguel and his circle retrograde, the Carta was imperfect but palatable. Conservative liberals thus sought common ground with those moderate liberals not enraptured by visions of restoring the 1822 constitution.

For the so-called *vintistas,* the liberals who had galvanized the 1820 revolution and written the 1822 constitution, the Carta's arrival was not unreservedly embraced. As in Brazil, the possibility of a Cortes playing a role in the redaction of the Lei Fundamental was obviated by the promulgation of a royal charter, a "gift" from the throne. However, even these more radical liberals perceived the Carta as a partial victory, endowing constitutionalism with the royal imprimatur, something which Dom João's vacillation and un-delivered promises, not to mention Dom Miguel's reactionary tendencies, had precluded between 1823 and 1826.[60] Still, the same men who had favored the Cortes in its struggle with Pedro in 1822 and 1823 to keep Portugal and Brazil united and had witnessed Dom Pedro's subsequent erratic, high-handed treatment of representative institutions in Brazil in 1823 and 1824, were inevitably uneasy. These unnatural allies would clash after 1831 when Dom Pedro put himself, probably in violation of the Carta, at the head of his daughter's regency.[61] In 1826, however, the rising tide of ultra-royalism—in both its popular and elite manifestations—encouraged pragmatism, which translated into grudging acquiescence or at least tepid support for the Carta.

In voicing support for the Carta, some of its adherents repudiated the 1822 constitution and strove to highlight its distinct origin. The *Velho Liberal* newspaper described the constitution of 1822 as "eminently democratic in its organization, for not having been issued by the governors for the governed, but rather by the latter for the former, attacking monarchical principles, and exposing the Portuguese to the disasters that harmed Naples and Spain."[62] The disavowal of the constitution of 1822, now dismissed by moderates as "the offspring more of desperation and suffering than ingenuity in the service of patriotism," was coupled with the assumption that the "old system" was equally untenable. The Carta's "middle way" (*meio termo*) was embraced as a viable alternative.[63] Interestingly, though it drew its inspiration from the political thought of French restoration and resembled the 1814 Chartre, the Carta was frequently compared to the British constitution. One enthusiast gushed at "the similarity of our constitutional charter with that of Great Britain, the origin of its greatness and splendor."[64]

But for other sections of public opinion, the Carta raised more problems than it solved. Part of the dissatisfaction may have stemmed from what the nineteenth-century historian J. P. Oliveira Martins described as the Carta's incomplete quality: "It was a statement of principles, a catechism, a skeleton still missing musculature. It was a sketch, or perhaps a map, on which the names of the rivers and cities were still to be marked."[65] Many of the initial negative reactions, most of which would not be published until after Dom Miguel's 1828 coup, stemmed from doubts over Dom Pedro's right to impose a constitution. The first objection was that the Carta was too similar to the 1822 constitution, reviled by Royalists, which also had sought to "reform the nation according to abstract theories, without heeding the instructive lessons of experience."[66] The Carta was deemed "perfectly antipathetic to our customs, our opinions, our sensibility and our character." It reflected the "system followed by all of the architects of new political edifices since 1789, to accommodate the land to the constitution and not the constitution to the land."[67] It repeated the "errors" of *vintismo,* but "with honey on its lips."[68] The embrace of the Carta by those who had previously favored the constitution of 1822 was therefore suspect. "The only enthusiasts are these men of a chaos causing instinct, without character, morals or sense of custom, who, in theaters and cafes, speak of nothing except liberty."[69]

Its transparent similarity to the 1824 Brazilian Constitution was obvious, spoke to its hasty composition, and caused consternation. Calmer critics noted that Pedro's decision to draft the 1824 constitution for Brazil was perfectly reasonable, for "a new nation, a new monarchy, a new government requires a new act, convention, constitution, charter or fundamental law," but that such a document was inappropriate for Portugal, where it could only undergo "dangerous mutation."[70] Its New World origins were therefore suspect, but more worrisome to many was Dom Pedro's interference in Portugal's internal affairs. "By the treaty of 29 August 1825, Brazilians are to be considered foreigners before the king of Portugal," one particularly prolific pamphleteer argued, "but the king of Portugal is the emperor of Brazil: therefore it follows that Brazilians are foreigners before the emperor of Brazil."[71] The shaky logic notwithstanding, it conveys the widespread sense of impropriety and confusion generated by Dom Pedro's activities. It also was a not-so-covert way of suggesting the forfeiture of the crown to which he was entitled by primogeniture. With his brother on the throne, such arguments could be voiced with impunity. Pedro's rights had been clouded by his conduct. Not only had he chosen to become the sovereign of another country, but he had "declared war on Portugal, his [native] country, and dismembered one of its most considerable dominions."[72]

But the imputed foreign nature of the Carta derived not only from its Brazilian provenance, but also from its purported "British" origins. Long before the Carta's appearance, the Portuguese mania for English institutions had been derided. With his characteristic biting wit, José Agostinho Macedo remarked that he was "impressed" by Portuguese travelers who, "after taking a stroll around Falmouth, or visiting the dunes, suddenly consider themselves very wise, literate, gifted, instructed, and capable of governing the world."[73] This suspicion drew strength not only from hostility toward Britain for its effective military occupation of Portugal after 1814 and its decisive role in separating Brazil from Portugal through the commercial treaties of 1808 and 1810. As a Miguelista observed in 1828, English involvement in Portuguese affairs from 1807 was "the beginning of Portugal's humiliation, the beginning of an era in which more was lost than during the sixty years that Portugal suffered under Spanish rule."[74] Stuart's role as the courier of the Carta generated further hostility toward British meddling in Portuguese affairs. The Englishmen brought "in his bag, or perhaps in his pocket, a fateful, insidious and treacherous gift."[75] Moreover, the Carta was derided as the work of an "anglo-maniac sect" who had persuaded the Portuguese people that by importing English institutions, like trial by jury, "Portugal would be raised suddenly to a power of the first rank."[76] Guided by mere fashion, not substance, the Carta's champions had failed to transfer "what is called the public spirit of England" along with its institutions.[77] "Imitators" of the British constitution thus came in for extreme criticism from the opponents of the Carta. Such efforts could never "produce anything useful, if only its exterior is copied," and it was much more advisable to explore alternate "arrangements" that reconciled long-established forms of national representation with hereditary monarchy.[78]

The notion that Dom Pedro had first violated and then torn asunder the Lei Fundamental of Portugal became a dominant theme in criticism of the Carta after 1828. The Carta had further weakened the Brazilian emperor's dynastic claims for it "arbitrarily destroyed the fundamental law of the kingdom."[79] Macedo pilloried the imprudence and impudence of the measure. Moving beyond the tired question of Dom Pedro's right to issue the Carta, he suggested it had been unnecessary: "to issue a new constitution, it must be demonstrated that [reform] cannot occur without it. . . . [I]t must be shown, through an examination of history, that the monarchy's present constitution is inadequate."[80] The mere fact of Pedro's succession, even if juridically valid, did not justify constitutional innovation. "All of these so-called chambers, moderating powers and such," Macedo argued, are merely "the acts of rebellion of children against their parents, of vassals against their monarchs."[81] A year later, Macedo enumerated the attributes of sovereignty: "an independent, free, and absolute king, executor of laws without restriction, author without competition from any other authority."[82] The Carta therefore served neither the king nor the people, for it made "a *fantasma* of [royal] power, coercing the king, or extinguishing his power whereas the people, instead of seeing the end of tyranny (as revolutionaries promise), merely witness the number of tyrants multiplied."[83]

These public debates concerning the Carta's merits must be contrasted with the private responses, whether expressed in private journals or correspondence, of those at the highest echelons of power. Usually either staunch monarchists or champions of aristocratic privilege, they often sought to ameliorate Portugal's political situation without tarrying long in the unpredictable, dangerous arena of popular politics. Their uncommon access to information concerning Dom Pedro's motives colored their discourse with a different hue from that of the public debate. Several leading political figures saw the Carta as a savior, a document that ended rancorous partisan conflict. Soon after its arrival, Palmela wrote: "If well-intentioned men of different parties join together to support moderate liberty, legitimately acquired, instead of the abstract theories of democrats and the stagnation caused by absolute power, the *Carta* will usher in an era of alliance [between different parties] and will come to be seen as a gift from heaven."[84] Yet after the Carta was cast aside by Dom Miguel, this enthusiasm turned to despair. In particular, Dom Pedro's chimerical actions were perplexing, his motives far from transparent. Even Mouzinho da Silveira, later chief architect of Dom Pedro's policy, first during the regency on the Azorean island of Terceira and then in Portugal in the final phases of the Civil War of 1828–1834, was confounded. He failed to understand "what caused Pedro to issue the Carta or why he later seemed to abandon it and remain in Brazil." With characteristic acuity, Mouzinho da Silveira identified the Carta's flaws. Besides the absence of the prince who had issued it, the Carta was doomed because it arrived "without auxiliary laws, but instead found itself mixed together with millions of pre-existing statutes that conflicted or were inconsistent with it." "Liberty," Mouzinho da Silveira argued, "is an exotic plant, and when its growth is stunted, it cannot become acclimatized."[85]

The most important response to the Carta, of course, was that of Dom Miguel, still exiled in Vienna.[86] In October 1826, the regent, Dona Isabel Maria, informed Dom Pedro that their brother still had not sworn allegiance, noting that his failure to do so jeopardized his status as future regent. Leaving little doubt concerning her fears, she prophesied, "When Miguel enters the country, Portugal will be swimming in blood and all shall be lost. For the love of God, dear brother, do not delude yourself on this point."[87] Princess Isabel Maria's fears proved justified and Dom Pedro was compelled to plead his case directly to Dom Miguel. After imploring his brother to "sustain the *Carta* will all his strength," Pedro called it an "anchor, which can save the ship of state from the great political tempest that threatened [Portugal] with total ruin."

The Carta, Pedro continued, was merely a means to a greater end: "Constitutional liberty, correctly conceived, is a safeguard that should be defended by all men of religion and good sense. Extremes should be avoided, for in politics it is the middle course (*meio termo*) that should be followed."[88] Dom Miguel's project was already well advanced by the time this letter was received. The Viscount of Barbacena tried to convey to Dom Pedro some of the "indisposition" in England toward his constitution, advising him to disassociate the cause of his daughter from that of the Carta, to go as far as to claim for her "full and absolute power." He begged the emperor to consider whether this arrangement, eminently more agreeable to the courts of Europe, would make the "Portuguese nation less free, less happy than it formerly was, and could be, without such a scrap of paper (*tal folheta*)?"[89] Given Dom Pedro's master plan to entrust the throne to his daughter and harness Portugal's remaining resources to prop up his own throne in Brazil, it is unclear why he failed to act decisively.[90] It was attributable in part to his troubles in Brazil, particularly the ill-fated war with Argentina over the Banda Oriental, but it also was due to the strong, negative reaction by other European powers to his Carta.

The European Reaction to the Carta

Barbacena's description of European, especially British, discomfort with the Carta was largely accurate, but it must be placed in a wider context. Already in 1823, George Canning remarked that "the counter-revolution [in Portugal] is just what one could wish," disparaging "those revolutionists [as] the scum of the earth, and the Portuguese earth, fierce, rascally, thieving, ignorant ragamuffins, hating England and labouring with all their might to entrap us into war."[91] Nor would adherence to principles stand in the way of expanding British influence in Portugal. The Duke of Wellington thought that propping up Dom João's throne following the Vilafrancada was good politics: "Indeed, it must tend to give [Britain] all the weight it would desire to have in the settlement of the affairs of the peninsula, and of those between Portugal and the Brazils."[92] Disdain for revolution, combined with exasperation with the Portuguese Crown's inept conduct, then, informed British policy in the years preceding the issue of the Carta. But British policy was far from clearly defined, as officials waited for events to play out in Portugal. Here Dom João's failure to frame and issue a constitution before his death loomed large, for such a document would have clearly stipulated the order of succession and likely would have excluded Dom Pedro from it. Canning noted that

Britain was unable "to guarantee beforehand an unknown settlement which is to be established by any authority, the nature of which is not yet known."[93]

Yet British intervention in the settlement of affairs between Brazil and Portugal in 1825 and then the role of one of its senior diplomats in transporting the Carta from Rio de Janeiro to Lisbon did not permit such detachment. Though Canning insisted that Stuart had possessed "no authority to act in any matter of this kind," Canning conceded that he could not "justly disapprove of what [Stuart] had done."[94] For his part, Stuart was proud of his handiwork, boasting in a letter to Lord Lowther, "[My] operations have been attended with all the success I could wish. I do not know if you and your friends approve of the course that has been followed, but, depend on it, it will be the salvation of [Portugal], and that it places us on higher ground than ever."[95] These private exchanges did nothing to diminish the public perception that Stuart's role of courier between kings was evidence for British approval of both the grant of the Carta and Pedro's abdication of the Portuguese Crown. In a speech in the House of Commons, Canning daintily sought to dispel these ideas, denying that Britain was the "contriver and imposer of the Portuguese constitution." He affirmed, "It is not [Britain's] duty or her practice to offer suggestions for the internal regulation of foreign states." This disavowal notwithstanding, Canning noted that it was "impossible for an Englishman not to wish [the Carta] well," since it was "founded on principles in a great degree similar to those of our own, though differently modified."[96] Canning's speech aimed to rally support for the dispatch of four thousand British troops to Lisbon at the Portuguese government's request, purportedly to discourage Spain from further meddling in its neighbor's affairs. Canning justified sending troops to prevent Portugal from being "trampled down." British involvement was necessary, he claimed, "not to rule, not to dictate, not to prescribe constitutions, but to defend and preserve the independence of an ally," and to prevent full-blown "national degradation."[97]

Canning's florid speech merely masked the pervasive distaste for the Carta, and for England's guardianship of it, that percolated in official circles. Writing from Buenos Aires, Lord Ponsonby remarked, "Dom Pedro hates liberty as much as Sir Toby Belch did water," noting that the Carta's genesis lay in the emperor's collaboration with his "pimp [O Chalaça] and Benjamin Constant (I mean his book, not the great philosopher in his proper person). And so one morning after breakfast they sat down and by dinner, out came the constitution, now the palladium of Lusitania, the despair of Spain, the envy of the Turk, and care and Nursling of great statesmen, governments and kings."[98]

Reactions to the Carta beyond England's shores were equally unflattering. Prince Metternich lamented, "Nothing is more problematical than the application of the deplorable work of Dom Pedro. It would be difficult to know how Portugal is governed now, for each day presents singular anomalies."[99] In Spain, Dom Pedro's actions caused a "great and widespread disgust" while the Spanish emissary to Russia reported that Tsar Nicholas was alarmed by the "maniacal and unexpected" events transpiring in Portugal.[100] These sentiments made the establishment of the *Carta* almost impossible and serves to explain why Dom Miguel's coup would face scant protest, and no active resistance, from the European powers in 1828. Dom Pedro had promised order, but his *Carta* had not fulfilled that promise. As a leading Miguelista noted, the *Carta* was misused by the "enemies of order" to "overthrow legitimate government." The Carta, then, was prone to disorder, and other more extreme measures were necessary to prevent Portugal from descending into anarchy.[101]

The Carta during the Portuguese Civil War

Dom Pedro's involvement in the Portuguese Civil War emerged less from commitment to his daughter's cause or liberal ideas than from the fact that his disgraceful exit from Brazil in 1831, culminating in his hasty abdication, left him casting about aimlessly in Europe, bereft of throne and funds. Before these events catalyzed the search for a new vocation, his ambivalence toward the Portuguese liberal cause, which had made the restoration of the Carta and Dona Maria to the throne its rallying cry, had alienated and exasperated its advocates. Expelled from Portugal for their defense of the Carta and forced to eke out a precarious, exiled existence in England, France, and Belgium, the liberal refugees mounted a force capable of seizing the Azorean island of Terceira and there established a regency in Dona Maria's name. Dom Pedro's grudging moral support for the regency was not complemented by significant material assistance, a parsimony that infuriated the exiles. Nor did he recognize the regency as the sole legitimate government of Portugal, something which the exiles believed was an indispensable precondition for gaining broader support from the European powers and ensuring their continued non-recognition of Dom Miguel's regime. Palmela explained to Dom Pedro that, without funds, "our position is necessarily passive, and we cannot sustain without great privation more than 4,000 men. . . . [T]here cannot be an effective reaction in Portugal [against Dom Miguel] unless it has the support of an external force, and the indispensable condition for this [force] is money."[102] But these arguments seemed to produce little effect until the emperor's forced departure from Brazil in 1831.

Furthermore, Pedro's embrace of liberalism in Europe in the early 1830s was far-fetched given his authoritarian turn in the late 1820s. Events in Brazil had left him wary of liberal ideas and skeptical of the efficacy of constitutions. By the late 1820s, he was convinced that the 1824 constitution, the model for the 1826 Carta, required modification. In March 1829, Pedro sent a circular to his confidants, the most important features of which were two questions: First, "would it be possible under the present circumstances to amend the constitution?" Second, should he issue another, new constitution, one that would be 'truly monarchical' (*verdadeiramente monarchica*)?" All of his advisors recoiled at the political tumult augured by such a plan, whereas Frei Antônio de Rabida candidly expressed his "horror," advising the emperor to "burn every paper on which this suggestion is made." If such proclivities were widely known, he claimed, "our most frightful ruin" would be imminent.[103] From the extant correspondence, Dom Pedro's views of his Carta remain unclear, but his monarchical tendencies probably led to his diminished estimation of that document as well.

Yet the advent of the July Monarchy in France greatly augmented the prospects of the Carta and diminished those of Dom Miguel. Its supporters sought to take advantage of such "propitious conditions in Europe."[104] Recently dethroned, Dom Pedro adapted himself to this new environment and placed himself at the head of the regency, assuming the title of the Duke of Braganza and casting himself as the champion of constitutionalism. The flurry of legislation, authored by Mouzinho da Silveira but brandishing Dom Pedro's signature, further embellished his liberal credentials. With international support for Dom Miguel waning (only the Vatican and the United States had recognized him as king), and with England intent on preventing further Spanish interference in Portuguese affairs, the liberal cause eventually triumphed in 1834. The Carta was reinstated, and Dona Maria was placed on the throne. After the incessant political turbulence that characterized the late 1830s and early 1840s subsided, the Carta finally became ensconced as Portugal's constitution, with several modifications made in the 1850s, until the fall of the monarchy in 1910.

~

This essay has sought to reconstruct the Brazilian origins of the 1826 Portuguese Constitution as part of a broader effort to underscore the mutual influence that Brazil and Portugal exerted on each other after the former colony gained its independence. The transoceanic connections that characterized the Luso-Brazilian Empire (and the wider Atlantic world) did not cease abruptly, but rather persisted, and sometimes quickened, after the demise of formal dominion.[105] The second half of the 1820s (and first half of the 1830s) was a period in which the consequences of the incomplete, unfinished nature of independence asserted themselves and demanded resolution. Dom Pedro's behavior with regard to the Portuguese succession in 1826 indicates that the eventual reunification of Portugal and Brazil was not a far-fetched fantasy, and it is clear that European statesmen feared this prospect.

Nor did his abdication in 1831 dispel such speculation. The military victory of the Azorean regency over Dom Miguel's government, apparent from 1833, raised new hopes (and fears) in Brazil that Dom Pedro might seek to reclaim his New World crown, using a freshly vanquished Portugal as a base. Brazilian governmental correspondence is littered with anxiety of this sort: "The Duke of Braganza will attempt to invade Brazil to restore his throne. . . . [W]e must destroy the miserable horde of slaves who support the Duke, who seeks to destroy our liberties and re-impose the insupportable yoke of tyranny."[106] An active Sociedade Restauradora flourished in Brazil from 1832. It was not unusual for Portuguese residents in Brazil (and their native-born collaborators) to be accused of fomenting a restoration. In Recife and elsewhere, urban riots were purportedly accompanied by the ubiquitous cries of "Viva Dom Pedro, Rei de Portugal, e do Brasil,"[107] whereas several of the major rural revolts of the Brazilian regency period (1831–1840) routinely invoked Dom Pedro's name to legitimate their expressions of discontent. Fear of such a possibility led the Chamber of Deputies to pass a resolution in 1834 to exclude Dom Pedro from ever returning from Brazil, though this attempt was rebuffed by the Senate.[108] Dom Pedro's premature death in 1834 abruptly ended such speculation (and popular mobilization), but there exists a superabundance of evidence to support the claim for the persistence of significant political and intellectual connections between Portugal and Brazil in the decade following independence.

The history of the 1826 Portuguese Constitution suggests two more general conclusions about the decade of the 1820s. First, Latin American politics and political ideas continued to reverberate in Europe, creating unexpected havoc for politicians (and contemporary historians) accustomed to operating in a closed system composed solely of European states, with their established norms and predictable tendencies. Second, there is a clear need to dispense with models of ideological diffusion that overstate the unrequited movement from a European center to a non-European periphery and of Latin American borrowings of European intellectual fashions and institutions. Instead, a model of mutual and reciprocal influence seems to fit the evidence more accurately. Certainly, the impact of Europe's institutions, manufactured goods, fashions, and ideas in newly independent Latin America was enormous. The ubiquity of Europe's influence is prodding Latin Americanists to study European history more closely in order to understand how ideas were appropriated and adapted to American circumstances. But if the history of the 1826 Portuguese Carta is not an isolated and anomalous episode, European historians, too, would benefit from examining the ways that Latin America's history resonated in Europe after the demise of formal empire.

Notes

This chapter was originally published under the same title in *European History Quarterly* 41, no. 3 (2011): 444–71. I thank SAGE Publishing for permitting its publication in this volume as well as The University of Alabama Press for making an exception to its usual policy by republishing it here. I wish to reiterate my thanks to the following institutions for their support of my research: the British Academy; the Brazil Studies Program at Harvard University; the Center for History and Economics at Harvard University; the Lilly Library at Indiana University; the Portuguese Fulbright Commission; and Trinity College, University of Cambridge. An early draft of this chapter benefited immensely from the comments and criticism of my colleague and coeditor Matthew Brown as well as the suggestions offered by two anonymous *European History Quarterly* reviewers.

1. For a sampling, see Gargarella, "Towards a Typology of Latin American Constitutionalism," 141–53.

2. With notable exceptions, chief among these are Hale, *Mexican Liberalism in the Age of Mora*; Lewin, *Surprise Heirs,* vol. 2; Chust, *Doceañismos, Constituciones e Independencias*; and Breña, *El Primer Liberalismo Español y los Procesos de Emancipación de América.*

3. The chief exception is the 1787 US Constitution's pervasive influence in France. See Higgonet, *Sister Republics,* esp. 228–29.

4. Maurizio Isabella has recently shown how Latin American, particularly Mexican, debates about federalism influenced the political thought of Italian exiles. See Isabella, *Risorgimento in Exile.*

5. These modifications did not significantly modify the Crown's authority: not only did the royal person remain inviolable and sacred, but the king could dismiss

ministers without providing a justification, dissolve the assembly, and veto laws emanating from the legislative branch while retaining the leading role in public life. See Magalhães, *Tradicionalismo e Constitutionalismo,* 23. Perhaps the only real limitations on Crown authority as a result of the 1852 amendments were the ratification of all foreign treaties by the Cortes and the abolition of the death penalty for political crimes. See Miranda, *O Constitucionalismo Liberal Luso-Brasileiro,* 37.

6. On the relationship between these two documents, see Oliveira Torres, "As Origens da *Carta* Portuguesa," 21–28; and Melo Franco, "Introdução."

7. The best biography in any language remains Macaulay, *Dom Pedro.* On the "Restorationist" current in Brazilian politics in the early 1830s, see Barman, *Brazil.*

8. On the creation of a "Tropical Versailles" between 1808 and 1821, see Schultz, *Tropical Versailles.*

9. For an overview, see Kenneth Maxwell, "Why Was Brazil Different? The Contexts of Independence," in Maxwell, *Naked Tropics.*

10. Mascarenhas Barreto, *Memórias do Marquês de Fronteira e d'Alorna,* pt. 2, 194.

11. See Berbel, "A Retórica da Recolonização," 791–808.

12. *Reverbero Constitucional Fluminense* (Rio de Janeiro), no. 19, March 19, 1822, 230.

13. Dom Pedro to Dom João, letter, March 14, 1822, in *Cartas de D. Pedro I a D. João VI,* ed. Lima Junior, 58–59 (letters are hereafter cited as in *Cartas*).

14. Dom Pedro to Dom João, July 26 1822, in *Cartas,* 69.

15. Dom Pedro to Dom João, September 22, 1822, in *Cartas,* 74.

16. On the Assembléia Constituinte, see the classic study by J. H. Rodrigues, *A Assembléia Constituinte de 1823*; more recently, see C. Rodrigues, *Assembléia Constituinte de 1823.*

17. Dom Pedro (*Fala do Trono*) to the Assembléia Constituinte, May 3, 1823, in *Falas do Trono,* ed. Calmon, 37.

18. Vale, *The Audacious Admiral Cochrane,* 151–54.

19. Dom Pedro, "Manifesto de sua Majestade o Imperador aos Brasileiros," November 16, 1823, in *Falas do Trono,* ed. Calmon, 81–83.

20. Silva Lisboa, *Contestação da Historia e Censura de Mr De Pradt Sobre Successos do Brasil,* 7–8; on Silva Lisboa's political thought, see Gabriel Paquette, "José da Silva Lisboa and the Vicissitudes of Enlightened Reform in Brazil, 1798–1824," in *Enlightened Reform in Southern Europe,* ed. Paquette, 361–88.

21. Dom Pedro to Antonio Telles da Silva, February 2, 1824, Arquivo do Museu Imperial Petrópolis, RJ, Brazil (hereafter cited as AMI), II-POB.00.02.1824. PI.B.C.1-3.

22. On moderate constitutionalism in the Luso-Brazilian world, see Cruz Canaveira, *Liberais Moderados e Constitucionalismo Moderado.*

23. Royer-Collard, quoted in Starzinger, *The Politics of the Center,* 27.

24. Guizot, quoted in Neely, *Lafayette and the Liberal Ideal,* 185; on Guizot, see Craiutu, *Liberalism under Siege.*

25. As Robert Alexander points out, "the Restoration preserved much of the legacy of the Revolution of 1789, but it did so through the filter of reforms instituted under Bonaparte. Retention of the Napoleonic codes meant that legal equality would be maintained, and there would be no return to the *ancien régime* fiscal or office-holding privileges." Alexander, *Re-writing the French Revolutionary Tradition,* 2–3.

26. Palmela to Dom João VI, November 18, 1820, in *Despachos e Correspondencia do Duque de Palmela,* ed. Reis e Vasconcellos, 1:144–45.

27. Lord Cochrane to Dom Pedro, November 14, 1823, AMI, I-POB.14.11.1823. Coc.c; on Cochrane's memory of this consultation, see Cochrane, *The Life of Thomas, Lord Cochrane,* 1:250–51.

28. More conservative voices, such as Silva Lisboa's, would argue that "the imitation of foreign institutions, though they are themselves good, does not always produce beneficent results in all countries"; see the speech given by Silva Lisboa, October 21, 1823, in *Annaes do Parlamento Brazileiro,* 6:156–57; a similar sentiment was expressed subsequently by Pinheiro Ferreira in his *Observações sobre a Constituição do Imperio do Brasil,* 176.

29. Antônio Carlos Andrada, April 24, 1840, in the Câmara dos Deputados, quoted in Braga de Menezes, *As Constituições Outorgadas ao Império do Brasil,* 25. Such boasts received further credence through their repetition by historians who did not consult the archival documents relating to the framing of the 1824 and 1826 constitutions, including Leal, *História das Instituições Políticas do Brasil,* esp. 195–96.

30. Sampaio, "Projecto," reproduced in Braga de Menezes, *As Constituições Outorgadas ao Império do Brasil,* 63.

31. Ibid., 64–66, passim.

32. Gomes da Silva, "Bases," in Braga de Menezes, *As Constituições Outorgadas ao Império do Brasil,* 76–79, passim.

33. Constant, quoted in B. Fontana, *Benjamin Constant and the Post-Revolutionary Mind,* 64. On the reception of Constant in 1820s Brazil, see Lynch, "O Discurso Político Monarquiano e a Recepção do Conceito," 611–54.

34. A copy of the 1824 constitution is reprinted in Campanhole and Campanhole, *Tôdas as Constituições do Brasil.*

35. The Confederation of the Equator is treated in detail by Mosher, *Political Struggle, Ideology, and State Building.*

36. Dom Pedro to Felisberto Caldeira Brant, January 27, 1825, AMI, II-POB.27.01.1825.PI.B.c.1-11.

37. Hespanha, *Guiando a Mão Invisível,* 35.

38. Martins, Rangel, and Santiago, "Projecto Institucional do Tradicionalismo Reformista," 1:155.

39. Palmela, quoted in Rodrigues Dias, *José Ferreira Borges,* appendix, doc. 2, 302. The recollections of one of the moderate members of the junta give a sense of the uncompromising absolutism of the majority of its members. See Campos de Andrada, *Memórias de Francisco Manuel Trigoso de Aragão Morato,* 181–87.

40. Archbishop of Évora, quoted in Rodrigues Dias, *José Ferreira Borges,* appendix, doc. 7, 322–23. The Ultras' conception of the "ancient" Cortes is a complex subject and beyond the scope of this article. For a meticulous reconstruction of competing conceptions of the powers and attributes of the Cortes under the Old Regime, see Cardim, *Cortes e Cultura Política no Portugal do Antigo Regime.*

41. Maria Thereza to Dom João VI, letters of June 3 and 24, 1824, AMI, I-POB .03.06.1824.MT.P.c.1-3.

42. Dom João, untitled document, dated May 9, 1824, and published in the Impressão Regia, located in "Collection of Portuguese Broadsides and Other Documents Relating to *Miguelismo* (1799–1835)," Harvard University, Houghton Library, MS *90–300F; Dom João, quoted in Manique, *Portugal e as Potencias,* 107.

43. Anonymous, *Refutação Methodica das Chamadas Bazes da Constituição Politica,* 12–14, passim.

44. Anonymous, *Revolução Anti-Constitucional em 1823,* 9, 39.

45. Hespanha, in ibid., 19, 150. The junta's "Projecto de Lei Fundamental" is analyzed expertly in Mesquita, *O Pensamento Político Português no Século XIX,* 118–19. In the older historiography, there was some suggestion that this 1823 "Projecto" was the model for the Carta. It is true that they share some similar features, making such a claim plausible. I concur with Mesquita, who argues that there is no direct evidence for this older claim. Furthermore, as I strive to demonstrate in this chapter, the 1824 Brazilian Constitution is a more likely inspiration and model.

46. Dom Pedro to Dom João, July 15, 1824, Biblioteca da Ajuda, Lisbon (hereafter cited as BA), 54-X-7, nos. 161 and 175.

47. Palmela to Porto Santo (Oficio Reservado #26), January 10, 1825, Arquivo Nacional da Torre do Tombo, Lisbon (hereafter cited as ANTT), Arquivo Particular de António de Saldanha da Gama, Cx. 1, Maço 2.

48. Dom Pedro's status as heir to the Portuguese throne prompted ranking Portuguese officials to fret about the 1824 constitution, fearing that Pedro would remodel Portuguese institutions so that they conformed to those of Brazil. Some went so far as to argue for the abolition of the Brazilian constitution as a condition for Pedro's accession to the Portuguese throne. See Bonnabeau, "The Pursuit of Legitimacy," 42–47, passim.

49. Stuart to George Canning, October 20, 1825, the National Archives, Kew, England (hereafter cited as TNA), FO 13/5, fos. 22v.–23.

50. Dom Pedro, quoted in AMI, I-POB.25.04.1826.PI.B.do/MFN 10841.

51. All of the documents related to this topic are found in an unbound, unfolioed folder in AMI, I-POB.25.04.1826.PI.B.do/MFN 10841, from which the material in the next paragraphs is taken.

52. This last proposal was a non starter. In a 1826 letter to Palmela, Canning declared that he had "no hesitation in saying that any attempt by the Brazilian government to make itself master of the remaining colonial possessions of Portugal would entitle his Most Faithful Majesty to call upon his ally the King of Britain for prompt and effectual interposition." Canning to Palmela, February 3, 1826, in *Some Official Correspondence of George Canning,* ed. Stapleton, 1:11. On Portuguese policy toward its remaining African colonies after 1825, see Gabriel Paquette, "After Brazil: Portuguese Debates on Empire, c. 1820–1850," *Journal of Colonialism and Colonial History* 11, no. 2 (2010): online only.

53. This process is well known. Besides the documents cited below, also reproduced in *O Constitucionalismo de D Pedro I no Brasil e em Portugal* (Rio de Janeiro: Arquivo Nacional, 1972), it is described at length in Gomes da Silva's *Memorias Oferecidas a Nação Brasileira,* 88–91.

54. Dom Pedro, quoted in AMI, II-POB.29.04.1826.PI.B.do.1-6.

55. Miranda, *O Constitucionalismo Liberal Luso-Brasileiro,* 33; Hespanha, in Anonymous, *Revolução Anti-Constitucional em 1823,* 259.

56. Even prior to Dom João's death, Dom Pedro had struck upon this arrangement, but he later discarded it. As Stuart explained to Canning, "the possible contingency of further male issue, and the desire to retain the moveable part of his inheritance (jewels, gold etc), have, for the present, banished the idea from [Dom Pedro's] mind." Stuart to Canning, March 11, 1826, TNA, FO 13/18, fos. 123v.–24.

57. There is some discrepancy in the records about how and when it was intended to be presented to the Portuguese public. Certain documents indicate that it was supposed to be endorsed or ratified by the traditional Cortes (*Tres Estados do Reino*) before its presentation to the public. It is clear that Dom Pedro published it in Rio de Janeiro soon after Charles Stuart's departure, and it also is known that news of the grant of the Carta reached Paris before Stuart's ship arrived in Lisbon.

58. Francisco d'Almeida to the Marquis of Palmela, January 27, 1827, ANTT, MNE, cx. 153.

59. Hespanha, in Anonymous, *Revolução Anti-Constitucional em 1823,* 365.

60. As the British ambassador to Portugal noted, "the Liberals would certainly rather submit to D. Pedro's continued rule than run even the slightest chance of the alternative put forward by the Ultras, of Don Miguel as absolute king." See William

Á Court to Canning, October 28, 1826, in Webster, *Britain and the Independence of Latin America,* 2:275.

61. The clearest and most influential case against Dom Pedro in the period after 1831 is made in Silva Passos and Silva Passos, *Parecer de Dous Advogados da Caza do Porto,* 6–7.

62. Anonymous, *Considerações do Velho Liberal,* 3.

63. Anonymous, *A Funda de David Defonte do Clarim Portugues,* no. 3, n.p.

64. Anonymous, *Resumo Histórico do Parlamento de Inglaterra.*

65. Oliveira Martins, *Portugal Contemporaneo,* 1:74.

66. *O Amigo do Bem Publico, ou o Realista Constitucional* [Lisbon], no. 1, September 14, 1826, 1.

67. Lobo, "Rezumida Noticia da Vida de D. Nuno Caetano Alvares Pereira de Mello," 2:386. For a recent overview of the political ideas animating *Miguelismo,* see Barreiros Malheiro da Silva, *Miguelismo: Ideologia e Mito.*

68. Macedo, *A Besta Esfolada,* no. 2, September 21, 1828, 13.

69. *O Realista: Amigo da Observacia da Lei* [Lisbon], no. 1, September 26, 1826, n.p.

70. Lemos Seixas e Castel-Branco, *Memoria Justificativa come que Pertende Provar-se,* 31. Though the Brazilian origins of the Carta have been revealed by archival research, its similarity to some of the *projectos* circulating in Lisbon in 1823 and 1824 led some opponents to believe that it was a purely Lusitanian product. As late as 1831, one anonymous pamphleteer noted, "We can affirm that the charter Sir Charles Stuart brought from the Brazils was manufactured in Lisbon." See Anonymous, *A Few Words in Answer to Certain Individuals respecting the Present State of Portugal.*

71. Madre de Deos, *Absurdos Civis, Politicos e Diplomaticos,* 9.

72. Anonymous, *Golpe de vista, em que compendio,* 5–6.

73. Macedo, *O Espectador Portuguez,* vol. 2, no. 3, 12.

74. "A Conspiração contra o Principe D. Miguel" (1828), BA, 54-VI-52, Doc. 38, fos. 49–52, passim.

75. Lobo, "Rezumida Noticia da Vida de D. Nuno Caetano Alvares Pereira de Mello," 2:387. Though he exerted significant influence on Dom Pedro in the weeks leading up the Carta's composition, it appears that Stuart did not play a role in drafting it, though he did assist Dom Pedro in deciding which members of the Portuguese nobility would obtain a seat in the Pares.

76. Anonymous, *Exposição Genuina da Constituição Portugueza de 1826,* 29–32. On this pamphlet, see Hespanha, in Anonymous, *Revolução Anti-Constitucional em 1823,* 155, fn. 368.

77. Lobo, "Rezumida Noticia da Vida de D. Nuno Caetano Alvares Pereira de Mello," 2:386–87.

78. Anonymous, *Sobre a Constituição da Inglaterra e as Principaes Mudanças que tem soffrido*, 69.

79. Anonymous, *Golpe de vista, em que compendio*, 5–6.

80. Macedo, *A Besta Esfolada*, no. 4, December 3, 1828, 10.

81. Ibid., no. 22, August 2, 1829, 14.

82. Macedo, *O Desengano. Periodico Politico, e Moral*, September 6, 1830, 11.

83. Ibid., September 26, 1830, 7.

84. Palmela (August 11, 1826), quoted in Vianna, *Apontamentos para a Historia Diplomática Contemporânea*, 3:38–39.

85. Halpern Pereira, et al., eds., *Mouzinho da Silveira, Obras*, 3:639.

86. The best recent study of Dom Miguel and his reign is Lousada and Ferreira, *D. Miguel*.

87. Princess (and Regent) Isabel Maria to Dom Pedro, October 14, 1826, AMI, II-POB.14.10.1826.IM.P.c. the regent's fears were shared by many others, including Sir Charles Stuart, who told Henry Wellesley that "everything which has come to my knowledge since my arrival here shows the wisdom of the determination taken by the emperor of Brazil. . . . I urge you to use your influence with the Cabinet of Vienna in order to prevent by very practical means the departure of D. Miguel." Stuart to Wellesley, July 1826, Lilly Library, University of Indiana–Bloomington, Stuart MSS.

88. Dom Pedro, in AMI, II-POB.1828.P1.B.doc.1-152 (Pasta 1). It should be noted here that Dom Pedro sternly requested that Dom Miguel travel to Rio de Janeiro to hash things out, an offer (or command) that was refused.

89. Barbacena to Dom Pedro, May 6, 1829, AMI, II-POB.1829.Hor.do.1-27.

90. Dom Pedro had stated this hope explicitly to Sir Charles Stuart as he was drafting the Carta: "[Dom Pedro] then talked of conciliating the affections of the Portuguese by giving them a constitutional charter and, if the war should turn out unsuccessfully in [the Banda Oriental], of obtaining military succor from Portugal with a view to diminish the burthen which is already severely felt in [Brazil]." Stuart to Canning, April 30, 1826, TNA, FO 13/18, fos. 245–49, passim.

91. Canning to Bagot, July 14, 1823, in *George Canning and His Friends*, ed. Bagot, 2:183. For a broad overview of Portugal's place in Europe in the first half of the nineteenth century, see Manique, *Portugal e as Potências Europeias*.

92. Wellington to Canning, August 3, 1823, in Wellington, *Despatches, Correspondence, and Memoranda of Field Marshall Arthur Duke of Wellington*, 2:113–14.

93. Canning to Palmela, February 3, 1826, in *Some Official Correspondence*, ed. Stapleton, 10. But this was a departure from Canning's earlier view, expressed to William Á Court in a letter dated November 23, 1825: "Don Pedro remains undoubted heir to the crown of Portugal, according to the fundamental laws of that kingdom" (in Webster, *Britain and the Independence of Latin America*, 2:272).

94. Canning to Granville, July 2, 1826, in *Some Official Correspondence,* ed. Stapleton, 117.

95. Stuart, quoted in Franklin, *Lord Stuart de Rothesay,* 188.

96. Canning, *Corrected Report of Speeches delivered by the Right Hon. George Canning,* 28–29.

97. Ibid., 61, 39.

98. Lord Ponsonby to Bagot, October 17, 1826, in *George Canning and His Friends,* ed. Bagot, 310.

99. Metternich to Count Bombelles, September 7, 1826, in *Memoirs of Prince Metternich,* ed. Richard Metternich, 4:330.

100. Duke of Villahermosa to Duque of Infantado, June 23, 1826. Second quotation is drawn from a report written by Don Juan Paez de la Cadena, Spanish emissary to Moscow, September 26, 1826. Both are quoted in Aquino Brancato, "A *Carta* Constitucional Portuguesa de 1826 na Europa," 470–71.

101. Viscount of Santarém to Palmela, March 22, 1828, and April 5, 1828, ANTT, MNE, cx. 154.

102. Palmela to Dom Pedro, March 20, 1830, ANTT, MR (Regência em Angra do Heroísmo), Livro 451.

103. These quotations are taken from the unfoliated documents found in a folder, AMI, I-POB.17.03.1829.PI.B.c.

104. Luis Antonio de Abreu e Lima to Luis da Silva Mouzinho de Albuquerque, January 20, 1831, ANTT, MNE, Livro 469.

105. On the persistence of other types of connections, see Luiz Cervo and Magalhães, *Depois das Caravelas*; on inter-connected histories in the nineteenth century, see Rothschild, "Late Atlantic History."

106. Arquivo Público Estadual Jordão Emerenciano [Recife], PP8, José Marciano de Albuquerque e Cavalcanti to Manuel Seferino do Santos, August 8, 1833.

107. "Oficios do Presidente," April 25, 1832, Instituto Arqueológico, Histórico e Geográfico Pernambucano, Recife, Brazil, Cx. 215, Maço 4.

108. Reinert, "A Political History of the Brazilian Regency," 139; more generally, see Barman, *Brazil.*

6

An American System

The North American Union and Latin America in the 1820s

Jay Sexton

The people of the North American union had reason to identify with the links Latin Americans cultivated with the Old World in the 1820s. Like their "southern brethren," as James Monroe called them in his famous 1823 message, the inhabitants of the United States found that political independence did not mean isolation, a point that has attracted much attention in recent historiography.[1] The English-speaking republic remained within the orbit of the Old World, particularly its former colonial master, Britain. Its economy relied on access to European markets and British capital; its security hinged upon great power rivalry; and its culture drew liberally from the traditions of the Old World. If many in the United States feared that they remained trapped in a neocolonial system, experiments such as the ill-fated Jeffersonian embargo (1807–1809) taught them that transatlantic engagement was preferable to isolation. For all their harangues about British economic imperialism, most in the United States recognized that foreign investment and transatlantic trade provided the key to establishing their economic independence. The intellectuals of the new republic similarly drew inspiration from the culture and ideas of the Old World, which they hoped to refashion into a distinctively American identity.

Yet nineteenth-century US statesmen were uncomfortable with the political and economic relationships the newly independent states of Latin America cultivated with the Old World.[2] This sentiment found expression in James Monroe's 1823 message and its subsequent corollaries, which sought to restrict European involvement in Latin America and establish the United States as the hemispheric hegemon. Having exploited connections with the Old World for decades, US statesmen sought to deny Latin Americans from doing the same. This chapter will examine the roots, rationale, and consequences of US policy toward Latin America in the formative decade of the 1820s.

I

As Latin Americans achieved their independence in the 1810s and 1820s, the United States was itself still in the process of consolidating its independence and internal unity. This point is often lost in the historiography, which tends to assume US power and project back the dynamics of its late nineteenth-century imperialism. There were important continuities, of course, in US policy toward Latin America across time, and one can find throughout the nineteenth century evidence of virulent racism and the expansionist nature of the capitalist economy of the new republic. Yet the North American union of the 1820s was not the United States of 1898. In the earlier period, the United States remained vulnerable to the great powers of the Old World, particularly Great Britain. To be sure, the young republic had weathered the storm of the Napoleonic Wars, even finding ways to profit from Europe's distress through shrewd diplomatic maneuvers such as the Louisiana Purchase. Notwithstanding such fortuitous acts and the young republic's advantageous geographical position, the United States remained vulnerable, struggling to free itself from an expanding British Empire. It is worth remembering that, with the possible exception of slavery, the central political issue in the United States in the 1820s concerned how best to free the nation from the chains of British economic neocolonialism.

The North American union of the early nineteenth century was a complex and paradoxical political beast, notable both for its internal fragility and for its remarkable capacity to adapt to the challenges it faced. Its political structure sought to balance the interests of its divergent states, sections, and political persuasions. It drew power from an emerging nationalism, which was rooted in republican and expansionist ideologies, networks of trade and communication, and the states' experience of collectively fighting the British during the Revolutionary War. Yet for all of its actual and potential power, the idea of the "American nation" co-existed alongside other identities and political structures—those of states, sections, religious groups, political persuasions, and so on. These layered identities and structures were at times symbiotic and mutually reinforcing. But they also came into conflict, at times even threatening the union itself.

Chief among these threats was the precarious balance between states and sections. As the contentious debates of the 1787 Constitutional Convention demonstrated, the states were deeply divided. Small and large states argued over the form of political representation; Atlantic seaboard states worried about their status in a westwardly expanding union; and, most ominously, southern slaveholding states and those abolishing the institution in the North looked upon each other with great suspicion. The extent to which certain states and individuals were committed to the national project was an open question. Leaders in independent Vermont toyed with re-entering the British Empire, and renegade frontiersmen schemed to detach various parts of the trans-Appalachian West. After all, "Americans" most often thought of themselves in this period as "Virginians" or "New Englanders" or "Westerners," revealing the draw of state and sectional identities.

That the North American states remained united until 1861 owed much to the interlocking relationship between union and independence.[3] Even before the Revolutionary War, American leaders feared that independence would result in a cluster of unstable and weak states or federations that would invite further European meddling. In this scenario the American states would have traded formal colonialism for an even less desirable position as pawns of the European powers, pitted against one another in conflicts waged to maintain the balance of power in the Old World. "Weakness and divisions at home would invite dangers from abroad," John Jay asserted in *Federalist 5,* "nothing would tend more to secure us from them than union, strength, and good government within ourselves."[4] The US Constitution of 1787 aimed to consolidate the achievements of the Revolutionary War by creating a union powerful enough to maintain its independence. It sought to walk the tightrope of conferring new powers to the federal government, while at the same time satisfying individual states by retaining elements of home rule. David Hendrickson recently has argued that the Philadelphia convention should be viewed in relation to the era's international congresses, such as that in Vienna in 1815. Indeed, the political language of the early republic—which spoke of states, congresses, and treaties—applied the vocabulary of international relations to the internal politics of the union. When Henry Clay helped broker one of the many internal compromise agreements of this period in 1833, he labeled it "a treaty of peace and amity."[5]

The logic of union and independence appealed to Americans of all regions and political stripes. It helped fuel a powerful nationalism that found expression in tributes to the union, Fourth of July celebrations, and commitment to the ongoing struggle to consolidate independence from the British. The War of 1812—the so-called second war of American independence—fortified these new and stronger ties between the states. Andrew Jackson's victory at New Orleans inspired a new spirit of popular nationalism that saw the divisive first party system wither away, replaced by a brief era of political consensus and economic nationalism. Yet, even during this heyday of nationalism in the years following 1815, US statesmen continued to fear disunion. The decentralized character of the federal union, a precondition of its formation and continuation, paradoxically stood in the way of greater national integration: states regulated banks; the military power of the young republic largely lay within state militias; and, though the central state exerted more power than is traditionally assumed, moves to expand federal authority triggered stiff political opposition. As Latin Americans fought for their independence in the 1810s and 1820s, the North American union remained in danger of dissolving. New England Federalists threatened to undermine the union at the Hartford Convention of 1814. More ominous was the great debate, from 1819 to 1821, concerning the admission of Missouri as a slave state, the "title page to a great tragic volume," as John Quincy Adams called it. Though moderate nationalists carried the day in both episodes, they served as reminders of the precariousness of the union. Even a nationalist like Henry Clay feared "that within five years from this time [1820], the Union would be divided into three distinct confederacies."[6]

The internal dynamics of the union shaped its early foreign policy. The statecraft of the early republic sought two interrelated objectives: the fulfillment of international ambitions and the preservation and consolidation of the union at home. These two goals often went hand in hand. Territorial expansion or the negotiation of liberal commercial agreements, for instance, could bind together divergent interests. But they could have the opposite effect, pitting sections or political persuasions against one another, perhaps even leading to disunion. US statesmen thus had to balance international ambitions with domestic politics—a tightrope act that some did better than others. The greatest danger to the union lay in the possibility that internal sections or factions would ally with European powers, thus fusing internal and external threats.

A central means of mitigating the union's internal vulnerabilities was to limit political commitments with the powers of the Old World, while seeking to expand American commercial interests. One of the cornerstones of nineteenth-century American foreign policy, Washington's Farewell Address (1796), argued that a foreign policy of non-entanglement and commercial expansion should be pursued in order to mitigate the threats to the union from within. Washington's address dealt primarily not with foreign threats, but with the dangers to the union posed by separatist movements and the entrenchment of ideologically opposed political parties, particularly his political opponents who, he feared, had been seduced by the French Revolution. Washington's "great rule" of having "as little political connection as possible" with the Old World was a means of preempting these internal threats to the union, not an end in itself.[7]

II

The response of the United States to the "Western question" should be viewed in relation to the internal dynamics of the union.[8] This is not to dismiss the proto-imperialism of the Monroe Doctrine, nor the importance of capitalist expansion, nor the salience of racism and anti-Catholicism, nor the persistence of anticolonialism and republicanism. Far from discounting these important themes, the "union paradigm" provides a framework through which to understand their significance.[9]

The great paradox of the United States' response to the dissolution of Spain's American empire is that it embodied both the insecurity and the confidence of the young republic. Proponents of extending diplomatic recognition to the new Latin American republics, such as Henry Clay, were not lacking in ideological certitude. To Clay and his allies, the struggles in Latin America portended the universal application of the US ideals of 1776. Clay's early speeches advocating recognition are notable for their absence of racism and their admiration of Latin American leaders. As much as Clay emphasized the ideological stakes in Spanish America, his argument for an active policy also rested on how recognition would advance the economic interests of the union, particularly those of the agricultural-exporting and capital-starved trans-Appalachian West, which would profit from the opening of potentially lucrative markets in Spanish America.[10]

Clay premised his argument for recognition on the ideological and economic ambitions of the United States. Yet in the end it was heightened perceptions of threat that compelled the Monroe administration in 1822 to recognize the Spanish American governments of Buenos Aires, Chile, Colombia,

Mexico, and Peru.[11] The move was prompted, in part, by the ratification in 1821 of the Transcontinental Treaty with Spain, which ceded Florida to the United States and gave the republic a claim to the Pacific Coast. With this long-sought agreement in hand, Monroe and Adams could move more boldly on the issue of Spanish American independence. Yet recognition also stemmed from the identification of a new threat: the prospect that the new Spanish American states would not embrace the political and economic principles favored by the United States. Despite the analogies with the North American Revolutionary War made by Clay and his supporters, the reality on the ground was more complex. Monarchy remained an attractive political form, especially in Brazil and also in Mexico, where monarchists emerged temporarily victorious with the crowning of Emperor Agustín I in 1822. Many Spanish Americans looked toward the Old World, rather than the United States, for political inspiration and economic sustenance.

It was this very political gulf that prompted the Monroe administration to reverse its previous policy and to extend recognition. Though several Spanish American states had consolidated their independence by 1822, the Monroe administration feared that they remained unstable and vulnerable to European intervention. Monroe predicted that Spanish Americans would feel "resentment towards us" if recognition continued to be withheld, making them all the more susceptible to "the artful practices of the European powers, to become the dupes of their policy." The prospect of a monarchical Spanish America allied with European powers led the Monroe administration to fear for its own security. If surrounded by hostile states, the United States would be under siege: its preexisting internal divisions would be exacerbated and its decentralized political system might require alteration, such as increased taxation and military build-up, in order to confront these new threats. "There was danger in standing still or moving forward," Monroe asserted. By 1822 Monroe and Adams embraced moving forward, despite the risk that it would trigger European reprisals. That the Monroe administration made this move—and did so unilaterally without the British support it previously had sought for recognition back in 1818 and 1819—represented the emergence of a bolder approach to foreign policy. As James Lewis recently has argued, the move to recognition prefigured the more celebrated Monroe Doctrine of the following year.[12]

Indeed, there is little question that Monroe's 1823 message long has enjoyed an inflated reputation (incidentally, it was not known as the Monroe Doctrine until expansionists in the 1840s and 1850s reinvented it as such to justify their aggressive acts in Oregon, Mexico, and Central America). An examination of the background to the message, which pronounced the Western Hemisphere no longer open to European colonization and political intervention, reveals reluctance on the part of the Monroe administration to issue a unilateral pronouncement. To be sure, John Quincy Adams argued forcefully against accepting George Canning's offer of a joint Anglo-American declaration warning the Holy Allies not to intervene in Spain's former colonies, on the grounds that Britain had not yet recognized the Spanish American republics and that the proposal included a provision that would preclude US annexation of Cuba and Texas. Yet other members of the cabinet, as well as former presidents Jefferson and Madison, urged acceptance of Canning's offer out of a heightened perception of threat and a desire to detach Britain from the Holy Allies. Such thinking reflected an awareness of the indispensability of the Royal Navy to US objectives, as well as a nascent warming of relations between the historic adversaries. Even after the Monroe cabinet drafted the famous message of December 2, 1823, it kept the door open to cooperation with the suddenly reticent British. Though later observers could look back at Monroe's message and see a turning point in US foreign policy, the statesmen at the time did not intend it as the "diplomatic declaration of independence" that it is often portrayed as. Acutely aware of the limits of its power, the Monroe administration moved cautiously, careful to keep Britain and its powerful navy on board.[13]

If Monroe's message of 1823 fell short of a diplomatic declaration of independence, it did articulate the expansive security requirements of the United States. The message was written not out of concern for the new states in Latin America, but because the Monroe administration deemed European intervention in the Western Hemisphere as dangerous to its peace and safety. That the Monroe administration's conception of national security encompassed potential European actions thousands of miles from the borders of the United States might come as a surprise, especially considering the almost complete absence of US interests in places such as Buenos Aires (which, incidentally, is further from Washington than is Moscow). One can be forgiven for asking why statesmen in Washington regarded the installation of a Bourbon prince in Buenos Aires or the monopolization by Russia of the maritime rights off the Alaska coast as a threat to their national security.

The answer to this question in part resides in the ideological lens through which the Monroe administration viewed potential threats. The reactionary doctrines promulgated by the Holy Allies reinforced the view in the United

States that their republic was engaged in an ideological struggle with the monarchies of the Old World. "The political system of the allied powers is essentially different . . . from that of America," the 1823 message asserted.[14] The protagonists in this struggle viewed each others' political system as inherently expansionist, not unlike the Cold War thinking of the twentieth century, thus necessitating strategies of containment. The Holy Allies' Troppau Circular made it clear that the continental monarchies would oppose the forces of republicanism and constitutionalism in Europe, just as Monroe's 1823 message declared that European colonization and political intervention in the New World constituted a threat to the United States.

When the members of the Monroe cabinet considered a single European intervention in the New World, they ended up envisioning multiple interventions. It was taken as a given that a move by one power—France installing a puppet monarch in Buenos Aires, for example—would set in motion a series of land grabs throughout the Western Hemisphere. John Quincy Adams recorded in his diary the administration's doomsday scenario: France first would seize Buenos Aires and Mexico; Russia would counter by gobbling up California and the Pacific coast of South America; Britain would have no choice but "to take at least the island of Cuba for her share."[15] Surrounded by hostile states with antagonistic political and economic systems, the United States would have no choice but to alter its own domestic practices. Increased taxation, a standing army, the centralization of political power—all of these and more would be required to counter such a threat. But these actions would in themselves endanger the union by running counter to established political practices, perhaps even leading disillusioned groups into the arms of Old World powers. In this way, the presence of monarchies in Spanish America, particularly in neighboring Mexico, would inflame domestic conflict and threaten the union itself. "Violent parties would arise in this country," John C. Calhoun prophesized in a cabinet meeting, "one for and one against them, and we should have to fight upon our own shores for our own institutions."[16]

The Monroe administration's perception of threat in 1823 thus linked foreign dangers to internal politics. The differing views within the cabinet on the likelihood of a successful Holy Alliance intervention, however, led to different conceptions of what constituted the greatest threat. Calhoun's fear that the Holy Allies could succeed in establishing puppet monarchies in Spanish America led him to argue that the United States should prevent them from acquiring a foothold in the New World at all costs. Calhoun was prepared to ally with the hated British, as well as to give a pledge not to annex the two territories he viewed as central to national security, Texas and Cuba. The future advocate of states' rights from South Carolina went even further, contemplating increased powers for the federal government to deter the Holy Allies from intervening in Spanish America. "Our country ought to omit no measures necessary to guard our liberty and independence against the possible attacks of the Armed Alliance," Calhoun argued. "They are on one side, and we the other of political systems wholly irreconcilable. The two cannot exist together. One, or the other must gain the ascendency."[17]

Adams, in contrast, contended that the greatest threat to the union was precipitate action to forestall a phantom threat. Adams did not think the Holy Allies were on the verge of intervening in Latin America. Even if they were, the secretary of state thought the venture certain to fail. The greater threat in Adams's estimation was that Calhoun's saber rattling—which found expression in the first draft of what became Monroe's 1823 message—might provoke the Holy Allies into the very actions they were unlikely to take. Above all, Adams sought to avoid war with the Holy Allies. Such a conflict would place "different portions of the Union in conflict with each other, and thereby endangering the Union itself." The United States thus "should retreat to the wall before taking up arms."[18]

Though Calhoun and Adams conceived of the threat differently, they both endorsed the final draft of the 1823 message, which was a compromise that addressed both of their concerns.[19] Monroe's 1823 message kept the door open to joint action in future with the British, without bowing to the conditions of Canning's offer. It informed the Holy Allies that the United States would consider any intervention in Spanish America as a threat to its own security, but sugarcoated this warning by pledging not to interfere in European affairs, as well as to respect functional colonial arrangements established before December 2, 1823. Finally, it articulated the expansive conception of national security that, despite their differences, both Calhoun and Adams held. Premised upon the need to insulate the union from foreign threats, the national security of the United States required more than just the safety of its borders—it required an entire hemispheric system conducive to its political system and economic practices.

III

Historians once viewed Monroe's 1823 message as inaugurating a new diplomacy for the New World. It allegedly proclaimed that the old rules of European colonial rivalry no longer applied to the Western Hemisphere, which would now be governed by non-intervention, republicanism, and economic liberalism. Yet this interpretation sat uncomfortably with the imperial ambitions of the expansionist United States. If the message stopped short of explicitly calling for territorial expansion, there is no question that the Monroe administration wanted to keep open the possibility of annexing Cuba and Texas. In his diary Adams, ever the anticolonialist, predicted that the annexation of Texas and Cuba would be acts of self-determination.[20] The process of Texas annexation in 1840s, as well as the attempted purchase of Cuba, justified on the grounds of preemptive preservation of slavery there in the 1850s, proved otherwise (a point Adams himself would recognize when he opposed the acquisition of both Texas and Cuba).

The novelty of Monroe's message is also called into question by the striking extent to which it followed the lead of the British. During the cabinet deliberations, Adams famously declared, "It would be more candid, as well as more dignified to avow our principles explicitly . . . than to come in as a cockboat in the wake of the British man-of-war."[21] Yet this is precisely what happened, even if the Monroe cabinet rebuffed Canning's offer of joint action. The two non-intervention paragraphs in the 1823 message closely resembled Canning's Polignac Memorandum, a record of a secret meeting between the foreign secretary and the French ambassador that similarly warned the Holy Allies to stay out of Spanish America. Indeed, upon receiving Monroe's message in early 1824, the London *Times* applauded it on the grounds that it articulated "a policy so directly British." In terms of immediate diplomatic impact, it hardly needs to be mentioned that it was the Polignac Memorandum of October 1823, not Monroe's message of that December, which thwarted whatever interventionist designs the French might have had.[22]

The message of 1823 also drew upon the forms and style of Old World statecraft. Many in the United States at the time (and not a few historians since) viewed the message as inaugurating a new style of open diplomacy.[23] But the form of Monroe's message was not as innovative as it appeared. Just as Washington's Farewell Address drew from the Old World tradition of the "political testament,"[24] the 1823 message should be viewed in the context of the circulars, memoranda, and protocols issued in the same period by the European powers. Monroe's message was similar in form to the Troppau Circular of 1820 and the Russian Ukaz of 1821 (which proclaimed exclusive rights for Russia along the northwest Pacific coast of North America). The monarchies of continental Europe, of course, did not appeal to the wider public—indeed, a roused populace was exactly what they sought to avoid. The 1823 message therefore differed from the Troppau Circular in being aimed not only at other governments, but also at ordinary people, both in and out of the United States. Canning, however, did not share these reservations about appealing to popular sentiment. Indeed, the British foreign secretary packaged his statecraft for domestic and overseas consumption in an even more sophisticated manner than did the statesmen from the more democratic United States. Canning appealed to popular sentiment through public addresses, as well as the previously unused tactic of publishing diplomatic correspondence (including, famously, one of his dispatches composed in rhyming verse!). A sympathetic biographer has even suggested that Canning be credited with establishing "open diplomacy," something US historians typically reserve for Woodrow Wilson.[25]

It is true that the Polignac Memorandum does not best exemplify this characteristic of Canning's statecraft. But Canning quickly recognized the public relations value of Monroe's 1823 message. He scoffed at the Americans, as his biographer put it, for blowing "a blast on the republican trumpet, while sheltered behind the shield of England." Though Adams had outfoxed him in the run-up to the message, Canning quickly fired back when he released the hitherto confidential Polignac Memorandum in March 1824. Canning deleted all references to the United States in this version of the memorandum, which was one of the first state papers to be reproduced through the new technology of the lithograph. British agents in Spanish America circulated this version of the Polignac Memorandum to demonstrate their government's decisive role in thwarting the designs of the Holy Alliance. "Its date is most important," the foreign secretary wrote of the Polignac Memorandum, "in reference to the American speech which it so long preceded." Canning would continue to trumpet Britain's role in supporting the independence of Spanish America. Though it was the United States that had first recognized the independence of the new governments from Spain, Canning declared in 1826 that he himself had "called into existence the New World."[26] Statesmen in Washington played a similar game. Both Monroe and Adams saw, in a unilateral message to Congress, the key advantage: it would enhance the United States' reputation in Spanish America, where they hoped to counter Britain's influence. Adams's insistence that the separate spheres be included in the message, as well as his references to the fact that Britain had not yet recognized Spanish American independence, similarly sought to group Britain with the reactionary powers of Europe in order to invoke suspicion of the British in Latin America.

In their respective attempts to secure credit for protecting Spanish America from the Holy Alliance, one sees the playing out of what is called today "public diplomacy." Far from providing closure to the diplomatic crisis of 1823, Monroe's message and the Polignac Memorandum kicked off what would be a protracted Anglo-American struggle for preeminence in Latin America. The non-colonization clause, the only paragraph that Adams later would consider the "Monroe Doctrine," is important in this regard. British statesmen did not endorse this statement—unlike the two paragraphs dealing with non-intervention—which they rightly interpreted as intending to limit their future reach in the Western Hemisphere. In a letter written in the 1830s, Adams made clear that the non-colonization clause not only aimed at countering Russian activities in the Northwest, but also was "a warning to Great Britain herself." As was so often the case in the nineteenth century, Anglo-American relations in 1823 paradoxically entailed both collaboration and competition.[27]

These points should make historians think twice before interpreting US policy in purely ideological terms. The two English-speaking powers, of course, had different ideological objectives: the United States was firmly republican; Britain, mildly monarchical. These hopes, however, did not prevent the United States from recognizing monarchical Brazil, nor Britain from recognizing the republics in Spanish America. Nor did the differing ideological aims of the two nations preclude them from the aggressive pursuit of their economic and strategic interests. When Mexico and Colombia threatened to liberate Cuba from Spanish rule, anticolonialism and republicanism took a back seat to the United States' interest in avoiding a potential race war on the island and British annexation. The Adams administration went so far as to launch a diplomatic offensive in Europe aimed at preserving Spanish control of the island. The scheme did not unfold smoothly, but the United States achieved its desired objective of perpetuating Spanish rule of this strategically important island.

The two English-speaking powers pursued their interests with similar vigor in Mexico, where US minister Joel Poinsett and British representative Henry Ward locked horns in a battle to advance the economic interests of their respective governments. The competition between Poinsett and Ward quickly took on a life of its own, with each diplomat drawing support from rival Masonic lodges in Mexico City. There certainly was an ideological dimension to this rivalry—Poinsett allied himself with Mexican liberals and Ward sought the support of conservatives and the Catholic Church. Yet cultivation of relations with collaborating elites in Mexico was a means to the end of securing commercial agreements and, in the case of the United States, territorial adjustments, rather than an end in itself. For all the talk in Washington of a new diplomacy, the Anglo-American struggle in Mexico was an old-fashioned battle for political influence and commercial gain.[28]

IV

The political genius of Monroe's 1823 message was that it did not call for any action. All Monroe did was declare what European powers could not do in the New World. The message dodged all of the important questions—Canning's offer of alliance, future relations with the new states of Spanish America, and, of course, the matter of if and how the United States would uphold the prohibitions it placed on European actions ("the only really important question to be determined," in Adams's mind).[29] When approached by representatives of Colombia and Brazil to enter into defensive treaties of alliance, Adams informed them that Monroe's message did not pledge the United States to defend the new states in Latin America against European intervention. The message did not even explicitly endorse future territorial expansion, though this clearly remained popular in the Monroe cabinet. Eschewing all commitments and costs yet trumpeting the ideals of the United States, it is not surprising that Monroe's message met with overwhelming popularity at home.

But the consensus of 1823 proved ephemeral. Only two years later Latin American policy would be the subject of one of the most vitriolic congressional debates on foreign affairs in American history. The source of this discord was the proposal of now president John Quincy Adams to participate in the Panama Congress organized by Simón Bolívar. A former opponent of Henry Clay's hemispheric "American system," Adams, with Clay as his secretary of state, now argued that the United States needed to take a leading role in hemispheric affairs.

Similar to the move toward recognition in 1822, this change of heart was motivated by fears that new states of Latin America were falling under the control of an Old World power. This time the chief threat was the British, whose trade and investment in Spain's former colonies dwarfed that of the United States. In a telling symbol of Britain's economic dominance, the new US ministers and consuls in Latin America relied on drafts supplied by the

London bank of Baring Brothers. US representatives in Latin America reported to Washington that the new states were fast becoming "de facto colonies" of Britain. From Buenos Aires, John Murray Forbes reported that while the people of Buenos Aires spontaneously celebrated England's St. George's Day, US representatives had to choreograph Fourth of July celebrations.[30] Indeed, if there was a state outside of Spanish America that was central to Bolívar's plans for the Panama Congress, it was Britain, not the United States. "England is the envy of all Countries in the world, and the pattern all would wish to follow in forming a Constitution and Government," Bolívar asserted. A combination of strategic calculations, economic interests, and political sympathies led Bolívar to seek a formal alliance with Britain. As late as 1826, he called for a "union of the new states with the British Empire."[31]

The Adams administration was fortunate to even receive an invitation to participate in the Congress of Panama (Bolívar initially saw no need to include the United States in his plans and changed his mind only after lobbying from Colombian and Mexican officials). Despite barely being invited, the administration was not bashful about using the conference to advance its interests. The conference offered the president the opportunity to advance all of the goals he had long sought: enhancing the security of the union, limiting the reach of the British and Europeans in the New World, and promoting the economic interests of the United States. In two important messages to the US Congress (December 1825 and March 1826), Adams outlined his objectives at Panama: reinforcement of Monroe's 1823 message through a "joint declaration" signed by the participating governments, the establishment of liberal commercial agreements enshrining the most favored nation principle, codification of neutral shipping rights, and the "advancement of religious liberty" in Spanish America.[32]

Adams's two messages delineating his objectives at Panama should be considered his pro-active complement to the negatively framed message of 1823. Whereas Monroe had declared in 1823 what the European powers could not do, Adams now presented a vision of what the United States would do. This pro-active hemispheric vision was intimately intertwined with the administration's domestic agenda of internal development and the liberation of the republic from its economic dependence upon Britain. Adams first advocated participation in Panama in his landmark 1825 annual message to congress, which outlined an ambitious set of measures such as federal assistance for internal improvements and the creation of a national university. Indeed, the phrase "American system" denoted not only a hemispheric diplomacy, but also a set of domestic policies aimed at strengthening the bonds of union through measures designed to counter Britain's economic hegemony. The foreign and domestic components of the American system were two halves of the same whole. The erection of protective tariffs, for example, sought to end Britain's dominance in manufacturing. The subsequent increase in American manufacturing would necessitate the negotiation of trade agreements with Spanish America to provide markets for these new goods.[33]

The "American system" of Adams and Clay fused the paradoxical forces of the early statecraft of the United States: traditional anticolonialism and nascent imperialism. Both of these forces sought to strengthen the union of states at home. Though the American system was not devised as a plan to dominate Latin America, its logic led in that direction. Just as independence from Britain had entailed control over Native Americans in 1812, liberation from Britain's economic control in the 1820s necessitated the establishment of economic supremacy in the Americas. "It is in our power to create a system of which we shall be the centre," Clay asserted, "and in which all South America will act with us."[34] Even as Clay denounced British economic imperialism, he used Britain's informal empire as a model for his vision of economic and political relations with the new American states.[35] While "American system" boosters emphasized their ideological solidarity with the new states of Spanish America, many of them racially and culturally identified with their former colonial master.

The Adams administration's plans to participate in the Panama Congress provoked vituperative domestic opposition in Congress. Ostensibly at issue were the approval of the diplomats Adams nominated to attend the conference (in the Senate) and the appropriation of the required funds (in the House). But lurking behind these procedural matters were fundamental questions about the form and future direction of the North American union.[36]

Most ominous was the sectionalism unleashed by the administration's proposed participation in the Panama Congress. Given tensions from the recent Missouri crisis, it should come as little surprise that a group of pro-slavery southerners regarded the Panama Congress as a threat to their peculiar institution. Southern extremists such as Robert Hayne (South Carolina) and John Randolph (Virginia) feared that the American system had an anti-slavery tilt: John Sergeant of Pennsylvania, one of Adams's nominees to represent the United States at the Panama Congress, had been an outspoken advocate of restricting slavery in Missouri; possible items on the agenda in Panama in-cluded cooperation with Britain to prohibit the international slave trade and relations with the black republic of Haiti; and, though slavery remained en-trenched in Cuba and Brazil, southerners took note of its weakness elsewhere in Latin America, where it was in the process of gradually being phased out. As the debates progressed, southerners such as Hayne stepped back from the specifics of the Panama Congress to proclaim that new rules must be followed if the union was to remain intact. "With nothing connected with slavery can we consent to treat with other nations," Hayne asserted, before warning that any federal intervention within the South would prompt disunion.[37]

The proslavery opposition to the Panama Congress was one of many such political controversies in this period that foreshadowed the dissolution of the union. Yet the significance of the Panama debates lay not just in that they prefigured secession and civil war, but also, paradoxically, in how they dem-onstrated the potential for the shrewd exploitation of partisan conflict and ra-cialized nationalism to hold the union together. The Panama debates played an important early role in the reconfiguration of US politics from the in-terregnum of the so-called era of good feelings to the second-party system of Whigs and Democrats. The establishment of two cross-sectional parties would be instrumental in preserving the union in the coming decades (in-deed, it is no coincidence that secession and civil war came only after the col-lapse of the second-party system).[38]

Ambitious party builders such as Martin Van Buren and James Buchanan seized the opportunity to unite the disparate critics of the Adams adminis-tration. They exploited recent memories of the "corrupt bargain" between Henry Clay and John Quincy Adams that had allegedly denied Andrew Jack-son the presidency in the contested election of 1824. They capitalized on the popularity of Monroe's 1823 message and Washington's Farewell Address by contending that the administration's foreign policy violated the maxims of unilateralism and political non-entanglement. They claimed that the Adams administration sought entrance into a new super-federal system at Panama, a political structure that would infringe upon the sovereignty of the North American union. And they used the Panama issue as a means of discredit-ing the larger American system, which many, particularly proponents of free trade from the South and West, equated with corruption and mercantilism. The "American System," Hayne declared, was a term "which, when applied to our domestic policy, mean[s] restriction and Monopoly, and when applied to our foreign policy, mean[s] 'entangling alliances.'"[39]

Most significant was how the opponents of the Panama Congress articulated a racialized notion of the North American nation. Racist views of Latin Americans, of course, were not new. But they became increasingly pronounced as the 1820s progressed. When compared to the congressional debates a decade earlier on the recognition of Spanish American independence, the racist nature of the Panama debates immediately jumps out. The evidence for this is not hard to find. Speaker after speaker on the floor of Congress pointed to the racial (and religious, it should be pointed out) inferiorities of Latin Americans. "I do not believe that there ever can be any cordial fraternity between us and them," Virginian William Rives stated, before warning that Mexico was more likely to be an enemy than an ally of the United States. Even friends of the administration, though generally less virulent in their racism, portrayed Spanish Americans as "pupils in the school," struggling to adapt to the responsibilities of self-government.[40] A recent study of US statesmen's perception of Mexicans in this period similarly found a marked rise in racism.[41]

As historians long have argued, racist conceptions of Latin Americans became an important element of US imperialism.[42] It also played a key role in the emerging nationalism that held the union together in the subsequent Jacksonian era. The British threat long had united the disparate elements of the North American union and, in differing ways, would continue to do so in the intra-party politics of both the Whigs and Democrats. Now party builders in the nascent Jacksonian coalition exploited racist conceptions of Latin Americans as a means of bringing together their constituencies in the North and South. Opponents of the Panama Congress particularly emphasized the racial inferiority of black Haitians and the undesirability of diplomatic engagement with that state, a message that united slaveholders and non-slaveholders alike. Racialized nationalism diminished sectional identities and united white Americans from across the union.

After months of repetitive debate, both houses of Congress approved participation in the hemispheric conference. It was a pyrrhic victory for the Adams administration and its American system. Neither of the administration's representatives arrived in Panama in time to take part in the deliberations, which accomplished little. In the longer term, the opponents of the Panama Congress emerged even more victorious. Though they failed to block congressional support for participating in the conference, they fatally undermined the idea of hemispheric cooperation within the United States until the late nineteenth century. The coalition that opposed the Panama Congress—comprised of many disparate elements, but most notably southern slavers, midwestern expansionists, and northeastern radicals—soon coalesced into the Democratic Party. Following Adams's unsuccessful single term in the White House, three of the next five presidents came from the ranks of those who vociferously had opposed the Panama Congress: Andrew Jackson, Martin Van Buren, and James K. Polk.

Like Adams and Clay, these Jacksonian Democrats sought to establish the United States as the leading power of the hemisphere. But if the goal was the same, the means were very different. In stark contrast to Adams and Clay, the Democrats proposed disengagement from the new states of Latin America and the unilateral and aggressive pursuit of more narrowly defined interests, particularly, the consolidation of control over the North American continent. The racialized nationalism on display during the Panama debates helped fuel two projects central to Jacksonian America: Indian removal (in the 1830s) and the war of conquest against Mexico (1846–48). Latin America might have been most important to Jackson as a dumping ground for spoils-system diplomatic appointments. Selected as a reward for their political support, many of Jackson's representatives to the region spoke no Spanish and achieved little apart from alienating Latin American governments. Nor did the Jackson administration adhere to a strict definition of the 1823 message when the British seized the Malvinas/Falkland Islands in the early 1830s. Despite its legendary Anglophobia, the Jackson administration calculated that British ownership of the islands was preferable to them being in the hands of Buenos Aires, which had blocked American fishing and sealing rights off of the islands the previous year.[43]

Much divided the statesmen of the United States when it came to Latin American policy in the 1820s. Yet, for all their differences, Americans from across the political spectrum came to agree that the interests of their union necessitated the establishment of a dominant position within the Western Hemisphere. Two central conceptions emerged regarding the form this position of preponderance should take. Proponents of the American system, such as Henry Clay and John Quincy Adams, argued that hemispheric engagement at the Panama Congress would bind together the North American union and complete its liberation from British neocolonialism. The idea that internationalism best advanced national interests would have much traction throughout the nineteenth century, shaping the policies of a diverse group of statesmen, including William H. Seward and James G. Blaine. Opponents of Clay and Adams proposed an alternative policy: disengagement from Latin America and the vigorous pursuit of narrowly defined interests, particularly continental expansion. This thinking, too, would have much traction in the future, influencing statesmen such as Jackson, Polk, Stephen Douglas, and, later in the century, Grover Cleveland. The seeds of divergent forms of US imperialism, in short, were sown in the 1820s.

Notes

1. Two recent works provide a good starting point for the US history in global context: Thomas Bender, *A Nation among Nations: America's Place in World History* (New York: Hill and Wang, 2006); and Ian Tyrrell, *Transnational Nation: United States History in Global Perspective since 1789* (London: Palgrave Macmillan, 2007).

2. This chapter uses the term "Latin America" to refer to the newly independent countries and peoples of the Spanish and Portuguese American empires. As Aims McGuinness has demonstrated, US imperialism in part lies behind the formation of this term, which was a creation of the 1850s. The projection of US power in the hemisphere led Latin Americans to see themselves as separate from and unified against Anglo-Americans. McGuinness, *Path of Empire.*

3. For recent explorations of these themes, see Onuf, "A Declaration of Independence for Diplomatic Historians," 71–83; Hendrickson, *Peace Pact*; Hendrickson, *Union, Nation, or Empire*; Ratcliffe, "The State of the Union," 3–38; J. Lewis, *The American Union and the Problem of Neighborhood*; Earl Weeks, *John Quincy Adams and American Global Empire*; Hammond, *Slavery, Freedom, and Expansion in the Early American West.*

4. John Jay, quoted in Goldman, *The Federalist Papers,* 26.

5. Henry Clay, quoted in Hendrickson, *Peace Pact*; Hendrickson, *Union, Nation, or Empire,* 130.

6. John Quincy Adams, quoted in Hendrickson, *Union, Nation, or Empire,* 118–23.

7. Washington's Farewell Address (1796) can be found at the following web address: http://avalon.law.yale.edu/18th_century/washing.asp (accessed March 31, 2012).

8. Blaufarb, "The Western Question," 712–41.

9. For the "union paradigm," see Hendrickson, *Peace Pact,* ix–xiv.

10. Weeks, *John Quincy Adams and American Global Empire,* 91–94.

11. J. Lewis *The American Union and the Problem of Neighborhood,* 157–78.

12. Monroe, quoted in J. Lewis, *The American Union and the Problem of Neighborhood,* 157–78; Monroe to Madison, May 10, 1822, in Murray Hamilton, *Writings of James Monroe,* 6:284–91.

13. McGee, "The Monroe Doctrine—A Stopgap Measure," 233–50; B. Perkins, *Castlereagh and Adams,* 305–47; D. Perkins, *The Monroe Doctrine, 1823–1826.*

14. James Monroe, "Seventh Annual Message," December 2, 1823, available online at http://www.gutenberg.org/dirs/1/0/9/1/10919/10919.txt (accessed March 31, 2012).

15. J. Q. Adams, "Diary," November 26, 1823, 6:204–10.

16. John C. Calhoun, quoted in ibid.

17. Calhoun, quoted in May, *The Making of the Monroe Doctrine,* 48.

18. J. Q. Adams, "Diary," November 22 and December 2, 1823, 6:196–98, 223–25.

19. For this consensus, see ibid., November 26, 1823, 204–10.

20. J. Q. Adams, "Diary," November 7, 1823, 6:177–81.

21. Ibid.

22. *Times,* January 6, 1824; B. Perkins, *Castlereagh and Adams.*

23. See, for example, D. Perkins, *The Monroe Doctrine, 1823–1826,* 260.

24. Gilbert, *To the Farewell Address.*

25. Harold Temperley, *The Foreign Policy of Canning,* 297–316, 307.

26. Temperley, *The Foreign Policy of Canning,* 127–29; Hinde, *George Canning,* 355; Webster, *Britain and the Independence of Latin America,* 50; Canning, quoted in Boyd Hilton, *A Mad, Bad, and Dangerous People? England, 1783–1846* (Oxford: Oxford University Press, 2006), 292.

27. Crapol, "John Quincy Adams and the Monroe Doctrine," 413–18; Brauer, "1821–1860," 72–82.

28. Rippy, *Rivalry of the United States and Great Britain,* 247–302; Moseley, "The United States and Mexico," 122–96; Gover, "Plunging at Spectres?"

29. J. Q. Adams, "Diary," November 26, 1823, 6:204–10.

30. Allen to Clay, April 4, 1826, in *Diplomatic Correspondence,* ed. Manning, 2:1112; Forbes to Adams, April 30, 1823, in *Diplomatic Correspondence,* ed. Manning, 1:620–21; Humphreys, *Tradition and Revolt in Latin America,* 130–53; Goodwin, "Initiating United States Relations with Argentina," 102–21.

31. J. Lynch, *Simón Bolívar,* 212–17; Shepherd, "Bolivar and the United States," 270–98; Rippy, *Rivalry of the United States and Great Britain,* 152; Bolívar, "Views of General Simón Bolívar on the Congress of Panama," 154–55.

32. J. Q. Adams, "Messages to the Senate of the United States," December 26, 1825; and J. Q. Adams, "To the House of Representatives of the United States," March 15, 1826 (the "advancement of religious liberty" only appeared as a US objective in Adams's message to the Senate). Both of these addresses from Adams are available at http://www.gutenberg.org/dirs/1/0/9/1/10919/10919.txt (accessed March 31, 2012).

33. R. Campbell, "The Spanish American Aspect of Henry Clay's American Sys-

tem," 3–17; Brauer, "The United States and British Imperial Expansion," 19–37; Walker Howe, *What Hath God Wrought,* 251–60, 271.

34. Quoted in R. Campbell, "The Spanish American Aspect of Henry Clay's American System," 8.

35. Brauer, "The United States and British Imperial Expansion."

36. The most recent examination of the Panama debates is Malanson, "The Congressional Debate over U.S. Participation in the Congress of Panama," 813–38.

37. *Register of Debates,* 19th US Cong., 1st sess., 165–66; N. Cleven, "The First Panama Mission and the Congress of the United States," 225–54; Matthewson, *A Proslavery Foreign Policy.*

38. Cayton, "The Debate over the Panama Congress," 219–38.

39. *Register of Debates,* 19th US Cong., 1st sess., II, part 1, 166–67, 2276–77; J. Q. Adams, "Diary," 7:75, 111, 117; Niven, *Martin Van Buren,* 168.

40. *Register of Debates,* 19th US Cong., 1st sess., 2086; Gleijeses, "The Limits of Sympathy," 481–505.

41. Navarro, "Our Southern Brethren."

42. Horsman, *Race and Manifest Destiny*; Schoultz, *Beneath the United States.*

43. Belohlavek, *"Let the Eagle Soar!,"* 10, 191, 192–96, 254–56; Maisch, "The Falkland/Malvinas Islands Clash of 1831–32," 185–209.

7
The Chilean-Irishman Bernardo O'Higgins and the Independence of Peru

Scarlett O'Phelan Godoy

Now that the Fatherland no longer needs my weak efforts . . . and now that [I am] separated from the difficult and thorny post of Supreme Director, I can dedicate myself to my private activities, I hope that the government will be dignified enough to allow me to spend some time in Ireland, in the bosom of my paternal family.

—Bernardo O'Higgins, February 12, 1823

Bernardo O'Higgins Riquelme was born in 1778 in Chillán, Chile. He died in Lima in 1842. His active public life spanned the crucial transformative decades of the age of revolution, and he was one of the examples cited by Eric Hobsbawm in his seminal work on the subject.[1] His life was a transatlantic one: like his sometime mentor Francisco de Miranda, O'Higgins became conscious of his "American identity" while resident in Europe. From 1797 O'Higgins was schooled in London and came into contact with Miranda's circle of liberal, often Masonic, brothers who would be so vital in the subsequent wars for the independence of Spain's American colonies. In Karen Racine's argument, O'Higgins became Miranda's "surrogate son," his "disciple" in the quest to bring liberation to the revolutionary Atlantic and the colonies of Spain in the Americas.[2]

Hobsbawm's and Racine's work is representative of the way that O'Higgins's name frequently crops up in studies of the age of revolution and in works that examine the Atlantic connections of the process of independence in Spanish America. Yet until now, studies of Bernardo O'Higgins's life and work have tended to be restricted to the national, Chilean paradigm, without giving full interpretative value to the Atlantic contexts of his movements, his thoughts, and his dreams. This chapter seeks to remedy this omission and in doing so to contribute to the question under study in this volume: To what extent did the imperial networks that underpinned the Atlantic in the early nineteenth century evolve or change in the decade of the 1820s? Does O'Higgins's life reflect the continuities with the colonial period or demonstrate the radical novelty of the leaders who came to the forefront of the new successor states? Both interpretations are considered below, based on a detailed reading of O'Higgins's life and travels, with particular reference to his relationship with the vice-regal capital of Peru, Lima.

Bernardo O'Higgins Riquelme was an active participant in his country's early war of independence until the disaster of Rancagua, in 1814, which closed the period known as the Patria Vieja.[3] After this event, O'Higgins—like other patriotic families—was forced to seek refuge in Argentina, where he forged a solid friendship with Don José de San Martín, whom he had met earlier in Spain,[4] encouraging him to cross the Andes in 1817, a decision that was later crowned with the victory of Chacabuco, February 18 of that year, followed by the entry into Santiago. It was under these circumstances that the Patria Nueva was inaugurated and the Open City Council (Cabildo Abierto) proclaimed San Martín as the supreme director of Chile. He immediately resigned from the post in favor of his friend and companion-in-arms O'Higgins.[5] The independence of Chile was later sealed with the battle of Maipú, on April 5, 1818, led by San Martín in O'Higgins's absence away from the capital.[6]

During the first years of O'Higgins's term as supreme director of Chile, a series of state crimes were perpetrated—between 1818 and 1821—that removed from the political arena the rival caudillos and potential conspirators, such as the Carrera brothers (Juan José, Luis y José Miguel) and Manuel Rodríguez, whose assassinations were ordered by the Tucumanian Bernardo Monteagudo, San Martín's right-hand man.[7] An alternative interpretation suggests that the Lautaro Masonic Lodge was behind the assassinations.[8] These murders may help to explain why Chile did not endure a period of caudillos after independence, as did the majority of its neighbors, precisely because the potential caudillos had been systematically eliminated at the dawn of the Chilean Republic. Regardless of the actual causes, on January 28, 1823, O'Higgins presented his resignation in order to avoid an imminent civil war that was threatened by the followers of the leaders who had disappeared. O'Higgins left for Peru, a country that he knew, where he had studied and forged friendships, and that was indebted to him for his deployment of the liberating army in Peruvian territory, composed of Argentines and Chileans and commanded by General San Martín.

The Irish in the Viceroyalty of Peru

If we want to place Bernardo O'Higgins Riquelme in his appropriate imperial and international context, we have to start with the fact that he was the illegitimate son of the Irishman Don Ambrosio O'Higgins (Ambrose Bernard O'Higgins, 1720–1801), who had been educated and worked in Cádiz, Spain, before he went to Chile in 1764 as the assistant of another Irishman, John Garland, who at the time was the acting military governor of Valdivia.[9] Throughout his successful administrative career, Don Ambrosio performed the roles of intendant-governor of Concepción, Chile (1786–1788), governor of Chile (1788–1796) and finally, Viceroy of Peru (1796–1801). In 1795 he would be recognized with the title of Baron of Ballenary, that his predecessors in Ireland had enjoyed, and the following year the title of Marquis of Osorno was created for him.[10] In that his father was Irish and his mother—Isabel Riquelme y Meza—was Chilean, Bernardo O'Higgins can therefore be described as a "Chilean-Irishman." Moreover, the weight that his Irish side was going to receive in his education would be notable. In many respects, therefore, Bernardo O'Higgins's rise to political power in Chile was reflective of a continuity with the colonial period, where Irishmen—and in particular the O'Higgins family—continued to enjoy significant influence within the Hispanic world, regardless of the political changes that were ongoing in the period.

The point of interest of this case is that an Irishman born in Sligo and raised in Meath, like Don Ambrosio, would assume the post of viceroy of Peru. A similar case—though not identical—could have been that of the last viceroy of Mexico, Don Juan O'Donoju O'Rian (O'Donahue O'Ryan), who, even though he descended on both sides from Irish parents, was born in Seville.[11] This can be explained by the opening that the House of Bourbon demonstrated in the second half of the eighteenth century with regard to the Irish and their descendants in important administrative and military posts. The Irish were not only well-known Catholics, they were also renowned as experienced merchants and, more than anything, were appreciated for their military competence and prestige. For example, Ferdinand VI and Charles III included Irishmen among their military advisors. This is how the Irishman Ricardo Wall, of Limerick, occupied the enviable position of minister of state for war in Spain (1754–1763), being known as "the powerful man of the Monarchy."[12] Being skeptical about being able to return to Ireland, the Irishmen adopted Spain as their fatherland and lent their services unconditionally. Wall declared in 1758, "I have no other country than this one [Spain] yet despite more than forty years of service, the people are not fully convinced that I love this country as much as its natives do."[13] Nevertheless, during his time as minister, Wall never forgot his origins and, indeed, surrounded himself with various Irishmen. Among them were Alejandro O'Reilly, Guillermo Bowles, Bernardine Ward, and Ambrosio O'Higgins.[14]

Following this tendency of gifts and favors, it should not be surprising that Don Ambrosio would take advantage of his post as viceroy of Peru to get his nephew, the Irishman Demetrio O'Higgins, named intendant of Huamanga in 1799, a position that he assumed in 1802.[15] In 1795 Don Ambrosio had pulled strings for another of his nephews, Don Tomas O'Higgins, having him named captain of the Dragoon Regiment and later designated as the governor of Huarochiri.[16] But these kinds of concessions were not limited to the family. Viceroy O'Higgins would also place his compatriots in high-level administrative positions, as happened with the Irishman Juan Mackenna O'Reilly, whom he named superintendent of Osorno on August 11, 1797.[17] What is more, after Mackenna O'Reilly assumed the position, various Irish and English artisans were sent to him in the expectation that, with their introduction into small industry and mechanical occupations, they would contribute to the development of the population.[18]

The ties of mutual support that were woven among the Irish in Spain, especially in the port of Cádiz, were transferred with them to Spanish America.[19] When Don Ambrosio began to look for trusted people to be in charge of educating his son and when Don Bernardo was searching for high-quality property auditors and managers, they searched within the circle of their Irish countrymen. Don Ambrosio chose his close friend, the Irishman Tomas Dolphin, to pick Bernardo up from his mother's home and to send him to Lima to study in the prestigious Convictorio de San Carlos.[20] In Lima, Don Ambrosio chose another compatriot to be in charge of his son's education, the Irish merchant Don Juan Ignacio Blake, whom Jaime Eyzaguirre describes in his book *O'Higgins* as "a wealthy man."[21] According to the Tribunal del Consulado of Lima in 1775, he was "a single Irish person who has a public store of merchandise in the coves of the cathedral."[22] That is to say, Blake was a small retailing merchant or, in other words, a *cajonero*, which was how shopkeepers were denominated at this time. By the early 1790s, when Don Bernardo arrived in Lima, it is most likely that Blake had increased his fortune.[23]

On the other hand, in 1811, in the middle of the war for independence, when Don Bernardo was in need of consultation and advice, he thought to bring back two of his closest acquaintances, his cousin Tomas O'Higgins and Don Juan Mackenna, who had been placed by his father as governor of Osorno, in 1797. Finally, O'Higgins would later decide in favor of the latter, considering his cousin Tomas to be too committed to the Spanish Crown.[24] Later on, when he retired in 1823, Don Bernardo O'Higgins was accompanied to Peru by John Thomas Nowland, a native of Ireland, who would become his closest confidant and with whom he had established a close friendship before leaving Chile. Nowland was put in charge of reorganizing the deteriorated haciendas of Montalván and Cuiba, both located in the Cañete Valley, which had been awarded to O'Higgins by San Martín in recognition of his commitment to Peruvian independence. These properties, which had belonged to the Spanish official Don Manuel Arredondo y Pelegres, Marquis of San Juan Nepomuceno, were confiscated from their owner during the merciless anti-peninsular campaign unleashed in Lima by Bernardo Monteagudo.[25] The Montalván hacienda alone was estimated to be worth around 600,000 pesos, with its buildings, equipment, land, and slaves.[26] These properties, having been occupied for extended periods by the royalist army, were found—after the war of independence—in a lamentable state and, under Nowland's supervision, it was necessary to repair the irrigation system, collect the dispersed livestock, and replant the vineyards and sugarcane plantations that had been the economic axis of production.[27] Nowland was also in charge of surveying Don Bernardo's activities and looking after his field journal, which is why he was referred to as "his faithful chronicler."[28]

The O'Higgins family demonstrated their propensity for establishing endogamous relationships with their fellow countrymen that transcended the circle of relatives and entered as well into the professional sphere. It should not surprise us that the Irish formed businesses together, that they supported each others' dealings in their bureaucratic and military careers, and that they designated each other as tutors, executors, and front men.[29] Many Irishmen in Spanish America formed emotional relationships with local women, perhaps partially because they understood that having American women as their partners facilitated their possibilities of inserting themselves conveniently into colonial society and that their children could then establish themselves in a more permanent and advantageous way in Spanish America. This pattern of Irish assimilation and influence appears—from the case of Bernardo O'Higgins at least—to have continued through the 1820s and into the republican period.

The Convictorio de San Carlos

Bernardo O'Higgins's education provides a useful case study to see the divergence from the colonial past that became apparent at the very beginning of the nineteenth century. At first his education followed a very traditional colonial pattern: he would study from the age of twelve at the Convictorio de San Carlos in Lima. Although the Colegio Carolino functioned in Santiago de Chile—it had replaced the ancient Convictorio de San Francisco Javier, governed by the Jesuits—it was decided that Bernardo O'Higgins (Bernardo Riquelme back then) would move to Lima for a course of study in the Convictorio de San Carlos. He was following a tradition well rooted in the Chilean elite.[30] This emblematic center of studies had been founded on July 7, 1770, during the government of Viceroy Amat y Juniet, replacing the San Felipe and San Martín colleges after the expulsion of the Jesuit order from Peru.[31] The vice-regal government's long-lasting control over the Convictorio was from the beginning very tight.

When O'Higgins was studying at San Carlos, Toribio Rodríguez de Mendoza (1785–1817) was the rector. In the thirty years that he held this position he aimed to convert the Convictorio into the principal educational center in the Viceroyalty of Peru. Rodríguez de Mendoza is considered one of the most brilliant representatives of the enlightened clergy in the end of the eighteenth century: "He was a decided defender of Bourbon royalism and had certain characteristics in common with the Jansenists, like his anti-Jesuitism, his rejection of popular baroque religiosity and of scholastics."[32] Rodríguez de Mendoza was able to count, among his team, professors of a high academic level, like José Baquiano y Carrillo (author of "Elogio a Jáuregui"), and of unquestionable intellectual capacity, such as José Faustino Sánchez Carrión, who notably influenced the pupils with his reformist ideas. Even if Rodríguez de Mendoza left his position in 1817, the new ideas transmitted to the Carolino students allowed many of them to take up even more radical positions than those of their teachers, getting to actively participate in the process of independence.

Teachers at the Convictorio Carolino included prominent members of the Sociedad de Amantes del Pais and active collaborators from the newspaper *Mercurio Peruano*. They included José Baquijano y Carillo, Vicente Morales Duárez, Joaquín de Olmedo, Ramón Olaguer Feliú, Blas de Ostolaza, Mariano de Rivero, and José Antonio Navarrete. Morales Duárez was later elected president of the Cortes of Cádiz on May 26, 1812, after the inauguration of the liberal constitution.[33] According to Felipe Barreda y Laos, Morales Duárez "was distinguished by his very advanced doctrines, his liberal tendencies and by his vigorous defence of the rights of America."[34]

Bernardo O'Higgins received his education within this reformist environment and atmosphere of change. One of his classmates was the Limeño aristocrat Bernardo de Tagle y Portocarrero. The friendship that developed from then on would be actively maintained but took on unexpected directions. During the later 1810s and 1820s they reactivated the bonds that had been forged in the Convictorio, even though they did not share political ideals with anything like the same clarity or intensity.

One explanation for their dissimilar political trajectories must be the fact that after four years at the Convictorio de San Carlos, in 1794 O'Higgins was sent to continue his studies in Richmond, England, where he entered into contact with the Venezuelan activist Francisco de Miranda y Rodríguez—his political mentor.[35] With this departure from the colonial model of education, O'Higgins became representative of a new order, a new generation of potential leaders, who owed more to liberal currents of thought in London than to established colonial centers of education in the Americas. O'Higgins became involved in the formation of the Lautaro Masonic Lodge in London, which aimed to win the independence of Spanish America following the North American model. As his correspondence shows, Bernardo O'Higgins was the only Chilean Miranda ever met.[36] But an allegation that O'Higgins was part of Miranda's circle of conspirators led to Don Ambrosio being ejected from office on June 19, 1800, and subsequently, he cut all economic assistance to his son.[37] Only in 1802, after his father's death, did O'Higgins return to Chile after residing for some years in Spain. He first joined the Provincial Council of Chillán, only later to voice the insurgent politics. Torre Tagle, in contrast, did not study in England, and neither did he have the opportunity to meet such a great interlocutor as Miranda or participate in the European lodges of political character. His training, thus, was much more discrete. He maintained a political position that was similar to his contemporaries in Spain. He was elected as a deputy to the Cortes of Cádiz, though he did not arrive until 1813. He opted to stay in Spain for three long years after the absolutist monarchy of Ferdinand VII was reinstated in 1814.

San Martín's arrival in Peru motivated the explicit support of a significant number of Carolino alumni for the cause of independence. The liberal formation that had been taught in the Convictorio's classrooms began to bear its fruit at the dawn of the 1820s. As the Gaceta de Lima recognized in 1822, the progressive work of Rodríguez de Mendoza had "sowed the seeds amidst the dangers and despite the despotic forces."[38] Understandably then, several of the pupils were the first people to sign and swear on the act of independence, by their own initiative and not forced by the circumstances, and another group would fulfill an active role in the Protectorate.[39] One of these would be, without doubt, the Marquis of Torre Tagle. The 1820s witnessed the flourishing of long-term changes in Peruvian society and a political culture that had evolved in the late colonial period. O'Higgins, with his British schooling and international and inter-imperial contacts, was at the forefront of those changes.

O'Higgins, San Martín, and the IV Marquis of Torre Tagle

When on August 20, 1820, O'Higgins was bidding farewell to the liberating squadron that embarked at Valparaíso for Peru, he charged San Martín with contacting Bernardo de Torre Tagle in Lima. For San Martín, no doubt acting on O'Higgins's advice, Torre Tagle would be the perfect person with whom to establish an alliance, in that "his name and influence add a certain prestige to the blossoming cause of liberty."[40]

But, who was José Bernardo Tagle y Portocarero? Born in Lima in 1779, he was a descendent of *montañeses* and carried the noble title of IV Marquis of Torre Tagle.[41] Viceroy Abascal had named him, in 1811, sergeant major of the Concordia Regiment, though that did not necessarily mean that he would have received rigorous military training. Nominated as a deputy to the Cortes of Cádiz, he arrived there in 1813, remaining in Spain until 1817. He returned to Peru with the post of intendant of La Paz, but Viceroy Pezuela sent him to serve in the Intendancy of Trujillo, where he took charge in 1819.[42] In this post Torre Tagle was a royal civil servant. When San Martín landed on the Peruvian coasts, he immediately contacted Torre Tagle, who, in a gesture of patriotism, declared Trujillo's independence on December 29, 1820.

This may have been a political decision, or one of calculated self-interest by Torre Tagle. We should also take into account the importance of the family ties, both consanguineous and spiritual, that Torre Tagle maintained with O'Higgins, on one side, and with San Martín, on the other. His closeness with Don Bernardo, even though it had originated in the Carolino classrooms, had been recently reinforced by familial ties. Since their schooldays together, the IV Marquis of Torre Tagle, a widower, had remarried with the

Creole Doña Mariana de Echevarría y Ulloa, who was herself the widow of Don Demeterio O'Higgins, cousin of Don Ambrosio and uncle of Don Bernardo. At the time of the wedding in 1819, Bernardo O'Higgins was supreme director of Chile. Doña Mariana's mother, Doña Ana María Santiago de Ulloa, was a native of Valparaiso and, therefore, Chilean, so the wedding was a Peruvian-Chilean alliance as well as a link in the chain between O'Higgins and Torre Tagle.[43] The matrimonial bond was sworn in the parish of El Sagrario of Lima on July 20, 1819.[44]

In addition to these family ties, Torre Tagle tried to maintain correspondence with Bernardo O'Higgins in this key period of warfare and indecision, to whom he remitted, in 1821, Ambrosio O'Higgins's family genealogy, which had been preserved by his then-wife, Doña Mariana.[45] Without a doubt, Torre Tagle hoped to convince O'Higgins of the relevance of the family ties that united them.

Torre Tagle used a similar practice as he cultivated his relationship with San Martín. When the Marquis of Torre Tagle baptized his daughter, Josefa Manuela, in the Chapel of the Supreme Government in Lima on March 26, 1822, the Protector Don José de San Martín signed in person, as the child's godfather.[46] It was perhaps no coincidence that the Torre Tagles chose the name Josefa for their daughter, as it was the feminine version of José, which was the name of the girl's godfather and her father's new friend. From then on the flow of familiarity between the two men was ever more cemented. The following month, in a letter sent by the protector to the marquis, San Martín requested of him, "*My compadre,* if the inventory of the O'Higgins estate is in your hands, send it to me."[47] San Martín certainly seemed to trust the marquis implicitly. He quickly conferred on him, first, the title of Marquis of Trujillo and, subsequently, promoted him to the presidency of Peru, in addition to decorating him with the recently inaugurated Orden del Sol medal. Despite that, in the official communications, Tagle y Portocarrero continued signing consistently as the Marquis of Torre Tagle instead of Marquis of Trujillo.[48]

One thing that seemed to acquire less relevance than it perhaps deserved, as family relations were foregrounded in San Martín's construction of a new Peruvian governmental elite, was the question of whether Torre Tagle was actually the most suitable person to lead the process of independence in Peru. Although San Martín never become publicly disillusioned with his friend's political actions, Antonio José de Sucre and Simón Bolívar's arrival in Peru created a new scenario. Both became frustrated at what they saw as the Marquis of Trujillo's prevarication, ambiguity, and indecision. He became plagued with doubts regarding the path that should be taken in order to achieve Peruvian independence. Not without reason, the English traveler Robert Proctor, a firsthand witness of the events of 1823 and 1824, held the opinion that Torre Tagle "probably never would have existed as a politician, if he weren't condescending and apt as an instrument of foreign hands; for this reason only San Martín, the Congress and Bolivar busied him."[49] This was a pretty pejorative comment, which Bolívar and Sucre would probably have agreed with in the end. Torre Tagle's difficulties showed the complexity for elite individuals in negotiating the ever-shifting sands of political developments in 1820s Peru. Proctor's dismissal of Torre Tagle's ability, however, was not necessarily shared by the marquis' old classmate, Don Bernardo O'Higgins, in spite of his declared animosity toward aristocracy.[50]

O'Higgins and Peru under Bolívar

When O'Higgins disembarked in Callao on July 28, 1823, it was little more than a week after his good friend Bernardo de Torre Tagle had assumed the presidency of Peru. The Chilean general was warmly received in the Peruvian lands, although that did not prevent him from noticing sharply the chaotic situation that engulfed the country. Don Bernardo O'Higgins had intended on going to Ireland, the land of his ancestors that he so desired to know, but after arriving in Lima, he changed his mind, deciding that it was a priority to finish the work that the patriot army had begun in 1821.[51] He wrote immediately to San Martín, commenting, "The country suffers from all the maladies associated with its past disorders, in that it is enveloped in ignorance and ambition *without leadership or direction.*"[52] He had hardly settled down in Lima before he received news of Bolívar's arrival at Callao on September 1, 1823. Bolívar intended to assume leadership of the war and complete it, as the Congress of Peru had requested.

Two subjects bothered O'Higgins after making contact with Bolívar. The first was to investigate the possibility of moving a contingent of 2,500 soldiers up from Valparaiso to Callao, in order to re-enforce the Gran Colombian army. Bolívar explicitly asked O'Higgins to return to Chile to solicit "all the help that only your grace could rally for the strong influence of your grace's own character and friends."[53] But O'Higgins would not travel to Chile, and therefore the requested troops would not be sent to Peru. It is probable that O'Higgins considered it a bad moment to return to his country, which not so long ago he had abandoned. Despite his courteous treatment of O'Higgins,

Bolívar most likely was discomforted by his presence, connected as he was with Bolívar's rival, San Martín, and with President Torre Tagle, of whom, in contrast to O'Higgins, Bolívar had the poorest of opinions. The request that Bolívar made of O'Higgins to return to Chile was probably at least partially motivated by the Chilean's personal and familial ties with Torre Tagle and San Martín. Bolívar wanted to remove him from the political arena in order to consolidate Peruvian independence in collaboration with Sucre and the Gran Colombian army.

Bernardo O'Higgins's first intention, to bring more Chilean troops to Peru, did not materialize. His second preoccupation was his own distance from the "Libertador" and the military campaign. To be closer to the action, O'Higgins offered, as a gesture to Bolívar, to move to Huanchaco, the port of Trujillo, in order to serve there. O'Higgins was taking into account that former president Riva Agüero had already fled the northern city. When the Libertador did not respond to his offer, O'Higgins pleaded once more to his friend, President Torre Tagle, who had remained in Lima at the head of the government. O'Higgins was struggling to negotiate the new political affiliations of the 1820s. Torre Tagle must have accepted O'Higgins's proposal, as at the end of 1823 O'Higgins had moved to Trujillo with his family, even though he was still recovering from malaria.[54] It seems likely that O'Higgins was desperate to be close to Bolívar, and also that Torre Tagle wanted him there too. Settling in Trujillo in early 1824, O'Higgins would learn, not without dismay, that his co-disciple and now political relative, Torre Tagle, had been seen in conversations and negotiations with the Royalists. This indicated that Bolívar's intuition about the marquis' ambiguous stance was not all wrong. Bolívar loved being proven right. In the correspondence, which in 1824 Bolívar regularly exchanged with Sucre, the latter did not shy from referring to "the perversity of Torre Tagle," advising even "to disregard the perfidious advice of Tagle and other tainted Americans who had so vilely sold the interests of the Fatherland and the trust that Peru instilled in them, that they continue working constantly against the Spanish." Similarly, in March of the same year, Bolívar did not have any qualms about communicating with Vice President Francisco de Paula Santander, "I assure you that we are, in Peru, little less than in Hell."[55]

According to the English traveler Proctor, the situation became unsustainable when Torre Tagle made a public appearance in the company of Royalist military chiefs and emitted a comment proclaiming against Bolívar, "calling him an invader and destructor of the country and praising the Spanish as the only legitimate owners of Peru."[56] In this context the well-known intimacy shared by O'Higgins and Torre Tagle must have raised serious suspicions in the Liberator. In the wake of these turbulent events, the marquis manifested his intention to return to Chile, sacrificing his personal ambitions for the good of the country. Proctor explained this by pointing to the fluid friendship between Torre Tagle and the Chilean patriots—namely, O'Higgins.[57] The catalyst for Torre Tagle's departure, however, was his apparent incapacity to effectively manage Peruvian politics.

Nevertheless, Marquis Torre Tagle had considerable family in Chile that was not reducible to his wife's maternal relatives. A branch of the Tagles, the Ruiz Tagles, who like him were descendants of José de Tagle y Bracho, first Marquis of Torre Tagle, was established in Santiago. Thus, Don Bernardo Ruiz Tagle and Don Francisco Ruiz Tagle were two successful *montañés* merchants covering the route between Chile and Peru. Moreover, the former was married in Lima to Doña María Josefa Ortiz de Torquemada, and their three sons had been educated in colleges in Lima. One of these children, Francisco Ruiz Tagle, would maintain a clear intimacy with San Martín and O'Higgins during the process of independence, being named director of the Urban Police of Santiago (Director de la Policía Urbana) and member of the Sanitation Committee (Junta de Salubridad) by the supreme director of Chile in 1822.[58] This is to say that for the IV Marquis of Torre Tagle seeking refuge in Chile was not at all out of the question. The connections between the O'Higginses and the Tagles were as strong in Chile as they were in Peru. Theirs was a new reconfiguration of the Chilean-Peruvian networks that had persisted in the late colonial period, into which Don Ambrosio O'Higgins had successfully integrated himself, his Irish countrymen, and their families.

Simón Bolívar's attitude toward Bernardo O'Higgins was one of politeness suffused with distrust. Bolívar avoided O'Higgins's presence when he could. When O'Higgins reiterated his desire to enroll in the liberating army, Bolívar at first accepted the offer with enthusiasm. Bolívar wrote from Huaráz, "On my part, I offer you control in it [the army] . . . because a contingent from Colombia under your command should be victorious."[59] In early August, O'Higgins was finally able to visit Bolívar after he had triumphed at the Battle of Junín. Bolívar was affable, but again he declined to confer any position of responsibility in his army upon O'Higgins, which was what he had promised, including in writing. Later, on December 18, 1824, in Lima, O'Higgins heard the news of the victory of Ayacucho, which sealed Peruvian independence.

O'Higgins had suspected that he would not be involved. A little earlier he had expressed his complaints to English general Guillermo Miller—who had arrived with San Martín's army and now fought for Bolívar's side—telling him in a letter, "Is it possible that Chile, that incited the work of liberating Peru, creating from nothing a powerful squadron and sending an excellent army, is not represented by one division, not even one battalion, in the army in charge of accomplishing this task?"[60] His intuition was, therefore, that the Liberator would not call upon him for the final battle.

It was obvious for Bolívar that O'Higgins was clearly a man of San Martín, and his long-standing friendship with Torre Tagle did not help him at all. It should not be forgotten that when San Martín returned to Chile, after the upsets of his campaign in Peru, he stayed in O'Higgins's home, and it was San Martín who persuaded O'Higgins to return to Peru to consolidate independence.[61] Later on, when he had established himself in Lima, O'Higgins would convert himself into San Martín's proxy, managing the pending salaries of the ex-protector of Peru.[62] These antecedents were obviously influential in Bolívar's marking of a subtle but firm distance with the former supreme director of Chile.

If Bernardo O'Higgins de Ballenary y Riquelme—as he called himself in his testament—did not return to Chile in 1823 when he could have been recruiting troops to support Bolívar, then in reality he would never return to his country.[63] This was a desire that he could never materialize, since on October 24, 1842, at the age of sixty-four, O'Higgins passed away in Lima, the city he chose for his voluntary retirement and where he lived the last twenty years between independence and his death. He lived through the Confederation of Peru and Bolivia (1836–39), during which General Andrés de Santa Cruz requested his favor as a mediator.[64] O'Higgins's funeral was held with pomp in La Merced Church, as instructed in his will, on October twenty-sixth, presided over by Don Santiago O'Phelan, Bishop of Ayacucho, son of an Irishman from Waterford who had established himself in Arequipa, Captain Raymundo O'Phelan.[65] Even in his last moments, O'Higgins asked for a priest with Irish ascendancy to perform his mourning prayers.

This chapter has demonstrated the interesting ways in which Bernardo O'Higgins's life and relationships chime with the themes of the age of revolution and Atlantic connections post-independence. At first glance, O'Higgins might appear a classic example of the Atlantic connections that fostered independence, a protégé of Francisco de Miranda, who traveled back from London to Chile inspired by ideals he acquired in non-Hispanic Europe. Nevertheless, the detailed analysis of his political and social networks back in Chile and Peru demonstrates some quite resounding continuities with the public life of his own father, Ambrosio O'Higgins (who, of course, renounced his son in disgust and shame when news reached him of the young man's activities in London). Like his father, he was closely linked to aristocratic *limeño* circles, his relationships cemented through kinship and friendship. Colonial social practices shaped his ascent to political authority, but also contributed to undermining that authority and prohibited him from returning to Chile.

I will conclude by pointing out that although it has been stressed that it was Diego Portales, the Chilean minister, who fostered the project to make Valparaiso the most important port in the Pacific Coast, it is possible to demonstrate that it was actually Bernardo O'Higgins who began that policy. It was during O'Higgins's position as supreme director of Chile that the British community of Valparaiso started to grow noticeably. It is not surprising, therefore, that when the British traveler Samuel Haigh visited Valparaiso in 1828, after eleven years had passed since his first stay, he observed that in 1817 "there were only two English residents in the whole port, and now there are about two thousand."[66] One fact that could have attracted the presence of foreigners, and particularly the British, was the religious tolerance embraced by O'Higgins's government, as O'Higgins was very liberal on religious matters. Another facility that he did give to the foreign investors was to enable them "to take part in the nation's mining industry with the same privileges enjoyed by the Chileans."[67] He must have felt the impact of the competition that existed between Callao and Valparaiso for the control of the Pacific and made use of his political power to favor the Chilean port. Although he lived some twenty years in Peru and died in Lima, his short period of government in Chile left important economic bases that marked the economic development of his homeland during the rest of the nineteenth century.

Notes

I am grateful to the John Simon Guggenheim Memorial Foundation of New York for sponsoring this research project.

1. Hobsbawm, *The Age of Revolution,* 139.
2. Racine, *Francisco de Miranda,* 145–50.
3. Villalobos, *El proceso de la emancipación,* 377.

4. Mehegan, *O'Higgins of Chile,* 35, 84. Mehegan states that San Martín, who at the time was lieutenant in the Spanish army in the regiment of Murcia, had met O'Higgins in Cádiz; both had been born in the same year, 1778.

5. Villalobos, *El proceso de la emancipación,* 393, 394. Also see Jocelyn-Holt Letelier, *La Independencia de Chile,* 251.

6. Sergio Villalobos, *El proceso de la emancipación,* 398.

7. Bernardo O'Higgins's period as supreme director of Chile lasted six years, beginning in February 1817 and ending in January 1823, when it was toppled by a conservative military coup.

8. Vicuña Mackenna, *Vida del Capitán General Don Bernardo O'Higgins,* 292. The person who claimed to have received this confession from the lips of one of the accomplices was none other than the English general Guillermo Miller, although he took care not to reveal the name of his informant.

9. The transcript that was opened when he requested the title of Castilla signals that Don Ambrosio O'Higgins was the son of Charles O'Higgins, squire of Ballenary, and Margarita O'Higgins; paternal grandson of Roger O'Higgins, squire of Ballenary, and Margarita de Breham; and, on his mother's side of William O'Higgins, squire of Longarough, and Winifrida O'Fallon. For more on this, see Campos Harriet, *La Vida Heroica de O'Higgins,* 9. According to Orrego Vicuña (*O'Higgins,* 30), Don Ambrosio O'Higgins resided in Cádiz between 1751 and 1756. In 1761 Spain naturalized him, as it had done with other Irishmen, so that he could reside and trade in Spain's peninsular and American territories.

10. It was his nephew, Demeterio O'Higgins, who was in charge of providing the transcript of the accreditation of the title of Baron of Ballenary, arguing for the legitimate descent of Don Ambrosio, by direct line, from Juan Duff O'Higgins, who would be Baron of Ballenary in the County of Sligo, Kingdom of Ireland. For more details, see Donoso, *El marqués de Osorno Don Ambrosio O'Higgins,* 278–79; Arias de Saavedra Alías, "Irlandeses en la Alta Administración," 50.

11. Ibid., 51.

12. Sarrailh, *La España Ilustrada de la segunda mitad del siglo XVIII,* 323–25.

13. Wall, quoted in López-Guadalupe, "Irlandeses al servicio del Rey de España en el siglo XVIII," 173.

14. Boylan, *A Dictionary of Irish Biography,* 297. There were other distinguished Irishmen in the eighteenth-century Spanish administration, like Guillermo Lacy, born in the County of Limerick, who in 1750 was named a member of the Council of War; his son, Francisco, was named plenipotentiary minister to Russia in 1772, entering the Council of War in 1780. See Arias de Saavedra Alías, "Irlandeses en la Alta Administración," 57.

15. Fisher, *Government and Society in Colonial Peru.*

16. Donoso, *El marqués de Osorno,* 416.

17. Ibid., 366.

18. Ibid., 369. Many of these individuals had been prisoners in the last wars in the peninsula.

19. Fernández Pérez, "Comercio y familia en la España pre-industrial," 134; Fernández Pérez, *El rostro familiar de la metrópoli.*

20. Donoso, *El marqués de Osorno,* 388.

21. Eyzaguirre, *O'Higgins,* 1:24.

22. Archivo General de la Nación, Lima (AGNP), Tribunal del Consulado, Leg. 127. Doc.734, Año 1775.

23. Campos Harriet, *La Vida Heroica de O'Higgins,* 18.

24. Clissold, *Bernardo O'Higgins and the Independence of Chile,* 88. O'Higgins wrote, in a letter to Colonel Juan Mackenna, on January 5, 1811: "My first idea was to direct myself to my cousin Don Tomas O'Higgins, to obtain instruction and advice, since they had told me that he was a good soldier and distinguished tactician . . . but I have reasons to suppose that his opinion has not been very prudent since I have committed myself to the revolution." Vicuña Mackenna, *Vida del Capitán General,* 116.

25. Rosas Siles, "La nobleza titulada en el virreinato del Perú," 221. The title was conceded to Don Manuel Arredondo y Pelegres in 1808 by King Carlos IV. Monteagudo was described as "staunch enemy of the entire Spanish race" according to the traveler Basil Hall. B. Hall, "Lima independiente," 1:262. According to Clissold, Monteagudo was "an Argentine-born mulatto, who combined in his person the destructive instincts of the terrorist with utter ruthlessness in the pursuit of power and the indulgence of his own passions, he was the evil genius of the Revolution." Clissold, *Bernardo O'Higgins and the Independence of Chile,* 168.

26. Pruvonena (pseudonym of José de la Riva Agüero y Sanchez Boquete), *Memorias y Documentos para la Historia de la Independencia del Perú,* 1:58. The author indicates that San Martín gave his property as a gift to O'Higgins, taking it away from its legitimate inheritors.

27. Eyzaguirre, *O'Higgins,* 12:444–45. According to Eugenio Orrego Vicuña, the cultivation of sugarcane was the prime industry of the hacienda, although *panllevar* and *vid* were also cultivated, the labor force being composed of sixty black slaves. Orrego Vicuña, *O'Higgins,* 366.

28. Orrego Vicuña, *O'Higgins,* 338.

29. O'Phelan Godoy, "Una doble inserción," 439.

30. Campos Harriet (*La vida heroica de O'Higgins,* 18) signals that it was customary for the Chilean aristocracy to send their children to study in Lima in this period.

31. Espinoza Ruíz, "La reforma de la educación superior en Lima," 221.

32. Cubas, "Educación, Elites e Independencia," 301.

33. Ibid., 303, 311.

34. Ibid., 311.

35. This education included, according to a letter sent by Bernardo in 1799 to his father, English, French, ancient and modern history, geography, music, drawing, and "exercise of arms" classes. Clissold, *Bernardo O'Higgins and the Independence of Chile,* 57. In his frequent trips from Richmond to London, Bernardo O'Higgins had the opportunity to meet and to become friends with Francisco de Miranda in 1798. Díaz, *O'Higgins,* 13. Later, O'Higgins would declare in a letter directed to the Admiral Hardy and dated in his Montalván hacienda, September 1, 1828: "I owe to Miranda the first inspiration that launched my career of revolution and saving my Fatherland." Vicuña Mackenna, *Vida del Capitán General,* 121.

36. Clissold, *Bernardo O'Higgins and the Independence of Chile,* 59. Miranda wrote to O'Higgins, "In my long connection with South America, you are the only Chilean whom I have met."

37. Orrego Vicuña, *O'Higgins,* 49. After his destitution, Don Ambrosio would be replaced by one of his staunchest enemies, the Marquis of Aviles, but he died on March 18, 1801, before his substitute could take office. See Galván Moreno, *Don Ambrosio O'Higgins,* 6–7.

38. Valencia Avaria, *Bernardo O'Higgins,* 23.

39. Anna, *The Fall of the Royal Government;* Anna, "The Peruvian Declaration of Independence," 221–23.

40. Proctor, "El Perú entre 1823 y 1824," 2:250.

41. Atienza, *Nobiliario español,* 200. The title had been created in 1730 for Don Jose de Tagle y Bracho, who was a native of Ruiloba, in Burgos, Spain.

42. Vivero, *Galerías de Retratos de los Gobernantes del Perú Independiente,* 5.

43. Protocolos Notariales, Escribano José María La Rosa, Prot. 629, Año 1813, AGNP. Doña Mariana was the daughter of Juan de Echeverria, who had acted as the director of the Mining Tribunal, and Doña María Santiago de Ulloa, native of Valparaiso.

44. Archivo de la Parroquia de El Sagrario, Lima (APEL), Libro de Matrimonio, no.11, 299. The marriage of Don Bernardo de Tagle y Portocarrero—gentleman of the order of Santiago, Marquis of Torre Tagle, widower of Dona Juana Rosa Garcia de la Planta—with Doña Maria de Echeverria y Ulloa, widow of Don Demetrio O'Higgins, was registered on July 20, 1819.

45. O'Phelan Godoy, "Sucre en el Perú," 398–99.

46. Ortiz de Zevallos, *El norte del Perú en la Independencia,* 102.

47. San Martín, quoted in ibid., 100.

48. Vicuña Mackenna, *Vida del Capitán General,* 329. In the same way, the Count of Vega del Ren, the Count of Valle Oselle, and the Count of Torre Velarde signed an official document on December 24, 1821.

49. Proctor, "El Perú entre 1823 y 1824," 2:250.

50. J. Lynch, *José de San Martin,* 158.

51. Orrego Vicuña, *O'Higgins,* 331. O'Higgins requested a passport to visit Ireland, which was granted for two years.

52. O'Higgins, quoted in Eyzaguirre, *O'Higgins,* 2:435–36.

53. Bolívar, quoted in Eyzaguirre, *O'Higgins,* 438.

54. O'Higgins traveled accompanied by his mother, Isabel Riquelme; his half-sister, Rosa Rodriguez Riquelme; his illegitimate son, Pedro Demetrio; and two domestic servants. On the warship *Fly,* Governor Zenteno, don Felipe Santiago del Solar, Colonel Don Pedro Ramón Arriagada, Lieutenant Colonel Martínez, and Captain Don Tomás Sutcliffe, an English official serving in Chile, also accompanied him. See Díaz, *O'Higgins,* 197.

55. Sucre, *De mi propia mano,* 162.

56. Proctor, "El Perú entre 1823 y 1824," 2:329–30.

57. Ibid., 282.

58. Amunátegui Solar, "Mayorazgo Ruíz Tagle," 2:279–93. Francisco Ruíz Tagle maintained a good relationship with O'Higgins and San Martín, the latter of whom had stayed in his La Calera hacienda in 1817 so that the general could recover from a grave illness. On these familial networks, see Sánchez, "Familia, Comercio y Poder," 29–63.

59. Bolívar, quoted in Eyzaguirre, *O'Higgins,* 2:440.

60. According to Proctor, "El Perú entre 1823 y 1824," 2:215. Guillermo Miller was an English general born in Kent, who joined the Chilean patriot army, becoming one of the confidants of San Martín, having combated in the battle of Maipú that sealed Chilean independence. Miller would be decorated at the age of twenty-four with the Order of the Sun, in recognition of his merits and services lent in favor of independence.

61. Clissold, *Bernardo O'Higgins,* 201.

62. Díaz, *O'Higgins,* 199.

63. Sección Notarial/Testamentos, Escribano Gerónimo de Villafuerte, Protocolo 1025, folio 136, Año 1842, AGNP. Including in his name the word *Ballenary,* Don Bernardo was adopting, in some ways, the nobility title granted to his father, don Ambrosio O'Higgins, Baron de Ballenary, in 1795.

64. Parkerson, *Andrés de Santa Cruz y la Confederación Perú-boliviana.* O'Higgins

argued for the suspension of the war between Chile and the Confederation in light of the friendship that should have existed between the two countries. Santa Cruz backed his conciliatory posture, and it is probable that he was not sure that success would accompany the Confederation and that, in any case, it was not the opportune moment for armed confrontations when the confederate state was not yet facing revolt.

65. Valencia Avaria, *Bernardo O'Higgins,* 478. Archivo Departamental de Arequipa (ADA), Testamentos, Escribano Francisco Xavier de Linares, Protocolo 376, Año 1797, 282–86. Don Raymundo O'Phelan was the captain of the local army and graduate colonel; he was married to Doña Bernardina Recavarren.

66. Samuel Haigh, quoted in Kinsbruner, "The Political Influence of the British Merchants," 27.

67. Kinsbruner, "The Political Influence of the British Merchants," 31.

8
Corinne in the Andes

European Advice for Women in 1820s Argentina and Chile

Iona Macintyre

The time may arrive, when South America may have to boast her Madame
de Staels and a host of female literati; and another Corinna may conduct her
lover over Southern scenery, the snow-topt Andes, and Imperial Cusco, with
as much soft enthusiasm as belongs to her Italian rival.

—Anonymous, *A Five Years' Residence in Buenos Aires*

I take the title of this chapter from the words of the anonymous author of *A
Five Years' Residence in Buenos Aires, during the Years 1820–1825: Containing Remarks on the Country and Inhabitants,* who conjures up the image of
a Spanish American answer to the European literary figure of Corinne.[1]
Corinne is the erudite half-English and half-Italian heroine of the French-
Swiss writer Germaine de Staël's best-selling novel of 1807, *Corinne, or Italy,*
which follows the fate of a learned woman, a character connoting modernity
in nineteenth-century European literature. The main themes in the novel
are women and learning, but cultural differences are also explored: the di-
vergences between the north and the south and between the Anglo-Saxon
world and Latin people.

The woman question was a liberal transatlantic concern during the 1820s.
The focus of this chapter is the Spanish liberal José Joaquín de Mora (1783–
1864), who, alongside other revolutionary activities, drew on his knowledge
of British and French culture and spread advice on the education of girls and
women in Latin America. During his lifetime Mora worked in elevated political and civic circles as a lawyer, writer and poet, newspaper editor, translator, and educator in Spain, Britain, and South America and lived in Argentina
and Chile during the second half of the 1820s, helping to shape intellectual
life wherever he took up residence. As such, Mora sheds light on initiatives,
connections, and networks between Europe and Latin America during the
decade.

Raised in Cádiz, Mora studied law at the University of Granada, where
he subsequently took up a teaching post in logic.[2] During the Napoleonic

Wars he fought at the 1808 Battle of Bailén. As a prisoner of war in France he met his future wife, Françoise Delaunay (1791–1887), the daughter of a justice of the peace in Autun, Burgundy. They married in January 1814 and left for Spain. During the Trienio Liberal (a historical period), the couple resided in Madrid, where, politically committed and active, Mora was a newspaper editor (founding the weekly *Crónica Literaria y Científica* in 1817) and journalist (for periodicals such as the *Minerva Nacional* in 1820). Throughout his life Mora also worked as a translator, mainly working contemporary French texts into Spanish, for example, Charles Brifaut's play of 1813, *Ninus II, tragédie en 5 actes* (1818), and François-René de Chateaubriand's pamphlet against Napoleon Bonaparte, *De Buonaparte et des Bourbons,* of 1814 (translated that same year). Mora corresponded with Jeremy Bentham and translated his pamphlet on the Spanish Cortes in 1820. He translated the moral philosopher Baron d'Holbach's *Essai sur les préjugés* (1770) in 1823. Mora twice translated French writers who were interested in the woman question. In 1812 he translated Jean-Nicolas Bouilly's *Contes á ma fille* of 1809, and in 1825 he translated work of the seventeenth-century writer François Fénelon, who had also written a treatise on the education of daughters in 1681.

With the return of absolutism in Spain, Mora was forced to go into exile in 1823. Following his arrest in connection with subversive activities at his debating club in Madrid, the couple sought refuge in London. There, German publisher Rudolph Ackermann had established a successful business providing middle-brow and presentable prints, books, and journals to the British public, and he was now expanding into the Spanish American book market.[3] Ackermann had already published Spanish Bibles for the British and the Foreign Bible Society to sell in Spanish America.[4] Now he responded to reports that foreign books on useful subjects were needed in Spanish America and employed a number of Spanish exiles resident in London as writers and translators with the aim of providing modern concepts in modern books. Ackermann's texts in Spanish met calls for more reading material in Spanish America, for example, by Chilean priest and writer Camilo Henríquez (1769–1825). Henríquez wrote in the *Aurora de Chile* in favor of popularizing British thinkers in Spanish America.[5] Mora very much shared Henríquez's views on the improving effects of British culture, and he entered into Ackermann's employment. In Mora's translator's note in the Ackermann edition of Walter Scott's 1825 novel, *El Talisman* (1826), he expresses a belief that the translation of the novel would help Spanish Americans develop good taste.

Under Ackermann's employment, Mora wrote, compiled, and translated a number of books for distribution in Spanish America. His work and translations covered history, for example, William Davis Robinson's *Memorias de la revolución de Méjico* (1824); Francisco Javier Clavigero's *Historia antigua de Méjico* (1826); the anonymously written *Cuadros de la historia de los Árabes: Desde Mahoma hasta la conquista de Granada* (1826), which Mora dedicated to Vicente Rocafuerte; and *Persia: Descripción abreviada del mundo* (1824), by Frederic Schoberl (1775–1853). He also translated fiction, such as Walter Scott's *Ivanhoe* (1825). At the same time he edited the periodicals *Museo Universal de Ciencias y Artes* (1825) and *Correo literario y político de Londres* (1826), where he published José Joaquín de Olmedo's epic poem, *La Victoria de Junín. Canto a Bolívar.*

In general, the Ackermann texts transferred new ideas in humanities, science, the arts, and other fields into useful information for a general audience that would include school children, juveniles, and women. Most emblematic of the enterprise are the Ackermann catechism school books produced between 1823 and 1829.[6] The series covered topics such as rhetoric, mythology, chemistry, literary studies, Greek and Roman history, modern history, geography, natural history, and geometry. Book dedications and featured advertisement pages demonstrate that the schoolhouse was an important target market for Ackermann and was, therefore, a subsystem of Latin American society that received Eurocentric narratives. The superiority of European civilization (here Europe is a vague concept that does not necessarily encompass Spain) was both implicit and explicit in the catechisms:

Q. Why is Europe famous?
A. Because of the knowledge, culture, intelligence and activity of its inhabitants.[7]

Mora would also emphasize this point, perhaps seeing himself as an intercontinental voice and as a transmitter of knowledge from the west to the east and from the north to the south, from the knowledgeable to the inexperienced: "From the great cities of Europe the sacred fire of knowledge spreads with incalculable speed, and arrives at the most far off countries. What a simple journalist puts on paper in Edinburgh is transmitted like an electric spark to the Banks of the Ganges and of the River Plate, to the foot of the Alps and to the foot of the Andes."[8]

In Britain, Ackermann targeted the ladies' market with fashion plates, albums, annuals, souvenirs, keepsakes, calendars, and other kinds of gift books, sometimes publishing women artists. In 1824 Mora compiled an annual entitled *No me olvides,* which aimed to continue from the success of the 1823 English-language *Forget Me Not,* though it was not published until 1827. These books were highly illustrated and clearly intended to be given as gifts. They consisted of verse, short stories, and fragments of travelogues. Mora's 1824 text was not entirely the same as the 1824 *Forget Me Not,* but they share several characteristics, for example, the inclusion of the story *The Adventure of Two Englishmen in South America,* about two adventurers who travel to South America to fight alongside Simón Bolívar. Mora promoted women writers from time to time in his other writings. For example, the dialogue that precedes Mora's 1825 translation of *Ivanhoe* states that, contrary to popular belief, it was not Walter Scott who pioneered the historical novel, but rather a French woman writer. This is presumably a reference to Stéphanie de Genlis (1746–1830), who hailed from the same town as Mora's wife, also wrote on education, and was the author of *Jeanne de France, nouvelle historique* of 1816. In another example, in 1826 the *Museo Universal de Ciencias y Artes* journal, edited by Mora, reviewed an instructive book for children, *Harry and Lucy,* by Ango-Irish writer Maria Edgeworth (1768–1849).

The culmination of Mora's interest in the woman question came about in 1824. That year Ackermann brought out *Cartas sobre la educación del bello sexo por una señora americana.*[9] Written anonymously in epistolary form, its real author was Mora himself. Although Mora had already translated thinkers on the woman question, we must remember that Joseph Blanco White's letters report that Ackermann often interfered in the writing of the books that he commissioned.[10] Ackermann himself was open to new ideas in education; his sons George (who would take the family business to Mexico during the 1820s) and John had attended a Pestalozzi school, and his daughter Selina (married name was Butler) would run a boarding school for girls in Oxford during the 1830s.

The first noticeable feature in the title of *Cartas* is the deceit involved in the presentation of the text, the counterfeit intimacy produced by the anonym "una señora americana." The authorial persona (a generic Spanish American woman from a distinguished revolutionary family, as she recounts in the introduction) was purposely designed to appeal to the intended market. The second aspect of importance is that *Cartas* presents a secular vision of education with no mention of the supremacy of the Roman Catholic Church. This arrangement was a great success. An undated edition of the book was printed in Paris by the Librería de A. Mezin later that decade. In Latin America the book was reproduced a number of times: in Buenos Aires in 1826 and Havana in 1829. Fragments of the text were reproduced in the Brazilian journal *O Mentor das Brasileiras* in Minas Gerais between 1829 and 1832, and an edition was brought out in Rio de Janeiro in 1838. For example, the entire book was published in Portuguese in Rio in 1838 as *Cartas sobre a educação das meninas por uma senhora americana,* by João Candido de Deos e Silva, and distributed to schoolteachers in Minas Gerais at the instruction of the president of the province. The book's dedication stated:

To the ladies of Brazil,
For your instruction and that of your daughters I have translated this book into our language. Its aim is not to form women for dances or games, but rather to form good mothers and good wives, who can provide the State with useful and virtuous citizens.[11]

Another Portuguese version was translated by educator Francisco Freire de Carvalho and published in London in 1850. Carvalho was the instructor to the daughter of liberal king Pedro I of Brazil. Versions followed in Morelia in 1855, Valparaíso in 1856, and Managua in 1869.[12] The Spanish American editions were promoted as being more affordable than the British import.

Cartas opens describing Northern Europe: "The magnificence of the cities, the beauty, the excellent cultivation of the fields, the general application to useful tasks, the brilliance of the public institutions, the urbanity of the manners, the artistic production, and above all, the welfare universally diffused in the immense population."[13]

Taking inspiration from these achievements, the author of *Cartas* expressed "her" wish to defend the role of women, a social group that was ignored by colonial Spain. *Cartas* explained the female population's special responsibility in establishing order and progress in the new republics. The book expressed a positive view of women's domestic role in society and argued that emulation of the English model of education for girls, which particularly instilled the virtues of hard work, was one of the most effective ways to modernize Spanish America. In contrast, nations in the East and Italy, Portugal, and Spain condemned the fair sex to ignorance. In general, Spanish customs were rejected in *Cartas*. Mora's preference for British culture even extended to cuisine; *Cartas* advised against spicy food. The text also advocated the study of the English language.[14]

More than just being in circulation, we know that Mora's book was read in Latin America. Argentinian president-to-be Domingo Faustino Sarmiento (1811–1888), writing in Chile in 1849, reported that *Cartas* was used for reading aloud, memorization, and recitation in a school for girls in San Juan:

> Forty four volumes were read in the space of a year and a half in these activities whose utility is unquestionable as long as there is discernment in the selection of materials. *Consejos a mi hija, Cuentos a mi hija, La moral en acción, La juventud, Cartas sobre la educación del bello sexo, Robinson Crusoe,* and a multitude of works whose titles I cannot remember, made up a long period of reading which was as enjoyable as it was instructive, enriching the memory with valuable facts and filling the heart with soft emotions. Encouraging this daily activity fosters a taste for Reading which is the fountain of all knowledge. Few men in that country had, as these girls did, the habit of reading aloud with careful pronunciation and an accent and a tone perfectly suited to the subject matter.[15]

Ackermann and Mora followed the success of *Cartas* in 1824 with *Gimnástica del bello sexo: Ensayos sobre la educación física de las jóvenes. Gimnástica* attacked the inactivity of rich women (assuring them that physical exertion was not plebeian) and the use of constricting clothes. The text identified the Hispanic siesta and the hammock as particularly harmful. Sedentary habits were criticized while fresh air, games, activities, and horse riding in the English style were all recommended. *Gimnástica* suggested a number of pastimes, such as swings, see-saws, tennis, wooden toys such as yoyos, running games such as *el juego de las cuatro esquinas, el juego de la gallina ciega* (something along the lines of blind man's bluff), and other guessing games, singing, dancing, horse riding in the English style, hoop rolling, skipping, and skittles, and also recommended eating sugar in moderation. It advised a happy medium between being lazy and being boyish. Below is an example of verse from *Gimnástica* that expounds the merits of physical exercise:

> There is no life without movement;
> The death of thought
> Is the languid repose
> Of an inert and pleasure-seeking man.
> Of a swamp full
> Of useless reeds,

Of venomous beasts.
Fetid air,
Deathly emanations,
Are born from deep inside.
Meanwhile free and serene
The babbling stream
Moves its crystal waves.
Simple birds sing,
On its green banks;
Thousands of bushes surround it,
And they thrive and flower,
And in the immense meadow
The sap moistens the plants
And gives freshness to the air
And beauty to the fields.[16]

Here we see individual inertia, like stagnant water, contrasted with the re-
plenishing movement of a stream that creates flowering nature. Lethargy is
also attacked in *Cartas,* where it is very much associated with colonial policy.
Cartas states that Spanish America must adopt "all useful thinking" now that
the "mortiferous lethargy" of Spanish absolutism is in the past. This theme
of lethargy also appears in the "indolent idleness" in *Silva a la agricultura en
la zona tórrida* of 1826 by Venezuelan Andrés Bello (also written in exile in
London), which addresses the concept so hated by Jean-Jacques Rousseau and
cited in *La nouvelle Heloise,* his novel of 1761: "If indolent idleness engenders
only melancholy and boredom, the delight of pleasant leisure is the result of
a laborious life."[17] In *Gimnástica* activity and productivity are promoted as
modern feminine virtues.

Cartas and *Gimnástica* set out to bring productivity to the periphery by arguing that the Spanish American republics needed educated women in order
to become orderly and productive modern societies. Spanish national character and everyday life were condemned and Hispanic women were urged to
improve their judgment through education and to swap their vanity, idleness,
and prattling for British plainness, practicality, and rationalism.

Mora was by no means unusual in his thinking on education for girls. During the 1820s pamphlets circulated and laws were drafted on education for
girls across Spanish America. The behavior of women was considered at the
highest levels of revolutionary society. In 1825, shortly after the death of his

wife, Remedios Escalada, the Argentinean general José de San Martín wrote a set of maxims for his daughter Mercedes:

> Maxims for my daughter
>   1. Humanise your character and be sensitive even with harmless insects. Sterne has said to a fly as he opened the window for it to leave: "This world surely is wide enough to hold both thee and me."[18]
>   2. Love truth and hate lies.
>   3. Build trust and friendship but retain respect.
>   4. Be charitable to the poor.
>   5. Respect private property.
>   6. Know how to keep a secret.
>   7. Be indulgent to all religions.
>   8. Be sweet to servants, the poor and the elderly.
>   9. Speak little and precisely.
>   10. Be formal at the dinner table.
>   11. Be clean and reject luxuries.
>   12. Love the patria and freedom.[19]

Anecdotal evidence suggests that San Martín's maxims, secular like Mora's texts, endured and were memorized in schools in Argentina in civics classes as recently as during the 1980s.

The urgent need for the education of girls and women was an idea that was also starting to come from North America by the late 1820s. In 1827 Emma Willard of the Troy Female Seminary in New York wrote to Bolívar on the subject of founding a school for girls in Bogotá:

> For what purpose has Bolivar so long bared his generous bosom to the storm of war—for what purpose given his devoted head a prey to the sleepless care of administering present and providing for future governments,—to give to South America, Liberty and Independence?— From what foes, in the hour of melancholy musing, does he fear that on some evil day Slavery will return? It is not from a Spanish force? This he can conquer again. The foes he dreads are ignorance and superstition. How can he best vanquish these? Where is their stronghold, and from whence do they sally forth most effectually to enslave mankind? It is the uncultivated mind of woman. Rout them there, and they fly for ever. Emancipate the future mother and the child must be free.[20]

It is one thing establishing that attempts were made from Britain and the United States to reform female behavior in Spanish America, but it is another to trace the actual effects of these efforts. Here we turn to Mora's practical activities. Mora's employment with Ackermann ended in 1826 when Mora and his family left London for Buenos Aires at the invitation of President Bernardino Rivadavia (1780–1845). Buenos Aires was fertile ground for liberal activity during the mid-1820s and, indeed, Rivadavia was sympathetic to the improvement of education for girls.[21] There the Moras, working alongside Neapolitan liberal Pedro de Angelis (1784–1859) and his Swiss wife, Melanie Dayet (another intellectual European married couple employed in post-independence regeneration in South America), founded the Colegio Argentino, a school for girls, while Mora and de Angelis founded the periodicals *La Crónica Política y Literaria de Buenos Aires* (1827) and *El Conciliador* (1827). Well connected in Europe, de Angelis had been the tutor of the children of Joaquín Murat and Carolina Bonaparte, Napoleon's sister. Dayet had been a lady-in-waiting to Countess Orloff (1777–1842), a famous literary salon hostess in Paris.

In Buenos Aires, Mora and his collaborators found that, rather than starting from scratch, they were joining a preexisting educational community focused on girls as well as boys. This community was made up of foreign and local participants. The Edinburgh Baptist James Thomson had been in the province of Buenos Aires between 1818 and 1821 to advise the government on education, promote the introduction of the Lancaster teaching method, and distribute Spanish New Testaments on behalf of the British and the Foreign Bible Society and the British and Foreign School Society. Thomson set up elementary schools in Buenos Aires before departing for Chile in 1821 at the invitation of Bernardo O'Higgins. He was a strong supporter of education for girls, writing, "Female education, in my opinion, is the thing most wanted in every country; and when it shall be properly attended to, the renovation of the world will go on rapidly."[22]

The experiments in female education in Buenos Aires ended in 1827. Rivadavia's resignation coincided with conflict between the Mora and de Angelis families over the running of the school.[23] De Angelis remained in the city in the employment of Juan Manuel de Rosas, rising to prominence in Federal circles as a historian. In contrast, Mora accepted an invitation from Chilean president Francisco Antonio Pinto (1785–1858), who had fought alongside San Martín and was now a committed educationalist belonging to the liberal party, to travel to Santiago de Chile.[24] The Moras arrived in Santiago early in 1828. Mora, in a letter to Florencio Varela, the Argentine minister for the interior, reported "education-mania" in Chile.[25] Mora was contracted to run the Liceo de Chile in 1828 (where he hoped to form the public figures so needed in the country), drafted the 1828 Chilean liberal constitution, and edited the periodicals *El Mercurio Chileno* (1828–29) and *El Constituyente* (1828).[26] He also wrote a catechism on geography to be used in the Liceo.[27] Mora's high regard for the British work ethic had not yet waned; in another letter to Varela he wrote: "In England I worked a lot because everyone worked a lot; here I work a lot because everyone works little."[28] During the public exams in August 1829 the students were tested in Christian doctrine, English (for which the pupils recited Shakespeare), Spanish, French, geography, and ancient history. The following day there was a music recital with a selection of popular opera, including the German composer Giacomo Meyerbeer (1791–1864) and the Italians Gioachino Rossini (1792–1868), Girolamo Crescentini (1766–1846), and Saverio Mercadante (1795–1870). They also sang the Chilean national anthem by Catalan Ramón Carnicer (1789–1855). Françoise Delaunay founded a state-run girls' school using the Lancaster method, which the president's daughters attended.[29] The school taught Christian doctrine, reading and writing, English, French, geography, and sewing. There were clear policies on pedagogical methods. For example, some subjects were taught using the monitorial method, some by a technique based on the questions and answers in catechisms, and French was taught via a system called the Hamilton method, which emphasized idiomatic phraseology according to individual topics that included literature, drama, the arts, manners, morals, and health.

The Moras' time in Chile was also of short duration. Pinto left office in August 1829, and Mora was forced to leave Chile in 1831 following the rise of conservative government. The 1830s would see an end to the liberal and modernizing experimentation of the 1820s in Buenos Aires and Santiago. But a seed was sown: in the 1850s president Manuel Montt (1809–80) promoted education, including education for girls and teacher training for women in Chile. In the same decade his Argentinean ally Sarmiento founded a girls' school in San Juan and brought sixty-three women teachers from the United States to teach in Argentina. After further residence in Peru and Bolivia, Mora returned to London in 1838 as an envoy of Andrés de Santa Cruz (1792–1865). This ended more than a decade during which Mora had worked as a lawmaker, writer, and educator in South America. Mora's *Cartas* is evidence of a flourishing transatlantic print community during the 1820s. In addition, the fact that *Cartas* was reproduced during the nineteenth century many times more than other Ackermann texts in Latin America supports the conclusion that reading material for girls and ladies was perceived to be necessary and that the idealized images of British utility, activity, and reserve had a clear appeal. In the long term this Eurocentric cultural and educational connection between Europe and Latin America during the 1820s prevailed, re-surfacing in Chile and Argentina in the 1850s. Mora, a Spaniard with firsthand knowledge of Britain and France, is therefore an example of fitful European influence in Latin America during the 1820s: first, discursively and successfully with his involvement with Ackermann in London and his development of lasting instructional materials, and then, practically and insufficiently, through his and his wife's employment as public servants by liberal politicians eager to engage skilled migrants. Ultimately, and in line with other projects that connected Europe and Latin America during the decade, the Moras' practical work in education for girls was truncated due to the fact that their local Europhile patrons, Rivadavia and Pinto, were not installed securely enough in power.

Notes

1. The author is thought to be George Thomas Love, the editor of the English-language newspaper in Buenos Aires, *The British Packet*. In the text that follows the quotation, the author states his belief that Spanish men traditionally dislike learned women, which for him explained why Spanish American women remained uncultivated in comparison to their European counterparts.

2. Gabino F. Campos believes there is sufficient anecdotal evidence to show that Mora was a Protestant convert.

3. Roldán Vera, *The British Book Trade and Spanish American Independence*.

4. See Racine, "Commercial Christianity," 78–98.

5. Will, "The Introduction of Classical Economics into Chile," 8.

6. See Roldán Vera's "The Catechism as an Educational Genre in Early Independent Spanish America" and *The British Book Trade and Spanish American Independence*.

7. Anonymous, *Catecismo de geografía natural* (London: Ackermann, 1823), 3–4. In addition to Eurocentric views such as these, white supremacy was advanced in the Ackermann texts, for example, in José de Urcullo's *Catecismo de historia natural* (London: Ackermann, 1826), 13. All translations are my own unless otherwise stated.

8. *Crónica de Buenos Aires* in 1827, cited in Amunátegui, *Don José Joaquín de Mora*, 13.

9. In 1825 Ackermann published an instructional book for men, *Lecciones de moral, virtud y urbanidad,* by José de Urcullu.

10. Letter from Joseph Blanco White to Robert Southey, March 16, 1823, Bodleian Library, Oxford University, MS.Eng.lett.d.74 ff.98.

11. João Candido de Deos e Silva, *Cartas sobre a educação das meninas por uma senhora americana* (Rio de Janeiro: Tipografia Nacional, 1838), 3.

12. Other editions were printed in Mexico City and Veracruz.

13. Mora, *Cartas sobre la educación del bello sexo por una señora americana,* 2.

14. Not all of *Cartas* was Mora's own work, containing as it does two English translations, a conduct book to be used by girls attending boarding schools, and a list of maxims on marriage from Ackermann's monthly magazine *Repository of Arts, Literature, Commerce, Manufactures, Fashions and Politics* (1809–29).

15. Sarmiento, *De la educación popular,* 82.

16. Mora, *Gimnástica del bello sexo,* 98.

17. Rousseau, *La nouvelle Heloise Julie,* 204. Mora's *Gimnástica del bello sexo* also quotes William Shakespeare.

18. The reference to Laurence Sterne comes from *Tristam Shandy* (1759).

19. San Martín, quoted in Zago, *José de San Martín,* 84.

20. Willard, "Female College at Bogota," 279.

21. See Macintyre, *Women and Print Culture in Post-Independence Buenos Aires.*

22. James Thomson, *Letters on the Moral and Religious State of South America Written during a Residence of Nearly Seven Years in Buenos Aires, Chile, Peru, and Colombia* (London: James Nisbet, 1827), 129.

23. In a letter to Florencio Varela in 1828 Mora reported that parents had complained that de Angelis was rough with the girls, kicking them and calling them brutes. G. Rodríguez, *Contribución histórica y documental,* 510–11.

24. Andrés Bello arrived in 1829. In April 1832 he wrote in *El Aracauno* that censorship had prohibited the entry of *Delfina* by Staël. The relationship between Bello and Mora is discussed in Avila Martel, *Mora y Bello en Chile,* 39–42.

25. Stuardo Ortiz, "El Liceo de Chile," 55.

26. Mora taught the liberal writer José Victorino Lastarria (1817–88) at the Liceo de Chile.

27. Stuardo Ortiz, "El Liceo de Chile," 49.

28. Letter dated April 15, 1828, reproduced in G. Rodríguez, *Contribución histórica y documental,* 514–16.

29. Conservative families preferred the girls' school run by Madame Ana Versin.

9
Heretics, Cadavers, and Capitalists

European Foreigners in Venezuela during the 1820s

Reuben Zahler

The night of December 8, 1825, was a very bad one for Colonel Feudenthal. A German aristocrat, he had come to Venezuela during the war years and fought for the republican cause. He settled in Venezuela and lost himself in the shameful habits of drinking and gambling. On the night in question, he got into a fight with Luis Stahl. Stahl had also come to Venezuela as a mercenary and now owned the City Hotel in Caracas, where Feudenthal was a guest. Though Stahl was a commoner, he bested the aristocrat. Feudenthal, thoroughly despondent from his sinful habits and wounded pride, went to his room, put a pistol to his head, and blew his brains out. His problems, however, did not stop there. He was a practicing Protestant, which posed a problem because this Catholic country possessed no Protestant cemeteries. Fortunately, when he lived in Bogotá a few years earlier, he had purchased a certificate that claimed he was Catholic so that he could marry a local woman. Based on this document, the Catholic Church allowed him a proper burial.[1]

The following year, Luis Stahl also found himself in a tight spot. He had designed the City Hotel to emulate European styles and appeal to an elite clientele, but apparently it did not meet certain standards. The British consul, Sir Robert Ker Porter, described the place as "a sad, miserable hotel—filthy and fleay [*sic*]." Porter complained of the rats and the noise from boisterous soldiers that prevented his sleep.[2] By 1826, less than a year after the hotel's construction, Stahl could not pay his creditors, and one of them, Lope Buros, sued. Stahl placed much of his defense upon the fact that he was a foreigner and therefore didn't understand the Spanish language, his rights, or the local laws. For these reasons, Stahl requested that the court dissolve the renter's contract, forgive his debts, and excuse any wrongdoing on his part. The judge, however, sided with Buros, dismissing Stahl's argument that foreigners should receive special consideration: "a general principle of laws is that ignorance of the laws does not preclude punishment for those who break them."[3] Stahl appealed and lost again.[4] Both the first judge and the appeals judge rejected Stahl's attempt to hide behind his status as a foreigner and instead required him to uphold his contract and obey the law, as they would a native Venezuelan.

These two anecdotes offer some insights into the diverse fortunes of North Atlantic immigrants in Venezuela during the 1820s and how these foreigners affected the young republic. Unlike during colonial times, Venezuelans could now freely trade with merchants from throughout the Atlantic world.[5] Further, the liberal principles that the republic adopted allowed for the immigration of non-Catholics, so that for the first time Protestants and Jews freely lived and traded on Venezuelan territory. The presence of these outsiders caused new problems, as the locals were unaccustomed to religious pluralism and to competing with merchants from beyond the Hispanic world. There is not a lot of research on foreigners in Venezuela at this time. Nonetheless, two patterns emerge from the sources that illuminate the disruptive dynamism caused by these new immigration and trade policies. First, foreigners in Venezuela experienced a wide variety of fates, and their fortunes depended in part on both their socioeconomic status and their ethnic/religious identity. Second, the presence of foreigners helped the Venezuelan state to solidify its power and its commitment to liberal reform.

Foreigners came principally to gain wealth from trade, and their fate was quite uncertain as individuals enjoyed very different levels of social and economic success on South American soil. Officially, foreigners enjoyed legal status much like that of citizens. Nonetheless, while foreigners found generally hospitable conditions in the young republic, some ethnic groups (particularly Spaniards and Jews) had a harder time than others. Further, foreigners with means maintained a cultural distance from the locals; wealthy foreigners segregated themselves socially from the Venezuelans, while poorer foreigners tended to integrate much more with the locals. Not surprisingly, Venezuelan civilians periodically challenged the inflow of people whom they considered to be heretical, commercially competitive, and aloof.

Under these circumstances, the presence of foreigners provided the state with an opportunity to assert its authority and promote its liberal agenda as it periodically defended the rights of foreigners against local interests. Official defense of foreign interests could take the form of tariff policies, religious tolerance, or the physical protection of merchant communities. Pressure from foreigners was not the main the driving force behind these policies, and such governmental actions should not be interpreted as buckling under to outside influence. Rather, the state embraced liberal values and promoted free trade as the path to national prosperity. Consistent with these principles, the state sought to create a hospitable environment for foreign merchants and to weaken the power of the Catholic Church. The presence of foreigners aggravated the debate within a society that was ambivalent toward liberalism and at times rallied opposition to these new policies. The state suppressed violent opposition and thereby strengthened its position and its fidelity to liberal reform.

The 1820s, then, warrant particular attention for a number of reasons. Venezuelans integrated themselves into trans-Atlantic trade, intellectual milieu, and immigration to a far greater degree than during the colonial regime. Consequently, these were the first years with a strong presence of non-Hispanic, non-Catholic foreigners. This heightened integration brought political and social strains that marked the trajectory of the emerging republic. Also, foreign interference was at a low point during this period. Numerous foreigners came to Venezuela, but the merchants and diplomats from no single foreign country had preponderant influence, and none dominated Venezuelan economic or political life. The first three to four decades after independence mark a period in which there was not formal, neo-, or informal colonialism. Venezuela was not sovereign as it was a part of Gran Colombia. Still, with regards to North Atlantic influence, this decade marked a high point of sovereignty. This chapter will consider these observations regarding foreigners, ending with an examination of some particular problems faced by non-Catholic minorities.

Liberalism in the Early Republic

Venezuela's leaders charted a highly liberal course for the young republic, due both to colonial precedents and to revolutionary ideology. Bourbon reforms had greatly increased the power and prestige of Caracas, as between 1776 and 1803 it became the seat of Venezuela's Intendencia, Capitanía General, Audiencia, merchant guild, and archdiocese. By the end of the colonial period, therefore, the region enjoyed almost complete autonomy within the viceroyalty of Nueva Granada. Additionally, by the late colonial period the powerful *hacendado* (merchant) class enjoyed considerable control over their export activities, as peninsular merchants did not exert nearly as much control as they did in most other parts of the empire.[6] The region benefited greatly from the policy of *comercio libre* and became "Spain's most successful agricultural colony."[7] During the final years of the empire, economic elites advocated greater economic liberties and developed a nearly liberal sense of individual, inviolate property rights.[8]

The revolutionary wars broke out early in Venezuela, as radical liberal ideologues took control of the Caracas *cabildo* and declared full independence in 1811. Venezuela's war proved to be the most destructive in all of Latin America; it periodically descended into race, class, and regional warfare as nonwhites took revenge on the dominant class and various regions resisted Caracas's hegemonic ambitions. By the time republicans secured victory in 1821, over one-third of the population had died or gone into exile. From 1821 until 1830, Venezuela existed as a province within Gran Colombia, an enormous country that included what are today the countries Colombia, Ecuador, and Panama, with its capital in Bogotá. In 1830, Venezuela and Ecuador peacefully seceded and became independent.

Though Venezuela faced numerous postwar obstacles after 1821, liberal reform benefited from relative stability and a near consensus among elites. Banditry and pockets of Royalist opposition persisted, but throughout the 1820s violence never spread beyond the local level. Further, post-independence elites maintained widespread agreement in their promotion of liberal principles. The leaders of the independence movement had been liberals, and they commanded the political landscape during the 1820s peace. The great majority of landowners, merchants, and military leaders sought a government that would be secular, representative, and transparent, as well as a free market economy, civil rights, an end to racial and social castes, and the separation of church and state. The press stressed the notion that they had made a sharp break with the "tyranny" of Spanish rule and that "our new liberal laws" should guide the republic.[9] In this regard, for the most part they were in ideological harmony with Francisco de Paula Santander's regime in Bogotá. While Venezuela's elites disagreed with each other over many issues, they tended to do so within a liberal context and never forced a pendulum swing toward conservatism. These conditions enabled Venezuela to pursue liberal reform with far less conservative opposition than found in most other Latin American republics.

As during the late colonial period, political and economic leaders looked to free, trans-Atlantic trade as the means to economic health. The war had ravaged the economy, destroying haciendas, infrastructure, and cattle herds, and displacing the population. Nonetheless, agricultural production (mostly coffee, cacao, cotton, and cattle products) rebounded, and reduced import tariffs facilitated rapid expansion.[10] In 1822, export values were 22 percent of the average from 1800 to 1810; from 1828 to 1830, export values had grown to 99 percent of what they had been from 1800 through 1810.[11]

Throughout the 1820s, Venezuela's largest source of imported goods was Britain, and the largest recipients of Venezuelan exports were the United States and France.[12] The local government granted British merchants special concessions as gratitude for the number of wartime mercenaries and postwar loans from that country. Nonetheless, during this decade no single country clearly dominated Venezuela's foreign trade—Britain would not attain that position until later in the century.[13] By 1823, British, French, American, and Dutch businessmen owned a dozen merchant houses throughout Venezuela.[14] By 1828, the newspaper *Gaceta del Gobierno* listed 215 individuals who had received visas to reside in Venezuela. The single largest group was composed of Spanish and Canary Islanders (26 percent), then British and French (21 percent each), then, in descending order, United States, Dutch, German, Italian, Danish, Swiss, Portuguese, and Haitian.[15] The total number of foreigners, however, probably exceeded those with visas.[16]

Foreigners in Venezuela

As we consider conditions for foreigners, we must keep in mind that the concept of "foreigner" was somewhat complicated. There was not a sense of national unity in Venezuela, and even less so in Gran Colombia.[17] So we can't assume that a Venezuelan from the city of Coro considered somebody from Britain or Curacao to be more foreign than somebody from Caracas or the Andes. Nonetheless, the foreigners discussed here, who came from the North Atlantic, had distinct status and catalyzed distinct problems.

As the story about Luis Stahl illustrates, foreigners enjoyed legal protections and responsibilities much like natives. Article 183 of the 1821 constitution stated that foreigners could freely enter Colombia and "enjoy in their persons and property the same security as other citizens, as long as they always respect the laws of the Republic." Further, the constitution defined a "Colombian" in terms that could include foreigners; technically, a "Colombian" was any free person born in Colombia or located in Colombia at the time of independence who "remain[ed] loyal to the cause of independence." This definition, then, included people without regard to race, caste, religion, economic status, or place of origin.[18] Foreigners could not vote, but they enjoyed certain advantages over locals: they didn't have to serve in the militia, they enjoyed the protection of their home country's consular officials, and, interestingly, they could be elected to either house of Parliament.[19]

Throughout Hispanic America's young republics, the presence of foreigners facilitated a stronger sense of national identity and sovereignty, which found expression in laws on attaining citizenship.[20] Under the colonial regime, automatic membership within a municipality depended on being born there, being Catholic, being of European or American (not African) descent, and demonstrating loyalty to the sovereign. A foreigner gained membership primarily through residence and willingness to participate in the community, for example, performing communal duties such as holding an administrative office. Place of origin and language, therefore, were not essential criteria for achieving membership in colonial municipalities.[21] After independence, Spanish American republics modeled themselves on the notion of the nation-state, in which membership is equal but dependent on characteristics such as residence and place of birth. Notably, race, religion, estate, and wealth did not affect one's ability to become a citizen, though wealth requirements restricted access to the franchise. Like the Old Regime, republics required new members to swear loyalty to the sovereign, now represented by the laws and constitution rather than the king.[22] Consistent with these broader trends, Gran Colombia's naturalization requirements focused on issues of loyalty, residence, and usefulness. The foreigner had to renounce all ties to other governments and all hereditary titles, swear loyalty to the republic's constitution and laws, and have some useful occupation or skill with which to sustain himself.[23]

At the moment of Venezuela's independence, there already were some Europeans in place, particularly Britons who had fought for the republican armies as mercenaries. Some of the adventurers did quite well, principally by marrying into prominent Venezuelan families. Alternatively, Colonel Edward Stopford became wealthy during the war and later became a powerful member of Venezuelan society. He financed and edited eminent newspapers, moved in top circles, and served as the governor of the province of Cumaná. On the other hand, most foreign veterans who remained after the war did not flourish to this degree. Many of these veterans had trouble earning a living and remained relatively poor. Of a sample of 391 mercenary veterans, 82 percent remained in the military or led lives too obscure to remain in government

records. By the 1820s, many of the poor British mercenaries had married local women and settled into domestic lives.[24]

At the same time as these ex-mercenaries of modest means assimilated into
Venezuelan life, they maintained a level of group cohesion and identity. For
example, on the evening of May 31, 1823, a noisy fight between an English
couple, William and Harriet Matilda Alton, caught the attention of their Caracas neighbors. William was an ex-mercenary and now a tailor, and on this
night he beat Matilda so savagely that she nearly died. Five neighbors, all British ex-mercenaries, came into the house and intervened on her behalf. They
threatened to kill William, removed Matilda from the house, and served as
witnesses in the trial against her husband. When interrogated, William appeared unrepentant and rather blandly explained that he beat her so badly
simply because he lost patience with her. Matilda formally suggested that
they separate and that William provide her with alimony of sixteen pesos per
month, and he accepted the arrangement. The court agreement also stipulated
that William would face no criminal charges, "that this proceeding cannot
now or at any time be used prejudicially against his good reputation,"[25] and
that he would pay the court costs. Though this agreement offered little deter-
rence to domestic abuse, it was typical of similar cases and indicated no special treatment for foreigners. The entire event demonstrated that this group
of ex-mercenaries both maintained internal cohesion and had integrated into
local conditions; they lived near each other, they looked after another British
family, and they used the local justice system to resolve a domestic conflict.

The second main group of foreigners was composed of merchants who arrived in the wake of independence, hoping to make a fortune in transatlantic
trade. Compared both to Venezuelan merchants and to foreign war veterans,
these new arrivals tended to be much wealthier and better situated to take advantage of transatlantic trade. They had trade networks already established
throughout the Atlantic world, which the local merchants were only just beginning to create. The foreigners also enjoyed the protection of the government from their respective countries and exemption from military service.

While poor war veterans blended into their surroundings, the wealthy merchant class did not integrate into Venezuelan society, but rather remained distant and aloof. Like British merchants elsewhere throughout Latin America,
wealthy foreigners in Venezuela tended to live apart;[26] they socialized among
themselves, imported cooks and artisans to have things done in the familiar
way, and married among each other. John Hankshaw, who lived in Venezuela
from 1832 to 1834, observed, "The English, Americans, and Germans, who

compose the largest part of merchant activity, do not copy the natives in their manner of living," and would eat or live like the natives only if they lacked money.[27]

Foreign attitudes facilitated this segregation, as, apparently, Europeans had a rather dim view of the natives. Sir Robert Ker Porter, Britain's envoy in Caracas from 1825 to 1842, recorded in his diary in 1825: "I have seen many uncivilized states and have lived years amongst them and have found that there must be a certain degree [of] education (but more particularly *Moral*) wove into the mass ere *freedom or liberty* is let loose amongst them. If I can judge from the very short time I have been here—then these of the South Americans are still wide of the time—ignorant, bigoted, prejudiced—insolent—proud—and literally wanting the common politeness of a savage."[28]

Hankshaw had a somewhat more positive view of the locals, but he also considered them to be morally deficient ("cruel and licentious"), and he quite casually wrote about the "mental superiority" of whites and Europeans.[29] He spoke of Venezuelans in highly racialized terms, noting, "They suffer pain with great stoicism, partly because of the apathy of their minds, and partly perhaps on account of the less [*sic*] degree of refinement of their nervous systems. Comparatively indifferent to pain themselves, they are prepared to inflict it upon others, and in their nature they are generally cruel."[30]

In the same pages where Hankshaw described the intellectual and moral inferiority of Venezuelans, he blamed the lack of social mixing not on the Europeans but rather on the fact that local elites were jealous of the foreigners: "A jealousy of foreigners prevails to a considerable extent; perhaps because they find themselves outstripped by them in commercial enterprise, or outshone by them in their establishments, and greater means: hence, [the foreign merchants] are confined chiefly to associating with each other, except at public places. Occasionally they intermarry with foreigners, but even this is not effectual in removing the barrier to social intercourse."[31] Notably, neither Hankshaw nor Porter seemed to consider that the foreigners' condescending attitude contributed to these social problems.

For their part, Venezuelans from all strata resented the wealth and aloofness of the foreigners. The artisans suffered because the foreigners imported their own goods or artisans and thus denied opportunities to locals. In 1828, a prominent Creole named Alamo wrote to President Bolívar to complain, "These [foreign] men offer nothing useful to the country, because they bring their own dependents, their cooks, all their food . . . to the point of sending their clothes to Europe or the colonies to be washed . . . they have put all the artisans in a final state of misery . . . the foreigners cause not just these evils, but also they are extracting gold and silver which they buy from indigent and desperate families, for a third of its value, and often they pay in rice, grain, or biscuits."[32]

However, this shabby treatment did not go entirely unrequited; Venezuelans proved they could treat foreigners quite poorly, as well. For instance, Hankshaw observed that among judges of the lower courts of justice "there is also a strong prejudice against foreigners, and a disposition to allow their own countrymen to escape, if it is only upon strangers that they have been the aggressors."[33] The 1820s witnessed many misunderstandings and conflicts as foreigners mingled with locals who had suffered a decade of warfare, were undergoing a rapid political transformation, and often found the presence of foreigners to be politically, economically, culturally, and religiously threatening.

Of the foreigners, the Spanish got the worst. In Venezuelan court cases and public debates, opponents frequently referred to each other as *godo* (literally, "Goth," but connoting Spaniard, Royalist, conservative), a synonym for enemy of freedom, enlightenment, and the republic. In 1823, the Bogotá government expelled Spaniards from Gran Colombian territory, excepting those who had served in the republican military, on the grounds that Spaniards "discredit the government . . . foment disorder against the Constitution. . . . [They are] truly dreadful enemies." Venezuelans, however, protested this edict, as they considered it to be unjust, illiberal, and bad for business. They enforced the expulsion inconsistently and Iberians continued to live in Venezuela throughout the 1820s.[34]

Notably, in other countries in the circum-Caribbean, the threat of a Spanish invasion also caused governments and citizens to suspect and mistreat Spaniards. Due both to fears of an attack and to rivalry between Mexican and Spanish merchants, Mexico expelled Spaniards in 1827, 1829, and 1833. In response to Spain's attack on Mexico in 1829, the Central American federation forbade Spaniards from serving in the legislature, and member-state Guatemala expelled all Spaniards suspected of disloyalty. As in Gran Colombia, the calls for expulsion in Mexico and Guatemala were never carried out fully. On the other hand, Argentina, which was geographically very far removed from a Spanish threat, never reduced the civil rights of Spaniards or expelled them.[35]

Another category of foreigners, the Protestants and Jews, also endured precarious conditions. The colonial government had prohibited the practice of any religion other than Roman Catholicism. With independence, the government opened its doors to non-Catholics, but the legal status of religious tolerance remained ambiguous. The 1821 constitution itself made no mention of religion. Nonetheless, the constitution's epilogue, which took the form of a letter from the constituent congress to the people of Colombia, referred to Catholicism as "the religion of our fathers, and it is and will be the Religion of the State. . . . [T]he Government authorizes the necessary contributions for the Sacred Religion." Such language offered some solace to Catholic loyalists, but it neither secured the church's monopoly nor declared toleration. Bible societies, which promoted Protestantism and openly opposed the Catholic Church, arrived from Britain and the United States in 1821 and 1825, respectively. By 1823, there were eighteen Masonic lodges found throughout the country, including ones founded by American and British ex-patriots. In 1825, two hundred Scots arrived to establish a community, and they brought their own pastor.[36] The government, therefore, did not clearly define the status of non-Catholic religions but in practice supported pluralism.

Though liberal intellectuals promoted religious tolerance and recognized such a policy as necessary to attract immigrants and foreign capital, popular sentiments also viewed non-Catholics with discomfort.[37] In 1826, a Caracas priest named Santana published a pamphlet entitled *The Serpent of Moses,* which attacked proponents of religious freedom, particularly liberals and Masons. The pamphlet caused so many street disturbances that authorities charged Santana with sedition.[38] Sir Robert Ker Porter made frequent reference in his journal to bigotry against Protestants. One of the topics he mentioned numerous times was the problem of burial. All cemeteries in the country were Catholic, and the church would not allow non-Catholics to be interred in its ground. In 1825, he complained that deceased Protestants typically "get taken up in the night, by the bigoted population, and thrown to the Vultures, who prowl in multitudes in the vicinity of the city."[39] His journal contains numerous instances in which he performed the funeral services over Protestants from various countries and buried them in any decent land he could find.[40]

These problems with burial were fundamentally religious rather than national. Priests also forbade Venezuelan Protestants from being buried in church cemeteries.[41] Yet they interred foreign Catholics without problem.[42] Indeed, struggles over burials may have preceded independence. Pamela Voekel shows that late colonial Mexican urban elites promoted an "enlightened" piety that embraced a more individualistic, rational religiosity and that conflicted with the baroque, ornate, and hierarchical practices of the Catholic Church. As one sphere of this reform, proponents advocated simpler burials in cemeteries away from churchyards in order to simplify the ritual and comply with new medical standards of hygiene.[43] No study on this subject exists for Venezuela. Nonetheless, we find similar arguments in 1824, in the coastal town of San Pablo, when the mayor and priest got into a lengthy legal battle because the priest refused to intern a local man suspected of being a Protestant. The mayor insisted that the priest could not simply bury the body in open ground because it was unhygienic and that the deceased deserved a proper burial because he was a loyal, enlightened republican.[44]

By the 1830s, some of these problems had been resolved. On February 12, 1834, Congress legislated freedom of religion. Two weeks later, Ker Porter inaugurated Venezuela's first Protestant cemetery. Several hundred prominent Venezuelans attended, including the president and other officials, to demonstrate their support.[45] That same year, President José Antonio Páez assisted in the establishment of the country's first Anglican chapel, led by a bishop from Barbados.[46]

In another part of the country, a colony of foreign Jewish merchants from the Dutch-Caribbean island of Curacao did not fare so well. Throughout the eighteenth century, Curacao merchants had done a brisk business in contraband with the Spanish mainland. The independence wars, however, had disrupted Spanish American trade and, by the 1820s, commercial activity had not revived. From the 1810s to the 1830s, therefore, Curacao merchants emigrated to find more prosperous locations throughout the Caribbean, in New York City, and, principally, in the port cities of Gran Colombia. The Gran Colombian government encouraged this immigration in order to stimulate economic activity; as early as 1819, independence leaders officially invited Jewish merchants to settle in their territory.[47] Thus, in 1823, a contingent of Curacao Jews settled in the western Venezuelan city of Coro, which is the mainland port closest to Curacao.

Despite the government's approval of these immigrants, native *corianos* (residents of Coro) disliked the Jews for the same reasons that Venezuelans objected to other foreigner merchants: they benefited from their well-established trade networks throughout the Dutch and British Empires and remained somewhat isolated, living in their own quarter of town, marrying only other Jews, and integrating into the local society at a minimal level. Additionally, this particular foreign group evoked traditional anti-Semitic hatred.

By 1830, several *vecinos* of Coro became so distressed that they complained to the central government. They lamented the presence of this "horde of

Jews," whom they considered "monopolists, bad debtors, usurers, locusts, and vagabonds." The Jews lacked "good customs, national character, a spirit to conserve virtues . . . and they have no respect for Christianity."[48] Tensions rose to the point that, in 1831, a mob attacked the Jewish community, beat several Jews, and damaged their property. The local government quelled the mob and, though some of the Jews returned to Curacao, the majority remained in Coro.

Conclusion

With the advent of independence in Latin America, the 1820s opened up the potential for a rapid leap in transatlantic trade and migration. This decade set a precedent that has been in place ever since, in which the flow of goods and peoples is far more free and of much higher volume than in the preceding centuries. Increased trade and immigration will always bring sociopolitical stresses as open doors threaten local customs and benefit people unevenly. Consequently, not all Venezuelans welcomed the spirit of openness, and foreigners lived under precarious conditions. Trade relations were clearly the dominant theme of foreign relations and migration during these years. Europeans came not so much for military purposes, entertainment, or adventure, or to found utopian societies, but rather to trade. The story of foreigners in the young republic also shows how very different cultures throughout the Atlantic world intermingled both amicably and abusively but continued to jostle along together in the interest of trade.

Among the many changes that this decade brought to Venezuela, one of most dramatic was the presence of numerous non-Hispanic foreigners. During the colonial period, peninsular visitors and immigrants were foreigners, but they were members of the same Hispanic empire. Further, though Jews and Protestants had engaged in contraband with colonists in *tierra firma,* their presence in Venezuela occurred at a clandestine, superficial level—they remained in the shadows and tended not to venture beyond the coast.[49] In contrast, in the 1820s for the first time non-Hispanic non-Catholics lived, worked, befriended, traded, and married with the local population.

Foreigners enjoyed virtual legal equality with nationals as well as additional benefits such as consular protection, established trade networks, and forgiveness from militia service. The number of foreigners was fairly small and, for the most part, composed of two groups: mercenaries who had fought in the war and more recently arrived merchants. Foreigners integrated into the local society to different degrees depending on their status. By and large, poor foreigners integrated far more than did those who could afford to segregate themselves. For their part, Venezuelans benefited economically from the foreigners and also resented their distant, aloof attitude.

One of the most obvious shifts during this decade was the practice of religious toleration, which marked a change in popular sentiments and offered the state an opportunity to consolidate its power. The liberal theories of the day, the cultural requirements for international trade, and the daily practices of accommodating the foreigners forced even resistant Venezuelans to tolerate diverse religions. As Charles-Louis Secondat Montesquieu had written some eighty years earlier, commerce has the potential to improve manners and bring peace between nations.[50] Though some Venezuelans treated non-Catholics poorly, the governments in Bogotá and Caracas welcomed and protected foreign merchants in order to foster international trade. Government officials showed public support for the first Protestant cemetery and chapel and convinced the Jews to remain in Coro. Though foreigners complained about Venezuelans in general, they had great praise for José Antonio Páez, the regional military leader and strongman.[51] The state's desire to ensure religious tolerance overall was effective and, therefore, served as an area for the government to exert its authority. The presence of foreigners, then, helped the state to pursue its liberal agenda: to foster free trade, promote the standard of a unitary legal code, support religious diversity, and dominate the Catholic Church.

Though a part of Gran Colombia, in a certain sense Venezuelan sovereignty was at an all-time high as no foreign entity could dictate domestic economics or politics. This condition would become yet more solidified with full independence in 1830 and would persist until the emergence of a neocolonial order in the 1870s. Ironically, political-economic practices in the 1820s foreshadowed the neocolonial conditions that would make sovereignty so tenuous decades later. Elites of the 1820s intentionally designed the economy around the export of primary commodities to foreign markets and, therefore, were dependent on foreign demand. The state promoted free trade and the interests of foreigners, even to the point of suppressing opposition from fellow Venezuelans. Such policies were, at the time, consistent with revolutionary ideologies of liberalism, secularism, and nationalism. In this first decade after independence there was a real optimism that expanding trade and Enlightenment ideals would bring unparalleled wealth, order, and sovereignty. Ironically, some fifty years later, these very conditions had morphed into a neocolonial regime in which the economy depended on foreign demand for commodities, foreign economic influence eroded the state's sovereignty, and the government supported foreign and local elite interests rather than national interests. In the 1820s, however, few could have foreseen such an outcome.

Notes

1. Porter, *Sir Robert Ker Porter's Caracas Diary,* December 9 and 10, 1825. Ker Porter's diary does not mention Colonel Feudenthal's first name.

2. Ibid., December 3, 1825, and January 6, 1826.

3. Archivo General de la Nación de Venezuela (hereafter cited as AGN), Civiles y Criminales (CC), 1826, B-06.

4. For more on Stahl and his ill-fated hotel, see Walter, *Los Alemanes en Venezuela,* 85–88.

5. For the most part, colonial Spanish American merchants could trade only with other Hispanics. Occasionally, during wartime when Spanish shipping was over-extended, Spanish Americans could trade with merchants from neutral countries.

6. See McKinley, *Pre-Revolutionary Caracas,* 63.

7. Deas, "Venezuela, Colombia, and Ecuador", 511. Also see Bushnell, *Santander Regime,* 1.

8. For example, in 1799 the *consulado* and *cabildo* of Caracas argued against the Crown's trade restrictions. Their discourse about property rights sounded nearly liberal in content in that they asserted, "Their private rights practically entitled them to violate political dictates, which came close to claiming that private property rights came before political decisions." Adelman, *Sovereignty and Revolution,* 113.

9. *El Venezolano,* Caracas, Venezuela, no. 84, May 1, 1824; *El Argos,* Caracas, Venezuela, April 8, 1825, 1–2.

10. Polar, *Diccionario,* "Comercio exterior."

11. Carrillo Batalla, *Proyecto Cuentas Nacionales,* 67.

12. Polar, *Diccionario,* "Comercio exterior."

13. Walter, *Los Alemanes en Venezuela,* 82–84. Buenos Aires housed Latin America's largest British population; by 1825, this city's 1,355 British merchants were clearly the dominant foreign presence. Shumway, *The Case of the Ugly Suitor,* 56.

14. The majority of these foreigners were in the vicinity of Caracas, though there were also concentrations in the cities of Angostura, Puerto Cabello, and Maracaibo. Cunill Grau, *Geografía,* 124; Tosta, "Extranjeros," 34.

15. "Gaceta del Gobierno," July 4, 1828, found in Perazzo, *Historia de la Inmigración,* 18–22.

16. In the early 1830s, one English mining operation near Puerto Cabello employed two hundred Englishmen, who served as administrators and foremen to Venezuelan workers. Hankshaw, *Reminiscences,* 168.

17. See Eastwood, *The Rise of Nationalism,* chapter 5.

18. 1821 Venezuelan Constitution, Article 4.

19. Ibid., Articles 88 and 96. In Central America and Argentina, also, foreigners enjoyed such a comfortable status that there was little incentive to naturalize. Dym, "Citizen of Which Republic," 509; Vogel, "New Citizens," 126–27.

20. Benton, *Law and Colonial Cultures,* chapter 6; Dym, "Citizen of Which Republic"; Vogel, "New Citizens."

21. Herzog, *Defining Nations,* introduction.

22. For naturalization requirements in Central America and Argentina, see Dym, "Citizen of Which Republic," 488–89; and Vogel, "New Citizens," 116–17, respectively.

23. Law of July 4, 1823. Naturalization requirements for Central America in the 1820s also specified residency or usefulness (the "exercise of a science, art, or office"). Dym, "Citizen of Which Republic," 489.

24. M. Brown, *Adventuring,* 174–83.

25. AGN, CC, 1823, A-02, f7b.

26. Guenther, *British Merchants,* 69–70. Also see David Rock's chapter on the British in Buenos Aires in this volume.

27. Hankshaw, *Reminiscences,* 172.

28. Porter, *Sir Robert Ker Porter's Caracas Diary,* December 31, 1825.

29. Hankshaw, *Reminiscences,* 207.

30. Ibid., 214.

31. Ibid., 211.

32. Cunill Grau, *Geografía,* 124–25.

33. Hankshaw, *Reminiscences,* 219.

34. Cunill Grau, *Geografía,* 120–23.

35. Vogel, "New Citizens," 124–25.

36. Giacomo Cassese, "The Religious Conflict in Venezuela during the Revolutionary Age of 1810 to 1830" (diss., Lutheran School of Theology, 1996), 155–59. Masons, who overtly challenged the power of the Catholic Church, had established their first lodge by 1808. Most of the independence heroes were Masons.

37. See Mary Watters, *A History of the Church in Venezuela, 1810–1930* (Chapel Hill: University of North Carolina Press, 1933), 129–30.

38. AGN, CC, 1826, S-07.

39. Porter, *Sir Robert Ker Porter's Caracas Diary,* December 11, 1825.

40. For instance, see ibid., April 26, 1826, and March 7, 1828.

41. Archivo Arquidiocesano, Caracas, Sección Judicial, Carpeta 141, año 1824.

42. E. Lambert, "Muerte."

43. Voekel, *Alone before God.*

44. AGN, CC, 1824, A-19.

45. Porter, *Sir Robert Ker Porter's Caracas Diary,* February 26, 1834. Buenos Aires established its first Protestant cemetery in 1821. See Jeremy Howat, *Register of Burials in the First Protestant Cemetery, 1821 to 1833,* http://www.argbrit.org/StJBurials/Socorro1821-1825.htm (accessed September 4, 2009).

46. Cassese, "Religious Conflict in Venezuela," 161.

47. Bakkum, *La Comunidad Judeo-Curazoleña,* 11–16.

48. Archivo de la Asamblea Nacional, Caracas, Senado, vol. 39, 103–11, Coro 24 de abril de 1830, f3b. See also AGN, I&J, Tomo 38 (1831), Expediente 2.

49. See Ramón Aizpurua, *Curazao y la costa de Caracas: Introducción al estudio del contrabando de la provincia de Venezuela en tiempos de la Compañía Guipuzcoana, 1730–1780* (Caracas: Academia Nacional de Historia, 1993).

50. Montesquieu, *The Spirit of the Laws,* 20:1–2.

51. See Mondolfi Gudat, *Páez visto por los ingleses.*

10

Porteño Liberals and Imperialist Emissaries in the Rio de la Plata

Rivadavia and the British

David Rock

In their introduction, Gabriel Paquette and Matthew Brown stressed continuity and transition—the taints of the past and the markers of the future—as the principal features of the 1820s in Latin America. Following emancipation, transatlantic contacts prolonged ties with Western Europe and "resurgent empire" followed the re-exploration of the region by Europeans. The decade also marked a cycle linked to European investment. The London financial bubble of mid-decade disrupted the flow of funds into Latin America and contributed to an economic collapse that weakened the early post-independence regimes. Toward 1830, the outward-looking liberal states dissolved; introspective, rural-based caudillos commonly displaced them.

The categories defined by Paquette and Brown grew strikingly visible in the Rio de la Plata under Bernardino Rivadavia.[1] His liberal reforms affecting land, government, civil liberties, the church, and the military were based largely on European precedents or derived from European intellectuals. They included modernizing measures, headed by the attempt to build a postcolonial liberal state—a task completed in Argentina only after 1860—alongside conservative, regressive legislation like the effort to re-impose the *conchabo,* a local form of serfdom. The Rivadavian reforms provided instances of complex re-synthesis between the old and the new. As an example, the constitution of 1826 juxtaposed forms of representation from the "age of democratic revolutions" with centralized government inherited from the Spanish Bourbon era of 1776–1810. Against those who stressed Rivadavia's innovative and progressive credentials, Vicente Fidel López, the distinguished nineteenth-century

Argentine historian, emphasized his ties with the Spanish Enlightenment and his aspirations to emulate it. In López's view, he never transcended the idea that "Charles III and its counselors had made Spain the most brilliant and attractive country in Europe."[2]

In the Rio de la Plata, resurgent empire during this period took two principal forms. One appeared in the influence of contemporary European intellectuals, headed by Jeremy Bentham and Benjamin Constant. Rivadavia's supporters frequently invoked Benthamite themes like the freedom of the press, the value of public debate, and the importance of "beneficent and liberating institutions" such as the newly founded University of Buenos Aires.[3] Meanwhile, members of the Buenos Aires legislature read lengthy citations from Constant in discussions of voting reform.[4] Political forms of neocolonialism grew visible in the efforts of British merchants and investors to strengthen their influence in Buenos Aires. The British first arrived during the late colonial period in 1806 and began putting down roots in the city following the May Revolution against Spanish rule in 1810.

As early as 1811, the British claimed to command what a merchant called a "beneficial though quite indirect influence over public affairs and public opinion at the seat of government."[5] In 1817, a US diplomat accused the British of planning to establish a protectorate in the Rio de la Plata. He reported he had heard British merchants arguing that the Porteños of Buenos Aires should be "placed under the guardianship of some other nation for twenty or thirty years. . . . The drift of all this was not hard to be discovered . . . [and] it meant the guardianship of England."[6] In 1821, a US consul described British influence in terms identical to a textbook definition of informal empire. He complained that the British "practically control the public institutions. . . . England derives from [La Plata] and from Chile all the advantages of colonial dependence, without the responsibility or expense of civil or military administration."[7] In this period, the liberal press in Buenos Aires recurrently denied charges by critics that Rivadavia intended to encourage the British to replace the Spaniards as the province's colonial masters.[8]

Paquette and Brown noted "the persistence of mutual influence" as another hallmark of the 1820s, implying that Latin America influenced Europe as well as the reverse. The Latin American impact on Europe became visible as a form of European rediscovery of the Americas led by the British. As R. A. Humphreys once noted, "It is doubtful whether there has ever been so general a demand in England for information about this vast area and, proportionately, so liberal a supply, as in the eighteen-twenties."[9] In the Plata region,

British soldiers, entrepreneurs, and explorers traversed the westward colonial routes from Buenos Aires into Chile or went northwest to the silver mines of Potosi and to Peru. They assessed the area for trade, settlers, and mining and sized it up as a field for British investors.[10] They became classic "vanguard" figures of capitalism who, to cite Mary Louise Pratt, adopted "a goal-oriented rhetoric of conquest and achievement."[11]

The liberal regime dominated by Rivadavia formed in late 1820 and collapsed in late 1829. Ties with the British evolved in a similar circular form. In the ascendant early years of the decade, British settlers established a niche in Buenos Aires, but in its downward phase after 1825 their position weakened. As the regime itself disintegrated, numerous merchants fell bankrupt. Ethnic and religious tension erupted between Britons and Porteños, and British informal influence diminished. A commentary in the *Edinburgh Review,* particularly valid for the Rio de la Plata, exemplified the way British attitudes changed in the course of the decade: pessimism replaced high expectations; mistrust displaced confidence. "Everything involving the mention of South America was shunned as fatal, or abandoned with a horror fully as undiscriminating as the previous calenture. . . . Our extravagant folly one season could only be surpassed by our alarm and despondency the next."[12]

Rivadavia: A Sketch

Bernardino Rivadavia (1780–1845) embodied the Janus-faced qualities of early Porteño liberalism that looked toward the future and the past. He belonged to an upper-class family of Spanish origin, formerly linked to the colonial administration and to Spanish commerce. His career revealed a progressive pro-European outlook, mingling British and French influences with conservative orientations from the Spanish Bourbons. Serving in the second triumvirate in Buenos Aires in 1811 and 1812, for example, he supported a ban on the slave trade as instituted in Britain in 1807 and a lowering of tariff duties as sought by British merchants. Simultaneously, he promoted a centralized administration reminiscent of *borbonismo* that foreshadowed both the regime known as *unitarismo,* during his presidency in 1826 and 1827, and the Argentine liberal oligarchy of the post-1860 period.

As a diplomat in Europe from 1814 to 1819, Rivadavia appeared a conservative, as, for instance, when he attempted to recruit a European prince for the throne he hoped to establish in Buenos Aires. Yet he was no absolutist and his monarchism proved pragmatic and tactical. By exalting constitutional monarchy, he flattered the British while attempting to enlist other allies to fit Buenos Aires into the European system established by the Congress of Vienna. Monarchism formed part of a strategy aiming to neutralize Spain and consolidate independence. In other respects Rivadavia appeared a progressive figure. When he visited London, he committed himself to a program of port works, agrarian colonization, and mining and formed an attachment with Bentham. "Je n'ai cesse de mediter vos principes en matière de legislation," he claimed in a letter to Bentham in 1823.[13]

Many of Rivadavia's reforms during his term as chief minister in Buenos Aires from 1821 to 1824 attacked the foundations of colonial society. He established a citizens' militia to undermine notions of the military inherited from Spanish rule as a privileged corporate elite. He closed monastic houses and eliminated the Cabildo of Buenos Aires, which he condemned as bastions of the colonial regime. He promoted the diffusion of printing and the importation of books in Spanish translation published in Europe that "offered a space in which the [new] values of the postcolonial order were contested and defined."[14] His government encouraged foreign merchants to establish banks and urged immigration by northern European farmers in order to promote the Protestant work ethic. He endorsed the controversial Baring Loan of 1824, whose funds were swallowed up in brokers' commissions or dissipated in warfare.[15] The universal suffrage law of 1821 in Buenos Aires appeared a progressive measure in advance of even Bentham, (whose conversion to democracy occurred later), although it aimed to promote stability rather than enfranchise the masses. Following the political unrest of 1820, the so-called Year of Anarchy, the Partido del Orden that eventually took power urged increasing the size of the electorate in an attempt to dilute the power of factions.[16]

Reform applied to the denizens and institutions of the city alone. Reverse orientations inflected most measures in rural areas, where Benthamism remained absent. Convicted beggars faced compulsory military service, the same fate meted out under the colonial system.[17] Land legislation perpetuated Iberian practices based on Roman law. Under the emphyteusis system, the government leased state land in large units, which tended to disseminate *latifundismo* rather than smallholder capitalism. Under the proposed Unitario Constitution of 1826, the president appointed and controlled provincial governors, while the powers of the governors largely replicated those of the late colonial *intendentes*. Ideological and institutional eclecticism—the old mixed with the new, the colonial with the postcolonial, interwoven British, French,

Spanish, or North American models—permeated the repertoire of government legislation.

The British in Buenos Aires

Porteño liberals argued that greater contact with Britain would promote growth, consolidate revenue and government authority, and fit the country into the European system of alliances. Their views contrasted with previous colonial attitudes. Tainted by clerical influence, colonial policy toward Britain shunned all contact with a nation epitomizing "greed, cruelty, deceit and unlimited avarice."[18] When Rivadavia became chief minister in 1821, the British residents of Buenos Aires welcomed the positive climate for business and trade. "It is wonderful to observe," wrote William Parish Robertson, a leading Scottish merchant, "the different aspect which affairs in general have taken. Everything breathes activity and public spirit; and public prosperity is the natural result."[19] He added that "since the present Executive Government came into power, it has pursued one undeviating line of protection to ourselves individually and encouragement to the community of Great Britain."[20]

Ignoring Catholic opposition, the Rivadavians sponsored British immigration and extended civil liberties to British residents. They were permitted to own property and to become naturalized citizens; they enjoyed religious freedom and were authorized to build churches; they could intermarry with *criollas* so long as they raised their children as Catholics; they were allowed to consecrate a cemetery and were no longer forced by Catholic priests, as had sometimes occurred previously, to cast the dead into the Rio de la Plata. The Treaty of Amity, Commerce, and Navigation of 1825 granted the British a special position in Buenos Aires as a resident mercantile community. Their privileges included exemption from military service, a prized status in a society susceptible to civil war, where men were subject to forced enlistment. The treaty represented another re-synthesis between the old and the new. It intertwined the eighteenth-century principle of privileged standing for a favored group with nineteenth-century liberal objectives of development and modernization.[21]

In the early 1820s, British trade with Buenos Aires surpassed that of all the other Spanish American states combined, climbing to around half that with Brazil (where Rio de Janeiro commanded exceptional importance as a re-export center for British goods).[22] Robertson noted the expanding sales of "plain and simple Calicoes. . . . England is the great Mart for the Producer of

Buenos Ayres; and British imports . . . are consumed over the whole country and by all classes."[23] British commercial practices embodied the principles proposed by Adam Smith in *The Wealth of Nations,* in which merchants attempted to increase the size of the market and the range of suppliers. They sold imported factory goods as cheaply as possible and attracted local sellers by paying higher prices than their competitors in the export trade. As Robertson noted, the British merchants operated in a directly opposite fashion to Spanish colonial merchants, who based their business on monopoly, scarcity, and low turnover: "While the colonial system existed, all Manufacture and other European goods sold here at three times their present prices; while the Produce of the Country was given in exchange at a fourth part of what is now paid for it."[24]

As trade surged, the British community in Buenos Aires grew to around four thousand by 1830, a larger number than everywhere else in Spanish America, in a total city population of seventy thousand. In 1825, the peak year of immigration, around forty ships arrived at Buenos Aires bringing British settlers, many of them artisans.[25] During the first phase of contact around 1810 through 1820, men comprised an overwhelming proportion of the settlers, and at this point, up-and-coming young British merchants married upper-class Porteño women. The trend toward assimilation diminished around 1820 with the arrival of larger numbers of British women as wives, siblings, and servants. In Robertson's view, matriarchal influence promoted cultural and ethnic segregation between Britons and Porteños: "[With the] increase in English families many of the female heads gradually withdrew from native society; while new arrivals, finding an ample sufficiency of English [people], looked for no other or farther society."[26]

In the 1820s, the British residents of Buenos Aires developed into an expatriate cluster with their own associations and commemorative festivals. The merchants promoted ethnic mutualism and in 1827 attempted to establish a philanthropic fund covering the entire British and Irish community.[27] As intended by the commercial treaty, religion became a prominent instrument in cementing ethnicity.[28] A Presbyterian Church founded in Buenos Aires in 1825 was followed in 1826 by an Anglican Church on passage of the Consular Chaplaincy Act by Parliament, which committed the British government to match funds raised locally for churches and hospitals. The clerics preached fidelity to the homeland, encouraged endogamy, and founded Anglophone schools. As ethnic identity strengthened, marriage, education, religion, and national origins grew closely connected. "The religious clanship is the secret of the progress and power of the community," wrote a late-nineteenth century Scots-Argentine historian. "It is only logical that the history of the [Scots] colony should be intimately interwoven with that of its pastors."[29] Ethnicity, reinforced by religion, strengthened the separate identity of British residents, facilitating their role as a mercantile nexus between Britain and Buenos Aires.

Scouts and Prospectors

From 1817 to 1825, British promoters, entrepreneurs, and adventurers explored the interior of the Plata and scouted out gold and silver mines in the Andes. In this guise they became vectors for the transmission of Latin American influences to Western Europe. The Rio de la Plata enjoyed a particularly high reputation in Britain, originating in the brief British conquest of Buenos Aires in 1806. The invaders seized a hoard of silver en route to Buenos Aires from the mines of upper Peru, which they sent to England and paraded through the city of London.[30] Early British promoters of the Plata included Major Alexander Gillespie, who in 1818 published an account of his experiences of 1806 as a soldier and prisoner of war. Gillespie advertised Buenos Aires in the light of the revolution of 1810. The revolution became the source of the "elevated independent rank [the country] has finally attained among the nations. . . . No country in the world offers a more enviable situation at the moment." He emphasized the liberal orientations of the governments of Buenos Aires, visible in the efforts to eliminate "papist superstition," and predicted the city would surpass Boston and Philadelphia as a center of commerce.[31] Notions of the Plata as a fabulously rich, unknown, but now accessible and exploitable area of the world permeated British writings. Alexander Caldcleugh, for example, a visitor from 1819 to 1821, referred to a "great field being thrown open to British enterprise by revolutionary changes and the adoption of a liberal and enlightened policy."[32]

A sophisticated piece published anonymously in 1819 compared several different parts of Spanish America in order to assert the superior qualities of Buenos Aires against everywhere else. The points of comparison included the impact of the wars of independence on each area or social institutions as defined by criteria of equality and the prevalence of slavery. In all these respects, the Plata enjoyed superiority. "Not the slightest connection" tied the Plata with an area like Venezuela currently devastated by civil war or with slaveholding societies like St. Domingue because in the Plata "no class [existed] which has an interest in the depression or destruction of any other." In this part of the continent, greater equality and a very low population density would provide a buttress against the formation of a dictatorship. Consequently, "there is no country which better deserves the attention of Britons than the provinces of the River Plate. They contain an immense extent of fertile soil, blessed with a salubrious climate, and fitted for the growth of every species of product. Under a liberal government they must soon teem with inhabitants and wealth. They must every day abound with new commodities. . . . To England therefore they open the prospect of a constantly increasing market for the sale of her goods."[33] Prospects for mining and trade also drew the British into the region. Samuel Haigh, only twenty-two years old at the time of his voyage to Buenos Aires in 1817, typified the adventurous young men lured by greed, imagination, and naiveté. Haigh was working as a clerk in the city of London when he received an unexpected summons from a relative: "I found my wealthy kinsman seated at his desk upon a high counting house stool. . . . [G]reat news had just been received from South America, no less than the opening up of Chile to foreign trade, in consequence of the victory of Chacabuco, gained by the patriots; that this was the time to push for a fortune; he and two partners contemplated sending out a cargo to get the cream of the market; if I would undertake its management, I should have an opportunity of filling my coffers with ingots of gold and silver."[34] John Miers, too, was impelled by the "immense fortune" he expected to make in Spanish America. His plan required transporting tons of copper-refining equipment by ship round Cape Horn to Valparaiso while he traveled to Chile by land from Buenos Aires. Miers exemplified contemporary British attitudes toward Spanish America. He praised the newly minted (often Bentham-inspired) institutions of the former Spanish colonies and the republican elites who embodied "the rising spirit of illumination and freedom" but disparaged the South American people as backward and uncouth. Using a nineteenth-century trope, he assimilated the Argentine gauchos with Middle Eastern and North African Arabs. Thus, a gaucho minstrel he encountered "played nearly all the day, and all the evening, some wild notes on an old guitar, occasionally singing through his nose a melancholy, barbarous, Saracenic air."[35]

Miers illustrated another feature of European discourse about Latin America when relating the experience he and his pregnant wife endured attempting to cross the Andes. The couple set off from the western city of Mendoza, but only fifty miles out in the foothills, the woman gave birth at the roadside. They endured days of privation out in the wild, but fortunately they were traveling with a local resident, Scottish physician "Dr. Gillies," who helped Miers carry the woman and child back to Mendoza. The story dramatized the stereotype of an inhospitable, depopulated, and uncivilized American wilderness into which Europeans ventured at their peril.[36] Miers met the same fate as most other British mining entrepreneurs seeking fortunes in Spanish America. His mistakes included attempting to apply water-driven technology developed for British conditions to a semi-arid region of seasonal rainfall. His copper-refining enterprise failed.[37]

In 1825, the Rio Plata Mining Association commissioned Francis Bond Head, a military engineer, to explore mining sites in western Argentina and Chile. He published the best book of the period by a British author: *Rough Notes Taken during Some Rapid Journeys across the Pampas and among the Andes*. The book's fame became evident in references by Charles Darwin and many other subsequent visitors. Head's reputation derived partly from his equestrian prowess. Surpassing the feats of the gauchos, "Galloping Head" could ride more than 150 miles a day across the pampas. During his year in La Plata and Chile he covered 6,000 miles on horseback on a diet of beef and water. Head created a romantic cult of the gauchos and the pampas. He described the unconquered pampas Indians "as fine a set of men as ever existed under the circumstances in which they are placed." His writing about the pampas conveyed a sense of an idyllic environment and of an area of immense productive potential: "The whole country is in such beautiful order that if cities and millions of inhabitants could suddenly be planted at regular intervals and situations, the people would have nothing to do but drive out the cattle to graze, and, without any previous preparation, plough whatever quantity of ground their wants might require."[38]

Eminent mid-nineteenth-century Argentine writers, including Juan Bautista Alberdi and Domingo F. Sarmiento, drew extensively on Head's book. Another British writer, Joseph Andrews, also won a reputation, particularly in Alberdi's eyes, for his lyrical descriptions of the Spanish American terrain. Andrews testified to the way Latin America had captured the European imagination. In the northwestern province of Tucumán, he encountered landscapes that appeared "to an Englishman [like] the fiction of the Arabian nights, or some land of fairy imagination. . . . Nothing that the mind could dwell upon could surpass the scene in beauty and luxuriance."[39] Andrews formulated a uniquely explicit version of informal empire as he described the benefits the British could bring if they were allowed to settle in the country and develop it:

The English are going to take possession of your country, not, indeed, by force of arms against the government; but by a mode of conquest which will be equally beneficial to you and to themselves by bringing the resources of their capital and industry as machinery to raise the hidden treasures of your neglected mountains, and to render your impoverished plains fruitful. They will take possession of your country by placing it under the rule of a spirit of diligence, active labour, and sound moral feelings. They will take possession of your country when they settle amongst you by mingling British blood with that of the fair and lovely daughters of Tucuman.[40]

The invitation met a cold reception. Women and men alike shunned and condemned Andrews, who left Tucumán under a cloud but retained fond memories of his stay: "Farewell delicious Tucuman and hospitable Tucumeses; farewell to your delightful plains, and mighty romantic mountains. Though Englishmen are not to be your brothers in your country's bosom, there is one Englishman who will ever bear towards you the kindly feelings of a brother."[41]

Regime Failure

Difficulties also plagued the small groups of British rural settlers attracted by Rivadavia's promises of land grants on the pampas. In 1825, around 220 mostly Scottish lowlanders, men, women, and children, arrived under contract to William Robertson and his brother John Parish Robertson.[42] The organizers expected to receive free land, but the government failed to deliver on its promises. With the colonists already on their way from Scotland, the brothers purchased an expensive site for their planned settlement at Monte Grande near Buenos Aires. The colony cost far more to set up than it could ever expect to produce and appeared intrinsically doomed. In 1825, too, another 250 prospective British and Irish colonists sailed to Buenos Aires in a second colonizing project organized by John Barber Beaumont, a London entrepreneur.

The colonizing proprietors fostered utopian illusions among their recruits. The Robertsons encouraged their settlers to believe they were setting out to a land of unparalleled freedom and opportunity. Beaumont promised to make "hundreds of families happy and independent [and to] implant on the fertile coasts of the River Plate, the people, customs and energies of industrious Englishmen. He handed out a 'Book of Instructions' founded on the most glorious system of equality, according to the most approved radical principles."[43] The Scots brought out by the Robertsons laid out a settlement at Monte Grande and set about constructing mud houses. Of Beaumont's followers, only fifty reached their destination northwest of Buenos Aires in Entre Rios, where they found themselves marooned in a wilderness. Beaumont's other recruits halted in Buenos Aires before mostly returning to the British Isles.

Many of the problems of the colonizers reflected the tenuousness of government authority. Rivadavia issued numerous grants to British miners and rural settlers but had no means to enforce them, particularly in areas beyond Buenos Aires, outside his jurisdiction. In Entre Rios, the local government ignored the concession to Beaumont, leaving the colonists alone and hungry. In the western Andean provinces, the dominant caudillos refused to recognize Rivadavia's mining grants to companies like the one represented by Francis Head.[44]

The opportunities available to the British deteriorated as the liberal regime weakened. In late 1825, in a conflict that soon drained the treasury of Buenos Aires, war erupted between the United Provinces and the Empire of Brazil for control over the Banda Oriental (modern Uruguay). In the inland provinces, forced enlistment of men and seizures of livestock provoked an anti-Porteño backlash under the clerical slogan "*¡Religión ó Muerte!*" A Brazilian naval blockade disrupted the commerce of Buenos Aires. Trade valued at around £900,000 in 1824 plummeted to only £155,000 in 1826 and 1827.[45]

One unfavorable trend led to another. The decline of trade provoked falling tariff revenues, accelerating the collapse of government finances. When the government printed money to support the army in the Banda Oriental, inflation fueled commercial, financial, and political meltdown. British importers became the victims of *curzo forzoso con efecto retroactivo*—a system of mandatory paper money that could be used to settle previously contracted debts. Rapidly depreciating "forced" paper money liberated indebted domestic consumers but crippled foreign suppliers and creditors. British merchants suffered mounting failures. As they lamented in 1827, worthless paper money and the destruction of trade had "broken their spirits and ruined their resources."[46]

In early 1826 Beaumont dispatched his son to the Plata, who later published an entertaining account of conditions in Buenos Aires and surrounding rural areas during the war with Brazil. The young author illustrated how British attitudes toward Rivadavia suddenly changed from enthusiasm to condemnation. In burlesque style, he noted how Rivadavia's demeanor altered when he became president of the United Provinces in mid-1826. He was no longer the prosaic figure the author once knew in London; the pompous president had become a caricature of Napoleon: "His Excellency slowly advanced towards me, with his hand clenched behind him; whether this too was done in imitation of the great well-known, or to gain something of a counterpoint to the weight and bulk which he bore before him, or to guard his hand from the unhallowed touch of familiarity, it might be equally difficult to determine."[47] Conviviality between Britons and Porteños vanished. Francis Head recalled how Rivadavia had exaggerated the prospects of the western mines to the mining association he represented. "[He had provided] a most brilliant account of the riches of the provinces of the Plata [showing] that the sweepings of the houses, and even the manure of the mules, produced gold, and that precious metal sprung up in the fields like weeds. We can affirm, without hyperbole, that [according to Rivadavia] the Rinconada and the Santa Catalina [mines] contain the greatest riches in the universe."[48]

In the late 1820s the power of the Rivadavian liberals, the so-called Unitarios, crumbled, while that of their opponents, the Federales led by General Juan Manuel de Rosas, increased. In rural Buenos Aires xenophobia and violence unleashed mainly by the Federales enveloped some of the British settlers. A colonist reported how desperadoes attacked his farm, robbed him, and left him for dead. In an outlying village, another British family barely escaped execution when they were accused of pro-Unitario sympathies. On this occasion, the Federales had received orders that "all foreigners should be shot, every man [killed] who from the colour of his hair . . . or by whose physiognomy it might be inferred that he was a Unitarian."[49] Disaster overtook the Monte Grande colony. The Scottish plowmen had never prospered in a rural economy dominated by cattle. They failed to find markets for their crops and dairy products, and their artisans migrated into the city in search of better wages. Foundering from the start, in April 1829 the colony suffered invasion, pillage, and murder by several hundred gauchos supporting the Federales.[50]

The Anglophobia persisted into the following decade, when opposition to the British derived from pro-clerical groups, echoing the bigotry of the colonial era and anticipating Catholic discourse hostile to British capitalism during later periods. In 1833, a Catholic member of the legislature of Buenos Aires denounced a proposal to relax existing matrimonial law and permit marriages between local women and so-called Protestants in non-Catholic ceremonies. He argued that British merchants married Porteñas as part of a deliberate strategy to subvert the Creoles as the country's ruling elite and to ransack the country's riches: "[In permitting] these avaricious and speculating men [to marry local women], nothing would then be reserved for the sons of the country. . . . Before the arrival of these guests, and the gaudy articles they introduced into the market, the country was rich, very rich; now it is poor, very poor." The speaker tied objections to intermarriage to the seizure of the Falkland Islands by the British (on New Year's Day 1833). He claimed the annexation of the islands marked another step in a machination to reduce the entire country to British bondage.[51]

Conclusion

The resurgence of clericalism in Buenos Aires became a marker in the defeat of the liberals and the rise of the Rosas regime in late 1829. By the early 1830s British trade had dwindled to meager levels. In 1822, 167 British ships arrived at Buenos Aires, but in 1831 the total fell to 44.[52] The British community shrank as its members fled Buenos Aires. When he departed from Buenos Aires in 1832 after an eight-year stint as British consul, Woodbine Parish lamented how "our countrymen have lost a good deal of their enthusiasm, which formerly distinguished them here, caused perhaps by the misfortunes which have befallen them."[53] The brief career of Francis Bond Head in South America exemplified the cycle that characterized the decade. Head set out for Buenos Aires with high expectations but returned to Britain in disillusionment. He warned future entrepreneurs to consider "whether in this and other countries of South America, it is prudent to embark [their] capital in any permanent establishment or speculation, or to furnish these Countries with the Loans which some of them are still requiring."[54] He blamed Rivadavia for a sham invitation "to work mines of gold and silver in a country which produced nothing but horses, beef and thistles."[55] The first British efforts to penetrate the Rio de la Plata thus concluded in failure. In the early 1820s, the British viewed Buenos Aires as the gateway to hidden treasure, where "boundless wealth [was] to be had for the gathering." Ten years later, having found "a strange dearth of reapers," they abandoned the quest.[56]

Rivadavia's failures in the 1820s highlighted the embryonic level of state formation and the barriers to political order that took decades to breach. Partly a relic of the Enlightenment, Rivadavia also became a precursor of many Latin American liberal modernizers who overrated the transformative potential of ties with Western Europe or North America. As president in 1826 and 1827, he overstated the capacity of the politicians of Buenos Aires to dictate to the provinces. His Benthamite enthusiasm betrayed the same flaws and ingenuousness as were commonly identified with Bentham himself. "Your position will always be delicate," the French intellectual Detutt de Tracy warned Rivadavia in 1822, "until you make your nation as reasonable as your government."[57]

Notes

1. Rivadavia served as the chief minister of the province of Buenos Aires from 1821 to 1824 and as president of the United Provinces of the Rio de la Plata from 1826 to 1827. The large literature on his career is summarized in Gallo, *The Struggle for an Enlightened Republic*. See also Ricardo Rees Jones, *Bernardino Rivadavia y su negocio minero: Rio de la Plata Mining Association* (Buenos Aires: Editores Librería, 2008).

2. Vicente Fidel López, quoted in Piccirrilli, *Rivadavia,* 2:21.

3. For the connections between Bentham and Rivadavia, see Williford, *Jeremy Bentham in Spanish America.*

4. Ternavasio, *La revolucion del voto,* 87.

5. J. Robertson and W. Robertson, *Letters on South America,* 2:105.

6. H. M. Brackenridge, *Voyage to South America Performed by Order of the American Government in the Years 1817 and 1818 in the Frigate Congress* (London: T. and J. Allman, 1820), 1:289.

7. Quoted in E. Pratt, "Anglo-American Commercial and Political Rivalry," 315.

8. Rees Jones, *Rivadavia y su negocio minero,* 112, citing *El Nacional.*

9. Humphreys, *British Consular Reports,* ix.

10. On mining, see Dawson, *The First Latin American Debt Crisis,* 89; Ricardo D. Salvatore, "Re-Discovering Spanish America: Uses of Travel Literature about Latin America in Britain," *Journal of Latin American Cultural Studies* 8, no. 2 (1999): 199–217. An outstanding recent study is Rees Jones, *Rivadavia y su negocio minero.*

11. M. Pratt, *Imperial Eyes,* 140.

12. *Edinburgh Review* 46, no. 92 (October 1827): 497.

13. Rivadavia, quoted in Humphreys, *British Consular Reports,* 9; also Williford, *Jeremy Bentham in Spanish America.*

14. Roldán Vera, *The British Book Trade,* 236.

15. For background, see Rippy, "Latin America and the British Investment"; Dawson, *The First Latin American Debt Crisis.*

16. On the suffrage law, see Ternavasio, *La revolución del voto,* 77–89.

17. Halperín Donghi, *Politics, Economy, and Society in Argentina,* 351–52.

18. Street, *Gran Bretaña,* 81, quoting the Audiencia of Buenos Aires in 1806.

19. William Parish Robertson, quoted in Humphreys, *Paroissian,* 106.

20. J. Robertson, "Statement by British merchants," August 17, 1823, the National Archives, Kew, Foreign Office Papers (hereafter cited as TNA), FO 6–1. The standard work is Reber, *British Mercantile Houses.*

21. On civil liberties, see Nidia Areces and Edgardo Ossuna, *Rivadavia y su tiempo: Selección y prologo* (Buenos Aires: Centro Editor de América Latina, 1984), 30–31.

22. A table of British exports to Latin America, 1812–1830, appears in Humphreys, *British Consular Reports,* 344–49.

23. Memorandum enclosed in Parish to Foreign Office, July 30, 1824, TNA, FO 6–4.

24. J. Robertson and W. Robertson, *Letters on South America,* 1:262.

25. Parish to FO, January 23, 1826, TNA, FO 6–11.

26. J. Robertson and W. Robertson, *Letters on South America,* 3:115.

27. *British Packet,* August 11, 1827. On ethnic associations in the 1820s, see Hanon, *Diccionario,* 21–66.

28. On the importance of Anglicanism abroad in the early nineteenth century, see Strong, *Anglicanism and the British Empire.* Buenos Aires provided an example of the same technique being used in Latin America.

29. *Standard* (Buenos Aires), June 19, 1896. Commentary in Dodds, *Records of the Scottish Settlers.*

30. Street, *Gran Bretaña,* 141.

31. Gillespie, *Gleanings and Remarks,* preface.

32. Caldcleugh, *Travels in South America,* 1

33. Apparently composed by a British merchant and published in London, the piece appeared as an introduction to a report submitted to the US Congress. C. A. Rodney and John Graham, *The Report on the Present State of the United Provinces of South America* (New York: Praeger, 1969), 4, 43 (first published by the US Congress in 1818).

34. Haigh, *Sketches of Buenos Ayres,* preface.

35. Miers, *Travels in Chile,* 45, 122.

36. Ibid., 149–86.

37. Hanon, *Diccionario,* 591–92. The leading work on mining is Rees Jones, *Rivadavia y su negocio minero.*

38. Head, *Rough Notes,* 4, 64.

39. J. Andrews, *Journey from Buenos Ayres,* 1:226. On the influence of Andrews and other travelers on Argentine intellectuals, see Ricardo Cicerchia, *Viajeros: Ilus-*

trados y románticos en la imaginación nacional (Buenos Aires: Traquel, 2005); Adolfo Prieto, *Los viajeros ingleses y la emergencia de la literatura argentina,* 2nd ed. (Buenos Aires: Fondo de Cultura Económica, 2003), 28.

40. J. Andrews, *Journey from Buenos Ayres,* 1:233. The invitation was delivered in a speech at a banquet set up by Andrews for the social elite of Tucumán on the birthday of George IV in September 1825.

41. J. Andrews, *Travels from Buenos Ayres,* 251.

42. Dodds, *Records of the Scottish Settlers,* 7–23.

43. *The British Packet,* February 10, 1827 (quoting *The Spectator*); Hanon, *Diccionario,* 133–34.

44. The story is recounted at length in Rees Jones, *Rivadavia y su negocio minero.*

45. Trade figures in Humphreys, *British Consular Reports,* 344–49; J. Williams, "The Establishment of British Commerce," 27.

46. Memorandum of British merchants to Consul Woodbine Parish, December 31, 1827, TNA, FO 6–20; Parish, quoted in Dodds, *Records of the Scottish Settlers,* 146.

47. Beaumont, *Travels in Buenos Ayres,* 157.

48. Head, *Rough Notes,* 143.

49. Based on "John Simon to Dr. Richard, 4 Jan. 1827," mimeograph copy of a private letter seen by the author; *British Packet,* March 28 and April 11, 1829.

50. Events are outlined in *British Packet,* March 28 and April 11, 1829.

51. Translation in *British Packet,* April 6, 1833.

52. Shipping figures in *British Packet,* August 3, 1833.

53. Woodbine Parish, quoted in *British Packet,* January 21, 1831.

54. Head, *Report Relating to the Failure,* vi.

55. Ibid., 9.

56. *Standard* (Buenos Aires), March 11, 1880, quoting *London Times.*

57. Letter of Destutt de Tracy to Rivadavia, quoted in José Carlos Chiaramonte, *Ciudades, provincias, estados: Orígenes de la nación argentina, 1800–1846* (Buenos Aires: Emecé, 2007), 179.

11

"There Is No Doubt That We Are under Threat by the Negroes of Santo Domingo"

The Specter of Haiti in the Spanish Caribbean in the 1820s

Carrie Gibson

In discussing events in the Caribbean during the era of Atlantic revolutions, it is only relatively recently, in historiographical terms, that the slave uprising of Saint-Domingue has taken its rightful place, sandwiched between North America's war for independence in 1775 and the emergence of Latin American republics from 1810 to 1825. Indeed, the growing body of scholarship that has resulted has enhanced the understanding of the events in Haiti and its hitherto overlooked impact around the world.[1] Less well known is Haiti's influence on the emerging republics of Latin America some twenty years later.[2] Haitian leaders failed to convince the Creole revolutionaries they aided—most notably Simón Bolívar (see part 3)—to carry out a true abolition of slavery, and throughout the independence period the island loomed ominously in the Creole imagination. As Kenneth Maxwell has pointed out, "in the 1780s would-be Latin American revolutionaries had found inspiration in George Washington; after the 1790s, they would recoil in fear before the example of Toussaint L'Ouverture."[3] Indeed, amid the upheaval of the independence struggles in Spanish America and the political unrest in Spain during the 1820s slavery remained a constant factor and would, for the most part, continue to be so for decades after the fighting had stopped.[4] Chile was the first Latin American republic to declare the outright abolition of its four thousand slaves in 1823. The other emerging states opted for laws of gradual emancipation. Many children of slaves were born free in the 1820s, but their parents and extended family members were often tied into apprenticeship contracts, which kept them in bondage. It was as late as the 1850s before slavery was finally abolished from Latin American republics.[5] And, as the work of Aline Helg and Marixa Lasso makes clear in their studies of *pardocracia* in Colombia, the *idea* of Haiti played a very important role in sustaining racial hierarchies.[6] What Haiti had come to represent was a connection between free people of color and the possibility of race war. New imaginings of Haiti began to emerge by the 1820s, and coupled with political and social uncertainties that surrounded Latin America, these visions took on extra potency.

However, where most of Haiti's influence lay was with its more immediate neighbors, especially Cuba, Puerto Rico, and Santo Domingo.[7] What makes the 1820s particularly important for the Caribbean is how the possibility of independence brought back those visceral fears of 1791. If Creoles in Cuba or Puerto Rico agreed to press forward with independence from Spanish rule, then would they, like the French republicans before them, suffer the same fate? Would they too experience the complete destruction of their world? This was an important question at a time when sugar wealth was beginning to soar, and it weighed very heavily on the minds of Cuban and Puerto Rican planters. Of course, Haiti symbolized something very different for the slaves on those islands, as well as for the free people of color, who, despite having their liberty, still lived under a repressive system. One area ripe for further research is the question of the importance of Haiti for these groups.

Haiti's reputation took on an even more menacing dimension in the eyes of Latin America when it assumed control of its Spanish-speaking neighbor, Santo Domingo, in 1822. The period around these events—and the permeation of fear and anxiety in Cuban and Puerto Rican Creole society—is crucial for understanding the trajectory of the Caribbean islands, especially the continued loyalty of Cuba and Puerto Rico, which remained in a "pacto colonial" with Spain.[8] Although it was clear that the fear of a slave uprising on the scale of what happened in Saint-Domingue stifled the development of nascent republicanism in Cuba and Puerto Rico, this accepted observation deserves some further examination. Ada Ferrer has pointed out, with regard to this issue, that "although the fear of Haiti is used to explain, it is not itself explained."[9] The remainder of this chapter will examine three aspects of this problem. The first is the issue of fear itself and its many-hued existence in the Spanish Caribbean. The threat of republicanism coupled with that of slave rebellion changed the contours of the ongoing social anxiety, and fear took on a unique tenor during the 1820s. The second aspect is the economic anxieties. Quite beyond the threat of a race war, the more likely reason there was so much concern in Cuba and Puerto Rico is that their sugar industries were booming. It is a sad irony that these two islands were becoming rich because of the failure of Haiti to maintain its pre-revolutionary levels of sugar output. This was compounded by Spain's realization of how desperately it needed its coffers to be refilled by sugar duties. Lastly is the failed independence bid and occupation of Santo Domingo in 1822. This was a crystallizing moment, when new fears and old prejudices converged, and was one of the many contributing factors to the continuation of colonial rule for Cuba and Puerto Rico. These events, no doubt, were in the forefront of the mind of Puerto Rico's governor, Miguel de la Torre, when he wrote the following year, "There is no doubt that we are under threat by the negroes of Santo Domingo."[10]

I

The issue of fear of a Haitian-style uprising is an awkward one because of the difficulty in assessing the levels of anxiety. The meaning of fear was also contingent on circumstances. This section aims to examine briefly the connection between different types fear and some of the ways they manifested themselves in Caribbean society. Even in examining responses to anxiety, fear has many hues. Anthony Maingot has argued that a "terrified consciousness" grew out of the slaves' journey to freedom because events in Saint-Domingue were an example of actual behavior, and so similar rebellions elsewhere became a possibility.[11] Arturo Morales Carrión blamed the "síndrome haitiano" for many of the repressive measures that arose at times of uncertainty.[12] Clarence Munford and Michael Zeuske have called Cuba's reaction an "ambivalent paranoia," meaning that the island was happy to take control of the sugar trade while at the same time having to face a growing possibility of similar social upheaval.[13] The 1820s proved to be a crucial juncture in this long "temporal arc" of fear that stretched from 1789 to 1844, as Maria Dolores González-Ripoll has described it.[14] Imaging this arc, both the nature of the fear and what "unspeakable" actions Haiti represented changed dramatically as it stretched over the 1820s. And these varieties of fear were manifested in myriad ways throughout the period.

This "fear" of slave rebellion, while having many meanings, also had different levels of intensity. On one level was immediate—for instance, the fear of a possible revolt, directly inspired by the slaves of Haiti. This manifestation was most prevalent during the first decade after the beginning of the Haitian Revolution, roughly to 1800, and colonial officials responded to it by prohibiting the entrance of people of color from the island, as well as arresting slaves thought to be in contact with anyone from Saint-Domingue and using weak pretexts as grounds for punishment. Like the "French negroes" in the Unites States—as black refugees from Saint-Domingue were called— free people of color in Cuba and Puerto Rico, especially if they had a connection to Saint-Domginue or there was anything considered to be "French" about them, were often blamed for a number of things, especially instigating unrest and possible race war.[15]

As the immediate fear transmogrified into a lower-level, ongoing anxiety, many of these measures persisted and intensified. Island officials were also often convinced that rebellions and conspiracies that they had suppressed were inspired by Haiti, such as the Aponte rebellion in Cuba in 1812.[16] In the case of that particular conspiracy, the supposed existence of a notebook full of drawings of Haitian leaders was used as a justification to send the alleged leader, a free black man named José Antonio Aponte, to his death. One of the intriguing aspects of this type of anxiety about Haiti is its longevity and its relationship to the possibility of such an event coming to pass: the potential of Haitian-inspired uprisings between whites and people of color was invoked even in the debates over the Morant Bay rebellion in Jamaica as late as 1865.[17] Yet the reality was that Haiti was poor, cut off from trade, shunned by most of the international community, and itself worried about a French invasion.

By the 1820s, the colonial administrations in Cuba and Puerto Rico also had honed their responses to the possibility of uprisings in the decades following the rebellion in Saint-Domingue. For instance, there were continual attempts to stop free people of color from that island coming to Cuba because they were seen as potential rebels. And life for the free people of color who lived there was full of strict regulations. British observer Robert Francis Jameson spent 1820 in Cuba and remarked on this treatment, noting that free people of color "are unchained but the collar remains on their necks. They are subject to most of the restrictions imposed on a slave, such as respect [to] carrying weapons, being out after dark without a lanthor, &c and they are equally deprived of information, their freedom by no means extending to their minds."[18] Additionally, there were concerted efforts to control runaway slave colonies, known as *palenques*. Although such groups had been part of colonial society since the introduction of slavery in the sixteenth century, these often-autonomous groups were a frequent cause for concern, especially as officials began to realize that these runaways could, in theory, meet and plot with Haitian "agents." At times of increased anxiety and vigilance there were repeated orders to suppress them or recapture slaves trying to join them. For

instance, in 1824, Puerto Rico's governor, Miguel de la Torre, issued a proclamation outlawing the concealment of any runaway and offering a reward of
up to ten pesos for their capture.[19]

Even domestic life was fraught. In his time in Havana, Jameson remarked
on the physical manifestations of this racialized paranoia: "The mass of being is forcibly conjoined—their bond of union is a real chain. Fear, say the
metaphysicians, first formed society, and it is undoubted that such is the elemental principal [sic] of West Indian society. Every house is a sort of garrison
filled with domestic conscripts serving without pay and whom it is necessary
to guard strictly."[20]

While such official orders and social anxieties were not unusual in any
slave society, this type of legislation and the concerted effort to contend with
runaway slave groups is a continual presence in archival documents from the
1820s, indicating, as with the numerous "suppressions" of conspiracies, that
keeping control of the situation was often only just within the grasp of colonial officials on the Spanish islands and that manipulation of fear allowed
them to maintain colonial order and racial hierarchies. And as the number
of slaves rose and the sugar wealth grew throughout the decade, this need for
order multiplied many times over.

II

It had become clear at the beginning of the century that the planters' loss
in Saint-Domingue was Cuba's and Puerto Rico's gain. After independence
Haiti never came close to reaching the level of its sugar output before the revolution, but Cuba was especially well positioned to pick up Saint-Domingue's
business. Although events in Saint-Domingue proved to be a catalyst, larger
economic reconfigurations and political changes in trade had been going on
for some time, under the later part of Carlos III's reign of reform.[21] Spanish thinkers in the mid-eighteenth century had been increasingly turning
their attention to the profitability of agriculture. Social structures, too, were
in place, with a growing interest in political economy and technological innovation, as illustrated by the growth of *consulados* and of economic societies.[22] Cuba eventually was permitted access to US markets, and it also received more flexible trading rights.[23] Additionally, elites in Cuba had been
given special privileges that over time would yield a closer and more loyal relationship between its powerful elites and the Crown.[24] Economically and politically, Cuba was poised in the early 1800s to begin massive sugar produc-

tion, which meant that by the 1820s considerable wealth had been amassed in this short period.

This changing economic world was evident on these islands. The slave population in Puerto Rico had reached 21,700 by 1820, and 286,900 in Cuba by 1827.[25] Correspondingly, sugar and coffee output had increased. In Puerto Rico, some 3,905 metric tons of sugar were produced in 1812; by 1830 output climbed to 14,126 metric tons.[26] A noted German naturalist, Alexander von Humboldt, had visited Cuba in the early years of the 1800s and kept track of its growing wealth before publishing accounts in his *Political Essay on Cuba* in 1826. Measuring sugar output by boxes, based on customs house returns, he calculated there were some 63,274 boxes in 1786 and 245,329 boxes by 1824.[27] But he also noted the corresponding changes to Cuba's demographics, including its growing population of free people of color, noting: "Do not let us forget that since Haiti became emancipated there are already in the Antilles more free negroes and mulattoes than slaves. The whites, and more particularly the free blacks, who may easily make common cause with the slaves increase rapidly in Cuba."[28]

By 1825 there had been much wider reconfigurations as well—most of Central and South America were no longer under Spanish rule. Cuba and Puerto Rico were now caught in a bind: at last they had full imperial attention, but with the heavy economic pressure that went with it. With the silver of Peru and the gold of Mexico now gone, Spain's Fernando VII was forced to turn to his remaining Caribbean possessions. These colonies were then forced to turn to their slaves to help them capitalize on opportunities created in the sugar market. And the colonial authorities were forced to turn against most of their people, controlling slaves and attempting to keep a stranglehold over free people of color, methods later used to stifle potential republican movements. Economic expansion left fear and uncertainty in its wake, though these anxieties were often expressed through racial ideas rather than economic ones. Later on in his book on Cuba, von Humboldt quotes at length a passage from the *Representación del ayuntamiento, consulado y sociedad patriótica* of July 20, 1820, to illustrate attitudes among the elite: "In all matters concerning changes in the situation of the servant class, the important issue is not so much our fear of a decrease in agricultural prosperity as it is the safety of white people, who could so easily be harmed by an incautious measure."[29]

This rise in sugar production led to a similar boom in customs and treasury receipts, meaning that the two remaining American colonies were now financially vital to the Crown. By the 1820s, the deal had become clear: for Cuba and Puerto Rico, continued colonial rule could "protect" them from social upheaval, and they would provide the Crown with a much-needed economic lifeline. Now there was an added pressure on Cuba and Puerto Rico to generate revenue, but these islands were also struggling with the loss of the *situado* payments from Mexico that had long propped up their respective economies. To further complicate matters, Spain had also lost its status as the main trading partner with its former colonies, which were now free to pursue economic relationships with some of Spain's competitors. In 1792 the South American colonies accounted for 16.6 percent of Spain's export market, and Spain had provided some 20 percent of its imports. By 1827, however, the situation had changed dramatically. Cuba and Puerto Rico, which had absorbed some 4.3 percent of imports in 1792, were now, along with the Philippines, taking 16.6 percent. Likewise, imports in Spain from Cuba, Puerto Rico, and the Philippines rose from 6.8 percent to 20.3 percent, and those from the former colonies fell to 0.1 percent. Throughout the 1820s Cuba especially became a valuable market for Spanish exported goods. In 1826 the value of imports from Spain was 2,858,792 pesos, and this figure rose to 4,739,776 pesos by 1830.[30]

What became clear over the course of the 1820s was the increasingly symbiotic nature of the relationship between the Crown and its slave colonies. Small-scale rebellions could damage a sugar *ingenio,* but a large-scale Haitian-style uprising could destroy an entire economic project, leaving the island and its wealthy planters impoverished and the Crown without much-needed revenue or any remaining imperial prestige.

III

One of the underlying concerns about Haiti was its revolutionary past—not only its own uprising, but the later assistance that it provided to rebel leaders from Spanish colonies. For example, Javier Mina, who sought to liberate Mexico, secured support of an expedition from the leader of southern Haiti, Alexandre Pétion, in 1813. He was soon followed by Simón Bolívar, who arrived in Port-au-Prince on December 31, 1815. Mina's and Bolívar's paths appear to have crossed on the island.[31] Others followed, or at least enquired about the possibility of assistance. In 1819, the vice president of the Republic of Venezuela, Juan Bautista Arismendi, established contact with northern

Haiti's leader, Henri Christophe. The following year, an agent for Colombia, Juan Bernardo Elbers, managed to obtain one thousand rifles and six thousand pounds of lead from Pétion's successor in the south, Jean Pierre Boyer.[32]

So by the 1820s Haiti was feared not only for its abolitionism, but also for its support for Latin American republicanism—both considered threats to public "tranquility" in the minds of Spanish colonial officials and planters in Cuba and Puerto Rico. They worried that Haitians might invade, though they were not the only ones wanting to free the islands. When Simón Bolívar was taking refuge in Jamaica, where he wrote his famous *Jamaica Letter* before moving on to Haiti, he observed: "The islands of Puerto Rico and Cuba, with a combined population of perhaps 700,000 to 800,000 souls, are the most tranquil possessions of the Spaniards, because they are not within range of contact with the Independents. But are not the people of those islands Americans? Are they not maltreated? Do they not desire a better life?"[33] These were questions that many in the islands wanted to consider. By 1820, the Cuban organizers behind the pro-independence Soles y rayos de Bolívar conspiracy started formulating their answer, though the authorities, with their well-honed suppression techniques, stifled this dissent a few years later.[34] By 1825 Bolívar's plans to help Cuba and Puerto Rico had become well-known— Colombia and Mexico were to invade and liberate Cuba and Puerto Rico— though in the end he was unable to act upon them.[35]

The idea of Haitians being harbingers of destruction lingered in the white imagination across the Caribbean throughout the 1820s. Yet Haiti's first major political act as a reunited country—Boyer had brought it back together in 1820—in 1822 was quite different. And while its actions did bring freedom for more slaves, it did not bring bloodshed. In fact, in 1820 Haiti was still recovering from its own internal wounds. The Spanish side of the island, too, had been under duress. In December of 1821, fed up by imperial neglect in the shadow of their counterparts in Cuba and Puerto Rico, a group of pro-independence elites in Santo Domingo announced their freedom from Spain and their desire to join the republic of Gran Colombia, under Bolívar's leadership. They decided to give the new republic the somewhat confusing name of "Estado independiente de la parte Española de Haití."[36] Although the plan was to ally with Colombia, the name was invoked in the hopes that Haiti would provide arms and support for the fight. However, Boyer was keen for this state to join Haiti and not ally with Bolívar, and he had been agitating for this for some time. Boyer was driven by the fact that the Spanish side of the island was ill-equipped to stop any European forces that might have been looking for an easy point of entry to attempt a recolonization of Haiti. In an exchange of correspondence, Boyer said to the Creole movement's leader, José Núñez de Cáceres: "There is no obstacle that is capable of stopping me. . . . [O]pen your heart to enjoyment, to trust, because the independence of Haiti will be indestructible, due to the fusion of all hearts into one whole."[37] The new nation of Spanish Haiti was stuck—Spain was unwilling to intervene to reclaim it, and with a very small militia compared to Boyer's twelve thou sand troops, there was little choice. And so Boyer entered the city of Santo Domingo on February 9, 1822, and took control of the whole island.[38] A letter to the then governor of Puerto Rico, Francisco González de Linares, described how, when "Boyer took possession of the Spanish part of the Island of Santo Domingo, as a consequence of its disgraceful political change to a Republican system, his first steps were to bring together [public] opinion by means of popularity and [granting] equality to all classes of people of the island, by declaring absolute liberty from slavery."[39] Boyer then set about redistributing land to recreate the peasant smallholdings that had been instituted in Haiti and pushed for more agricultural output. While there had been some Dominican support for an alliance with Haiti, especially among free people of color, there were many more who were resistant to the idea, hence the initial efforts to make an alliance with Colombia. In 1823, three conspiracies were discovered and Boyer brutally suppressed them.[40] Yet, at the same time that Boyer was grappling with rebellious Dominicans, poor trade, and widespread poverty, across the Caribbean white planters seemed to believe that a Haitian invasion or a local race war instigated by the island's agents could take place at any time. The reality of Haiti was far more complicated than the version in the official mind.

IV

This chapter has sought to show another side to the issue of the continuity between Cuba, Puerto Rico, and Spain during the era of Latin American independence by considering the persistence of fear during the 1820s. While the issue of fear is a complex one because it is hard to measure or quantify, by looking around its edges it is possible to find its form. While there were myriad internal and external factors to the continued relationship between Cuba, Puerto Rico, and Spain, Haiti's role in the economic and political development of the Spanish Caribbean deserves examination. The specter of Haiti's achievement loomed over Cuba and Puerto for decades, while in the Latin

American republics it symbolized the potential destructiveness of a race war. Although the type of fear that emerged from the events in the 1820s receded as the republican threat to Cuba and Puerto Rico stopped temporarily, anxiety lingered on. Although fear was a constant part of the colonial condition, at this particular historical juncture in the Spanish Empire, fear of Haiti played a decisive role in the continuity of Cuba and Puerto Rico: racial hierarchies, repression, suspicion, and unease would reign. For Cuba, after a decade of relative quiet that followed the uncertainty of the 1820s, fevered anxiety would reappear again in 1844, during the brutal suppression of the La Escalera conspiracy, further tightening the colonial hold, fueled by the "Africanization" scares that had begun to take place a few years earlier.[41] In the same year, Santo Domingo obtained its independence from Haiti and was reborn as the Dominican Republic. But Cuba and Puerto Rico would carry on as colonies until 1898, increasing their sugar wealth and slave population. Abolition had only arrived a short time before, in 1873 for Puerto Rico and 1886 for Cuba. Haiti, meanwhile, descended into further internal political upheaval and poverty, while also suffering the continued rejection by much of the international community. Yet the stories that island's past inspired would live on, vivid in the imaginations of everyone who surrounded it; and Haiti's potential to act would continue to inspire hope in some people and fear in others.

Notes

I would like to thank Juan Cobo for his generous help with Spanish translations, though any errors are my own.

    1. There was a long historical pause after the publication of C. L. R. James's seminal work *The Black Jacobins* in 1938, prompting Michel-Rolph Trouillot to write about the "silencing" of Haiti's history in his work *Silencing the Past*. However, over the past thirty years a growing body of work has placed Haiti in a more Atlantic and revolutionary context. The works and edited volumes by David Geggus have been particularly important in this regard: see Geggus and Gaspar, *A Turbulent Time*; Geggus, *The Impact of the Haitian Revolution in the Atlantic World*; Geggus and Fiering, *The World of the Haitian Revolution*; and Geggus, *Haitian Revolutionary Studies*. Other recent contributions include L. Dubois, *Avengers of the New World*; Fischer, *Modernity Disavowed*; Garraway, *Tree of Liberty*; Nesbitt, *Universal Emancipation*; Buck-Morss, *Hegel, Haiti, and Universal History*. Other works about the Atlantic world or slavery more widely have also begun to address Haiti, for instance Blackburn, *The Overthrow of Colonial Slavery*.

2. Work on the wider impact of Haiti in Caribbean South America has emerged over the past couple of decades, such as Helg's *Liberty and Equality in Caribbean Colombia* and Lasso's *Myths of Harmony*. There has also been some work out of Peru, such as the volume edited by Claudia Rosas Lauro, *El miedo en el Perú siglos XVI al XX* (Lima: Pontificia Universidad Católica del Perú, Fondo Editorial, 2005), and Mexico as well in Von Grafenstein's *Nueva España en el circuncaribe*. The scholarship on Haiti's impact in the United States is not as extensive as might be expected, but Ashli White's recent *Encountering Revolution: Haiti and the Making of the Early Republic* (Baltimore: Johns Hopkins University Press, 2010) makes a welcome addition to that field.

3. Kenneth R. Maxwell, "Hegemonies Old and New," in *Colonial Legacies,* ed. Adelman, 88.

4. Schmidt-Nowara, *Empire and Antislavery.*

5. For a summary of emancipation in South America, see Herbert S. Klein and Ben Vinson, *African Slavery in Latin America and the Caribbean* (Oxford: Oxford University Press, 2007), 232.

6. Helg, *Liberty and Equality in Caribbean Colombia*; Lasso, *Myths of Harmony.*

7. See Gibson, "The Impact of the Haitian Revolution on the Hispanic Caribbean."

8. Fradera, *Colonias para después de un imperio,* 56.

9. Ferrer, "Noticias de Haití en Cuba," 677.

10. Miguel de la Torre to Francisco González de Linares, September 16, 1823, Archivo General de Puerto Rico, fondo Gobernadores Españoles, Asuntos Políticos y Civiles, caja 175. Spanish speakers sometimes referred to Saint-Domingue and later Haiti as Santo Domingo.

11. Anthony P. Maingot, "Haiti and the Terrified Consciousness of the Caribbean," in *Ethnicity in the Caribbean: Essays in Honor of Harry Hoetink,* ed. Gert Oostindie (London: Macmillan, 1996), 53–80.

12. Arturo Morales Carrión, "La revolución haitiana y el movimiento antiesclavista en Puerto Rico," *Boletin de la Academia Puertorriqueña de la Historia* 8, no. 30 (1983): 139–56.

13. Clarence J. Munford and Michael Zeuske, "Black Slavery, Class Struggle, Fear and Revolution in St. Domingue and Cuba, 1785–1795," *Journal of Negro History* 73, nos. 1–4 (1988): 12–32.

14. M. D. González-Ripoll Navarro, "Desde Cuba, antes y después de Haití: Pragmatismo y dilación en el pensamiento de Francisco Arango sobre la esclavitud," in *El rumor de Haití en Cuba: Temor, raza y rebeldía, 1789–1844,* ed. M. D. González-Ripoll Navarro (Madrid: CSIC, 2004), 16.

15. White, *Encountering Revolution*, 144–49.

16. Childs, *The 1812 Aponte Rebellion in Cuba*; Fischer, *Modernity Disavowed*, especially chapter 1.

17. Gad Heuman, *The Killing Time: The Morant Bay Rebellion in Jamaica* (London: Macmillan, 1994).

18. Jameson, *Letters From the Havana*, 37.

19. Miguel de la Torre, "Bando de policía y buen gobierno de 1824," in *Esclavos prófugos y cimarrones: Puerto Rico, 1770–1870,* ed. Benjamin Nistal Moret (Río Piedras: Editorial de la Universidad de Puerto Rico, 1984), 32–33.

20. Jameson, *Letters From the Havana,* 6–7.

21. See Fradera, *Colonias para después de un imperio*; G. Paquette, *Enlightenment, Governance, and Reform in Spain and Its Empire*.

22. G. Paquette, "State–Civil Society Cooperation and Conflict in the Spanish Empire," 263–98.

23. Anton L. Allahar, "The Cuban Sugar Planters (1790–1820): 'The Most Solid and Brilliant Bourgeois Class in All of Latin America,'" *The Americas* 41, no. 1 (1984): 48–49.

24. Knight, "Origins of Wealth and the Sugar Revolution in Cuba," 231–53.

25. P. D. Curtin, *The Atlantic Slave Trade,* 34–35.

26. Scarano, *Sugar and Slavery in Puerto Rico,* 7.

27. Von Humboldt, *The Island of Cuba,* 156.

28. Ibid., 124.

29. Ibid., 263.

30. Pablo Tornero Tinajero, *Crecimiento económico y transformaciones sociales: Esclavos, hacendados y comerciantes en la Cuba colonial (1760–1840)* (Madrid: Ministerio de Trabajo y Seguridad Social, 1996), 390.

31. W. Lewis, "Simón Bolívar and Xavier Mina"; Verna, *Petión y Bolívar.*

32. Elbers was a German who emigrated to the Caribbean and worked as a middleman during the wars of independence, selling arms. He later married into a Bogotá family. See Robert Louis Gilmore and John Parker Harrison, "Juan Bernardo Elbers and the Introduction of Steam Navigation on the Magdalena River," *Hispanic American Historical Review* 28, no. 3 (1948): 335–59; and Von Grafenstein, *Nueva España en el circuncaribe,* 250–51.

33. Bolívar, reproduced in his *Simón Bolívar: The Bolívarian Revolution,* 40–64.

34. Franco, *Ensayos Historicos,* 25.

35. Margarita González, *Bolívar y la independencia de Cuba* (Bogotá: El Ancora, 1985), 124.

36. San Miguel, *The Imagined Island*; Moya Pons, *The Dominican Republic.*

37. Jean Pierre Boyer to José Núñez de Cáceres, January 1822, *El Imparcial,* April 15, 1822, Madrid, Archivo General de Indias (hereafter cited as AGI), fondo Santo Domingo, Legajo 970.

38. This was not the first time this had happened. The Saint-Dominguen general Toussaint L'Ouverture had united the island under French control and abolished slavery on the Spanish side in 1801. It had been ceded to the French under the Treaty of Basle in 1795, but the order had been ignored until L'Ouverture decided to bring abolition to the East. After he was exiled to France, where he died in 1803, that side of the island remained under French control until a group of loyalist Creoles, fueled by Napoleon's invasion of Spain, fought them and reestablished the territory as a Spanish colony in 1808 and 1809. See Utrera, *Diario de la Reconquista.*

39. Juan Francisco Brenes to Francisco González de Linares, September 16, 1822, AGI, fondo Santo Domingo, legajo 970. Linares would be replaced later that year by Miguel de la Torre, who was governor until 1837.

40. Frank Moya Pons, "The Land Question in Haiti and Santo Domingo," in *Between Slavery and Free Labor: The Spanish-Speaking Caribbean in the Nineteenth Century,* ed. Manuel Fraginals Moreno et al. (Baltimore: Johns Hopkins University Press, 1985), 186.

41. R. Paquette, *Sugar Is Made with Blood.*

12
Bartolomé de las Casas and the Slave Trade to Cuba circa 1820

Christopher Schmidt-Nowara

Was it the age of revolution or the axial age? The global upheavals that took place from the later eighteenth century until the middle of the nineteenth unleashed apparently contradictory political, economic, and social transformations that reshaped but did not terminate the connections between Europe and Latin America. On the one hand, this was an era of liberation when Creoles across the Americas threw off the yoke of colonial domination and enslaved people struggled for their freedom and for political enfranchisement.[1] On the other hand, the period witnessed the enhancement of imperial state power in those parts of the Americas that remained under European control and the greatest surge of plantation slavery in the history of the Atlantic system.[2] Cuba was a place where these tensions manifested themselves vividly. Beginning in the later eighteenth century, Creole planters successfully lobbied the metropolitan state to liberalize the economic system so that they could expand the plantation belt around Havana and points east. They took a leading role in the management of the colony, enjoying terrific influence both in Havana and in Madrid. But this wave of economic and political liberalization brought with it a new system of violence and domination heretofore unknown in the Spanish overseas empire. The end of reform was a free trade in slaves that the Spanish Crown had never before permitted. Cuba became the biggest slave society in Spanish American history, as hundreds of thousands of enslaved Africans reached Cuban shores between the late eighteenth century and the closing of the traffic in 1867.

The 1820s were a pivotal moment in this process, during which the Spanish government and colonial planters and merchants fought off British anti-slavery and affirmed the centrality of the slave trade to Cuba's economy. Indeed, the 1820s would come to be the greatest decade of slave trading in the colony's history (though the 1830s would be the peak decade) in spite of an Anglo-Spanish treaty that was supposed to close the traffic in 1820. The decade also witnessed a significant rearrangement of state power in Cuba. Madrid eclipsed Creole influence by concentrating greater power in the office of its representative, the captain general based in Havana, and undercutting the institutions that had promoted local interests.[3]

In confronting this entwining of freedoms with new forms of domination, commentators on slavery and the slave trade turned to a historical figure who seemed to speak both the language of freedom and that of slavery in the Spanish Empire: Bartolomé de las Casas. The writings of las Casas influenced debates over the justice of Spanish rule and conquest in the Americas across the centuries. As Rolena Adorno has recently argued, las Casas's contest with Juan Gínes de Sepúlveda at Valladolid shaped the "polemics of possession" well beyond the era of Charles V. In the age of the Spanish American revolutions, American patriots such as Fray Servando Teresa de Mier appropriated las Casas and his works as the first voice of independence, vindicating the rights of the Americans against the Spanish conquerors. Adorno's study emphasizes the conflict over how to govern the natives of the Indies: "that polemic always centered on the rights of conquest and the treatment of the Amerindians."[4] Yet, las Casas also defined the terms of debate over the African slave trade to the Indies because the resort to the traffic in captives was always closely connected to the struggle over *encomienda,* the enslavement of Indians, and the rights of the conquerors.

Las Casas wrote extensively, and caustically, about Portugal's exploration of the eastern Atlantic and how it opened the slave trade from Africa in the fifteenth century in his *Historia de las Indias.* However, because the *Historia* remained unpublished until the 1870s, commentators on las Casas's role in the traffic's origins argued through inference.[5] Nonetheless, they placed him at the heart of the controversy, some arguing that las Casas convinced Charles V and his Flemish courtiers to commence the slave trade, others insisting that he was the traffic's bitter enemy, still others believing that he acted out of ignorance and good intentions. No matter the position, las Casas was a major protagonist in the telling of the traffic's history, especially during the revolutionary crises of the 1810s and 1820s. During that period, Spaniards and Americans argued over the slave trade's origins to understand, justify, and attack its unprecedented growth in Cuba, a place very familiar to las Casas himself.

~

Several factors leant new urgency to both defenders and critics of the slave trade in the early nineteenth century. On the one hand, the slave traffic, and slavery itself, was under siege in the French and British colonies and in the independent states of the New World. Revolutionaries in Saint-Domingue/ Haiti (1791–1804) destroyed the slave complex in the most productive Caribbean colony and threatened to spread their message of emancipation to neighboring islands and mainland colonies, such as Puerto Rico, Cuba, and Venezuela. At the same time, the British parliament, under great public pressure in the metropole, abolished the still booming slave traffic to its colonies. Thereafter, the British state took steps to suppress the trade from Africa to all American territories over the next several decades by deploying naval patrols in African, Caribbean, and Brazilian waters and by signing treaties with American and European governments. The United States agreed to abolish the transatlantic traffic to its shores in 1808, while the independent Spanish American nations quickly reached agreement with Britain to end the trade in the 1820s as they negotiated recognition.

On the other hand, even as plantation colonies such as Saint-Domingue and Jamaica saw slavery undermined or destroyed, the slave traffic to Spain's Caribbean colonies, with Cuba far out in front, was accelerating at an unprecedented rate. After centuries of heavy restrictions on the African slave trade to its colonies, the Spanish Crown began in the aftermath of the Seven Years' War to deregulate and encourage the traffic to Cuba, Puerto Rico, Trinidad, Santo Domingo, and Louisiana. By the second decade of the nineteenth century, Cuba was the largest importer of captives in the Caribbean, carrying on a trade that in scale more closely resembled Saint-Domingue and Jamaica in their heyday than it did other Spanish colonies (see table 1). Moreover, in response to the collapse of their main French and British competitors and to the rising global demand for tropical goods, *hacendados* in Cuba constructed plantations that far surpassed the size and productive capacity of Caribbean predecessors.[6] Thus, even as the slave trade came under attack in the Atlantic world, it became more central to Spain and Cuba during the crisis of Spain's American empire. Such was especially true by the 1820s when the metropole found itself clinging only to Cuba, Puerto Rico, and the Philippines.

In this period of dramatic economic and political transformation, Hispanic critics and defenders of the slave traffic turned to the past to make sense of

Table 1. Slaves disembarked in Cuba, Saint-Domingue, and Jamaica, 1781–1866

Decade	Cuba	Saint-Domingue	Jamaica
1781–1790	14,516	236,848	97,184
1791–1800	41,723	40,916	164,626
1801–1810	54,167	0	68,901
1811–1820	115,188	808	0
1821–1830	136,381	0	0
1831–1840	186,179	0	2,390
1841–1850	54,309	0	0
1851–1860	126,823	0	0
1861–1866	37,124	0	0
Totals	766,410	278,572	333,101

Source: Voyages Database, 2009, Voyages: The Trans-Atlantic Slave Trade Database, http://www.slavevoyages.org (accessed February 15, 2011).

contemporary positions. Understanding the role of las Casas in the origins of the slave traffic and his views on African slavery figured centrally in the controversy. Outside of Spain and Spanish America, historians and abolitionists had already zeroed in on his legacy during the "dispute of the New World" in the later eighteenth century.[7] William Robertson and other enlightened scholars believed that las Casas was a firm advocate of African slavery as a substitute for Indian labor. To save America, he sacrificed Africa by urging the "odious commerce."[8] In contrast, Thomas Clarkson heralded him as his ancestor of the abolitionists:

Among the well disposed individuals, of different nations and ages, who have humanely exerted themselves to suppress the abject personal slavery, introduced in the original cultivation of the *European* colonies in the western world, *Bartholomew de las Casas,* the pious bishop of *Chiapa,* in the fifteenth century, seems to have been the first. This amiable man, during his residence in *Spanish America,* was so sensibly affected at the treatment which the miserable Indians underwent, that he returned to *Spain,* to make a public remonstrance before the celebrated emperor, *Charles* the fifth, declaring, that Heaven would one day call him to an account for those cruelties, which he then had it in his power to prevent. The speech, which he made on the occasion, is now extant, and is a most perfect picture of benevolence and piety.[9]

The most influential foreign advocate of las Casas was the Abbé Gregoire, the French abolitionist.[10] In his 1800 *Apologie de Las Casas,* translated into Spanish in the 1820s but commented upon by Spanish and Spanish American admirers before then, Gregoire debunked the historical claims of Robertson and others. He noted that such claims rested upon one misconstrued paragraph from Antonio de Herrera's seventeenth-century chronicle of Spanish colonization (Herrera, as royal chronicler, was one of the few historians to have access to las Casas's manuscript of *Historia de las Indias*). No one actually cited the writings of las Casas himself. Gregoire also surveyed the historical record to reveal data that showed that the slave traffic was a going concern long before the intervention of the Bishop of Chiapa: the traffic was firmly in Portuguese hands by the middle of the fifteenth century, while African slaves were present in Columbus's first voyages and settlements in the Caribbean. To place the blame on las Casas thus flew in the face of the actual history of the slave trade's origins. Finally, Gregoire argued that, beyond documented facts, the tendency of las Casas's life and work was in defense of liberty, not slavery: "His actions and his principles are consistent: thus, Benezet, Clarkson, and in general friends of the Blacks, far from blaming las Casas, place him at the head of the defenders of humanity."[11]

Spaniards and Americans echoed these positions but with even greater urgency because of the unleashing of the slave trade to the Spanish Indies. They recognized the historical novelty of the situation and many opposed it. Beginning in the Habsburg era, the Spanish Crown regulated and limited the number of African slaves that could be imported into its American colonies. It also farmed out slaving to foreign merchants because Spain had no commercial presence on the west coast of Africa, unlike the rivals to whom it conceded the privilege to carry slaves to its colonies, including the Portuguese, Dutch, French, and English. The reforms of the late eighteenth century changed this situation completely. Spaniards and Cubans raced to Africa or to other Caribbean colonies to purchase slaves, while the number of captives that entered Cuba continued to swell.[12]

While the trade facilitated Cuba's transformation, it attracted criticism from Spaniards and Americans troubled by the scale of the changes. It also brought Spain and Cuba firmly into the sights of the British government, which was committed to suppressing the transatlantic traffic.

Debate over the trade came into the open beginning in 1808 with the war against the French, the uprisings in Spanish America, and the uneasy alliance formed with Britain. The Cortes de Cádiz, the provisional government that carried out the resistance to the French occupation in the absence of the monarch Ferdinand VII, briefly debated banning the trade, a measure supported by both Spanish and American deputies. However, an immediate challenge from Havana, penned by the impresario of the Cuban plantation complex, Francisco Arango y Parreño, brought that discussion to a close.[13]

But other voices sounded from outside the Cortes. Two passionately written pamphlets by learned and prominent intellectual figures sought to sway political opinion during the resistance to the French. One was written from abroad and likely had little circulation in Spain because it appeared at the time of Ferdinand VII's restoration, when open political debate was shutting down. The author was the expatriate and former priest Joseph Blanco White, who at the behest of British abolitionists translated, and effectively rewrote, one of William Wilberforce's denunciations of the slave trade in 1814. Wilberforce himself had hoped that Blanco White might draw upon an autochthonous antislavery tradition, including las Casas's work: "It has occurred to me as worthy of Consideration whether as Bartholomew (the Early Conveyor if not the first Spanish originator of the Sla. [sic] Trade) de la [sic] Casas, pleaded however the Cause of the Blacks, there might not be found in his Writings or those of some other of the Spanish divines, passages likely to have weight with the Ecclesiastics of the Country. Yr. Lordship knows, whether Mr. White is likely to be at all versed in Spanish Literature, especially in Ecclesiastical."[14]

Blanco White never cited las Casas directly in his *Bosquexo del comercio de esclavos y reflexiónes sobre este tráfico considerado moral, política y cristianamente*. Rather, the thrust of his arguments to potential Spanish readers (the pamphlet was circulated among Spanish officials by the British minister in Madrid) drew upon a familiar theme in Spanish criticisms of the slave trade: that Spain had never been a slave-trading power, differing significantly from its European rivals. Thus, the massive upsurge in slaving to Cuba was a historical aberration. He also turned to more immediate and intimate matters to provoke outrage by comparing Spanish and Cuban slaving in Africa to the French invasion and subjection of Spain.[15] Nonetheless, the most indefatigable biographer of Blanco White has shown that lascasian rhetoric shaped Blanco's defense of the Africans against the Spanish slave traders. In particular, Blanco appears to have plucked one of las Casas's most telling anecdotes to illustrate the evils of the transatlantic slave trade. While Cuban and Spanish defenders of the traffic frequently spoke of how enslavement in Cuba would benefit Africans by making them Christians, Blanco reported that many Africans were actually becoming Muslims because of their disgust at Christian slave traders, a rephrasing of las Casas's report that Indians recoiled from Christianity when confronted by the violence of their supposed Christian benefactors.[16]

Las Casas was a more explicit presence in the antislavery writing of Isidoro de Antillón, a geographer active in Madrid's learned societies before the French invasion. Among his works was an anti-slave-trade tract that sought to demonstrate that the deregulated slave traffic was not only anomalous but also unnecessary when understood within the structure of the Spanish colonial empire. Antillón insisted in his work, originally written and publicly delivered in 1803 but printed for the first time in 1811, that Spain must ban the traffic and instead rely on the indigenous population of the colonies, which had grown considerably in the eighteenth century, as the backbone of the labor force.[17] Antillón knew, of course, that this policy would have little appeal in Havana because the indigenous population had virtually disappeared, but to such objections he had a ready answer inspired by Toussaint L'Ouverture during the Haitian Revolution: "There can be no doubt. The blacks will one day find a valiant leader who will avenge them and assure their independence through force. And we must fear that finding the Crassus to this new Spartacus will not be easy."[18]

Antillón believed that Spain enjoyed considerable advantages over its French and British rivals because they relied too heavily on dangerous and unreliable enslaved African labor. The Saint-Domingue rebellion and the frequency of uprisings and maroonage in the British and French islands showed that the only way to stabilize tropical production in the rival empires would be by moving the plantations from the Antilles to Africa itself, where free laborers could be recruited. In contrast, Spain's American empire still had a large indigenous workforce. If Spain would effectively and faithfully apply its own venerable colonial legislation, the Laws of the Indies, then Indian workers would not only be more productive but also receive more just treatment from their employers and royal officials. The Bourbon reformers were mistaken in emulating Britain's and France's Atlantic empires by turning toward the slave traffic; instead, Spain should take advantage of its superior human and institutional resources in its efforts to catch up to its rivals by effectively inverting their formulae, substituting Indian labor for African: "It is uncontestable that in our Americas the Indians can take over the labor of the blacks, especially if they are treated with less harshness and arbitrariness than heretofore."[19]

A reading of las Casas and his actions was crucial to Antillón's attack on the slave trade and his defense of the indigenous population of the Spanish Indies. Antillón repeated the familiar charge that las Casas was responsible for convincing the Emperor Charles V to substitute enslaved African workers for Indians, a recommendation that Antillón was standing on its head almost three centuries later.[20] Yet in the endnotes of his work, Antillón included a lengthy and stirring endorsement of Gregoire's defense of las Casas. Indeed, so convinced was he by Gregoire's history that he claimed to have translated it into Spanish with additional notes on the life and career of the bishop of Chiapas. However, censorship under the Old Regime and then the disruption of war after 1808 kept him from publishing the work.[21]

After the restoration of Ferdinand VII in 1814, political circumstances in Spain and the Americas changed radically as the monarch and his supporters carried out an absolutist backlash, suppressing the Cortes and the constitution it ratified in 1812. Nonetheless, the slave trade remained on the agenda because Britain was pressuring its ally to sign a treaty suppressing it. At the same time, defenders of the Cuban trade actively lobbied and doled out bribes in Madrid to obstruct such a pact.[22] In the conversations taking place behind closed doors, las Casas continued to inform debate. In 1816, the Consejo de Indias discussed the proposed treaty with Britain. Despite the presence of firm advocates of the traffic on the Consejo, most notably the Cuban planter Arango y Parreño, the majority voted to enter into such an agreement. The majority opinion included a broad survey of the slave trade's history from the beginnings of European overseas exploration and colonization. It expressed the firm conviction that Spain was unlike the other European powers in that it had abstained from slaving, instead farming out contracts to foreign providers: "The Dutch and the Genoese, and afterwards, the English, gave greater extension to this Traffic: but the Spanish Court viewed with horror a commerce so contrary in its nature, to every feeling of humanity;—so much so, indeed, that, notwithstanding the repeated Applications from our American Colonies, the encouragement of such a Trade was constantly refused, and it went even so far as to prohibit, in the year 1516, under heavy penalties, the importation of Negroes into America."[23]

Slave trafficking to Cuba by Spaniards, which was in ascent in the first two decades of the nineteenth century, was thus a historical anomaly; banning the trade would restore the traditions of Spanish rule in the Americas. Included in this self-congratulatory overview was an aside about las Casas. The report's authors singled him out as the individual most responsible for the implantation of African slavery in the Spanish Indies. His zeal for defending the Indians against the colonists led him to favor the importation of enslaved Africans as a substitute for indigenous labor:

> The Licenciate, Bartolomeo de las Casas, urged his reclamations in favour of America, and, led away by his excessive attachment to that Country, he imagined it to be beneath the character and dignity of its Inhabitants to apply themselves to labour in the fields and proposed that Negroes from the African shores should be procured for that purpose.
>
> Yielding to his importunities, our Lord Charles V removed the then existing prohibition, and permitted him to introduce into the American islands, 4,000 Slaves, for the purpose of cultivating the land.
>
> This is the history of the first Resolution which was against those unfortunate Beings.[24]

The Spanish Crown soon followed the majority's recommendation by signing a treaty with Britain in 1817 that would close the slave traffic in 1820. However, as 1820 came and went, it became evident that Spanish officials would do little to halt the traffic to Cuba. Indeed, it grew to new heights in the 1820s (see table 1).

The slave trade to Cuba continued to bind Europe and Latin America beyond the threshold of the 1820s. So, too, did the evocation of Bartolomé de las Casas in Spanish and Spanish American debates over the traffic. During the restoration of the Constitution of Cádiz between 1820 and 1823, when there was some hope that the liberal regime would follow through on the 1817 ban, critics and defenders of the trade made their views public.[25] Among these works was Juan Antonio Llorente's two-volume collection of las Casas's writings, including a Spanish translation of the Abbé Gregoire's *Apologie de las Casas* and responses to it by Gregorio de Funes, Fray Servando Teresa de Mier, and Llorente himself about las Casas's views on the African slave trade. In his introduction, Llorente deplored the fact that

> the despicable and untrustworthy philosopher *Paw* [sic], and unfortunately the esteemed scholars *Rainald* [sic] and *Robertson* (who followed him without the necessary scrutiny), imputed to the venerable Bishop *Casas* authorship of the commerce of *black* African slaves to America to alleviate the Indians and to free them from slavery.

This (even though it certainly was), which in that time was not considered inhumane (the blacks being accustomed to slavery since ancient times), is now interpreted as a crime capable of defaming the memory of a hero.[26]

The responses to Gregoire included in the volume were mixed. The Mexican patriot Mier was an enthusiastic supporter. He, too, dismissed the careless scholarship of Robertson and Cornelius de Pauw. He also defended las Casas by contrasting what he could know during his lifetime with what enlightened Europeans and Americans knew in the nineteenth century. In the fifteenth and sixteenth centuries, the African slave traffic enjoyed religious and royal sanction, and most Europeans believed that the Portuguese were rescuing African captives from a terrible fate in Africa. Las Casas undoubtedly shared in this belief at the time, but if he lived now, he would be the first to recognize that slavers were "thieves of free men."[27]

In contrast, the Argentine patriot Gregorio de Funes argued that the slave traffic was licit during the era of las Casas and that the bishop of Chiapa was correct to recommend it as an alternative to indigenous labor: "it is impossible to believe that such a widely accepted institution was not looked upon with respect by the virtuous Las Casas."[28] Funes believed that the slave traffic was a form of *rescate* (rescue) for the enslaved Africans, who not only would be delivered from their native captors but also would benefit from their arrival in Spanish territories: "This tutelary angel necessarily concluded that it was a beneficial act to tear them from that sepulcher because at least they were to be transplanted in places with more gentle and fortunate climates, where their labors would be moderate and tolerable. One must acknowledge that in the greater part of the Spanish Colonies, the luck of the Black slaves has not been so unhappy as in the other nations, nor as that of the Indians."[29]

Such discrepant views of las Casas and the slave trade persisted after the restoration of Ferdinand VII in 1823 and beyond. The debate remained urgent because even though Spain lost most of its American empire in the 1820s, it retained control of Cuba, and the Cuban slave trade would thrive long beyond the 1820s, reaching its peak in the 1830s and showing great resiliency in subsequent decades despite the efforts of the British government and the Royal Navy. Given that the slave trade was unchecked and that the "polemics of possession" were still relevant, Spaniards and Cubans actively referenced him. In 1825 the director of the Royal Academy of Spanish History,

Martín Fernández de Navarrete, repeated the indictment of las Casas in his seminal collection of historical documents related to Spanish overseas exploration, the *Colección de los viages y descubrimientos que hicieron por mar los españoles desde fines del siglo XV*. After a detailed reconstruction of las Casas's use of his contacts with Charles V's Flemish courtiers, Navarrete concluded: "That the priest Casas, to relieve the Indians, established and authorized the traffic in blacks to the islands of the New World, as if they were not also rational. What an admirable contradiction of the human spirit!"[30] Navarrete and subsequent generations of Spanish scholars responded in part to the defense and endorsement of las Casas and his work by foreigners such as Alexander von Humboldt, William Hickling Prescott, and George Ticknor. Patriotic pride and defense of the status quo in Cuba made Spaniards bristle at versions of what would come to be known as the Black Legend, which the foreign reception of las Casas's works had stirred. But las Casas found defenders in both Spain and Cuba. The most outstanding of these was the Cuban José Antonio Saco, who beginning in the 1820s turned against the slave trade to the island. He defended the need for continued Spanish rule but criticized the despotic, exceptional rule that Madrid imposed in the aftermath of the Spanish American revolutions. In numerous pamphlets and articles, and in his multivolume study of the history of slavery, Saco followed the lead of Gregoire by vigorously and painstakingly demonstrating that las Casas could not be considered the instigator of the African slave trade to the Spanish Indies because slavery and trafficking were already so integral to the Iberian societies. In the 1860s, he vocally advocated the publication of the *Historia de las Indias* and criticized the Royal Academy of Spanish History for its hesitancy and foot-dragging: "nothing he can be accused of is enough to keep buried in a library's dust the extraordinary events and the great historical and moral truths written by the pen of one of the men who most honors Spain and humanity."[31]

∼

In the 1820s, for his defenders and critics, las Casas spoke to the emancipatory and abolitionist ideals of the revolutionary era while also confronting the harsh new dispensation of the axial age and the renewed Spanish and Cuban commitment to slavery and slave trafficking. Though the year 1820 was meant to mark the end of the Cuban slave traffic, the decade instead witnessed a huge surge in the movement of enslaved Africans to the island as Spaniards and Cubans crafted effective, illegal, slaving networks in tacit collaboration with the Spanish state and its representatives on the island. Far from a decline in slavery or the slave trade, this was a decade of innovation and expansion, as planters, traders, and officials adapted slavery in Cuba to new economic and technological conditions that allowed them to open sugar plantations of vast scale and productive capacity. Cuban plantation slavery from the 1820s onward thus represented more than another manifestation of the Caribbean sugar revolutions that began in Barbados in the mid-seventeenth century; it was part of a cycle of expansion that included southeastern Brazil and the southern United States, in which the number of enslaved workers in the Americas expanded greatly until the US Civil War. Plantation slavery and the slave trade continued to link Europe and the Americas; however, we must be attuned not only to the continuities in slavery but also to the significant ways in which it changed.[32] Though the defenders of slavery were triumphant in the 1820s, they faced many types of opposition, including slave rebellions, maroonage, and a heightened British naval and legal presence. They also faced criticism from Spaniards and Americans who rejected the innovations inaugurated by the deregulation of the slave traffic and advanced by modernizing planters and officials from the late eighteenth century to the mid-nineteenth. Interpreters of las Casas demanded the restoration of Spain's historic distance from the machinations of the slave traffic, which they construed as a foreign monstrosity without precedent in Spain's long history of overseas rule.

Notes

Support for this research was provided by Spain's Ministry of Science and Innovation (grant number HAR2009-07103).

1. For new synthetic works on the Hispanic world that emphasize the democratic and radical potential of the revolutionary era, see G. Andrews, *Afro-Latin America*; Blanchard, *Under the Flags of Freedom*; and Chasteen, *Americanos*.

2. The most influential view is Bayly, *Imperial Meridian*; and Bayly, *Birth of the Modern World*. On the Americas, see Spieler, "The Legal Structure of Colonial Rule"; and Fradera, *Colonias para después de un imperio*. On the growth of plantation slavery in the Americas and its causes, see Tomich, *Through the Prism of Slavery*; and Berbel, Marquese, and Parron, *Escravidão e política*.

3. See Fradera, *Colonias para después de un imperio*.

4. Adorno, *The Polemics of Possession,* 6. See also Brading, *The First America*.

5. Hanke, *Bartolomé de las Casas*; and Bataillon, "The *Clérigo* Casas," 415–18.

6. On the expansion of Cuban, Brazilian, and US slavery in the nineteenth century, see, most recently, Tomich and Zeuske, "Introduction, The Second Slavery,"

91–100. Specifically on Cuba, see Moreno Fraginals, *El ingenio*; Bergad, *Cuban Rural Society*. On the Spanish imperial context, see Fradera, *Colonias para después de un imperio*; and Schmidt-Nowara, "Continuity and Crisis."

7. Gerbi, *The Dispute of the New World*; Cañizares-Esguerra, *How to Write the History of New World*; and Arias, "Equal Rights and Individual Freedom." On shifting attitudes toward las Casas, see the indispensable Benjamin Keen, "Introduction: Approaches to Las Casas," in *Bartolomé de las Casas in History: Toward an Understanding of the Man and His Work*, ed. Juan Freide and Benjamin Keen (DeKalb: Northern Illinois University Press, 1971), 3–63.

8. W. Robertson, *The History of America*, 1:249.

9. Clarkson, *An Essay on the Slavery and Commerce of the Human Species*, ix.

10. On Gregoire and slavery, see Popkin and Popkin, *The Abbé Gregoire and His World*; and Sepinwall, *The Abbé Gregoire and the French Revolution*.

11. Gregoire, "Apología de don Bartholomé de las Casas," 2:349.

12. On Spanish restrictions on the slave trade and their eventual easing, see Delgado Ribas, "From Marginality to Centrality." On Spanish involvement in the slave traffic in the late eighteenth and early nineteenth centuries, see Fradera, *Indústria i mercat*.

13. Chust Calero, "De esclavos, encomenderos y mitayos"; Fradera, *Gobernar colonias*.

14. Wilberforce to Lord Wellesley, August 1, 1810, The National Archives, London, FO 72/104, folio 1.

15. See Schmidt-Nowara, "Wilberforce Spanished."

16. Pons, "Blanco White, abolicionista (3)," 144–45.

17. Antillón, *Disertación sobre el origen de la esclavitud*, 67.

18. Ibid., 75.

19. Ibid., 67, 53–67. On Spanish debates over policy toward the indigenous population in the late eighteenth and early nineteenth centuries, see Weber, *Bárbaros*. See also Andrien, "The *Noticias secretas de América*." For a recent discussion of emulation and the Bourbon reforms, see Paquette, *Enlightenment, Governance, and Reform*.

20. Antillón, *Disertación sobre el origen de la esclavitud*, 16–20.

21. Ibid., 89–91.

22. See D. Murray, *Odious Commerce*.

23. "Proceeding of the Council of the Indies of Spain, relative to the expediency of the Abolition by His Catholic Majesty, of the Slave Trade carried on by Spanish Subjects. Madrid, February, 1816," *British and Foreign State Papers* (BFSP) IV (1816–1817), 520.

24. Ibid.

25. Antillón's work was republished, *Disertación sobre el orígen de la esclavitud de los negros* (Barcelona: J. Busquets, 1820), though the author himself had been killed during the restoration of Ferdinand VII. The most notable pro-slave-trade tract was penned by one of the Cuban representatives to the Cortes, the priest O'Gavan, *Observaciónes sobre la suerte de los negros del África*.

26. Juan Antonio Llorente, "Prologo del Editor," in *Colección de las obras del venerable obispo de Chiapa*, ed. Llorente, 1:xi–xii (emphases in the original). On Llorente's collection, see Arias, "Equal Rights and Individual Freedom."

27. "Discurso del doctor don Servando Mier, natural de Mejico, Confirmando la apología del obispo Casas, escrita por el reverendo obispo de Blois, Monseñor Henrique Gregoire, en cara escrita a este año 1806," in *Colección de las obras del venerable obispo de Chiapa*, ed. Llorente, 1:430. See also Fray Servando Teresa de Mier's comments on las Casas and the slave trade in the prologue to his edition of las Casas's *Breve relación de la destrucción de las Indias Occidentales*, 37–40. On Mier during the revolutionary era, see Brading, *The First America*, 583–602. Mier's defense was flawed because he could not read the unpublished *Historia de las Indias*. Though las Casas did suggest African slaves as an alternative, he came to believe that the Portuguese were illegally enslaving Africans, who were born free.

28. "Carta del doctor don Gregorio de Funes, Deán de Cordova del Tucuman," in *Colección de las obras del venerable obispo de Chiapa*, ed. Llorente, 1:394.

29. Ibid., 396.

30. Navarrete, quoted in Schmidt-Nowara, *The Conquest of History*, 156.

31. Saco, quoted in Schmidt-Nowara, *The Conquest of History*, 146.

32. Blackburn, *The Overthrow of Colonial Slavery*; Tomich, *Through the Prism of Slavery*.

13
The 1820s in Perspective

The Bolivarian Decade

Matthew Brown

The Atlantic world changed but did not end in the 1820s. The chapters in this book make that very clear: imperial relationships were reconfigured and new political practices, such as the pronunciamiento, were born. The anticolonial and international wars that shook the Atlantic world in the period 1790–1820 morphed into civil wars, where regional elites and popular groups struggled over the control and direction of new nations and colonial legacies. Metropolitan leaders reacted with propaganda, pragmatic realism, or proud resistance. This was as true in Britain, with George Canning's imperial bluster in 1826, as it was in Spain with Fernando VII's refusal to recognize the loss of his continental American empire. In Spanish America, the surviving veterans of the wars of independence spent the 1820s positioning themselves for regional and then national power. The refugees of American royalism and loyalism assumed political protagonism elsewhere in Britain's and Spain's empires, as Maya Jasanoff and Natalia Sobrevilla Perea have shown.[1]

From another perspective, the Atlantic world hardly changed at all in the 1820s. Despite all the words spoken and battles fought, Latin America remained in a position of some subservience to Europe. The imperial chairs had been moved, but the dining arrangements remained the same. Latin America provided the silver service and waited the tables while European diners feasted themselves on its riches. The flow of raw materials and specie was disrupted by the wars of independence but was resumed with only a slight inflection of destination (from Seville and Lisbon to Amsterdam and London) in the 1830s. A comparative, continental perspective shows that, although statistics remain cloudy because of the fragmented, far-flung nature of commercial archives for this war-torn period (so we can never be entirely certain of our conclusions), relations between Europe and Latin America during and immediately after the 1820s seem to have maintained a considerable degree of continuity with the colonial period of the late eighteenth century.

As the chapters in this book have made clear, the 1820s was a paradoxical decade, where strengthened and ambitious empires overlapped and coexisted with newly independent and sovereign successor states. Contributors therefore stress both continuity and change. The overall conclusion encouraged by the works collected here, alongside other recent scholarship, is that the 1820s produced no outright winner: no European empire achieved hegemony in the Americas, no national political project proceeded untroubled, and no political ideology (monarchism, republicanism, or mixed constitution) was unequivocally ascendant. Simón Bolívar's own rise and fall neatly parallels this narrative: he declared victoriously on Mount Chimborazo in 1822 that "not even time could hold back freedom's march," whereas in 1830, on his way into exile, the Liberator lamented that "he who serves the revolution ploughs the sea."[2]

As a unit of study, the 1820s lend themselves to the study of imperfect beginnings and unfinished endings. Scarlett O'Phelan Godoy's account of Bernardo O'Higgins's life is a stringent defense of the continuities that linked the 1820s to the late colonial period, mixing the lure of new dreams with the defeats and disillusion caused when those dreams encountered hard political reality. O'Higgins's political successes were closely linked to his perceived influence in Britain and his educational heritage in London, just as his father Ambrosio O'Higgins's ascent to the apex of viceregal political power in Lima had been predicated upon his relations with a loyal and effective cohort of Irish-Hispanic officers and administrators in the Spanish Empire. As Oscar Recio Morales has demonstrated, the Irish were embedded in the Spanish Atlantic empire through the lives of both O'Higginses.[3] External connections were key in both of their political lives. Bernardo O'Higgins's career highlights the increasingly influence of the British navy in Pacific waters after 1815, perhaps, but social and economic structures seemed to have altered little by the end of his public career in the 1820s. His appearance in Iona Macintyre's chapter as a supporter of British publishing projects in Argentina, advocating female education and inviting British educationalists to set up schools in Chile, is an indication of the overlapping nature of many of the connections after colonialism analyzed in this book.

The chapters by Brian Hamnett and Josep M. Fradera also stress the deep roots of the changes that occurred in the 1820s. They view social and political change as being solidified in this decade, as the medium-term consequences of Bourbon reformism and the rise of Spanish and Portuguese liberalisms were played out. In Hamnett's words, "tensions between projects and processes ran continuously through this decade, which combined astonishing transformation of political forms with less ambitious tasks of renovation, innovation, and conservation."[4]

Other contributors focus particularly on new phenomena that emerged in the 1820s. Will Fowler's account of Rafael del Riego's pronunciamiento is the clearest example, opening the decade with a resounding and original call that had enormous impact in both Spain and the Americas throughout the 1820s and beyond. With his execution in 1823, Riego became one of the many martyrs that the 1820s provided to the growing gallery of heroes evoked by those who rallied to what Mónica Ricketts calls the "universal cry of liberty."[5] During the decade, Riego was joined by Lord Byron (1824), José María Córdova (1829), Antonio José de Sucre (1830), and Simón Bolívar (1830). The cause of liberty had good cause to look back to the 1820s as it sought its founding heroes during the rest of the nineteenth century.

One of the principal changes identified in the chapters collected here is the rapid spread and importance of news and communication during the 1820s. The fast transfer of news from colony to metropole, within empires and across nations, advanced apace in this decade. Many of the contributors rely heavily on newspaper coverage as they trace the ties that held the Atlantic together in the 1820s. Benedict Anderson's hypothesis on the influence of "print capitalism" and the growth of nations in the nineteenth century has been justifiably influential. But the newsprint revolution and the consequent proliferation of information had another, relatively understudied, influence, emphasized here, which was the way in which political movements on opposite sides of the Atlantic had now become not only related, but mutually constitutive—that is to say, they were more aware of each others' struggles, learned more quickly of each others' difficulties and opportunities, and adapted their strategies accordingly.[6] This has been detailed by Scott Eastman in his work on the links between Spanish and Mexican liberals in the 1820s.[7] The tight coupling between European and Latin American political activities is demonstrated most strikingly in Gabriel Paquette's contribution to this volume, arguing quite convincingly for the Brazilian origins of the Portuguese constitution of 1826. Drafts of constitutions, editions of newspapers, and many published pamphlets and broadsides shot across the Atlantic and across the Americas, triggering reactions and fomenting revolutions. These changes in the speed and nature of communication did not, nevertheless, assure political movements of success.

The growth of British influence is another theme touched on by several contributors, especially David Rock and Iona Macintyre. Macintyre uses another form of print culture, the catechism, to show how British culture began to permeate into the River Plate in the 1820s, a base from which it expanded rapidly during the nineteenth century. Rock focuses on the political influence of the British merchants in Buenos Aires, showing how they slipped into the power vacuum left by fleeing Spaniards. Rock's account shows how the 1820s saw the expansion of some types of transatlantic relations (i.e., trade, utopian dreams, print communication) and the contraction of others (i.e., formal diplomacy). Reuben Zahler takes a similar approach, but his broad treatment of foreigners in Venezuela suggests that, despite the evident social changes and political conflict he traces, there was also much continuity. Though new actors appeared on the scene in the 1820s, the way they were (or were not) integrated into the body politic—or the nation—differed little from how assimilation or exclusion had occurred in the late eighteenth century. For Zahler, the important new political and cultural changes—such as the introduction of religious toleration—came in Venezuela in the 1830s. The reconfiguration of imperial networks in the 1820s fed into new national reactions to those changes—in Zahler's case, the arrival of new categories of "foreigners" to live within the boundaries of the new states—in later decades. The changes that religious practice underwent during the age of revolution in Latin America remain an understudied aspect of the subject. Clément Thibaud and María Teresa Calderón's original recent work on "the majesty of the people" in Venezuela and Colombia shows quite startlingly how old beliefs died hard but were transformed under the weight of new political ideas and geopolitical reality.[8]

For Jay Sexton, too, the 1820s shifted the ground upon which later, more important changes could develop. US disengagement from Latin American affairs, most obviously after the Panama debates of 1826, led directly to the adoption of a more belligerent approach to obtaining and exercising US influence in the region.[9] Annexationist desires toward Mexico and Cuba received important boosts precisely as the new Hispanic American republics began to establish themselves as independent nations. The strength of Colombia and Mexico was potentially much more of a threat to US interests than had been the weak colonies of New Granada and New Spain that they had replaced, which had been tied into Hispanic interests in Europe. Carrie Gibson makes a similar point regarding Haiti. As Haitian independence became established in the 1820s—and, even more slowly, begrudgingly, and reluctantly, as it was recognized by the major powers—fear of violent upheaval amongst Haiti's neighbors was gradually replaced by a fear of economic disruption. The continued existence of Haiti was enough to remind slave owners in North America and around the circum-Caribbean of the very precarious nature of their own social and economic structures. In many areas, the decade of the 1830s was a pause in the process of the abolition of slavery across the Americas. This movement only recovered some momentum in the late 1840s.

Warfare, republicanism, and liberalism created new transatlantic networks in the 1820s that changed the way elites thought about the worlds they lived in. At the same time, the devastation of war and the discourses that motivated it opened up those elites to new groups. As Neil Safier has argued, travelers carried knowledge with them in many directions, creating unscheduled encounters and triggering unexpected changes in cultural and social practices. Hipólito da Costa founded journals and published obsessively in a way that, Safier argues, refracted and domesticated the British and other European influences that he absorbed from across the Atlantic.[10] Will Fowler's dissection of the birth and spread of the pronuciamiento reveals how political practices crisscrossed the Atlantic in the 1820s, sometimes finding fertile soil, as in Mexico, other times falling onto rocky ground. Unprecedented social mobility, especially through military mobilization in the Americas but also through the gradual opening up of electoral franchises on both sides of the Atlantic, meant that imperial and national leaders not only acted differently after 1820, but also emerged from a wider spread of ethnic, racial, regional, and occupational (but not gender) backgrounds.

～

Radical new political projects floundered on old barriers shaped by geography, economics, and geopolitics. Sometimes the leaders of independence were able to overcome them; on others they were tripped and left flailing. This point can be explored by tracing the rise to power, and fall from grace, of Simón Bolívar and his close associates during the first half of the nineteenth century. Their stories can illustrate the new mobility of the 1820s and also indicate its limits. In geopolitical and imperial terms, it can be argued that the increasingly explicit British involvement in Hispanic and Luso-America is a key development in the 1820s. The fulcrum of this change was the figure of Simón

Bolívar, prompting David Brading to speculate at our Cambridge symposium that, if anything, the 1820s were "the Bolivarian Decade."[11] Bolívar's trajectory through the 1820s, from "liberation to disappointment" as dreams of freedom crashed against the harsh reality of social and ethnic division, might seem an apt motif for the decade as a whole.[12] On another level, Bolívar's repeated flirtation with British "protection" and his quest for British military support and diplomatic recognition were far from unique. Throughout the Americas, the pressure Britain sought to exert in order to secure the abolition of the slave trade had important ramifications.[13] Republican elites perceived the specter of British imperialism in this pressure, particularly in those places, such as in the River Plate, where British naval forces had actually attacked or invaded within living memory. In imperial Brazil, frustrations with the terms of Brazil's trade treaty with Britain figured prominently in political debates in the late 1820s. But it remains far too simplistic to suggest, as Eduardo Galeano did in his influential *Open Veins of Latin America* (the book gifted to Barack Obama by Hugo Chávez at their first meeting in 2009, just weeks before the exchange of texts at the University of Cambridge that gave rise to this book), that Iberian colonialism gave way effortlessly into British imperialism in the 1820s, and henceforth to US neocolonialism in the twentieth century.[14]

Simón Bolívar's shadow dominates the 1820s on a variety of levels. The apex of his political career, his presidency of the Republic of Gran Colombia (1819–30), spans the entire decade. Of course, Bolívar is far from the only figure associated with the 1820s in this way: in Great Britain and Ireland King George IV reigned from 1820 through 1830, for example, and Bernardino Rivadavia's liberalism was dominant in Buenos Aires for most of the decade.

Yet one of the factors that set Bolívar apart was that he was already a global figure, a point of reference during his own lifetime. His story appeared in the popular annuals produced by José Joaquín de Mora (discussed in Iona Macintyre's chapter), his actions triggered debate in the US Congress and across the Italian diaspora (as mentioned in Jay Sexton's and Maurizio Isabella's chapters), and figures from across the world wrote to Bolívar requesting his advice or assistance for their personal projects. In death, already in the 1830s and, especially, in the 1840s, he became a symbol: first of Venezuelan nationalism, consecrated with the 1842 return of his remains from New Granada to Caracas; and then of continentalism, as in the resurrected dreams for pan-American unity. His growth into an all-purpose political symbol co-opted by all sides, along a transatlantic path being followed in the twenty-first century by Che Guevara, began only half a century after his death.[15]

There is a multiplicity of conflicting interpretations of Bolívar's political and social prominence in the Americas and in Europe. Historians have agreed on little beyond that his death in 1830 marked a turning point and that in death he gradually became a memory, a reference point, and a legend.[16] His name became synonymous with the liberation of Spain's American colonies. As David Bushnell has correctly observed, "the writings of the Libertador are so extensive and cover such a vast array of situations that by careful selection one can find passages to support even seemingly contradictory positions."[17] There are two particularly important considerations that continue to trigger debate amongst historians as well as contemporary politicians and that are of considerable relevance for the topics under discussion. First is Bolívar's reputation as a republican, which is complicated by his unpopular decision to argue for a life presidency to replace the monarch's divinely anointed power in the Americas (which is often ignored by present-day Bolivarians). Second is Bolívar's reputation as an anti-imperialist, which is blurred somewhat by his sometimes secret, sometimes public, but always pragmatic desire to replace Spanish authority with British protection in Latin America.

The two themes of monarchism and anti-imperialism are tied together in Bolívar's relationship with Great Britain. For the purposes of this volume, it seems to me that Bolívar's career perfectly illustrates the shift from Iberian toward British hegemony in the South Atlantic, which became manifest in the 1820s. Bolívar was no mere observer of this change; he was one of its architects and one of its most effective engineers.

Karen Racine has brilliantly captured this aspect of Bolívar's political makeup in her article "Simón Bolívar, Englishman."[18] Racine demonstrates how, as Bolívar and his generation "surveyed both the ancient past and contemporary polities for models upon which to base their reform projects," they were "powerfully attracted to the example of Great Britain" as a peaceful alternative to the violent upheavals experienced in France and Haiti. Bolívar's time in England in 1810 was particularly influential, Racine argues, in that his "association with progressive members of the British aristocracy clearly influenced his understanding of the responsibilities that privilege incurred" through charitable work and educational projects.[19]

When he came to power in the early 1820s, therefore, Bolívar possessed what Racine called an "Anglophile social vision" (David Bushnell calls it his "well-known Anglocentrism"), epitomized by the measures he passed in favor of a national Lancasterian school system. Bolívar, inspired by elements of the British aristocracy, tried to create structures that would further the common good: his rhetoric "assumed an instructive, tutelary guiding tone and abandoned the more egalitarian fervour that had initially fuelled [his] revolutionary fire."[20] "Inspired by England," Bolívar's social policies were based on a "paternalistic, aristocratic form of democracy that would allow [the elite] to maintain their own privileged position while the rest of the population caught up."[21]

Bolívar's political Anglophilia was paralleled by and informed by his geopolitical awareness of the unassailable might of the British Empire and, in particular, the Royal Navy, which continued its rise in dominance of the Atlantic in the 1820s. As Bushnell has observed, "there is no question but that he was entirely correct in thinking the goodwill of Great Britain was more important than that of the US in warding off the interference of other European powers" in Hispanic America.[22] But was Bolívar's courting of the British in the 1820s purely pragmatic and practical, part of the necessary maneuvering to assure recognition and independence, as some historians claim, or can we detect longer-term changes in the relationship of Hispanic America to the Atlantic world, in which the 1820s marked a decisive sea change? Was this the axial age, where Europe's imperial hold over the rest of the world was strengthened, even despite the apparent liberation of independence from Spanish colonial rule?

～

The life and writings of Simón Bolívar are of little use in finding an answer to this question. If we want to assess the role of the 1820s in changing Atlantic and global history, we must look beyond the decade and into the 1830s and 1840s. We cannot use Bolívar as a case study to analyze these changes because he was dead by the end of the 1820s. Instead, we must follow the paths of those who accompanied Bolívar through the 1820s and then struck out on their own in the years after his death. This is a more problematic exercise than repeating the well-trodden path of Bolivarian biography for, as John Lombardi has written, in comparison, "history [has been] unkind to those like José Antonio Páez, who labour long. With time in the limelight, the chances of failure accelerate rapidly. Bolivar's brilliant decade of rise and fall gave us the romantic, the triumphant and the tragic elements essential to an effective legend."[23]

An analysis of the post-1830 careers of some of Bolívar's followers may help to illustrate this point. It is useful, for these purposes, to think of the Bolivarians as a family in the 1820s and beyond. Defenders of Spanish imperial rule in the Americas in the 1810s had long spoken of the Spanish national family.

Bolívar himself took on this refrain and subverted it in the cause of independence, recasting the beloved *madre patria* (the mother country) into the *madrastra* (the wicked stepmother). As Catherine Davies has shown, Bolívar consciously presented himself as the *padre de la patria* (the father of the fatherland) who would replace Spain in the affections of its subject peoples. He imposed discipline on the *hijos de la patria,* the nation's sons who filled the army, though he was not beyond turning an indulgent blind eye to the misdemeanors of his favored sons, his *hijos predilectos.*[24] He was certain that women had a clear role to play in national life, but it would have to be a subordinate, domesticated one that left national politics and public life to men. Bolívar's vision of the national family was not without contradictions, of course; he relied heavily on the economic and personal support of his sister, María Antonia Bolívar, and on the political nous and emotional warmth of his long-term lover, Manuela Sáenz.[25]

Simón Bolívar's political family in the 1820s was extensive and complicated, and it is not my purpose to trace it or analyze its composition here.[26] Instead, I will use a comparative biographical treatment of two principal members of the Bolivarian family, José Antonio Páez from Venezuela and Tomás Cipriano de Mosquera from New Granada. Both spent part of the 1820s at Bolívar's side and outlived him into the second half of the nineteenth century. In what follows, I provide a biographical summary of each in turn, paying particular attention to their relations with the outside world in the 1820s and beyond. I conclude with some comparative and thematic observations on the transformative nature of the Atlantic 1820s.

The collective biography approach adopted here can provide the human edge to the broad-brush historical analysis presented elsewhere in this volume. Like other attempts to describe "colonial lives" through detailed biography, this story of the Bolivarian family cannot claim to be as representative or, indeed, as accurate as more depersonalized analyses adopted elsewhere or, for example, in the superb scholarly narratives of Fradera or Hamnett in this volume.[27] However, it hopes to add a human dimension to attempts to "find ways of conceptualising [the] connected histories of revolution" in the first half of the nineteenth century.[28] As the works of Emma Rothschild and Maya Jasanoff on regions far away from those under study here have shown, the humdrum details of everyday life can often shed unexpected light on drier structural developments and inter-imperial relationships.[29] The subsequent sections seek to use their insights to place the Bolivarian decade within its personal, revolutionary, and Atlantic contexts.

~

José Antonio Páez (1790–1873) is usually seen as a classic "caudillo" of the type who rose to prominence after independence in Hispanic America on the basis of charisma and control of dependent manpower in large, landed estates.[30] Páez's political career survived numerous apparently fatal challenges. Like Antonio de Santa Anna in Mexico, Páez appeared to become stronger with each failure, and each defeat or dishonorable exit only served to increase the intensity of the calls for his return in the next political crisis.[31] However, his career also perhaps unexpectedly encapsulates two of the major themes of this book: the many challenges posed by the rising hegemony of the Anglo-American empires in nineteenth-century Latin America and also the legacies of slavery after independence. Páez's relationship with Bolívar was a difficult one and deteriorated after 1826. Nevertheless, it is useful to analyze Páez's career within a Bolivarian paradigm, judging both men as members of the same generation who grappled with the same dilemmas of constructing postcolonial nations within the revolutionary Atlantic context.

Páez was born in Curpa in the Venezuelan llanos in 1790, the son of an official in the Spanish Royal Tobacco Monopoly. The quiet of his undistinguished education and early career was shattered when he killed a man in an altercation in 1807; Páez went on the run from the authorities and found work as a *peón* in rural Apure Province. His physical strength, horsemanship, and appetite for work gained him the respect of the *llaneros* he lived alongside; in the early rural conflict of the wars of independence in the llanos after 1811, Páez served on the Royalist side, before joining the republicans two years later. From then on his leadership of llanero lancers won him many victories, and he was incorporated into Bolívar's armies around 1816. After the Battle of Carabobo secured Venezuelan independence in 1821, Páez was established as the dominant figure in Venezuelan politics as Bolívar's trusted representative in the region. Páez occasionally made plain his difference concerning policies emanating out of the Colombian capital, Bogotá, but until 1826 he was seen as a reliable mediator between Venezuelan and Gran Colombian interests. He gradually, therefore, came to be seen, both in Caracas and Bogotá, as somehow representative of national sovereignty in Venezuela. This growing sense that authority and sovereignty had become invested in his person led Páez to lead the rebellion known as La Cosiata, which was ultimately diffused by Bolívar's personal appeals to Páez to respect the national integrity of Colombia. Nevertheless, historians mark 1826 as the beginning of the end of Gran Colombia. The first of the many nails hammered into the republic's coffin in early 1830 was administered by Páez himself in Caracas in January that year. Reacting to news of José María Córdova's rebellion in Antioquia three months previously (to which he had been alerted by a personal letter from Córdova, urging him to join the insurrection) and responding to the pleading of the economic and social elite in Caracas who could no longer stand being ruled from Bogotá, Páez announced Venezuela's separation from Bolívar's republic.[32] Páez had also been heavily encouraged by the British Royal Navy officer in charge of the West India station, Admiral Charles Elphinstone Fleeming, who visited Caracas in the week preceding the announcement and held a series of poorly concealed meetings with known secessionist conspirators, as well as with Páez himself.[33] Fleeming's wife gave birth to a daughter on her first day on Venezuelan soil, and she lived in Caracas as Páez's neighbor even after the departure of her admiral husband, remaining there and raising the infant for the next three years.[34] From March 1830 the New Granadan provinces began to follow Venezuela's lead with increasingly frequent rebellions against Bolívar's Colombian state.

Páez served one term as president of independent Venezuela, from 1830 to 1834. In these years, Páez fostered intimate relations with Great Britain, particularly through the figure of the British consul Sir Robert Ker Porter, with whom he dined regularly and whom he described as his "dear friend."[35] Páez's defeat in the *Revolución de las Reformas* (1836) left him in exile in Curacao. In 1838 Páez returned to the presidency after an overwhelming electoral victory. He stacked his cabinet with former Bolivarians, such as Diego Bautista Urbaneja in Interior and Justice, Rafael Urdaneta in War and Marine, and Guillermo Smith as minister of Finance. As the leader of a government representing what Venezuelan historians called "oligarchic conservatism," Páez and his ministers proposed and enacted measures that they thought would integrate the republic into the modern, prosperous world; for example, they encouraged private road-building schemes, national schools, immigration, and payment of the national debt. Tightly linked to the dominant landowners and slave owners who had emerged newly prosperous from the wars of independence (indeed, Páez himself became one of the biggest landowners in the country), the administration did not abolish slavery.

As Edgardo Mondolfi Gudat has shown and documented, Páez maintained the excellent reputation with British travelers and migrants that he had forged during the wars of independence. Writers queued up to exalt his charisma, endurance, and common touch.[36] Drawing on their publications, in the early twentieth century Robert Cunninghame-Graham wrote the first (and to this day, the last) full-length biography of Páez in English. He described Páez as "the most sympathetic character" of the wars of independence, with a "liberality of ideas surprising in a man who had passed his life on horseback with lance and lasso always in his hand."[37]

With Edinburgh-born Guillermo Smith in the Ministry of Finance (and later, also Foreign Affairs), it was clear that Venezuela's progress was firmly tied to British power in these years. The liberal opposition, grouped around the newspaper *El Venezolano,* criticized Smith's economic policies for undermining Venezuelan sovereignty. Páez's second presidency also witnessed the most long-lasting example of British hegemony in Venezuela. This was the inability of the Venezuelan state to resist growing British territorial incursions in Guayana. The unilateral boundary-marking expeditions led by Robert Schomburgk were denounced as British imperialism, as "abusive and unilateral theft" of national territory. It was lamented that the Venezuelan foreign minister, Guillermo Smith, and the British consul, Daniel O'Leary, could not have employed their excellent contacts and relationships with British imperial power in order to achieve a better settlement for Venezuela.[38]

Another example of the intimate links between Britain and Páez's government can be found in the nascent banking industry. In 1839 Páez gave the newly established Banco Colonial Británico substantial operating privileges in the hope that it would efficiently service and pay Venezuela's external debts.[39] The cozy relationship between the close-knit governing clique and the representatives of British imperial power was noticed and criticized by opposition politicians. Indeed, the axis between Páez's successor as president, Carlos Soublette, his brother-in-law Daniel O'Leary (Bolívar's old aide-de-camp), and Leandro Miranda, London-born son of the early hero of Venezuelan independence, Francisco de Miranda (both were directors of the bank and had close links to London financiers) catalyzed national opinion and, as Nikita Harwich Valenilla has shown, led directly to the foundation of the Banco Nacional de Venezuela in 1841.[40]

Despite these close links to the financial and military aspects of British imperialism, in the 1850s Páez went into exile not in Britain, but in New York. His sons had been educated in the United States, and, of course, it was geographically closer to Venezuela than London. With Páez gone, some space for political change was opened. It was only after his departure that slavery was finally abolished and black Venezuelans fully entered the path to citizenship of the republic. Páez made some later incursions into Venezuelan politics in the 1860s, including a brief spell as an unelected stopgap leader, but spent most of the rest of his life in exile. In New York he wrote his autobiography and translated Napoleon's writings on the art of war into Spanish. In the late 1860s and early 1870s he undertook a lengthy tour of Latin America, where he was feted with honors. Páez died in New York in 1873.

⌒

The second life to be examined here is that of a Colombian. Tomás Cipriano de Mosquera (1798–1878) had such a long, complex, and, above all, public life that any attempt to summarize it or generalize from it is doomed to failure. Nevertheless, after a brief biographical description I want to show how the 1820s were of profound importance in shaping Mosquera's political and career trajectory, in particular, his subsequent role as a mediator between liberal and conservative factions and between Colombia and the Anglophone world.

Born in Popayán in 1798 into a slave-owning, land-owning family, the bastion of the Creole elite in the Cauca Valley, Mosquera joined the forces of independence as a teenager. Despite criticism of his limited military abilities from his contemporaries, Mosquera quickly ascended the ranks through service in his home region. As the 1820s opened, military campaigns dragged Mosquera out of local politics, in which he would otherwise have probably spent his whole life, and rocketed him out across Hispanic America. Remaining loyal to Bolívar in the late 1820s as others passed over into opposition, Mosquera was governor of various provinces in or around the Cauca Valley. Mosquera went to Peru as an emissary in the buildup to the Peru-Colombia war in 1828 and 1829. Here Mosquera developed the fiery Colombian nationalism that would characterize the rest of his career even as he slipped between and beneath the conservative/liberal divisions that marked national politics in the next half century. In the late 1820s, also, Mosquera began to correspond with a wide range of Anglo-American friends and contacts who started to shape his political ideas in favor of liberal, federalist ideas linked (but not slavishly) to those prevalent in the United States.

In January 1828, Belford Hinton Wilson wrote to Mosquera from Bogotá, commenting approvingly on Mosquera's own words, stating that recent elections showed that "in a country [like Colombia] where the mass of the populace lacks virtue, political intrigue is valued much more than the national interest."[41]

During the 1830s Mosquera traversed a political trajectory that led him into open conflict with those whom he saw as guilty of unpatriotic political intrigue. Mosquera would famously use any possible means in order to vanquish those who—he believed—did not act in the nation's best interests. In order to outflank two rebellious liberal generals in the Cauca region in the War of the Supremes (1839–42), Mosquera, as minister of war, was integral to the New Granadan invitation to Juan José Flores (at the time, president of Ecuador) to invade New Granadan territory. But, of course, Mosquera's actions were criticized for "selling the country and its honour so that a foreigner [Flores] can have his revenge upon his enemies [Obando and López]."[42] Mosquera's extremism fueled an apparently perpetual cycle of rebellion against institutions, factionalism against legitimacy, violence against violence, and order against anarchy. All sides claimed, like Mosquera, that they were "against tyranny, against conspiracy and against the spilling of blood."[43] Mosquera's growing military talents contributed to ministerial victory in the War of the Supremes.

Mosquera's offer to Flores allowed his opponents to characterize him as someone who was excessively and unpatriotically allied to foreign parties to the expense of the national interest. In March 1841 Colonel Salvador Córdova recurred to the threat of foreign intervention in New Granadan affairs. Arguing that "resistance is a duty and obedience a crime," Córdova stated that "the government in Bogotá has established the dreadful precedent of foreign intervention in domestic disputes, introducing in this way, in the land of liberty, the European Holy Alliance's international law." Córdova desperately evoked the language of national sovereignty against Mosquera, urging the population of Buenaventura and Cauca to "find a way to reorganise our patria, establishing a strong empire of democracy and liberty. If we work together, civil wars will no longer torment us, and aristocrats [such as Mosquera] will finally abandon the throne forever. Long live democracy! Long live liberty!"[44] We can see in Córdova's use of language ("aristocrats," "throne") that he was linking Mosquera back to his colonial and Bolivarian pasts. These legacies remained in historical and political memory, even as chameleon figures like Mosquera shed their old skins to acquire new identities.

Just two months later, Salvador Córdova and his friend and ally Manuel Antonio Jaramillo were captured by General Mosquera. After a summary and, by all accounts, cursory trial, they stood side by side as they were executed by firing squad. Mosquera claimed that "those men could not be allowed to live without endangering the Republic's health."[45] Many contemporaries saw Mosquera to be eliminating potential competitors for regional and national power. For Córdova's supporters, the "treacherous murders . . . were events that cannot be described, that produce such indignation and anger that cannot be rendered."[46] Colombian historians María Teresa Uribe de Hincapié and Liliana López Lopera confirm that Córdova was executed "without any trial" in a "completely arbitrary act."[47] Investigation of Mosquera's correspondence from the period shows that his decision to eliminate potential rivals from national politics had been shaped by the public and private humiliations he had received during his first experience of civil conflict, the Bolivarian wars of the late 1820s.[48] Comparably, Mosquera's womanizing and philandering of the 1830s and 1840s was catalyzed by his unhappy—but politically strategic—marriage in the 1820s.[49] In all aspects of his life, therefore—from politics and love to his memory of Bolívar and his relationship to the United States—it was events in the 1820s that had guided him toward his future actions.

As commander of forces in the New Granadan Caribbean during the War of the Supremes (1839–42), Mosquera benefited from the convert assistance of British diplomats.[50] But Mosquera had learned at Bolívar's side during the 1820s, and he was astutely aware of the imperial reconfiguration that occurred across the North Atlantic in the subsequent decade. From 1845 to 1849, as president of New Granada, he approved the Bidlack-Mallarino treaty, which guaranteed US rights in Panama and which proved to be, with hindsight, the US foot in the door, which opened the "path to empire" followed by the United States in Panama and beyond in the second half of the nineteenth century.[51] Mosquera's relationship with the new British minister in Bogotá, Bolívar's former aide-de-camp Daniel O'Leary, was cold, and he favored ties with the United States. Indeed, Mosquera's relations with Anglo-Americans in Colombia in the 1820s had most certainly shaped his exchanges with North Americans in the 1840s and beyond. After leaving the presidency in 1849 he spent five years living in New York (1850–54), returning to serve as a general (most notably in leading the liberals to victory in the 1861–63 civil war), regional governor, ambassador to France, and national president (1861–64, 1866–67). He died back at home in Popayán in 1878. Mosquera's path through life shows how ambitious men negotiated the treacherous changes occasioned by the 1820s rupture with the Spanish Empire. The recourse to violence was one of the principal motors of Mosquera's continued grip on power; loyalty to any one ideological or partisan grouping was not. As with many other individuals studied in this book, Mosquera's life was marked by profound continuities with the colonial period and punctuated by new, radical upheavals of nation- and state-building. He was marked by the 1820s: connections after colonialism shaped his life, his travels, and his political endeavors.

∽

The biographical approach carries obvious limitations in the attempt to understand a period of global history. As David Todd, Maya Jasanoff, and Emma Rothschild have shown, biography can cut to the heart of social and economic change. Robert Bickers demonstrated in *Empire Made Me* that the biographical approach allows the historian to tease out the personal and the political, the financial and the cultural, the imperial and the individual.[52] Each life is unique, and the lives of political leaders arguably even more so. But the colonial and postcolonial lives of Bolívar's associates do bring out the extent to which their world was changed during the 1820s. The circles in which Páez and Mosquera moved and rebelled against centralist power in the 1820s and 1830s, for example, were a whole new world away from previous Andean rebellions a generation earlier, from Túpac Amaru in 1780 and 1781 to the 1808–1810 proclamations of independence. Then the intervention of the French or British had been sometimes feared, occasionally dreamed of. In Madrid, ministers like Manuel de Godoy were consistently anxious that "Spain and its empire were [being] ground between English and French millstones."[53] Now, however, northern Europe had made its long-feared initial incursions into continental Hispanic America. The 1820s saw the flourishing of new relationships that had often been encouraged, not resisted, by Bolívar and his supporters. It was Bolívar's supporters and people close to them, like Juan José Flores in Ecuador, Mosquera in Colombia, and Páez in Venezuela, who won their spurs in the 1820s and who used their political capital in the 1830s and 1840s to bring Latin America even closer to Europe and North America through the use of trade, liberal ideology, and military force. The Bolivarians became the fixed points around which new transatlantic connections were negotiated.

We can see from these lives the growing volume of liberal ideology in the Americas after the 1820s. Mosquera and Páez both served Royalism in the early years of independence, just like other postcolonial leaders elsewhere in the Americas, such as Andrés de Santa Cruz in Peru.[54] It was liberalism and its accompanying discourse of national citizenship that shaped their political careers in the 1830s and 1840s; even if both became closely associated with conservative parties, their politics remained resolutely liberal in the classic Latin American sense.[55] The lives, choices, and experiences summarized here show that their ideologies changed under the influence of liberalism, although we certainly cannot exclude simple opportunism and careerism from the explanation of their rises to power. The popular support that their armies received in civil warfare drew significantly on rural actors who were mobilized by state promises of the benefits and rights promised by citizenship, but, as several of the contributors to this volume have shown, those promises were only infrequently fulfilled.

The location of the places of exile chosen by Páez and Mosquera is itself illustrative. Páez spent spells in Caribbean exile, in the Dutch colony of Curaçao, which was convenient for a return to Venezuelan politics. In the 1840s Mosquera sought exile in Ecuador and Peru. In the 1850s Páez settled finally in New York. Mosquera also had a second home in the United States. Neither of them sought permanent asylum in London or Kingston, Jamaica, the places which had so inspired Simón Bolívar during his own travels in 1810 and 1815. This seems as good an illustration as any of the fading influence of British power in the Andean region after the 1830s.

One final comparative point to take from these lives is that, for all the talk of "close relations" between the leaders and Great Britain in the 1820s and 1830s, neither Páez nor Mosquera married Anglophone wives. They were not pulled into the British imperial bed by what Ann Laura Stoler has identified as "geographies of intimacy."[56] Páez married Dominga Ortiz in Canaguá (Mérida, Venezuela) in 1809. Mosquera married his first wife, Mariana Arboleda y Arroyo, in Popayán in 1820. After her death in 1867 he married her sister, María Ignacia Arboleda, in 1872. Mosquera, in particular, is known to have had multiple affairs, and so not too much emphasis can be laid on the meanings of marriage. It is, however, a point worth noting that the Bolivarian family may have sought and exploited Atlantic relations during their political careers, but in their personal lives they sought love and stability much closer to home.

～

It may be hard to measure love, but trade can be tracked with much more reliability. In most literature up to now, the Bolivarian decade was marked in Latin America by a surge in British imports and loans, followed, after the 1826 crash, by the rapid withdrawal of investment and the departure of speculative migrants and investors. However, a recent wave of economic history literature can be employed to support the more political and more social hypothesis of this volume. Adrian Pearce has argued that the apparently spectacular rise in British trade with Spanish America after independence appears to have been little more than the formalization and legalization of a rampant preexisting contraband and "neutral" trade whose real expansion had taken place in the late eighteenth century.[57] In this, Pearce's conclusions can be linked to Rory Miller's overview; Miller traced the steady increase in the volume of British trade with Latin America over the period 1800–1850. Although the value of trade fluctuated massively, dependent on international warfare and the costs of transatlantic transport, Miller showed how the volume of trade in cottons produced in Lancashire mills grew by over two and a half times between the 1820s and 1840s.[58] Manuel Llorca's recent doctoral research confirms this trend and supports it with compelling and original archival data for the British export of textiles to the Southern Cone between 1800 and 1850.[59] Taken together, the work of Miller, Pearce, Llorca, and others suggests that after the 1826 London financial crisis the levels of growth and commerce and the amount of capital destined for Latin America returned pretty much to where they were before the beginnings of the wars of independence, despite all the British loans to Mexico, Central America, and South America in the first part of the 1820s and the considerable investments and new commercial relations that they catalyzed. This confirms the pattern of the endurance and reconfiguration of old patterns detected for political and intellectual links detailed elsewhere in this volume. Within this interpretation, the 1820s would be a crest rather than a blip, the wars of independence a momentary interruption of a long-term process of growth rather than a strange and momentary incursion.

~

In one of his many short periods of retirement from politics, in 1868, Tomás Cipriano de Mosquera wrote up his notes from the time of independence. Remembering Bolívar, Mosquera wrote that "the liberator was blessed with immortal genius, he created a republic out of nothing; and at the same time as he created and organised it, he directed the war and managed the armed forces, all without neglecting a single aspect of his great project."[60]

Bolívar is often presented in this light: as the exceptional "Liberator," whose star shone and fell during his decade, the 1820s. In this chapter I have tried to suggest that Bolívar was less unique and more representative than is often thought. Simón Bolívar's courting of Great Britain in the 1820s was not something peculiar to his life or his political outlook. Instead, this chapter has tried to show how Bolívar's political family continued this trajectory in the 1830s and 1840s, demonstrating how the 1820s witnessed a substantial reconfiguration of imperial relationships in the Iberian and British Atlantics and their ever-greater intersection. But neither were these relationships static: by the end of Mosquera's and Páez's lives, it was the United States, not Great Britain, that had become the dominant imperial power shadowing Colombia and Venezuela.[61]

The transition from one imperial power to another returns us to the themes explored in the introduction to this volume. The historical paradigms of Atlantic history and the age of revolutions both hang upon our still insufficient knowledge of the changes and continuities of the 1820s. The evidence and analysis presented within these covers has pushed back the boundaries of our ignorance and facilitated new dialogues within a comparative framework across the Atlantic. But there still remains much work to be done. One of the traditional problems in studying imperialism in the Americas in the 1820s is that European policies—the standard subject of historical investigation until relatively recently—were rarely enacted and seldom successful in the 1820s. Spain, Britain, and France all designed several strategies toward the new American republics in this period; most of these plans had little or no effect on the other side of the ocean. Imperial formations in the 1820s were shaped by factors that are particularly difficult for historians to pinpoint or describe, such as insufficient resources, a lack of trust, the paucity of effective institutions, or ideological ambivalence.[62] Many of these best-laid plans came to nothing in the 1820s, for example, the settler communities planted in Poyais, Topo, and across rural Brazil.[63]

However, the decade of the 1820s presents an array of encounters and mutual influences that highlight the centrality of international events and transnational actors in the collapse of the Iberian Atlantic empires.[64] In the case of Spanish America, the crucial role of the Napoleonic occupation and the abdications of Carlos IV and Ferdinand VII (1808), the polarizing impact of Ferdinand's restoration and "reconquest" efforts (1814–16), the disorientating shock of Rafael del Riego's revolt, and the implementation of a constitutional monarchy during the Trienio Liberal (1820–23) are recognized as having had major, discernible effects on the trajectory of Hispanic American independence.[65] British and Irish adventurers served in Bolívar's armies, played pivotal roles in the forging of new nations, and were integrated into post-independence local elites in remarkable, peculiar ways. In Brazil, Dom Pedro encouraged the recruitment of foreign (Irish, German, Swiss) mercenaries, disbanding these battalions in 1830 after a 1828 riot of foreign troops caused public outcry.[66] British diplomats mediated the war between the United Provinces of the River Plate and Brazil over the Banda Oriental, leading toward the creation of the independent state of Uruguay at the end of the decade.[67] A large British community was thriving by the 1820s, as David Rock shows in his contribution to this volume, a harbinger of a growing cultural influence to come in the River Plate for much of the next century.[68] Other exiles from the turmoil of Europe's revolutionary and Napoleonic wars sought and found new occupations and new identities in unexpected parts of the New World.[69] Even the tortuous negotiations and showman-like fanfare that accompanied George Canning's recognition of the independence of parts of Hispanic America in 1825 were intimately linked to affairs in the Iberian peninsula. Canning's famous declaration to "bring the New World into existence, to re-dress the balance of the Old," was made in a parliamentary debate over affairs in Iberia, not Latin America.[70]

The 1820s, therefore, may well have been the Bolivarian decade. Bolívar was typical of many leaders of his generation in that he was steeped in Enlightenment thought and was the scion of a wealthy planter family that was oriented toward the export economy. Bolívar, José de San Martín, Mosquera, and others like them nevertheless dedicated themselves to leading independence movements inspired by revolutionary ideology that at first glance might be thought to threaten their traditional privileges. This was the paradox that unsurprisingly led Bolívar and others to flirt with centralism, monarchism, and other symptoms of their distrust of very people they sought to liberate from colonial rule. The economic, social, political, and intellectual shifts that occurred under his star had medium-term effects that had precious little to do with Bolívar, however, and everything to do with the Atlantic networks, convergences, aspirations, and ambitions traced and analyzed in this book. If the 1820s belong to anyone, therefore, it is to the future historians who take up the challenges laid down by the contributors to this book, whose painstaking and necessarily creative research in forgotten archives will help us to understand these slippery but unmistakable connections after colonialism.

Notes

1. Jasanoff, *Liberty's Exiles*; Sobrevilla Perea, "From Europe to the Andes and Back."

2. Bolívar, "My Delirium on Chimborazo," 1822, and "Letter to Juan José Flores," in Bolívar's *Simón Bolívar: El Libertador,* ed. Bushnell, 135, 146.

3. Recio Morales, *Ireland and the Spanish Empire, 1600–1825.*

4. See Hamnett, "Themes and Tensions in a Contradictory Decade," in this volume.

5. Ricketts, "Together or Separate in the Fight against Oppression?"

6. Earle, "Information and Disinformation in Late Colonial New Granada"; also see Silva, *República Liberal*; and Sara Castro-Klarén and John Charles Chasteen, eds., *Beyond Imagined Communities: Reading and Writing the Nation in Nineteenth-Century Latin America* (Washington, DC: Woodrow Wilson Center and Baltimore: Johns Hopkins University Press, 2003).

7. Eastman, "'America Has Escaped from Our Hands.'"

8. Thibaud and Calderón, *La majestad de los pueblos.* See also Straka, *Las alas de Icaro.*

9. The argument is expanded in Sexton, *The Monroe Doctrine.*

10. Safier, "A Courier between Empires," 265–70.

11. See also Brading, *Classical Republicanism and Creole Patriotism.*

12. Bushnell, *Simón Bolívar: Liberation and Disappointment.*

13. Bethell, *The Abolition of the Brazilian Slave Trade*; D. Murray, *Odious Commerce.*

14. Reported widely, as in the *Guardian,* April 19, 2009. Galeano, *Venas abiertas de América Latina.*

15. Germán Carrera Damas, *El culto a Bolívar: Esbozo para un Estudio de la Historia de las Ideas en Venezuela* (Caracas: Universidad Central de Venezuela, 1973).

16. Even this one fact has been questioned by revisionist historians in Venezuela. See, for example, Mier Hoffman, *La carta que cambiará la historia.*

17. Bushnell, "The United States as Seen by Simón Bolívar," 135.

18. Racine, "Simón Bolívar, Englishman," 56–70.

19. Ibid., 57–58. The point is made more broadly in Racine, "'This England, This Now.'"

20. Racine, "Simón Bolívar, Englishman," 60–66; Bushnell, "The United States as Seen by Simón Bolívar," 141.

21. Racine, "Simón Bolívar, Englishman," 68.

22. Bushnell, "The United States as Seen by Simón Bolívar," 141.

23. Lombardi, "Epilogue: History and Our Heroes," 180.

24. Davies, "Colonial Dependence and Sexual Difference," 5–19.

25. Quintero, *La criolla principal*; P. Murray, *For Glory and Bolivar.*

26. For the details of Bolívar's family and personal relations, see J. Lynch, *Simón Bolívar: A Life*; and Polanco Alcántara, *Simón Bolívar.*

27. D. Lambert and Lester, *Colonial Lives across the British Empire*; also see Boyer and Spurling, eds., *Colonial Lives: Documents on Latin American History*.

28. Armitage and Subrahmanyam, *The Age of Revolutions in Global Context*, xxxi.

29. Rothschild, *The Inner Life of Empires*; Jasanoff, *Liberty's Exiles*; Jasanoff, *Edge of Empire*.

30. J. Lynch, *Caudillos in Spanish America*.

31. Fowler, *Santa Anna, of Mexico*.

32. Safford and Palacios, *Colombia*, 128–31.

33. The gradual Venezuelan disentanglement from Gran Colombia is nicely captured in Porter, *Sir Robert Ker Porter's Caracas Diary*.

34. Admiral Fleeming's daughter was the mother of the author Robert Cunninghame-Graham, who recounted the story of his mother's birth in an appendix to his *José Antonio Páez*, 310.

35. Páez, cited in Pérez Vila, *Vida de Daniel Florencio O'Leary*, 566–67.

36. Mondolfi Gudat, *Páez visto por los ingleses*.

37. Cunninghame-Graham, *José Antonio Páez*, x.

38. Ojer, *Robert H. Schomburgk*; also Graham Burnett, *Masters of All They Surveyed*.

39. Pérez Vila, *Vida de Daniel Florencio O'Leary*, 586; Nikita Harwich Valenilla, "Banco Central de Venezuela," in *Diccionario de historia de Venezuela* (Caracas: Fundacion Polar, 1999).

40. Harwich Valenilla, *Formación y crisis de un sistema financiero nacional*.

41. Wilson to Mosquera, January 17, 1828, Bogotá, in Archivo Central del Cauca (ACC), Sala Mosquera, Carpeta 52, d5147.

42. Anonymous, *Boletin número V* (Medellín: M. A. Balcazar, October 31, 1840), AGNC, Archivo de la Academia Colombiana de Historia, Colección Abel Botero, Serie Papeles Varios, Asuntos Familiares S. Córdova, Caja 1, Carpeta 1, 28. On the Ecuadorian intervention see Earle, "The War of the Supremes," 123–27; and Uribe de Hincapié and López Lopera, *Las palabras de la guerra*, 142–46.

43. Uribe de Hincapié and López Lopera, *Las palabras de la guerra*, 129.

44. Córdova, *Habitantes del Cauca i Buenaventura*. Córdova made similar points in a letter to Joaquín Posada Gutierrez, reproduced in Posda Gutierrez, *Memorias histórico-políticas*, 4:69. The message was reinforced in Anonymous, *Honor al valiente General Córdova: Boletín número XIII* (Medellín: M. A. Balcazar, April 11, 1841), found in Archivo de la Universidad de Antioquia (hereafter cited as UdA), Medellín, Colombia, HS1 D1 F1.

45. Cited in Uribe de Hincapié and López Loprera, *Las palabras de la guerra*, 117.

46. Anonymous, "Contestación al artículo publicado en el número 197 de *El Día,* suscrito por un Cartagueño" (1841), found in UdA, HS2 D195 F227.

47. Uribe de Hincapié and López Lopera, *Las palabras de la guerra,* 90–92.

48. Many of Mosquera's letters are published in Helguera and Davis, *Archivo epistolar de Tomás Cipriano de Mosquera.* His archive is in the Sala Mosquera of the Archivo Central del Cauca in his hometown of Popayán.

49. Lofstrom, *La vida íntima de Tomás Cipriano de Mosquera;* also P. Murray, "Mujeres, género y política en la joven república colombiana."

50. Deas, "Weapons of the Weak?," 173–86.

51. McGuinness, *Path of Empire.*

52. Todd, "John Bowring and the Global Dissemination of Free Trade"; Rothschild, *The Inner Life of Empires;* Jasanoff, *Liberty's Exiles;* Bickers, *Empire Made Me.*

53. Stein and Stein, *Edge of Crisis,* 423.

54. Sobrevilla Perea, *The Caudillo of the Andes.*

55. On the all-encompassing nature of small "l" liberalism in the Andes, see Larson, *Trials of Nation-Making.*

56. Stoler, *Haunted by Empire.*

57. Pearce, *British Trade with Spanish America.*

58. Miller, *Britain and Latin America,* 74.

59. Llorca, "British Textile Exports to the Southern Cone During the First Half of the Nineteenth Century."

60. Mosquera, *Memoria sobre la vida,* 229.

61. See Matthew Brown's introduction, in M. Brown, *Informal Empire in Latin America,* 18–19.

62. In the latter category, a key example is the ambivalence toward colonies and colonial trade in political economy in the 1820s and 1830s. Some writers, including David Ricardo, were skeptical of the economic wisdom of colonies and colonial trade as opposed to free trade policy. See Winch, *Classical Political Economy and Colonies,* 39–45, passim.

63. M. Brown, "Inca, Sailor, Soldier, King"; Rheinheimer, *Topo;* O. Marshall, *English, Irish, and Irish American Pioneer Settlers.*

64. As Rafe Blaufarb suggests, "the activities of foreign revolutionaries, mercenaries, spies and freebooters who lurked in the back alleys of Latin American independence furnish material for a transnational diplomatic history 'from below' in which states figure as just one among several types of actor." Blaufarb, "The Western Question."

65. For an analysis of the most recent literature see G. Paquette, "The Dissolution of the Spanish Atlantic Monarchy"; see also Waddell, "International Politics and Latin

American Independence"; for Brazil, see Nizza da Silva, *A Repercussão da Revolução de 1820 no Brasil.*

66. George P. Browne, "Government Immigration Policy in Imperial Brazil, 1822–1870" (PhD diss., Catholic University of America, 1972), 77–88, passim.

67. Winn, "British Informal Empire in Uruguay," 100–126; also Vale, *A War Betwixt Englishmen.*

68. Rock, "The British in Argentina," 49–77.

69. Blaufarb, *Bonapartists in the Borderlands.*

70. Canning, *Corrected Report of Speeches,* December 12, 1826.

Bibliography

Archives

ACC: Archivo Central del Cauca (Popayán), Sala Mosquera.

ACP: Archives, College Park, Maryland, RG 59, M28.

ADA: Archivo Departamental de Arequipa. Testamentos.

AGI: Archivo General de Indias (Seville) Fondo Estado, Fondo Santo Domingo.

AGNC: Archivo General de la Nación, Colombia (Bogotá), Archivo de la Academia Colombiana de Historia, Colección Abel Botero.

AGNP: Archivo General de la Nación, Peru (Lima), Sección Protocolos Notariales, Sección Notarial/Testamentos, Sección Tribunal del Consulado.

AGPR: Archivo General de Puerto Rico, Fondo Gobernadores Españoles.

AMI: Arquivo do Museu Imperial, Petrópolis, Rio de Janeiro, Brazil.

ANC: Archivo Nacional de la República de Cuba, Fondo Asuntos Politicos.

ANTT: Arquivo Nacional da Torre do Tombo, Lisbon.

APEJE: Arquivo Público Estadual Jordão Emerenciano, Recife, Brazil.

APEL: Archivo de la Parroquia de El Sagrario, Lima. Libros de Matrimonio.

BA: Biblioteca da Ajuda, Lisbon.

BFSP: *British and Foreign State Papers* IV (1816–1817).

HL: "Collection of Portuguese Broadsides and Other Documents Relating to *Miguelismo* (1799–1835)," Harvard University, Houghton Library.

IAHGP: Instituto Arqueológico, Histórico e Geográfico Pernambucano, Recife, Brazil.

LL: Stuart MSS, Lilly Library, University of Indiana–Bloomington.

TNA: The National Archives, Kew, Foreign Office Papers, London.

Newspapers

British Packet (Buenos Aires), 1824–1833.

Gaceta patriótica del ejército nacional (Mexico), 1820.

La Abeja Poblana (Mexico), 1821.

L'Industriel (Paris), 1828.

New Monthly Magazine, 1825.

O Amigo do Bem Publico, ou o Realista Constitucional (Lisbon), 1826.

Reverbero Constitucional Fluminense (Rio de Janeiro), 1822.

Times (London), 1820–1829.

Books, Articles, and Theses

Abel, Christopher, and Colin Lewis, eds. *Latin America, Economic Imperialism, and the State: The Political Economy of the External Connection from Independence to the Present.* London: Athlone Press, 1985.

Acemoglu, Daron. "The Colonial Origins of Comparative Development: An Empirical Investigation." With Simon Johnson and James Robinson. *American Economic Review* 91 (2001): 1369–1401.

Adams, Jane Elizabeth. "The Abolition of the Brazilian Slave Trade." *Journal of Negro History* 10, no. 4 (1925).

Adams, John Quincy. "Diary." In *Memoirs of John Quincy Adams,* 12 vols., edited by Charles Francis Adams. Philadelphia: J. B. Lippincott, 1874–1877.

———. "Messages to the Senate of the United States," 1826, http://www.gutenberg .org/dirs/1/0/8/7/10879/10879.txt, accessed March 31, 2012.

Adelman, Jeremy, ed. "Colonialism and National History: José Manuel Restrepo and Bartolomé Mitre." In *Interpreting Spanish Colonialism: Empires, Nations and Legends,* edited by Christopher Schmidt-Nowara and J. M. Nieto-Phillips, 163–86. Albuquerque: University of New Mexico Press, 2005.

———. *Colonial Legacies: The Problem of Persistence in Latin American History.* London and New York: Routledge, 1999.

———. "Institutions, Property, and Economic Development in Latin America." In *The Other Mirror: Grand Theory through the Lens of Latin America,* edited by Miguel Angel Centeno and Fernando López-Alves, 27–54. Princeton: Princeton University Press, 2001.

———. *Republic of Capital: Buenos Aires and the Legal Transformation of the Atlantic World.* Stanford: Stanford University Press, 1999.

———. *Sovereignty and Revolution in the Iberian Atlantic.* Princeton, NJ: Princeton University Press, 2006.

Adorno, Rolena. *The Polemics of Possession in Spanish American Narrative.* New Haven: Yale University Press, 2007.

Aguilar Rivera, José Antonio, and Rafael Rojas, eds. *El republicanismo en Hispanoamérica: Ensayos de historia intelectual y política.* Mexico City: CIDE/Fondo de Cultura Económica, 2002.

Albonico, A. "La Gran Colombia in una rivista milanese coeva, gli Annali Universali di Statistica." In *L'America Latina e L'Italia,* edited by A. Albonico, 61–72. Rome: Quaderni della Ricerca, 1984.

———. "Tra padri della patria italiana e 'próceres' locali: L'ambigua complessità dell' America Latina." *Rassegna Storica del Risorgimento* 47, nos. 1–2 (1997): 400–436.

Aldana Rivera, Susana. "Un norte diferente para la Independencia peruana." *Revista de Indias* 57, no. 209 (1997): 142 64.

Aldrich, Robert. *Greater France: A History of French Overseas Expansion.* London: Macmillan, 1996.

Alexander, Robert. *Re-writing the French Revolutionary Tradition.* Cambridge: Cambridge University Press, 2003.

Alexandre, Valentim. *A Questão Colonial no Parlamento.* Vol. 1, *1821–1910.* Lisbon: Publicações Dom Quixote, 2008.

———. *Os Sentidos do Império: Questão nacional e Questão Colonial na Crise do Antigo Regime Português.* Oporto: Edições Afrontamento, 1993.

Alonso Romero, María Paz. *Cuba en la España liberal (1837–1898).* Madrid: Centro de Estudios Políticos y Constitucionales, 2002.

Amunátegui, Miguel Luis. *Don José Joaquín de Mora: Apuntes biográficos.* Santiago de Chile: Imprenta Nacional, 1888.

Amunátegui Solar, Domingo. "Mayorazgo Ruíz Tagle." In *Mayorazgos y Títulos de Castilla,* edited by Amunátegui Solar. Santiago de Chile: Imprenta, Litografía y Encuadernación Barcelona, 1903.

Andrews, George Reid. *Afro–Latin America, 1800–2000.* New York: Oxford University Press, 2004.

Andrews, Joseph. *Journey from Buenos Ayres, through the Provinces of Cordova, Tucuman and Salta to Bolivia, to Potosi, thence by the Deserts of Caranja to Arica, and Subsequently, to Santiago de Chile and Peruvian Mining in the Years 1825–1826.* 2nd ed. 1827. Reprint, New York: Ams Press, 1971.

Andrien, Kenneth J. "The *Noticias secretas de América* and the Construction of a Governing Ideology for the Spanish American Empire." *Colonial Latin American Review* 7 (1998): 175–92.

Anna, Timothy E. *España y la independencia de América.* Mexico City: Fondo de Cultura Económica, 1986.

———. *The Fall of the Royal Government in Mexico City.* Lincoln: University of Nebraska Press, 1978.

———. *Forging Mexico, 1821–1835.* Lincoln and London: University of Nebraska Press, 1998.

———. "Iguala: The Prototype." In *Forceful Negotiations: The Origins of the Pronunciamiento in Nineteenth-Century Mexico,* edited by Will Fowler. Lincoln: University of Nebraska Press, 2010.

———. *The Mexican Empire of Iturbide.* Lincoln: University of Nebraska Press, 1990.

———. "The Peruvian Declaration of Independence: Freedom by Coercion." *Journal of Latin American Studies* 7, no. 2 (1975): 221–48.

———. *Spain and the Loss of America.* Lincoln: University of Nebraska Press, 1983.

Anonymous. "Claudio Linati (1790–1832)." In *Memorie Parmensi per la storia del Risorgimento.* Parma, 1935.

———. *Considerações do Velho Liberal.* Lisbon, 1826.

———. *Exposição Genuina da Constituição Portugueza de 1826.* Lisbon, 1828.

———. *A Few Words in Answer to Certain Individuals respecting the Present State of Portugal.* London, 1831.

———. *A Five Years' Residence in Buenos Aires, during the Years 1820–1825: Containing Remarks on the Country and Inhabitants.* London, 1825.

———. *A Funda de David Defonte do Clarim Portugues.* Lisbon, 1826.

———. *Golpe de vista, em que compendio . . . a legitimidade dos direitos d'El Rei o Senhor Dom Miguel I no Throno de Portugal.* Lisbon, 1829.

———. *Refutação Methodica das Chamadas Bazes da Constituição Politica da Monarquia Portugueza.* Lisbon, 1824.

———. *Remarks on the Philippines Islands and Their Capital.* Calcutta: Baptist Mission, 1828.

———. *Resumo Histórico do Parlamento de Inglaterra.* Lisbon, 1826.

———. *Revolução Anti-Constitucional em 1823: Suas verdadeiras causas e effeitos.* London, 1825.

———. *Sobre a Constituição da Inglaterra e as Principaes Mudanças que tem soffrido.* Lisbon, 1827.

———. "Viaggio nell'interno della Colombia del Colonnello Hamilton." *Annali Universali di Statistica* 14 (1827): 203–5.

Antillón, Isidoro de. *Disertación sobre el origen de la esclavitud de los negros, motivos que la han perpetuado, ventajas que se le atribuyen y medios que podrían adoptarse para hacer prosperar nuestras colonias sin la esclavitud de los negros.* Palma de Mallorca: Miguel Domingo, 1811.

Aquino Brancato, Bras Augusto. "A *Carta* Constitucional Portuguesa de 1826 na Europa: Um Exame a partir de Documentos Espanhóis." *Revista de História das Ideias* [Coimbra] 10 (1988): 457–73.

Arango y Parreño, Francisco de. "Reflexiones de un habanero sobre la isla de Cuba." In *Obras de Francisco de Arango y Parreño.* Havana: Ministerio de Educación, 1952.

Arias, Santa. "Equal Rights and Individual Freedom: Enlightenment Intellectuals and the Lascasian Apology for Black African Slavery." *Romance Quarterly* 55 (Fall 2008): 279–91.

Arias de Saavedra Alías, Inmaculada. "Irlandeses en la Alta Administración española del siglo XVIII." In *La emigración irlandesa en el siglo XVIII*, coordinated by María Begoña Villar García. Málaga: Universidad de Málaga, 2000.

Armitage, David, and M. J. Braddick, eds. *The British Atlantic World, 1500–1800*. New York: Palgrave Macmillan, 2002.

Armitage, David, and Sanjay Subrahmanyam, eds. *The Age of Revolutions in Global Context, c. 1760–1840*. Basingstoke: Palgrave, 2010.

Artola, Miguel. *La España de Fernando VII*. Madrid: Espasa-Calpe, 1968.

———. *Los orígenes de la España contemporánea*. Madrid: IEP, 1978.

Atienza, Julio de. *Nobiliario español: Diccionario Heráldico de apellidos españoles y de títulos nobiliarios*. Madrid: Aguilar, 1954.

Ávila, Alfredo. *En nombre de la nación: La formación del gobierno representativo en México (1808–1824)*. Mexico City: CIDE/Taurus, 2002.

———. *Para la libertad: Los republicanos en tiempos del imperio 1821–1823*. Mexico City: UNAM, 2004.

Ávila Martel, Alamiro de. *Mora y Bello en Chile, 1829–1831*. Santiago: Ediciones de la Universidad de Chile, 1982.

Badura, Bohumil. "Los franceses en Santiago de Cuba a mediados del año de 1808." *Ibero Americana Pragensia* 5 (1971).

Bagot, Josceline, ed. *George Canning and His Friends*. 2 vols. London: John Murray, 1909.

Bailyn, Bernard. "The Idea of Atlantic History." *Itinerario* 20 (1996): 19–44.

Bakkum, Maarten-Jan. *La Comunidad Judeo-Curazoleña de Coro y el Pogrom de 1855*. Carcacas: Instituto de Cultura del Estado Falcón, 2001.

Banti, Alberto. *La Nazione del Risorgimento*. Milan: Feltrinelli, 2006.

Banus, Carlos. *Tratado de historia y arte military*. Barcelona, 1881.

Baquer, Miguel Alonso. *El modelo español de pronunciamiento*. Madrid: Rialp, 1983.

Barman, Roderick. *Brazil: The Forging of a Nation, 1798–1852*. Stanford, CA: Stanford University Press, 1988.

Barreiros Malheiro da Silva, Armando. *Miguelismo: Ideologia e Mito*. Coimbra: Minerva História, 1993.

Bataillon, Marcel. "The *Clérigo* Casas, Colonist and Colonial Reformer." In *Bartolomé de las Casas in History: Toward an Understanding of the Man and His Work*, edited by Juan Freide and Benjamin Keen, 353–440. DeKalb: Northern Illinois University Press, 1971.

Bayly, C. A. "The Age of Revolutions in Global Context: An Afterword." In *The Age of Revolutions in Global Context*, edited by Armitage and Subrahmanyam.

———. *The Birth of the Modern World, 1789–1914: Global Connections and Comparisons*. Oxford: Blackwell, 2004.

———. *Imperial Meridian: The British Empire and the World 1780–1830*. London: Longman, 1989.

———. "The 'Revolutionary Age' in the Wider World, c. 1790–1830." In *War, Empire, and Slavery, 1770–1830,* edited by Richard Bessel, Nicholas Guyatt, and Jane Rendall, 21–43. Basingstoke: Palgrave, 2010.

Bayly, C. A., and Eugenio F. Biagini, eds. *Giuseppe Mazzini and the Globalisation of Democratic Nationalism, 1830–1920,* Oxford: Oxford University Press, 2008.

Beaumont, J.A.B. *Travels in Buenos Ayres, and the Adjacent Provinces of the Rio de la Plata: With Observations Intended for the Use of Persons who Contemplate Emigrating to that Country; or, Embarking Capital in its Affairs*. London: J. Ridgway, 1828.

Belohlavek, John M. *"Let the Eagle Soar!" The Foreign Policy of Andrew Jackson*. Lincoln: University of Nebraska Press, 1985.

Benavides, Christine. "Isidoro de Antillon y la abolición de la esclavitud." Lecture given at the conference "Las elites y la revolución en España (1808–1814)," Madrid, Casa de Velázquez, 2007.

Bentham, Jeremy. *Colonies, Commerce, and Constitutional Law: Rid Yourselves of Ultramaria and Other Writings for Spain and Spanish America*. Edited by Phillip Schofield. Oxford: Clarendon Press, 1995.

Benot, Yves. *La Révolution française et la fin des colonies, 1789–1794*. Paris: Éditions La Découverte, 1987.

Benson, Nettie Lee. *La diputación provincial y el federalismo mexicano*. Mexico City: El Colegio de México/UNAM, 1994.

Benton, Lauren. *Law and Colonial Cultures: Legal Regimes in World History, 1400–1900*. New York City: Cambridge University Press, 2002.

———. "No Longer Odd Region Out: Repositioning Latin America in World History." *Hispanic American Historical Review* 84 (2004): 423–30.

Berbel, Márcia Regina. *A Nação como Artefacto: Deputados do Brasil nas Cortes Portuguesas (1821–22)*. São Paulo: Editora HUCITEC, 1999.

———. "A Retórica da Recolonização." In *Independência: História e Historiografia,* edited by István Jancsó, 791–808. São Paulo: Editora Hucitec, 2005.

Berbel, Márcia Regina, Rafael Marquese, and Tâmis Parron. *Escravidão e política: Brasil e Cuba, 1790–1850*. São Paulo: Editora Hucitec, 2010.

Bergad, Laird. *Cuban Rural Society in the Nineteenth Century: The Social and Economic History of Monoculture in Matanzas*. Princeton: Princeton University Press, 1990.

Bernecker, Walther. "Comercio y comerciantes extranjeros en las primeras décadas de la independencia Mexicana." In *América Latina en la época de Simón Bolívar,* edited by Liehr, 87–114.

Bethell, Leslie. *The Abolition of the Brazilian Slave Trade: Britain, Brazil, and the Slave Trade Question, 1807–1869.* Cambridge: Cambridge University Press, 1970.

———. "The Decline and Fall of Slavery in Nineteenth-Century Brazil." *Transactions of the Royal Historical Society* (6th ser.) 1 (1991): 71–88.

Bickers, Robert. *Empire Made Me: An Englishman Adrift in Shanghai.* London: Penguin, 2003.

Bistarelli, Agostino. "Cittadini del mondo? Gli esuli italiani del 1820–21." *Archivio storico dell'emigrazione italiana* 4, no. 1 (2008): 5–21.

Blackburn, Robin. *The Overthrow of Colonial Slavery, 1776–1848.* London: Verso, 1988.

Blanchard, Peter. *Under the Flags of Freedom: Slave Soldiers and the Wars of Independence in Spanish South America.* Pittsburgh: University of Pittsburgh Press, 2008.

Blanco Valdés, Roberto L. "Paisanos y soldados en los orígenes de la España liberal. Sobre revoluciones sociales, golpes de Estado y pronunciamientos militares." In *Revolución, independencia y las nuevas naciones de América,* edited by Jaime E. Rodríguez O. Madrid: Fundación Mapfre, 2005.

———. *Rey, Cortes y fuerza armada en los orígenes de la España liberal.* Madrid: Siglo XXI, 1988.

Blanco White, Joseph. *Bosquejo del comercio de esclavos y reflexiónes sobre este tráfico considerado moral, política y cristianamente.* Edited by Manuel Moreno Alonso. Sevilla: Ediciones Alfar, 1999.

Blaufarb, Rafe. *Bonapartists in the Borderlands: French Exiles and Refugees on the Gulf Coast, 1815–1835.* Tuscaloosa: University of Alabama Press, 2005.

———. "The Western Question: The Geopolitics of Latin American Independence." *American Historical Review* 112, no. 3 (2007): 742–63.

Bleiberg, Germán, ed. *Diccionario de Historia de España.* 2nd ed. Madrid: Revista de Occidente, 1969.

Bolívar, Simón. *Simón Bolívar: The Bolivarian Revolution.* Edited and translated by Matthew Brown. New York and London: Verso, 2009.

———. *Simón Bolívar: El Libertador, Writings of Simón Bolívar.* Edited by David Bushnell. Translated by Frederick Fornoff. Oxford: Oxford University Press, 2004.

———. "Views of General Simón Bolívar on the Congress of Panama." In *The Monroe Doctrine: Its Importance in the International Life of the States of the New World,* edited by Alejandro Álvarez. New York: Oxford University Press, 1924.

Bonavides, Paulo. "Constitucionalismo Luso-Brasileiro: Influxos Recíprocos." In *Perspectivas Constitucionais,* edited by Jorge Miranda. Coimbra: Coimbra Editora, 1996.

Bonnabeau, Richard F. "The Pursuit of Legitimacy: The Stuart Mission and the

Recognition of Brazilian Independence, 1824–26." PhD diss., Indiana University, 1974.

Boyer, Richard, and Geoffrey Spurling, eds. *Colonial Lives: Documents on Latin American History, 1550–1850.* Oxford: Oxford University Press, 2000.

Boylan, Henry. *A Dictionary of Irish Biography.* Dublín: Gill and Macmillan, 1988.

Brading, David A. *Classical Republicanism and Creole Patriotism: Simón Bolívar and the Spanish American Revolution (1783–1830).* Cambridge: Centre of Latin American Studies, 1983.

———. *The First America: The Spanish Monarchy, Creole Patriots, and the Liberal State, 1492–1867.* Cambridge: Cambridge University Press, 1991.

———. *The Origins of Mexican Nationalism.* Cambridge: Centre for Latin American Studies, 1985.

Braga de Menezes, Paulo. *As Constituições Outorgadas ao Império do Brasil e ao Reino de Portugal.* Rio de Janeiro: Arquivo Nacional de Rio de Janeiro, 1974.

Brauer, Kinley J. "1821–1860: Economics and the Diplomacy of American Expansionism." In *Economics and World Power: An Assessment of American Diplomacy since 1789,* edited by William H. Becker and Samuel F. Wells. New York: Columbia University Press, 1984.

———. "The United States and British Imperial Expansion, 1815–1860." *Diplomatic History* 12 (1988): 19–37.

Breña, Roberto. *El primer liberalismo español y los procesos de emancipación de América, 1808–1824: Una revisión historiográfica del liberalismo hispánico.* Mexico City: El Colegio de México, 2006.

Brown, Christopher L. "Empire without Slaves: British Concepts of Emancipation in the Age of the American Revolution." *William and Mary Quarterly* 56, no. 2 (1999): 274–306.

———. *Moral Capital: Foundations of British Abolitionism.* Chapel Hill: University of North Carolina Press, 2006.

Brown, Jonathan C. *A Socioeconomic History of Argentina, 1776–1860.* Cambridge: Cambridge University Press, 1979.

Brown, Matthew. *Adventuring through Spanish Colonies: Simón Bolívar, Foreign Mercenaries, and the Birth of New Nations.* Liverpool: Liverpool University Press, 2006.

———. "Inca, Sailor, Soldier, King: Gregor MacGregor and the Revolutionary Caribbean." *Bulletin of Latin American Research* 24, no. 1 (2005): 44–71.

———, ed. *Informal Empire in Latin America: Culture, Commerce, and Capital.* Oxford: Blackwell, 2008.

———. "Not Forging Nations but Foraging for Them: Uncertain Collective Identities in Gran Colombia." *Nations and Nationalism* 12 (2006): 223–40.

———. "Rebellion at Riohacha, 1820: Local and International Networks of Revolution, Cowardice, and Masculinity." *Jahrbuch für Geschichte Lateinamerikas* 42 (2005): 77–98.

Brown, Matthew, and Martín Alonso Roa Celis, eds. *Militares extranjeros en la independencia de Colombia: Nuevas perspectivas.* Bogotá: Museo Nacional de Colombia, 2005.

Buarque de Holanda, Sérgio. *Dispersão e Unidade in História Geral da Civilização Brasileira Tomo 2: O Brasil monárquico.* Vol. 2. São Paulo: Difel, 1985.

Buck-Morss, Susan. *Hegel, Haiti, and Universal History.* Pittsburgh: University of Pittsburgh Press, 2009.

Buldain Jaca, Blanca E. *Régimen político y preparación de Cortes en 1820.* Madrid: Congreso de los Diputados, 1988.

Bumgartner, Louis. *José del Valle of Central America.* Durham, NC: Duke University Press, 1963.

Burga, Manuel. "El Perú central, 1770–1860: Disparidades regionales y la primera crisis agrícola republicana." In *América Latina en la época de Simón Bolívar,* edited by Liehr, 227–310.

Bushnell, David. *The Santander Regime in Gran Colombia.* Newark: University of Delaware Press, 1954.

———. *Simón Bolívar: Liberation and Disappointment.* New York: Longman, 2003.

———. "The United States as Seen by Simón Bolívar: Too Good a Neighbour." In *Simón Bolívar: Essays on the Life and Legacy of the Liberator,* edited by David Bushnell and Lester Langley. Lanham, MD: Rowman and Littlefield, 2008.

Busquets, Julio. *Pronunciamientos y golpes de estado en España.* Barcelona: Planeta, 1982.

Byers, Edward. *The Nation of Nantucket: Society and Politics in an Early American Commercial Center.* Boston: Northeastern University Press, 1987.

Caldcleugh, Alexander. *Travels in South America, during the Years 1819, 1820, 1821: Containing an Account of the Present State of Brazil, Buenos Ayres, and Chile.* London: John Murray, 1825.

Calmon, Pedro, ed. *Falas do Trono, desde o ano de 1823 até o ano de 1889.* Brasília/São Paulo: Instituto Nacional do Livro, 1977.

Campanhole, Andriano, and Hilton Lobo Campanhole, eds. *Tôdas as Constituições do Brasil.* São Paulo: Editora Atlas, 1971.

Campbell, Margaret V. "Education in Chile." *Journal of Inter-American Studies* 1, no. 3 (1959): 353–75.

Campbell, Randolph. "The Spanish American Aspect of Henry Clay's American System." *The Americas* 24, no. 1 (1967): 3–17.

Campos de Andrada, Ernesto de, ed. *Memórias de Francisco Manuel Trigoso de Aragão Morato.* Coimbra: Imprensa da Universidade, 1933.

Campos Harriet, Fernando. *La Vida Heroica de O'Higgins*. Santiago de Chile: Editorial del Pacífico, 1947.

Candeloro, Giorgio. *Dalla Restaurazione alla Rivoluzione Nazionale*. Milan: Feltrinelli, 1962.

Candido, Salvatore. "Appunti all'apporto italiano alla storia delle emigrazioni politiche dall'Italia ai paesi ibero-Americani durante il Risorgimento." In *Atti del Congresso L'Apporto Italiano all Tradizione degli Studi Ispanici*, 187–202. Napoli, 30 e 31 Gennaio 1992. Rome: Instituto Cervantes, 1993.

———. "Combattenti italiani per la rivoluzione bolivariana: Corsari e ufficiali." *Quaderni Latinoamericani* 9–10 (1983): 1–35.

Canga Argüelles. *Memoria sobre los presupuestos de los gastos, de los valores de las contribuciones y rentas públicas de la nación española, y de los medios para cubrir el déficit*. Madrid: Imprenta Nacional, 1820.

Cañizares-Esguerra, Jorge. *How to Write the History of the New World: Historiographies, Epistemologies, and Identities in the Eighteenth-Century Atlantic World*. Stanford: Stanford University Press, 2001.

Canning, George. *Corrected Report of Speeches delivered by the Right Hon. George Canning, in the House of Commons, December 12, 1826, on the motion for an address to the king in answer to His Majesty's Message relative to the Affairs of Portugal*. London, 1826.

Canny, Nicholas. "Atlantic History and Global History." In *Atlantic History: A Critical Appraisal*, edited by Jack P. Greene and Philip D. Morgan, 317–36. Oxford: Oxford University Press, 2008.

Capel, Horacio, et al. *Los ingenieros militares en España: Repertorio biográfico y su labor científica y espacial*. Barcelona: Universidad de Barcelona, 1983.

Cardim, Pedro. *Cortes e Cultura Política no Portugal do Antigo Regime*. Lisbon: Edições Cosmos, 1998.

Cardoso, José Luís. "A Abertura dos Portos do Brasil em 1808: Dos Factos á Doutrina." *Ler História* 54 (2008): 9–31.

Carr, Raymond. *Spain, 1808–1939*. Oxford: Clarendon Press, 1966.

Carreras, Albert. "Cataluña, primera región industrial de España." In *Pautas regionales de la industrialización española (siglos XIX y XX)*, edited by Jordi Nadal and Albert Carreras. Barcelona: Ariel, 1990.

Carrillo Batalla, Tomás Enrique. *Proyecto Cuentas Nacionales de Venezuela 1800–1830: Soportes Estadísticas, Tomo 2*. Caracas: Banco Central de Venezuela, 1999.

Castells, Irene. *La utopia insurreccional del liberalismo: Torrijos y las conspiraciones liberales de la década ominosa*. Barcelona: Editorial Crítica, 1989.

Castro, María de los Ángeles. "La lealtad anticolonial: Ramón Power en las Cortes de Cádiz." In *Las Antillas en la era de las Luces y la Revolución*, edited by José A. Piqueras. Madrid: Siglo XXI, 2005.

Castro Leiva, Luis. *La Gran Colombia: Una ilusión ilustrada*. Caracas: Monte Avila, 1985.

Cayton, Andrew. "The Debate over the Panama Congress and the Origins of the Second American Party System." *Historian* 47, no. 2 (1985): 219–38.

Centeno, Miguel Ángel. *Blood and Debt: War and the Nation-State in Latin America*. University Park, PA: Pennsylvania State University Press, 2002.

Chakrabarty, Dipesh. *Provincialising Europe: Postcolonial Thought and Historical Difference*. Rev. ed. Princeton, NJ: Princeton University Press, 2008.

Chasteen, John Charles. *Americanos: Latin America's Struggle for Independence*. New York: Oxford University Press, 2008.

———. *Born in Blood and Fire: A Concise History of Latin America*. London and New York: Norton, 2001.

Chiaramonte, José Carlos. "The 'Ancient Constitution' after Independence (1808–1852)." *Hispanic American Historical Review* 90, no. 3 (2010): 455–88.

———. "Gli illuministi napoletani nel Rio de la Plata." *Rivista Storica Italiana* 86, no. 1 (1964): 114–32.

——— *La Ilustración en el Rio de la Plata: Cultura eclesiástica y cultura laica durante el Virreinato*. 2nd ed. Buenos Aires: Sudamericana, 2007.

Childs, Matt D. *The 1812 Aponte Rebellion in Cuba and the Struggle against Atlantic Slavery*. Chapel Hill: University of North Carolina Press, 2006.

Chust, Manuel, ed. *Doceañismos, Constituciones e Independencias: La Constitución de 1812 y América*. Madrid: Fundación Mapfre, 2006.

———, ed. *1808: La eclosión juntera en el mundo hispano*. Mexico City: Fondo de Cultura Económica, 2007.

———. "Federalismo avant la lettre en las Cortes hispanas, 1810–1821." In *El establecimiento del federalismo en México, 1821–1827,* coordinated by Josefina Z. Vázquez. Mexico City: El Colegio de México, 2003.

Chust, Manuel, and Ivana Frasquet, eds. *La trascendencia del liberalismo doceañista en España y en América*. Valencia: Biblioteca Valenciana, 2004.

Chust, Manuel, and José Antonio Serrano, eds. *Debates sobre las independencias iberoamericanas*. Madrid: Iberoamericana, 2007.

Chust Calero, Manuel. "De esclavos, encomenderos y mitayos. El anti-colonialismo en las Cortes de Cádiz." *Mexican Studies/Estudios Mexicanos* 11 (July 1995): 179–202.

Clarkson, Thomas. *An essay on the slavery and commerce of the human species, particularly the African; translated from a Latin dissertation, which was honoured with the first prize in the University of Cambridge, for the year 1785*. 2nd ed., revised and considerably enlarged. London, 1788.

Clavero, Bartolomé. "Libraos de Ultramaria! El fruto podrido de Cádiz." In *Constitución en España: Orígenes y destinos,* edited by José María Iturriñegui and José María Portillo. Madrid: Centro de Estudios Políticos, 1998.

Cleven, N. Andrew. "The First Panama Mission and the Congress of the United States." *Journal of Negro History* 13, no. 3 (1928): 225–54.

Clissold, Stephen. *Bernardo O'Higgins and the Independence of Chile.* London: Rupert Hart-Davis, 1968.

Coatsworth, John. "Obstacles to Economic Growth in Nineteenth-Century Mexico." *American Historical Review* 83, no. 1, (1978): 80–100.

Cochrane, Thomas. *The Life of Thomas, Lord Cochrane, Tenth Earl of Dundonald.* 2 vols. London, 1869.

Collier, Simon. *The Ideas and Politics of Chilean Independence, 1808–1833.* Cambridge: Cambridge University Press, 1967.

Comellas, José Luis. *El Trienio constitucional.* Madrid: Ediciones Rialp, 1963.

———. *Los primeros pronunciamientos en España, 1814–1820.* Madrid: CSIC, 1958.

Connaughton, Brian F. *Dimensiones de la identidad patriótica: Religión, política y regiones en México: Siglo XIX.* Mexico City: Universidad Autonoma, 2001.

Contreras, Carlos. "Las contribuciones directas en la formación del Perú republicano." In *De riqueza e inequidad: El problema de las contribuciones directas en América latina, siglo XIX,* edited by Luis Jáuregui. Mexico City: Instituto Mora, 2006.

Cooper, Frederick. *Colonialism in Question: Theory, Knowledge and History.* London and Berkeley: University of California Press, 2005.

Córdova, Salvador. *Habitantes del Cauca i Buenaventura.* Medellín: M. A. Balcazar, 1841.

Coronil, Fernando. *The Magical State: Nature, Money, and Modernity in Venezuela.* Chicago: University of Chicago Press, 1997.

Corwin, Arthur F. *Spain and the Abolition of Slavery in Cuba, 1817–1886.* Austin: University of Texas Press, 1967.

Costeloe, Michael P. *Bonds and Bondholders: British Investors and Mexico's Foreign Debt, 1824–1888.* Westport, CT: Praeger, 2003.

———. *Response to Revolution: Imperial Spain and the Spanish American Revolutions, 1810–1840.* Cambridge: Cambridge University Press, 1986.

Coxe, Tench. *Views of the United States, in a Series of Papers.* Philadelphia, PA: William Hall, Wrigley and Berryman, 1794.

Craiutu, Aurelian. *Liberalism under Siege: The Political Thought of the French Doctrinaires.* Oxford and New York: Lexington Books, 2003.

Crapol, Edward. "John Quincy Adams and the Monroe Doctrine: Some New Evidence." *Pacific Historical Review* 48 (1979): 413–18.

Cruz Canaveira, Manuel Felipe. *Liberais Moderados e Constitucionalismo Moderado (1814–52).* Lisbon: I.N.I.C., 1988.

Cubas, Ricardo. "Educación, Elites e Independencia: El papel del convictorio de

San Carlos en la Emancipación peruana." In *La Independencia del Perú: De los Borbones a Bolívar,* edited by Scarlett O'Phelan Godoy. Lima: IRA/PUCP, 2001.

Cunill Grau, Pedro. *Geografía del Poblamiento Venezolano en el Siglo XIX.* Caracas: Ediciones de la Presidencia de la República, 1987.

Cunninghame-Graham, Robert. *José Antonio Páez.* London: William Heinemann, 1929.

Curtin, Philip D. *The Atlantic Slave Trade: A Census.* Madison: University of Wisconsin Press, 1969.

———. *The Rise and Fall of the Plantation Complex: Essays in Atlantic History.* Cambridge: Cambridge University Press, 1990.

Daughton, J. P. "When Argentina was 'French': Rethinking Cultural Politics and European Imperialism in Belle-Époque Buenos Aires." *Journal of Modern History* 80, no. 4 (2008): 831–64.

Davies, Catherine. "Colonial Dependence and Sexual Difference: Reading for Gender in the Writings of Simon Bolivar (1783–1830)." *Feminist Review* 79 (2005): 5–19.

Davis, John. *Naples and Napoleon: Southern Italy and the European Revolutions (1780–1860).* Oxford: Oxford University Press, 2006.

Dawson, Frank Griffith. *The First Latin American Debt Crisis: The City of London and the 1822–25 Loan Bubble.* New Haven, CT: Yale University Press, 1990.

Deas, Malcolm. "Venezuela, Colombia, and Ecuador: The First Half-Century of Independence." In *Cambridge History of Latin America,* vol.3, edited by Leslie Bethell. Cambridge: Cambridge University Press, 1989.

———. "Weapons of the Weak? Colombia and Foreign Powers in the Nineteenth Century." In *Informal Empire in Latin America,* edited by M. Brown, 173–86.

Debien, Gabriel. "Les colons de Saint-Domingue réfugiés a Cuba, 1793–1815." *Revista de Indias* 14, no. 54–56 (1953): 11–36.

———. "Refugies de Saint-Domingue expulses de la Havane en 1809." *Anuario de Estudios Americanos* 35 (1978): 555–610.

del Valle, José Cecilio. *Cartas Autógrafas de y para José Cecilio del Valle.* Introduction by Cesar Sepulveda. Mexico City: Editorial Porrua, 1978.

Delgado Ribas, Josep M. *Dinámicas imperiales (1650–1796): España, América y Europa en el cambio institucional del sistema colonial español.* Barcelona: Edicions Bellaterra, 2007.

———. "From Marginality to Centrality: The Slave Trade in the Spanish Imperial System, 1501–1808." In *Slavery, Empire, and Abolitionism,* edited by Fradera and Schmidt-Nowara.

Dérozier, Albert. *Manuel José Quintana y el nacimiento del liberalismo en España.* Madrid: Turner, 1978.

Dias, Tânia. "A escrita diária de uma 'viagem de instrucão.'" *Escritos: Revista da Casa de Rui Barbosa* 1 (2007): 17–42.

Díaz, Francisco Javier. *O'Higgins*. Buenos Aires: Biblioteca del Oficial, 1946.

Dodds, James. *Records of the Scottish Settlers in the River Plate and Their Churches.* Buenos Aires: Grant and Sylvester, 1897.

Donoso, Ricardo. *El marqués de Osorno Don Ambrosio O'Higgins, 1720–1801.* Santiago: Publicaciones de la Universidad de Chile, 1941.

Dore, Elizabeth. *Myths of Modernity: Peonage and Patriarchy in Nicaragua.* Durham, NC, and London: Duke University Press, 2006.

Dubois, Laurent. *Avengers of the New World: The Story of the Haitian Revolution.* Cambridge, MA: Belknap Press of Harvard University Press, 2004.

DuBois Shaw, Gwendolyn. "'Moses Williams, Cutter of Profiles': Silhouettes and African-American Identity in the Early Republic." *Proceedings of the American Philosophical Society* 149, no. 1 (2005): 22–39.

Dunkerley, James. *Americana: The Americas in the World, around 1850 (or "Seeing the Elephant" as the Theme for an Imaginary Western).* London: Verso, 2000.

Duran López, Francisco, ed. *Crónicas de Cortes del Semanario Patriótico.* Cádiz: Fundación Municipal de Cultura, 2003.

Dym, Jordana. "Citizen of Which Republic? Foreigners and the Construction of National Citizenship in Central America, 1825–1845." *The Americas* 64, no. 4 (2008): 477–510.

———. *From Sovereign Villages to National States: City, State, and Federation in Central America, 1759–1839.* Albuquerque: University of New Mexico Press, 2006.

Earle, Rebecca. "Information and Disinformation in Late Colonial New Granada." *The Americas* 54, no. 2 (1997): 167–84.

———. *Spain and the Independence of Colombia, 1810–1825.* Exeter: University of Exeter Press, 2000.

———. "The War of the Supremes: Border Conflict, Religious Crusade or Simply Politics by Other Means?" In *Rumours of Wars: Civil Conflict in Nineteenth-Century Latin America,* edited by Rebecca Earle, 119–34. London: Institute of Latin American Studies.

Earl Weeks, William. *John Quincy Adams and American Global Empire.* Lexington: University of Kentucky Press, 1992.

Eastman, Scott. "'America Has Escaped from Our Hands': Rethinking Empire, Identity, and Independence during the Trienio Liberal in Spain, 1820–1823." *European History Quarterly* 41, no. 3 (2011): 428–43.

Eastwood, Jonathan. *The Rise of Nationalism in Venezuela.* Gainesville: University of Florida Press, 2006.

Elliott, J. H. *Empires of the Atlantic World: Britain and Spain in America, 1492–1830.* New Haven and London: Yale University Press, 2006.

Espinoza Ruíz, Grover Antonio. "La reforma de la educación superior en Lima: El caso del Real Convictorio de San Carlos." In *El Perú en el siglo XVIII: La Era Borbónica,* edited by Scarlett O'Phelan Godoy. Lima: IRA/PUCP, 1999.

Eyzaguirre, Jaime. *O'Higgins.* Santiago de Chile: Editorial Zigzag, 1972.

Fernández Gómez, Emilio Manuel. *Argentina: Gesta británica, Revaloración de dos siglos de convivencia.* Buenos Aires: L.O.L.A., 1995.

Fernández Pérez, Paloma. "Comercio y familia en la España pre-industrial: Redes y estrategias de inmigrantes irlandeses en el Cádiz del siglo XVIII." In *La inmigración irlandesa en el siglo XVIII,* coordinated by María Begoña Villar García. Málaga: Universidad de Málaga, 2000.

———. *El rostro familiar de la metropolis: Redes de parentesco y lazos mercantiles en Cádiz, 1700–1812.* Madrid: Unicaja, 1997.

Ferrer, Ada. "Cuba en la sombra de Haití: Noticias, Sociedad y esclavitud." In *El rumor de Haití en Cuba: Temor, raza y rebeldía, 1789–1844,* edited by María Dolores González-Ripoll et al. Madrid: CSIC, 2005.

———. "Noticias de Haití en Cuba." *Revista de Indias* 63 (2003): 675–94.

———. "Temor, poder y esclavitud en Cuba en la época de la revolución haitiana." In *Las Antillas en la época de la Revolución,* edited by José A. Piqueras. Madrid: Siglo XXI, 2005.

Ferrone, Vincenzo. *La società giusta ed equa: Repubblicanesimo e diritti dell'uomo in Gaetano Filangieri.* Rome: Bari, Laterza, 2003.

Fick, Carolyn E. *The Making of Haiti: The Saint Domingue Revolution from Below.* Knoxville: University of Tennessee Press, 1990.

Filippi, Alberto, ed. *Bolívar y Europa, en el pensamiento politico y la historiografía.* 2 vols. Caracas: Ediciones de la Presidencia de la República, 1986, 1992.

Fischer, Sibylle. *Modernity Disavowed: Haiti and the Cultures of Slavery in the Age of Revolution.* Durham, NC: Duke University Press, 2004.

Fisher, John. *Government and Society in Colonial Peru: The Intendant System, 1784–1814.* Londres: Athlone Press, 1970.

Fladeland, Betty. "Abolitionist Pressures on the Concert of Europe, 1814–1822." *Journal of Modern History* 38, no. 4 (1966): 355–73.

Flórez Estrada, Álvaro. *Examen imparcial de las disensiones de América con España, de los medios de su reconciliación y de la prosperidad de todas las naciones.* Madrid: Biblioteca de Autores Españoles, 1950.

Fontana, Biancamaria. *Benjamin Constant and the Post-revolutionary Mind.* New Haven and London: Yale University Press, 1991.

Fontana, Josep. *La época del liberalismo.* Madrid: Marcial Pons, 2007.

———. *La quiebra de la monarquía absoluta, 1814–1820: La crisis del Antiguo Régimen en España.* Barcelona: Ariel, 1970.

———. *La Revolución Liberal (Política y Hacienda, 1833–1845).* Madrid: Instituto de Estudios Fiscales, 1977.

———. "Prólogo." In *La utopia insurreccional del liberalismo: Torrijos y las conspiraciones liberales de la década ominosa,* by Irene Castells. Barcelona: Editorial Crítica, 1989.

Fontana Lázaro, Josep. *La quiebra de la monarquía absoluta, 1814–1820 (La crisis del Antiguo regimen en España).* Barcelona: Ariel, 1971.

Ford, John. *Ackermann, 1783–1983: The Business of Art.* London: Ackermann, 1983.

Fowler, Will. "El pronunciamiento mexicano del siglo XIX. Hacia una nueva tipología." *Estudios de Historia Moderna y Contemporánea de México* 38 (2009): 5–34.

———, ed. *Forceful Negotiations: The Origins of the Pronunciamiento in Nineteenth-Century Mexico.* Lincoln: University of Nebraska Press, 2010.

———. "'I Pronounce Thus I Exist': Redefining the Pronunciamiento in Independent Mexico, 1821–1876." In *Forceful Negotiations: The Origins of the Pronunciamiento in Nineteenth-Century Mexico,* edited by Will Fowler. Lincoln: University of Nebraska Press, 2010.

———. *Mexico in the Age of Proposals, 1821–1853.* Westport, CT: Greenwood Press, 1998.

———. *Santa Anna, of Mexico.* Lincoln: University of Nebraska Press, 2007.

Fradera, Josep María. *Colonias para después de un imperio.* Barcelona: Edicions Bellaterra, 2005.

———. *Filipinas, la colonia más peculiar: La hacienda pública en la determinación de la política colonial, 1762–1868.* Madrid: CSIC, 1999.

———. *Gobernar colonias.* Barcelona: Ediciones Península, 1999.

———. *Indústria i mercat: Les bases comercials de la indústria catalana moderna, 1814–1845.* Barcelona: Crítica, 1987.

———. "L'esclavage et la logique constitutionelle des empires." *Annales: Histoire, Sciences Sociales* 63, no. 3 (2008): 533–60.

———. "Why Were Spain's Overseas Laws Never Enacted?" In *Spain, Europe, and the Atlantic World: Essays in Honour of John H. Elliott,* edited by Richard L. Kagan and Geoffrey Parker, 334–49. Cambridge: Cambridge University Press, 1995.

Fradera, Josep M., and Christopher Schmidt-Nowara, eds. *Slavery, Empire, and Abolitionism: Spain from Overseas Expansion to Cuban Abolition.* Cambridge: Cambridge University Press, forthcoming.

Franco, José Luciano. *Ensayos Históricos.* La Habana: Editorial de Ciencias Sociales, 1974.

———. *Política continental americana de España en Cuba, 1812–1830.* Havana: Publicaciones del Archivo Nacional de Cuba, 1947.

Franklin, Robert. *Lord Stuart de Rothesay.* Brighton: Book Guild Publishing, 2008.

Frasquet, Ivana, ed. *Bastillas, cetros y blasones: La independencia de Iberoamérica.* Madrid: Fundación Mapfre, 2006.

———. *Las caras del águila: Del liberalismo gaditano a la república federal Mexicana (1820–1824).* Castellón: Universitat Jaume I, 2008.

Frasquet, Ivana, and Manuel Chust. "Agustín de Iturbide: From the Pronunciamiento of Iguala to the Coup of 1822." In *Forceful Negotiations: The Origins of the Pronunciamiento in Nineteenth-Century Mexico,* edited by Will Fowler. Lincoln: University of Nebraska Press, 2010.

Freide, Juan, and Benjamin Keen, eds. *Bartolomé de las Casas in History: Toward and Understanding of the Man and His Work.* DeKalb: Northern Illinois University Press, 1971.

Galeano, Eduardo. *Venas abiertas de América Latina.* Mexico: Siglo XXI, 1971.

Gallagher, John, and Ronald Robinson. "The Imperialism of Free Trade." *Economic History Review* (2nd series) 6, no. 1 (1953): 1–14.

Gallo, Klaus. *The Struggle for an Enlightened Republic: Buenos Aires and Rivadavia.* London: London University, Institute for the Study of the Americas, 2006.

Galván Moreno, C. *Don Ambrosio O'Higgins: Padre del Capitán General Don Bernardo O'Higgins.* Buenos Aires: Revista de Correos y Telégrafos, 1942.

Games, Alison. "Atlantic History: Definitions, Challenges, and Opportunities." *American Historical Review* 111, no. 3 (2006): 741–56.

García, Gloria. "Vertebrando la resistencia: La lucha de los negros contra el sistema esclavista." In *El rumor de Haití: Temor, raza y rebeldía, 1789–1844,* edited by María Dolores González-Ripoll et al. Madrid: CSIC, 2005.

García Baquero, Antonio. *Comercio colonial y guerras revolucionarias: La decadencia económica de Cádiz a raíz de la emancipación americana.* Seville: CSIC, 1972.

García de los Arcos, María Fernanda. *Forzados y reclutas: Los criollos novohispanos en Asia (1756–1808).* Mexico: Potrerillos Editores, 1996.

García Rodríguez, Mercedes. *Entre haciendas y plantaciones: Orígenes de la manufactura azucarera en La Habana.* Havana: Editorial de Ciencias Sociales, 2007.

Gargarella, Roberto. "Towards a Typology of Latin American Constitutionalism." *Latin American Research Review* 39, no. 2 (2004): 141–53.

Garraway, Doris L., ed. *Tree of Liberty: Cultural Legacies of the Haitian Revolution in the Atlantic World.* Charlottesville: University of Virginia Press, 2008.

Garrett, Almeida. "Da Europa e da América e de sua mutual influência na causa da civilisação e da liberdade." In *Obras Completas: Obra Política (1824–27).* Lisbon: Ed. Estampa, 1991.

Garrido, Margarita. "Independencia y bicentenario." Lecture given at the Congreso Colombiano de Historia, Bogotá, July 26, 2010.

Garrigó, Roque E. *Historia documentada de la conspiración de los Soles y Rayos de Bolívar.* Havana: Imprenta "El Siglo," 1929.

Geggus, David Patrick. *Haitian Revolutionary Studies.* Bloomington: Indiana University Press, 2002.

———, ed. *The Impact of the Haitian Revolution in the Atlantic World.* Columbia: University of South Carolina Press, 2001.

Geggus, David Patrick, and Norman Fiering, eds. *The World of the Haitian Revolution.* Bloomington: Indiana University Press, 2009.

Geggus, David Patrick, and David Barry Gaspar. *A Turbulent Time: The French Revolution and the Greater Caribbean.* Bloomington: Indiana University Press, 1997.

Gerbi, Antonello. *The Dispute of the New World: The History of a Polemic, 1750–1900.* Translated by Jeremy Moyle. Pittsburgh: University of Pittsburgh Press, 1973.

Gibson, Carrie. "The Impact of the Haitian Revolution on the Hispanic Caribbean." PhD diss., University of Cambridge, 2011.

Gilbert, Felix. *To the Farewell Address: Ideas of Early American Foreign Policy.* Princeton: Princeton University Press, 1961.

Gillespie, Alexander. *Gleanings and Remarks; Collected during Many Months of Residence at Buenos Ayres, and Within the Upper Country; With a Prefatory Account of the Expedition from England, of the Surrender of the Colony of the Cape of Good Hope, under the Joint Command of Sir David Baird and Sir Home Popham by Major Alexander Gillespie, Illustrated with a Map of South America, and a Chart of Rio de la Plata, with Pilotage Directions.* Leeds: B. Dewhurst, 1818.

Gil Novales, Alberto, ed. *Rafael del Riego: La revolución de 1820, día a día. Cartas, escritos y discursos.* Madrid: Tecnos, 1976.

Glave, Luis Miguel. "Una perspectiva histórico-cultural de la revolución del Cuzco de 1814." *Revista de las Américas, Historia y Presente* 1 (2003): 11–38.

———. *Vida, símbolos y batallas: Creación y recreación de la comunidad indígena, Cusco, siglos XVI–XX.* Mexico City: FCE, 1992.

Gleijeses, Piero. "The Limits of Sympathy: The United States and the Independence of Spanish America." *Journal of Latin American Studies* 24, no. 3 (1992): 481–505

Goldman, Lawrence, ed. *The Federalist Papers.* Oxford: Oxford University Press, 2008.

Goldstone, Jack. "The Problem of the 'Early Modern' World." *Journal of the Economic and Social History of the Orient* 4 (1998): 249–84.

Gomes da Silva, Francisco. *Memorias Offerecidas a Nação Brasileira.* London, 1831.

Gómez, Alejandro. "José del Valle: A Benthamite in Central America." Paper presented at ISUS-X, Tenth Conference of the International Society for Utilitarian Studies, Kadish Center for Morality, Law, and Public Affairs, University of California, Berkeley.

———. "Le syndrome de Saint-Domingue: Perceptions et représentations de la Révolution haïtienne dans le Monde atlantique, 1790–1886." PhD diss., Université Sorbonne Nouvelle-Paris, 2010.

Gonzaléz, Adriana Luna. "La receptión de ideas de Gaetano Filangieri." *ISTOR, Revista de Historia Interncional* 8 (2007): 120–49.

González-Ripoll Navarro, María Dolores. "Vínculos y redes de poder entre Madrid y La Habana: Francisco Arango y Parreño (1765–1837). Ideólogo y mediador." *Revista de Indias* 61, no. 222 (2001): 291–305.

Goodwin, Paul B., Jr. "Initiating United States Relations with Argentina." In *United States-Latin American Relations, 1800–1850,* edited by Thomas Ray Shurbutt, 102–21. Tuscaloosa: University of Alabama Press, 1991.

Gootenberg, Paul. *Between Silver and Guano: Commercial Policy and the State in Post-independence Peru.* Princeton, NJ: Princeton University Press, 1989.

Gould, Eliga. "Entangled Histories, Entangled Worlds: The English-Speaking Atlantic as a Spanish Periphery." *American Historical Review* 112, no. 3 (2007): 764–86.

Gover, Tom. "Plunging at Spectres? Anglo-American Rivalry in Mexico, 1823–1827." PhD diss., University of Oxford, 2009.

Graham Burnett, D. *Masters of All They Surveyed: Exploration, Geography, and a British El Dorado.* Chicago: Chicago University Press, 2000.

Graham-Yooll, Andrew. *La independencia de Venezuela vista por The Times.* Caracas: Libros de Hoy Del Diario de Caracas, 1980.

Green, William A. "Periodizing World History." In *World History: Ideologies, Structures, and Identities,* edited by Philip Pomper, Richard H. Elphick, and Richard T. Vann, 53–65. Malden, MA, and Oxford: Blackwell, 1998.

Gregoire, Abbé. "Apología de don Bartholomé de las Casas, obispo de Chiapa, por el ciudadano Gregoire." In *Colección de las obras del venerable obispo de Chiapa,* edited by Llorente, xx.

Guardino, Peter F. *Peasants, Politics, and the Formation of Mexico's National State: Guerrero, 1800–1857.* Stanford: Stanford University Press, 1996.

Guedea, Virginia, ed. *La independencia de México y el proceso autonomista novo-hispano, 1808–1824.* Mexico City: UNAM/Instituto Mora, 2001.

———. "Las primeras elecciones populares en la ciudad de México, 1812–1813." *Mexican Studies/Estudios Mexicanos* 7, no. 1. (1991): 1–28.

Guenther, Louise. *British Merchants in Nineteenth-Century Brazil: Business, Culture, and Identity in Bahía, 1808–50.* Oxford: Centre for Brazilian Studies, 2004.

Guerra, François-Xavier. "El pronunciamiento en México: Prácticas e imaginarios." *Travaux et Recherches dans les Amerique de Centre* 37 (2000): 15–26.

———. *Modernidad e Independencias: Ensayos sobre las revoluciones hispánicas*. Madrid: Mapfre, 1992.

Guy, Alain. *Femme-philosophes en Espagne et en Amerique Latine*. Paris: CNRS, 1990.

Haigh, Samuel. *Sketches of Buenos Ayres, Chile, and Peru*. London: Effingham Wilson, 1831.

Hale, Charles A. *Mexican Liberalism in the Age of Mora, 1821–53*. New Haven and London; Yale University Press, 1968. Translated into Spanish as *El liberalismo mexicano en la época de Mora 1821–1853*. Mexico City: Siglo XXI, 1987.

Hall, Basil. "Lima independiente." In *Relaciones de Viajeros*, 262:1. C.D.I.P. Tomo 27.

Hall, Catherine. *Civilising Subjects: Metropole and Colony in the English Imagination, 1830–1867*. London: Polity, 2002.

Halperín Donghi, Tulio. "La apertura mercantil en el Río de la Plata: Impacto global y desigualdades regionales, 1800–1850." In *América latina en la época de Simón Bolívar*, edited by Liehr, 115–38.

———. *Politics, Economy, and Society in Argentina in the Revolutionary Period*. Cambridge: Cambridge University Press, 1975.

——— *Reforma y Disolución de los Imperios Ibericos, 1750–1850*. Madrid: Alianza Editoria, 1985.

Halpern Pereira, Miriam, et al., eds. *Mouzinho da Silveira, Obras*. Lisbon: Fundação Calouste Gulbenkian, 1989.

Hamilton, Charles C. *French Phraseology*. London: G & W. B. Whittaker, 1824.

Hammond, John Craig. *Slavery, Freedom, and Expansion in the Early American West*. Charlottesville: University of Virginia Press, 2008.

Hamnett, Brian R. *A Concise History of Mexico*. 2nd ed. Cambridge: Cambridge University Press, 2007.

———. *Juárez*. London and New York: Longman, 1994.

———. *La política española en una época de revolución, 1790–1820*. Mexico City: Fondo de Cultura Económica, 1985.

———. "Liberal Politics and Spanish Freemasonry, 1814–1820." *History* 69, no. 226 (1984): 222–37.

———. "Process and Pattern: A Re-examination of the Ibero-American Independence Movements, 1808–1826." *Journal of Latin American Studies* 29, no. 2 (1997): 279–328.

———. *Revolución y Contrarrevolución en México y el Perú: Liberalismo, Realeza y Separatismo (1800–24)*. Mexico City: Fondo de Cultura Económica, 1978.

———. *Roots of Insurgency: Mexican Regions, 1750–1824*. Cambridge: Cambridge University Press, 1986.

Hanke, Lewis. *Bartolomé de las Casas, Historian*. Gainesville: University of Florida Press, 1952.

Hankshaw, John. *Reminiscences of South America from Two and a Half Years' Residence in Venezuela*. London: Jackson and Walford, 1838.

Hanon, Maxine. *Diccionario de británicos en Buenos Aires (Primera época)*. Buenos Aires: distribution by the author, 2005.

Harland-Jacobs, Jessica. "'Hands across the Sea': The Masonic Network, British Imperialism, and the North Atlantic World." *Geographical Review* 89, no. 2 (1999): 237–53.

Harlow, Vincent T. *The Founding of the Second British Empire, 1763–93*. 2 vols. London: Longman, Green & Co., 1952–1964.

Harris, J. "An English Utilitarian Looks at Spanish American Independence: Jeremy Bentham's Rid Yourselves of Ultramaria." *The Americas* 58, no. 2 (1996): 217–33.

Harwich Valenilla, Nikita. *Formación y crisis de un sistema financiero nacional: Banca y estado en Venezuela 1830–1940*. Caracas: Editorial Buria y Editorial Antonio José de Sucre, 1986.

Hassel, Mary, and Lenora Sansay. *Secret History Or, the Horrors of St Domingo in a Series of Letter, Written By a Lady At Cape Francois, to Colonel Burr, Late Vice-President of the United States, Principally During the Command of General Rochambeau*. Philadelphia, 1808.

Head, Capt. Francis B. *Report Relating to the Failure of the Rio Plata Mining Association Formed under an Authority Signed by His Excellency Don Bernardino Rivadavia*. London: John Murray, 1827.

———. *Rough Notes Taken during Some Rapid Journeys across the Pampas and among the Andes*. 4th ed. London: John Murray, 1846.

Helg, Aline. "A Fragmented Majority: Free 'of All Colors,' Indians, and Slaves in Caribbean Colombia during the Haitian Revolution." In *The Impact of the Haitian Revolution in the Atlantic World*, edited by David Geggus, 157–75. Columbia: University of South Carolina Press, 2001.

———. *Liberty and Equality in Caribbean Colombia, 1770–1835*. Chapel Hill: University of North Carolina Press, 2004.

———. "Simón Bolívar and the Spectre of 'Pardocracia': José Padilla in Post-independence Cartagena." *Journal of Latin American Studies* 35, no. 3 (2003): 447–71.

Helguera, J. León, and Robert H. Davis, eds. *Archivo epistolar de Tomás Cipriano de Mosquera*. 3 vols. Bogotá: Academia Colombiana de Historia, 1978.

Hendrickson, David C. *Peace Pact: The Lost World of the American Founding*. Lawrence: University Press of Kansas, 2003.

———. *Union, Nation, or Empire: The American Debate over International Relations, 1789–1941.* Lawrence: University Press of Kansas, 2009.

Hernández González, Manuel. *Diego Correa, un liberal canario ante la emancipación americana.* Tenerife: Ayuntamiento de La Laguna, 1992.

———. "El liberalismo exaltado en el trienio liberal cubano." In *Cuba: Algunos problemas de su historia,* edited by Josef Opatrný. Prague: Universidad Carolina, 1995.

Herzog, Tamar. *Defining Nations: Immigrants and Citizens in Early Modern Spain and Spanish American.* New Haven, CT: Yale University Press, 2003.

Hespanha, António Manuel. *Guiando a Mão Invisível: Direitos, Estado e Lei no Liberalismo Monárquico Português.* Coimbra: Livraria Almedina, 2004.

Higonnet, Patrice. "Le fédéralisme américain et le fédéralisme de Benjamin Constant." *Annales Benjamin Constant* 8–9 (1988): 51–62.

———. *Sister Republics: The Origins of French and American Republicanism.* Cambridge, MA: Harvard University Press, 1988.

Hinde, Wendy. *George Canning.* London: Collins, 1973.

Hobsbawm, Eric J. *The Age of Capital, 1848–1875.* London: Weidenfeld and Nicolson, 1975.

———. *The Age of Empire, 1875–1914.* London: Weidenfeld and Nicolson, 1987.

———. *The Age of Revolution: Europe, 1789–1848.* London: Weidenfeld and Nicolson, 1962.

———. *Echoes of the Marseillaise: Two Centuries Look Back on the French Revolution.* London: Verso, 1990.

Hopkins, A. G. "Informal Empire in Argentina: An Alternative View." *Journal of Latin American Studies* 26 (1994): 469–84.

Horsman, Reginald. *Race and Manifest Destiny.* Cambridge, MA: Harvard University Press, 1981.

Humphreys, R. A., ed. *British Consular Reports on the Trade and Politics of Latin America, 1824–1826.* London: Offices of the Royal Historical Society, 1940.

———. *Tradition and Revolt in Latin America and Other Essays.* London: Weidenfeld and Nicolson, 1969.

Humphreys, R. A., and John Lynch, eds. *The Origins of the Latin American Revolutions, 1808–1826.* New York: Alfred A. Knopf, 1966.

Inikori, Joseph E. *Africans and the Industrial Revolution in England.* Cambridge: Cambridge University Press, 2002.

Irurozqui, Marta, ed. *La ciudadanía en debate en América Latina: Discusiones historiográficas y una propuesta sobre el valor público de la infracción electoral.* Lima: Instituto de Estudios Peruanos, 2004.

Isabella, Maurizio. *Risorgimiento in Exile: Italian Émigrés and the Liberal International in the Post-Napoleonic Era.* Oxford: Oxford University Press, 2009.

Jacob, Margaret. *Living the Enlightenment: Freemasonry and Politics in Eighteenth-Century Europe.* Oxford: Oxford University Press, 1991.

Jacobsen, Nils. "Taxation in Early Republican Peru, 1821–1851: Policy Making between Reform and Tradition." In *América Latina en la época de Simón Bolívar,* edited by Liehr.

Jaksic, Ivan. *Andrés Bello: Scholarship and Nation-Building in Nineteenth-Century Latin America.* Cambridge: Cambridge University Press, 2001.

James, C. L. R. *The Black Jacobins.* London: Penguin, 2001.

Jameson, Robert Francis. *Letters From the Havana, During the Year 1820, Containing and Account of the Present State of the Island of Cuba, and Observations of the Slave Trade.* London: John Miller, 1821.

Jasanoff, Maya. *Edge of Empire: Lives, Culture, and Conquest in the East, 1750–1850.* New York: Fourth Estate, 2005.

———. *Liberty's Exiles: The Loss of America and the Remaking of the British Empire.* London: Harper Collins, 2011.

Jáuregui, Luis, and Carlos Marichal. "Paradojas Fiscales y Financieras de la Temprana República Mexicana, 1825–1855." In *Latinoamérica y España, 1800–1850: Un crecimiento económico nada excepcional,* edited by Enrique Llopis and Marichal. Madrid: Marcial Pons, 2009.

Jocelyn-Holt Letelier, Alfredo. *La Independencia de Chile: Tradición, Modernización y Mito.* Santiago: Planeta/Ariel, 1999.

Jones, Calvin. "Images of Simon Bolivar as Reflected in Ten Leading British Periodicals, 1816–1830." *The Americas* 40, no. 3 (1984): 377–97.

Karras, Alan. "The Atlantic World as a Unit of Study." In *Atlantic-American Societies: From Columbus through Abolition, 1492–1888,* edited by Alan Karras and J. R. McNeill. London and New York: Routledge, 1992.

King, James F. "The Colored Castes and the American Representation in the Cortes of Cádiz." *Hispanic American Historical Review* 33, no. 1 (1953): 33–64.

Kinsbruner, Jay. "The Political Influence of the British Merchants Resident in Chile during the O'Higgins Administration, 1817–1823." *The Americas* 27, no. 1 (1970): 26–39.

Klooster, Wim. *Revolutions in the Atlantic World: A Comparative History.* New York and London: New York University Press, 2009.

Knight, Franklin W. "Origins of Wealth and the Sugar Revolution in Cuba, 1750–1850." *Hispanic American Historical Review* 57, no. 2 (1977): 236–53.

Knight, Franklin W., and Peggy K. Liss, eds. *Atlantic Port Cities: Economy, Culture, and Society in the Atlantic World, 1650–1850.* Knoxville: University of Tennessee Press, 1991.

Lahiri, Smita. "Rhetorical *Indios*: Propagandists and Their Publics in the Spanish Philippines." *Comparative Studies in Society and History* 49, no. 2 (2007): 243–75.

Lambert, David, and Alan Lester, eds. *Colonial Lives across the British Empire: Imperial Careering in the Long Nineteenth Century.* Cambridge: Cambridge University Press, 2006.

Lambert, Eric. "Muerte y Entierro del Brigadier General James Towers English." *Boletín Histórico* 8, no. 24 (1970): 317–27.

Larson, Brooke. *Trials of Nation Making: Liberalism, Race and Ethnicity in the Andes, 1810–1910.* Cambridge: Cambridge University Press, 2004.

las Casas, Bartolomé de. *Breve relación de la destrucción de las Indias Occidentales: Presentada a Felipe II siendo Principe de Asturias.* Impresa en Sevilla, reimpresa en Lóndres, en Filadelfia, en México, y en Guadalajara en la oficina de D. Urbano Sanromán, año de 1822. [Guadalajara?], 1822.

Lasso, Marixa. *Myths of Harmony: Race and Republicanism during the Age of Revolution, Colombia, 1795–1831.* Pittsburgh: University of Pittsburgh Press, 2007.

Laughlin, Robert M. *Beware the Great Horned Serpent! Chiapas under the Threat of Napoleon.* Albany, NY: Institute for Mesoamerican Studies, 2003.

Lavrín, Asunción. *Latin American Women: Historical Perspectives.* Westport, CT: Greenwood Press, 1978.

Leal, Hamilton. *História das Instituições Políticas do Brasil.* Rio de Janeiro: Estados de Guanabara, 1962.

Lemos Seixas e Castel-Branco, Joaquim Antonio de. *Memoria Justificativa come que Pertende Provar-se, e com effeito, Juridicamente se prova a Legitimidade dos Direitos que Assistem ao Serenissimo Senhor Infante Dom Miguel a Coroa e Sceptro de Portugal.* Lisbon, 1831.

Lewin, Linda. *Surprise Heirs.* Vol 2: *Illegitimacy, Inheritance Rights, and Public Power in the Formation of Imperial Brazil.* Stanford: Stanford University Press, 2003.

Lewis, James E., Jr. *The American Union and the Problem of Neighborhood: The United States and the Collapse of the Spanish Empire, 1783–1829.* Chapel Hill: University of North Carolina Press, 1998.

Lewis, William F. "Simón Bolívar and Xavier Mina: A Rendezvous in Haiti." *Journal of Inter-American Studies* 11, no. 3 (1969): 458–65.

Liehr, Reinhard, ed. *América Latina en la época de Simón Bolívar: La formación de las economías nacionales y los interesesen la epoca de Simon Bolivar: La formacion de las economias nacionales y los intereses económicos europeos, 1800–1850.* Berlin: Biblioteca Ibero-Americana, 1989.

Lima Junior, Augusto de, ed. *Cartas de D. Pedro I a D. João VI relativas á Independência do Brasil.* Rio de Janeiro: Jornal de Commercio, 1941.

Liss, Peggy K. *Atlantic Empires: The Network of Trade and Revolution, 1713–1826.* Baltimore: Johns Hopkins University Press, 1983.

Llorca, Manuel. "British Textile Exports to the Southern Cone during the First Half of the Nineteenth Century: Growth, Structure, and the Marketing Chain." PhD diss., University of Leicester, 2008.

Llorente, Juan Antonio, ed. *Colección de las obras del venerable obispo de Chiapa, don Bartolomé de las Casas, defensor de la libertad de los americanos.* 2 vols. Paris: Rosa, 1822.

Lobo, F. A. "Rezumida Noticia da Vida de D. Nuno Caetano Alvares Pereira de Mello." In *Obras de D. Francisco Alexandre Lobo, Bispo de Vizeu.* Lisbon, 1849.

Lofstrom, William. *La vida íntima de Tomás Cipriano de Mosquera.* Bogotá: El Ancora Editores, 1996.

Lombardi, John. "Epilogue: History and Our Heroes: The Bolivarian Legend." In *Simón Bolívar: Essays on the Life and Legacy of the Liberator,* edited by David Bushnell and Lester Langley. Lanham, MD: Rowman and Littlefield, 2008.

Lomnitz, Claudio. "Nationalism as a Practical System: Benedict Anderson's Theory of Nationalism from the Vantage Point of Spanish America." In *The Other Mirror: Grand Theory through the Lens of Latin America,* edited by Miguel Angel Centeno and Fernando López-Alvez, 329–59. Princeton: Princeton University Press, 2001.

Loomba, Ania. "Periodisation, Race, and Global Contact." *Journal of Medieval and Early Modern Studies* 37, no. 3 (2007): 595–620.

López-Guadalupe, Miguel Luis. "Irlandeses al servicio del Rey de España en el siglo XVIII. Caballeros de Hábito." In *La emigración irlandesa en el siglo XVIII,* edited by María Begoña Villar García. Málaga: Universidad de Málaga, 2000.

Lorente, Marta. "América en Cádiz (1808–1812)." In *Los Orígenes del Constitucionalismo Liberal en España e Iberoamérica: Un estudio comparado,* edited by Pedro Cruz Villalón. Seville: Junta de Andalucía, 1994.

Lousada, Maria Alexandre, and Maria de Fátima Sá e Melo Ferreira. *D. Miguel.* Lisbon: Círculo de Leitores, 2006.

Lucena Giraldo, Manuel. "La orden apócrifa de 1810 sobre la 'libertad de comercio' en América." *Boletín Americanista* 20, no. 28 (1978): 5–21.

Luiz Cervo, Amado, and José Calvet de Magalhães. *Depois das Caravelas: As Relações entre Portugal e Brasil 1808–2000.* Brasília: Editora Universidade de Brasília, 2000.

Luttwak, Edward. *Coup d'état: A Practical Handbook.* London: Penguin, 1968.

Lux, William R. "French Colonization in Cuba, 1791–1809." *The Americas* 29 (1972): 57–62.

Lynch, Christian Edward Cyril. "O Discurso Político Monarquiano e a Recepção do Conceito de Poder Moderador no Brasil (1822–24)." *Dados* [Rio de Janeiro] 48, no. 3 (2005): 611–54.

Lynch, John. *Argentine Dictator: Juan Manuel de Rosas, 1829–1852.* Oxford: Clarendon Press, 1981.

———. *Caudillos in Spanish America, 1800–1850.* Oxford: Clarendon Press, 1992.

———. "Foreign Trade and Economic Interests in Argentina, 1810–1850." In *América Latina en la época de Simón Bolívar,* edited by Liehr, 139–55.

———. *José de San Martín: Argentine Soldier, American Hero.* New Haven, CT: Yale University Press, 2009.

———, ed. *Latin American Revolutions, 1808–1826: Old and New World Origins.* Norman and London: University of Oklahoma Press, 1994.

———. *Simón Bolívar: A Life.* New Haven: Yale University Press, 2006.

———. *The Spanish American Revolutions, 1808–1826.* London: Weidenfeld and Nicolson, 1973.

Lynn, Martin. "British Policy, Trade, and Informal Empire in the Mid-nineteenth Century." In *Oxford History of the British Empire,* edited by Andrew Porter, 101–21. Oxford: Oxford University Press, 1999.

Macaulay, Neill. *Dom Pedro: The Struggle for Liberty in Brazil and Portugal, 1798–1834.* Durham, NC, and London: Duke University Press, 1986.

Macedo, José Agostinho de. *A Besta Esfolada.* [Lisbon] 1828.

———. *O Desengano: Periodico Politico, e Moral.* [Lisbon] 1830.

———. *O Espectador Portuguez: Jornal de Litteratura, e Critico.* Lisbon, 1816.

Macintyre, Iona. *Women and Print Culture in Post-independence Buenos Aires.* Woodbridge: Tamesis, 2010.

Madre de Deos, Faustino José de. *Absurdos Civis, Politicos e Diplomaticos.* Lisbon, 1828.

Magalhães, Luiz de. *Tradicionalismo e Constitutionalismo: Estudos de Historia e Politica Nacional.* Porto: Lello & Irmão, 1927.

Maisch, Christian J. "The Falkland/Malvinas Islands Clash of 1831–32: U.S. and British Diplomacy in the South Atlantic." *Diplomatic History* 24, no. 2 (Spring 2000): 185–209.

Malanson, Jeffrey J. "The Congressional Debate over U.S. Participation in the Congress of Panama, 1825–1826: Washington's Farewell Address, Monroe's Doctrine, and the Fundamental Principles of U.S. Foreign Policy." *Diplomatic History* 30, no. 5 (2006): 813–38.

Maluquer de Motes, Jordi. "La revolución industrial en Cataluña." In *La modernización económica de España, 1830–1930,* edited by Nicolás Sánchez-Albornoz. Madrid: Alianza Editorial, 1985.

Manchester, Alan K. *British Preeminence in Brazil: Its Rise and Decline, a Study in European Expansion.* Chapel Hill, NC: Duke University Press, 1933.

Manique, António Pedro. *Portugal e as Potências Europeias: Relações Externas e In-*

gerências Estrangeiras em Portugal na Primeira Metade do Século XIX. Lisbon: Livros Horizonte, 1988.

Manning, William, ed. *Diplomatic Correspondence of the United States.* 12 vols. Washington, DC: Carnegie Endowment, 1940–1944.

Marichal, Carlos. "Beneficios y costos fiscales del colonialismo: Las remesas americanas a España, 1760–1814." *Revista de Historia Económica* 14, no. 3 (1997): 475–506.

———. *A Century of Debt Crises in Latin America, from Independence to the Great Depression, 1820–1930.* Princeton: Princeton University Press, 1989.

———. *La bancarrota del virreinato: Nueva España y las finanzas del imperio, 1780–1810.* Mexico City: Fondo de Cultura Económica, 1999.

Marichal, Carlos, and Daniela Marino, comps. *De Colonia a Nación: Impuestos y política en México, 1750–1860.* Mexico City: El Colegio de México, 2001.

Marshall, Oliver. *English, Irish, and Irish American Pioneer Settlers in Nineteenth-Century Brazil.* Oxford: Centre for Brazilian Studies, 2005.

Marshall, P. J. *"A Free though Conquering People."* London: KCL, 1981.

Martinez, Jenny S. "Anti-slavery Courts and the Dawn of International Human Rights Law." *Yale Law Journal* 117 (2008): xx.

Martins, J., R. Rangel, and A. Santiago. "Projecto Institucional do Tradicionalismo Reformista: A Crítica da Legislação Vintista pela Junta de Revisão das Leis." In *O Liberalismo na Península Ibérica na Primeira Metade do Século XIX,* edited by Miriam Halpern Pereira et al. Lisbon: Sá da Costa Editora, 1982.

Martiré, Eduardo. *La Constitución de Bayona entre España y América.* Madrid: Centro de Estudios Políticos y Constitucionales, 2000.

Marx, Karl. "Revolutionary Spain." In *Collected Works.* Vol. 13: *Marx and Engels, 1854–55,* by Karl Marx and Frederick Engels. London: Lawrence and Wishart, 1980.

Mascarenhas Barreto, J. *Memórias do Marquês de Fronteira e d'Alorna. D. José Trazimundo Mascarenhas Barreto: Ditada por êle próprio em 1861.* Coimbra: Imprensa da Universidade, 1928.

Matthewson, Tim. *A Proslavery Foreign Policy: Haitian-American Relations during the Early Republic.* Westport, CT: Praeger, 2003.

Maxwell, Kenneth R. *Conflicts and Conspiracies: Brazil and Portugal, 1750–1808.* Cambridge: Cambridge University Press, 1973.

———. *Naked Tropics: Essays on Empire and Other Rogues.* New York and London: Routledge, 2003.

May, Ernest. *The Making of the Monroe Doctrine.* Cambridge, MA: Belknap Press, 1975.

Mayer, Arno J. *The Persistence of the Old Regime: Europe to the Great War.* New York: Pantheon Books, 1981.

McCarthy, Matthew. "Maritime Predation and British Commercial Policy during the Spanish American Wars of Independence, 1810–1830." PhD diss., University of Hull, 2011.

McFarlane, Anthony. "Identity, Enlightenment, and Political Dissent in Late Colonial Spanish America." *Transactions of the Royal Historical Society* (6th series) 8 (1998): 309–36.

McGee, Gale W. "The Monroe Doctrine—A Stopgap Measure." *Mississippi Valley Historical Review* (1951): 233–50.

McGuinness, Aims. *Path of Empire: Panama and the California Gold Rush.* Ithaca, NY: Cornell University Press, 2008.

McKeown, Adam. "Periodizing Globalization." *History Workshop Journal* 63, no. 1 (2007): 218–30.

McKinley, P. Michael. *Pre-revolutionary Caracas: Politics, Economy, and Society, 1777–1811.* Cambridge, UK: Cambridge University Press, 1985.

Mehegan, John J. *O'Higgins of Chile.* London: J. & J. Bennett Ltd., Century Press, 1913.

Mejía Ricart, Gustavo Adolfo. *Crítica de nuestra historia moderna: primer período del estado libre en la parte Española de la isla de Santo Domingo.* Santo Domingo: Sociedad dominicana de bibliófilos, 2007.

Melo Franco, Afonso Arinos de. "Introdução." In *O Constitucionalismo de D. Pedro I no Brasil e em Portugal.* Rio de Janeiro: Arquivo Nacional de Rio de Janeiro, 1972.

Méndez, Cecilia. *The Plebian Republic: The Huanta Rebellion and the Making of the Peruvian State, 1820–1850.* Chapel Hill, NC: Duke University Press, 2005.

Mendoza, Rosario. *Pangasinan, 1572–1800.* Quezon City: New Day Publishers, 1991.

Mendoza Aleman, Máximo. *Un soldado de Simon Bolivar: Carlos Luis Castelli.* Caracas: Academia Nacional de la Historia, 1991.

Mesquita, António Pedro. *O Pensamento Político Português no Século XIX: Uma Síntese Histórico-Crítica.* Lisbon: Imprensa Nacional-Casa da Moeda, 2006.

Metternich, Richard, ed. *Memoirs of Prince Metternich.* Translated by Alexander Napier. 5 vols. London, 1881.

Mier Hoffman, Jorge. *La carta que cambiará la historia.* Caracas: Lindarte, 2009.

Miers, John. *Travels in Chile and La Plata, Including Accounts Respecting the Geography, Geology, Statistics, Government, Finances, Agriculture, Manners and Customs and the Mining Operations in Chile Collected during a Residence of Several Years in These Countries.* New York: Ams Press, 1970.

Mignolo, Walter. *The Idea of Latin America.* Oxford: Blackwell, 2005.

Miller, Rory. *Britain and Latin America in the Nineteenth and Twentieth Centuries.* London and New York: Pearson, 1993.

Miranda, Jorge, ed. *As Constituiçoes Portuguesas: De 1822 ao texto actual da constituçao.* Lisbon: Livraria Petrony, 1992.

———. *O Constitucionalismo Liberal Luso-Brasileiro.* Lisbon: Outra Margens, 2001.

Mitre, Antonio. *El monedero de los Andes: Región económica y moneda boliviana en el siglo XIX.* La Paz: Hisbol, 1986.

Mondolfi Gudat, Edgardo. *Páez visto por los ingleses.* Caracas: Biblioteca de la Academia Nacional de la Historia, 2005.

Montesquieu, Charles-Louis Secondat. *The Spirit of the Laws.* Translated by Thomas Nugent. New York: Hafner Press, 1949.

Mora, José Joaquín de. *Cartas sobre a Educação das Meninas por uma Senhora Americana passadas do Espanhol a Português e ofrecidas as Senhoras Brasileiras pelo Dr João Candido de Deus e Silva.* Rio de Janeiro: Tipografia Nacional, 1833.

———. *Cartas sobre a Educação do Belo Sexo.* Translated by Francisco Freire de Carvalho. London, 1850.

———. *Cartas sobre la educación del bello sexo por una señora americana.* London: Carlos Wood, 1824.

———. *Cuadros de la historia de los Arabes, desde Mahoma hasta la conquista de Granada.* London, 1826.

———. *Gimnástica del bello sexo: Ensayos sobre la educación física de las jóvenes.* Madrid: Espasa Calpe, 1988.

———. *Museo Universal de Ciencias y Artes.* London, 1825.

———. *No me olvides: Colección de producciones en prosa y verso, orginales y traducidas por José Joaquín de Mora.* London: Carlos Wood, R. Ackermann, 1824.

Morel, Marco. "Entre estrela e satélite." In *Hipólito José da Costa e o Correio Braziliense,* edited by Alberto Dines and Isabel Lustosa. Sao Paulo: Imprensa Oficial do Estado, 2002.

Morelli, Federica. "Filangieri e l'altra America: Storia di una ricezione." *Rivista Storica Italiana* 119 (2007): 88–111.

Moreno Alonso, Manuel. *La forja del liberalismo en España: Los amigos españoles de Lord Holland, 1793–1808.* Madrid: Congreso de los Diputados, 1997.

———. *La generación española de 1808.* Madrid: Alianza, 1989.

———. *La Junta Suprema de Sevilla.* Seville: Alfar, 2001.

Moreno Fraginals, Manuel. *El ingenio: Complejo económico social cubano del azúcar.* 1978. Reprint, Barcelona: Crítica, 2001.

Morgan, Philip D., and Jack P. Greene. "Introduction: The Present State of Atlantic History." In *Atlantic History: A Critical Appraisal,* edited by Jack P. Greene and Philip D. Morgan. Oxford: Oxford University Press, 2009.

Morillo-Alicea, Javier. "Aquel laberinto de oficios: Ways of Knowing Empire in Late-Nineteenth-Century Spain." In *After Spanish Rule: Postcolonial Predicaments of the Americas*, edited by Mark Thurner and Andrés Guerrero. Durham, NC: Duke University Press, 2003.

Moseley, Edward. "The United States and Mexico, 1810–1850." In *United States–Latin American Relations, 1800–1850*, edited by Thomas Ray Shurbutt. Tuscaloosa: University of Alabama Press, 1991.

Mosher, Jeffrey. *Political Struggle, Ideology, and State Building: Pernambuco and the Construction of Brazil, 1817–1850*. Lincoln and London: University of Nebraska Press, 2008.

Mosquera, Tomás Cipriano de. *Memoria sobre la vida del General Simón Bolívar*. Bogotá: Instituto Colombiano de la Cultura, 1978.

Moya, José C. "Modernization, Modernity, and the Trans/formation of the Atlantic World in the Nineteenth Century." In *The Atlantic in Global History, 1500–2000* edited by Jorge Cañizares-Esguerra and Erik R. Seeman, 179–97. Upper Saddle River, NJ: Pearson Prentice Hall, 2007.

Moya Pons, Frank. *The Dominican Republic: A National History*. New Rochelle, NY: Hispaniola Books, 1995.

———. *La dominación haitiana, 1822–44*. Santiago, República Dominicana: Universidad Católica Madre y Maestra, 1978.

Múnera, Alfonso. *El fracaso de la nación: Región, clase y raza en el Caribe colombiano (1717–1821)*. Bogotá: El Áncora Editores, 1998.

Murray, David R. *Odious Commerce: Britain, Spain, and the Abolition of the Cuban Slave Trade*. Cambridge: Cambridge University Press, 1980.

Murray, Pamela. *For Glory and Bolívar: The Remarkable Life of Manuela Saenz*. Austin: University of Texas Press, 2008.

———. "Mujeres, género y política en la joven república colombiana: Una mirada desde la correspondencia personal del General Tomás Cipriano de Mosquera, 1859–1862." *Historia Crítica* 37 (2009): 54–71.

Murray Hamilton, Stanislaus, ed. *Writings of James Monroe*. New York: G. P. Putnam's Sons, 1898–1903.

Navarro, J. Alexander. "*Our Southern Brethren: National Identity and Pan-Americanism in Early U.S.-Mexican Relations, 1810–1830.*" PhD diss., University of Michigan, 2005.

Navarro García, Jesús Raúl. *Control social y actitudes políticas en Puerto Rico (1823–1837)*. Seville: Diputación de Sevilla, 1991.

———. *Entre esclavos y revoluciones (El colonialismo liberal de 1837 en Cuba)*. Seville: CSIC, 1991.

Needell, Jeffrey. "The Abolition of the Brazilian Slave Trade in 1850: Historiography, Slave Agency, and Statesmanship." *Journal of Latin American Studies* 33, no. 4 (2001): 681–711.

Neely, Sylvia. *Lafayette and the Liberal Idea, 1814–1824: Politics and Conspiracy in an Age of Reaction.* Carbondale: Southern Illinois University Press, 1991.

Nesbitt, Nick. *Universal Emancipation: The Haitian Revolution and the Radical Enlightenment.* Charlottesville: University of Virginia Press, 2008.

Niven, John. *Martin Van Buren: The Romantic Age of American Politics.* New York: Oxford University Press, 1983.

Nizza da Silva, Maria Beatriz. *A Repercussão da Revolução de 1820 no Brasil: Eventos e Ideologias.* Coimbra: Universidade de Coimbra, 1979.

O'Gavan, Juan Bernardo. *Observaciónes sobre la suerte de los negros del África, considerados en su propia patria, y trasplantados a las Antillas Españolas: Y reclamación contra el tratado celebrado on los ingleses el año 1817.* Madrid: Imprenta del Universal, 1821.

Ojer, Pablo. *Robert H. Schomburgk, explorador de Guayana y sus líneas de frontera.* Caracas: Universidad Central de Venezuela, 1969.

Oliveira, Luís A. De, ed. *D. Pedro, Imperador do Brasil, Rei de Portugal: Do Absolutismo ao Liberalismo: Actos do Congresso Internacional.* Porto: Universidade do Porto, 2001.

Oliveira Martins, J. P. *Portugal Contemporaneo.* 2nd ed. Lisbon, 1883.

Oliveira Torres, João Camillo de. "As Origens da *Carta* Portuguesa." *Revista de Ciencia Politica* [Rio de Janeiro] 6, no. 3 (1972): 21–28.

Oliver, Guillem. *Discusión que hubo en las Cortes españolas del año de 1820, sobre las nuevas leyes de aduanas y aranceles generales para ambas Españas.* Havana: Oficina de Arazoza y Soler, 1821.

Onuf, Peter. "A Declaration of Independence for Diplomatic Historians." *Diplomatic History* 22, no. 1 (1998): 71–83.

O'Phelan Godoy, Scarlett. "Sucre en el Perú: Entre Riva Agüero y Torre Tagle." In *La Independencia del Perú: De los Borbones a Bolívar,* edited by Scarlett O'Phelan Godoy. Lima: IRA/PUCP, 2001.

———. "Una doble inserción. Los irlandeses bajo los Borbones: Del puerto de Cádiz al Perú." In *Passeurs, mediadores culturales y agentes de la primera globalización en el Mundo Ibérico, siglos XVI–XIX,* edited by Scarlett O'Phelan Godoy and Carmen Salazar-Soler. Lima: IFEA/IRA, 2005.

Orrego Vicuña, Eugenio. *O'Higgins: Vida y Tiempo.* Buenos Aires: Editorial Losada S. A., 1957.

Ortiz de Zevallos, Javier. *El norte del Perú en la Independencia.* Lima: Centro de Documentación e Información Andina, 1989.

Ortiz Escamilla, Juan, and José Antonio Serrano Ortega, eds. *Ayuntamientos y liberalismo gaditano en México*. Zamora and Xalapa: Universidad Veracruzana, 2007.

Ortuño Martínez, Manuel. *Expedición a Nueva España de Xavier Mina*. Pamplona: Universidad de Navarra, 2006.

Ott, Thomas. *The Haitian Revolution, 1789–1804*. Knoxville: University of Tennessee Press, 1973.

Pagden, Anthony. *Lords of All the World: Ideologies of Empire in Spain, Britain, and France, c. 1500–1800*. New Haven: Yale University Press, 1995.

Paquette, Gabriel B. "The Dissolution of the Spanish Atlantic Monarchy." *Historical Journal* 52, no. 1 (2009): 175–212.

———, ed. *Enlightened Reform in Southern Europe and Its Atlantic Colonies, c. 1750–1830*. Farnham and Burlington, VT: Ashgate Publishing, 2009.

———. *Enlightenment, Governance, and Reform in Spain and Its Empire, 1759–1808*. London: Palgrave Macmillan, 2008.

———. "The Intellectual Origins of British Diplomatic Recognition of the Spanish American Republics, c. 1800–1830." *Journal of Transatlantic Studies* 2, no. 1 (2004): 75–95.

———. "State–Civil Society Cooperation and Conflict in the Spanish Empire: The Intellectual and Political Activities of the Ultramarine Consulados and Economic Societies, c. 1780–1810." *Journal of Latin American Studies* 39 (2007): 263–98.

Paquette, Robert L. *Sugar Is Made with Blood: The Conspiracy of La Escalera and the Conflict between Empires over Slavery in Cuba*. Middletown: Wesleyan University Press, 1988.

Parada, Alejandro E. *El mundo del libro y de la lectura durante la época de Rivadavia: Una aproximación a través de los avisos de La Gaceta Mercantil (1823–1828)*. Buenos Aires: Universidad de Buenos Aires, 1998.

Parham, Althea, trans. and ed. *My Odyssey: Experiences of a Young Refugee from Two Revolutions, by a Creole of Saint Domingue*. Baton Rouge: Louisiana State University Press, 1959.

Parker, F. D. "Josè Cecilio del Valle Scholar and Patriot." *Hispanic American Historical Review* 32, no. 4 (1952): 516–39.

Parkerson, Philip. *Andrés de Santa Cruz y la Confederación Perú-boliviana, 1835–1839*. La Paz: Libreria Editorial Juventud, 1984.

Payne, Stanley. *Politics and the Military in Modern Spain*. Stanford, CA: Stanford University Press, 1967.

Paz, Octavio. *El laberinto de la soledad*. 1950. Reprint, Mexico City: FCE, 2002.

Pearce, Adrian. *British Trade with Spanish America, 1763–1808*. Liverpool: Liverpool University Press, 2007.

Pécout, Gilles. "The International Armed Volunteers: Pilgrims of a Transnational Risorgimento." *Journal of Modern Italian Studies* 14, no. 4 (2009): 413–26.

Peixoto, Antonio Carlos, et al., eds. *O Liberalismo no Brasil Imperial: Origens, Conceitos e Prática*. Rio de Janeiro: Editora Revan, 2001.

Pepe, Guglielmo. *Epistolario*. Edited by R. Moscati. Rome: Istituto per la storia del Risorgimento, 1938.

———. *Memoirs: Comprising the Principal Military and Political Events of Modern Italy*. 3 vols. London, 1846.

Perazzo, Nicolas. *Histora de la Inmigración en Venezuela (1830–1850)*. Caracas: Ediciones del Congreso de la República, 1982.

Pérez Ledesma, Manuel. "Ciudadanía y revolución liberal." In *A Guerra da Independencia e o primeiro liberalismo en España e América,* edited by José María Portillo Valdés, 103–28. Santiago de Compostela: Universidade de Santiago de Compostela, 2009.

———. "Ciudadanos y ciudadanía. Un análisis introductorio." In *Ciudadanía y democracia,* edited by Manuel Pérez Ledesma. Madrid: Editorial Pablo Iglesias, 2000.

———. "Las Cortes de Cádiz y la sociedad española." *Ayer* 1 (1991): 167–206.

Pérez Vila, Manuel. *Vida de Daniel Florencio O'Leary: Primer edecán del Libertador*. Caracas: Imprenta Nacional, 1957.

Perkins, Bradford. *Castlereagh and Adams: England and the United States, 1812–1823*. Los Angeles: University of California Press, 1964.

Perkins, Dexter. *The Monroe Doctrine, 1823–1826*. Cambridge, MA: Harvard University Press, 1927.

Pérotin-Dumon, Anne. "French America." *International History Review* 6, no. 4 (1984): 551–69.

Petit, Carlos. "Una Constitución europea para América: Cádiz 1812." *Academia Peloriatana dei Pericolanti: Classe de Scienze Giuridici* 60 (1991).

Piccirrilli, Ricardo. *Rivadavia y su tiempo*. 2nd ed. Buenos Aires: Peuser, 1960.

Pinheiro Ferreira, Silvestre. *Observações sobre a Constituição do Imperio do Brasil e sobre a Carta Constitucional do Reino de Portugal*. 2nd ed. Paris, 1835.

Pino Iturrieta, Elías. *País Archipiélago: Venezuela, 1830–1858*. Caracas: Fundación Bigott, 2002.

Piqueras, José Antonio, ed. *Las Antillas en la era de las Luces y la Revolución*. Madrid: Siglo XXI, 2005.

———. "Leales en época de insurrección. La elite criolla cubana entre 1810 y 1814." In *Visiones y revisiones de la independencia Americana,* edited by Izaskun Alvarez Cuartero and Julio Sánchez Gómez. Salamanca: Ediciones de la Universidad de Salamanca, 2003.

Pi-Suñer, Antonia. *La deuda española en México: Diplomacia y política en torno a un problema financiero, 1821–1890.* Mexico City: El Colegio de México, 2006.

Platt, D. C. M. "Further Objections to an 'Imperialism of Free Trade,' 1830–1860." *Economic History Review* 26, no. 1 (1973): 77–91.

———. "The Imperialism of Free Trade: Some Reservations." *Economic History Review* 21 (1968): 296–306.

———. *Latin America and British Trade, 1806–1914.* London: Black, 1972.

Platt, Tristan. *Estado tributario y librecambismo en Potosí (siglo XIX): Mercado indígena, proyecto proteccionista y lucha de ideologías monetarias.* La Paz: Instituto de Historia Social Boliviana, 1986.

Polanco Alcántara, Tomás. *Simón Bolívar: Ensayo de una interpretación biográfica a través de sus documentos.* Caracas: Ediciones IG, 1994.

Polar, Fundación. *Diccionario de Historia de Venezuela.* CDROM. Caracas: Fundación Polar, 2000.

Pons, André. "Blanco White, abolicionista (3)." *Cuadernos Hispanoamericanos,* nos. 565–66 (1997): 144–45.

Popkin, Jeremy D., and Richard H. Popkin, eds. *The Abbé Gregoire and His World.* Dordecht: Kluwer Academic Publishers, 2000.

Porter, Robert Ker. *Sir Robert Ker Porter's Caracas Diary, 1825–1842: A British Diplomat in a Newborn Nation.* Edited by Walter Dupouy. Caracas: Editorial Arte, 1966. (Translated by Teodosio Leal as *Diario de un diplomático británico en Venezuela.* Caracas: Fundación Polar, 1997.)

Portillo, José María, and Jesús Viejo, eds. *José Blanco White: El Español.* Granada: Almed, 2006.

Portillo Valdés, José M. *Crisis atlántica: Autonomía e independencia en la crisis de la monarquía hispana.* Madrid: Marcial Pons Historia, 2006.

Posada Gutierrez, Joaquín. *Memorias histórico-políticas.* 4 vols. Medellín: Editorial Bedout, 1971.

Prados de la Escosura, Leandro. "Comercio internacional y modernización económica en la España del siglo XIX." In *Mercado y desarrollo económico en la España contemporánea,* edited by Tomás Martínez Vara. Madrid: Siglo XXI, 1986.

———. *De imperio a nación: Crecimiento y atraso económico en España (1780–1930).* Madrid: Alianza Editorial, 1988.

Pratt, E. "Anglo-American Commercial and Political Rivalry on the Plata, 1820–1830." *Hispanic American Historical Review* 9 (1931): 302–35.

Pratt, Mary Louise. *Imperial Eyes: Travel Writing and Transculturation.* London and New York: Routledge, 1992.

Proctor, Robert. "El Perú entre 1823 y 1824." In *Relaciones de Viajeros.* C.D.I.P. Tomo 28.

Pruvonena [pseudonym of José de la Riva Agüero y Sánchez Boquete]. *Memorias y Documentos para la Historia de la Independencia del Perú.* 2 vols. Paris, 1858.

Quijada, Mónica. "Una constitución singular: La carta gaditana en perspectiva." *Revista de Indias* 68, no. 242 (2008): 15–38.

Quintana, Manuel José. *Memorias del Cádiz de las Cortes.* Cádiz: Publicaciones de la Universidad de Cádiz, 1996.

Quintero, Inés. *La criolla principal: María Antonia Bolívar, hermana del Libertador.* Caracas: Fundación Bigott, 2003.

Racine, Karen. "Commercial Christianity: The British and Foreign Bible Society's Interest in Spanish America, 1805–1830." In *Informal Empire in Latin America,* edited by M. Brown, 78–98.

———. *Francisco de Miranda: A Transatlantic Life in the Age of Revolution.* Wilmington, DE: Scholarly Resources, 2003.

———. "Imagining Independence: London's Spanish American Community, 1790–1829." PhD diss., Tulane University, 1996.

———. "Simón Bolívar, Englishman: Elite Responsibility and Social Reform in Spanish American Independence." In *Simón Bolívar: Essays on the Life and Legacy of the Liberator,* edited by David Bushnell and Lester D. Langley. Lanham, MD: Rowman and Littlefield, 2008.

———. "'This England and This Now': British Cultural and Intellectual Influence in the Spanish American Independence Era." *Hispanic American Historical Review* 90, no. 3 (2010): 423–54.

Ratcliffe, Donald. "The State of the Union, 1776–1860." In *The American Civil War: Explorations and Reconsiderations,* edited by Susan-Mary Grant and Brian Holden Reid. London: Longman, 2000.

Reber, Vera Blinn. *British Mercantile Houses in Buenos Aires, 1810–1880.* Cambridge, MA: Harvard University Press, 1979.

Recio Morales, Oscar. *Ireland and the Spanish Empire, 1600–1825.* Dublin: Four Courts, 2010.

Reinert, Helen K. "A Political History of the Brazilian Regency, 1831–40." PhD diss., University of Illinois, 1960.

Reis, João José. *Rebelião escrava no Brasil: A história do levante dos Malês.* São Paulo: Companhia das Letras, 1987.

Reis e Vasconcellos, J. J. das, ed. *Despachos e Correspondencia do Duque de Palmela.* Lisbon, 1851.

Reyes Heroles, Jesús. *El liberalismo mexicano.* 3 vols. Mexico City: Fondo de Cultura Económica, 1974.

Rheinheimer, Hans P. *Topo: The Story of a Scottish Colony near Caracas, 1825–1827.* Edinburgh: Scottish Academic Press, 1988.

Riall, Lucy. *Garibaldi: Invention of a Hero*. New Haven: Yale University Press, 2007.

Ricketts, Mónica. "Together or Separate in the Fight against Oppression? Liberals in Peru and Spain in the 1820s." *European History Quarterly* 41, no. 3 (2011): 413–27.

Rippy, J. Fred. "Latin America and the British Investment 'Boom' of the 1820s." *Journal of Modern History* 19, no. 2 (1947): 122–29.

———. *Rivalry of the United States and Great Britain over Latin America, 1808–1830*. Baltimore: Johns Hopkins Press, 1929.

Robertson, J. P., and W. Robertson. *Letters on South America*. 1843. Reprint, New York: AMS Edition, 1971.

Robertson, William. *The History of America*. 8th ed. London: Printed by A. Strahan, for T. Cadell Jun. and W. Davies, and E. Balfour, Edinburgh, 1800–1801.

Robson, Nicholas. *Hints for a General View of the Agricultural State of the Parish of Saint James, in the Island of Jamaica*. London: John Stockdale, 1796.

Rocafuerte, Vicente. *Ensayo Politico: El Sistema Colombiano, popular, electivo, y representativo, es el que mas conviene á la America independiente*. New York: En la imprentas de A. Paul, 1823.

Rock, David. "The British in Argentina: From Informal Empire to Postcolonialism." In *Informal Empire in Latin America*, edited by M. Brown, 49–77.

Rodrigues, Celso. *Assembléia Constituinte de 1823: Idéias Políticas na Fundação do Império Brasileiro*. Curitiba: Juruá Editora, 2002.

Rodrigues, José Honório. *A Assembléia Constituinte de 1823*. Petrópolis: Editora Vozes, 1974.

———. *Brazil and Africa*. Berkeley: University of California Press, 1965.

———. *Independência: Revolução e contra-revolução*. 5 vols. Rio de Janeiro: F. Alves, 1971-1975.

Rodrigues Dias, José Henrique. *José Ferreira Borges: Política e Economia*. Lisbon: I.N.I.C., 1988.

Rodríguez, Gregorio F. *Contribución histórica y documental*. Buenos Aires: Peuser, 1921.

Rodriguez, Jaime E. "La transición de colonia a nación: Nueva España, 1820–1821." *Historia Mexicana* 43, no. 2 (1993): 265–322.

———. *O infame comércio*. Campinas: Editora Unicamp, 2000.

Rodriguez, Mario. *The Cadiz Experiment in Central America, 1808 to 1826*. Berkeley: University of California Press, 1978.

Rodríguez Demorizi, Emilio. *Invasiones Haitianas De 1801, 1805 Y 1822*. Santo Domingo: Ciudad Trujillo, 1955.

———. *Santo Domingo y la Gran Colombia*. Santo Domingo: Academia Dominica de la Historia, 1971.

Rodríguez O., Jaime E. "Ciudadanos de la nación española: Los indígenas y las elecciones constitucionales en el reino de Quito." In *La mirada esquiva: Reflexiones histórica sobre la interacción del estado y la ciudadanía en los Andes (Bolivia, Ecuador y Perú), siglo XIX,* edited by Marta Irurozqui. Madrid: CSIC, 2005.

———. "The Constitution of 1824 and the Formation of the Mexican State." In *The Origins of Mexican National Politics, 1808–1847,* edited by Jaime E. Rodríguez O. Wilmington, DE: Scholarly Resources, 1997.

———. *The Independence of Spanish America.* Cambridge: Cambridge University Press, 1998.

———. *La independencia de la América española.* Mexico City: Fondo de Cultura Económica, 1996.

———. "Los caudillos y los historiadores: Riego, Iturbide y Santa Anna." In *La construcción del héroe en España y México (1789–1847),* edited by Manuel Chust and Víctor Mínguez. Valencia: Publicaciones de la Universidad de Valencia, 2003.

———, ed. *Revolución, independencia y las nuevas naciones de América.* Madrid: Fundación Mapfre, 2005.

———. "Una cultura política compartida: Los orígenes del constitucionalismo y liberalismo en México." In *El imperio sublevado,* edited by Víctor Mínguez and Manuel Chust. Madrid: CSIC, 2004.

Roldán Vera, Eugenia. *The British Book Trade and Spanish American Independence: Education and Knowledge Transmission in Transcontinental Perspective.* Aldershot: Ashgate, 2003.

———. "The Catechism as an Educational Genre in Early Independent Spanish America." *Book History* 4 (2001): 17–48.

Roldán Vera, Eugenia, and Marcelo Caruso, eds. *Imported Modernity in Postcolonial State Formation: The Appropriation of Political, Educational, and Cultural Models in Nineteenth-Century Latin America.* Oxford: Peter Lang, 2007.

Rolo, P. J.V. *George Canning: Three Biographical Studies.* London: Macmillan, 1965.

Rosas Siles, Alberto. "La nobleza titulada en el virreinato del Perú." *Revista del Instituto Peruano de Investigaciones Genealógicas,* no. 21 (1995).

Rothschild, Emma. *The Inner Life of Empires: An Eighteenth-Century History.* Princeton: Princeton University Press, 2011.

———. "Late Atlantic History." In *The Oxford Handbook of Atlantic History,* edited by Nicholas Canny and Philip Morgan. Oxford: Oxford University Press, 2011.

Rousseau, Jean-Jacques. *La nouvelle Heloise Julie, or the New Eloise: Letters of Two Lovers, Inhabitants of a Small Town at the Foot of the Alps.* Translated by Judith H. McDowell. University Park: Pennsylvania State University, 1996.

Rubio Mañé, José Ignacio. "Los diputados mexicanos a las cortes españolas y el

Plan de Iguala, 1820–1821." *Boletín del Archivo General de la Nación* (2nd series) 12 (1971).

Safford, Frank. "Commercial Crisis and Economic Ideology in New Granada, 1825–1850." In *América Latina en la época de Simón Bolívar*, edited by Liehr, 183–206.

———. "Politics, Ideology, and Society." In *Spanish America after Independence, c. 1820–70*, edited by Leslie Bethell. Cambridge: Cambridge University Press, 1987.

Safford, Frank, and Marco Palacios. *Colombia: Fragmented Land, Divided Society*. Oxford: Oxford University Press, 2002.

Safier, Neil. "A Courier between Empires: Hipólito da Costa and the Atlantic World." In *Soundings in Atlantic History: Latent Structures and Intellectual Currents, 1500–1830*, edited by Bernard Bailyn. Cambridge, MA: Harvard University Press, 2009.

Saiz, María Dolores. "Liberalismo y ejército: La 'Gaceta patriótica del ejército nacional' (1820)." *Revista de Estudios Políticos* (Nueva Época) 38 (1984): 127–46.

Saiz Pastor, Candelaria. "Imperio de Ultramar y fiscalidad colonial." In *La Ilusión de un imperio: Las relaciones económicas hispano-cubanas en el siglo XIX*, edited by Salvador Palazón and Candelaria Saiz Pastor. Alicante: Universidad de Alicante, 1998.

———. "Las finanzas públicas en Cuba: La etapa de las desviaciones de fondos a la península, 1823–1866." In *Las haciendas públicas en el Caribe hispano en el XIX*, edited by Inés Roldán de Montaud. Madrid: CSIC, 2008.

Sánchez, Susy. "Familia, Comercio y Poder. Los Tagle y su vinculación con los Torres Velarde (1730–1825)." In *Los comerciantes limeños a fines del siglo XVIII: Capacidad y cohesión de una elite, 1750–1825*, compiled by Cristina Mazzeo. Lima: Pontificia Universidad Católica del Perú, 2000.

Sánchez i Sánchez, Carlos. *La "Independencía Boba" de Nuñez de Cáceres, ante la historia i el derecho público*. Ciudad Trujillo, Santo Domingo: Montalvo, 1937.

San Miguel, Pedro L. *The Imagined Island: History, Identity, and Utopia in Hispaniola*. Durham: University of North Carolina Press, 2005.

Sargant, Jane Alice. *Letters from a Mother to her Daughter, at or going to school, pointing out the duties towards her Maker, her governess, her schoolfellows, and herself: 1821*. London: Wetton and Jarvis, 1825.

Sarmiento, Domingo Faustino. *De la educación popular*. Santiago: Imprenta de Julio Belin, 1849.

Sarrailh, Jean. *La España Ilustrada de la segunda mitad del siglo XVIII*. Madrid/Mexico City: Fondo de Cultura Económico, 1985.

Scarano, Francisco A. *Sugar and Slavery in Puerto Rico: The Plantation Economy of Ponce, 1800–1850*. Madison: University of Wisconsin Press, 1984.

Schmidt-Nowara, Christopher. *The Conquest of History: Spanish Colonialism and National Histories in the Nineteenth Century*. Pittsburgh: University of Pittsburgh Press, 2006.

———. "Continuity and Crisis: Cuban Slavery, Spanish Colonialism, and the Atlantic World in the Nineteenth Century." In *The Atlantic in Global History, 1500–2000*, edited by Jorge Cañizares-Esguerra and Erik Seeman, 199–217. Upper Saddle River, NJ: Prenctice-Hall, 2007.

———. *Empire and Antislavery: Spain, Cuba, and Puerto Rico, 1833–1874.* Pittsburgh: University of Pittsburgh Press, 1999.

———. "Wilberforce Spanished: Joseph Blanco White and Spanish Antislavery, 1808–1814." In *Slavery, Empire, and Abolitionism*, edited by Fradera and Schmidt-Nowara.

Schoultz, Lars. *Beneath the United States: A History of U.S. Policy toward Latin America*. Cambridge, MA: Harvard University Press, 1998.

Schroeder, Paul. *The Transformation of European Politics, 1763–1848*. Oxford: Oxford University Press, 1994.

Schultz, Kirsten. *Tropical Versailles, Empire, Monarchy, and the Portuguese Royal Court in Rio de Janeiro, 1808–1821*. New York and London: Routledge, 2000.

Scott, Julius Sherrard. "The Common Wind: Currents of Afro-American Communication in the Era of the Haitian Revolution." PhD diss., Duke University, 1986.

Scott, Walter. *El Talismán, cuento del tiempo de las Cruzadas*. Translated by José Joaquín de Mora. London, 1826.

———. *Ivanhoe*. Translated by José Joaquín de Mora. London, 1825.

Segreti, Carlos S. A. *Bernardino Rivadavia: Hombre de Buenos Aires, ciudadano argentino: Biografía*. Buenos Aires: Planeta, 2000.

Sepinwall, Alyssa Goldstein. *The Abbé Grégoire and the French Revolution: The Making of Modern Universalism*. Berekeley: University of California Press, 2005.

Serrano Ortega, José Antonio, and Luis Jáuregui, eds. *Hacienda y política, las finanzas públicas y los grupos de poder en la Primera República federal Mexicana*. Mexico City: Instituto Mora, 1998.

Sexton, Jay. *The Monroe Doctrine: Empire and Nation in Nineteenth-Century America*. New York: Hill and Wang, 2011.

Shaikh, Farida. "Judicial Diplomacy: British Officials and the Mixed Commission Courts." In *Slavery, Diplomacy, and Empire, 1807–1975*, edited by Keith Hamilton and Patrick Salmon. Brighton and Portland, OR: Sussex Academic Press, 2009.

Shepherd, William R. "Bolívar and the United States." *Hispanic American Historical Review* 1, no. 3 (1918): 279–84.

Shumway, Jeffrey. *The Case of the Ugly Suitor: And Other Histories of Love, Gender, and Nation in Buenos Aires, 1776–1870.* Lincoln: University of Nebraska Press, 2005.

Silva, Renán. *República Liberal, intelectuales y cultura popular.* Medellín: La Carreta Histórica, 2005.

Silva Dias, Maria Odila. "A interiorização da Metrópole (1808–1853)." In *1822: Dimensões,* edited by Carlos G. Mota, 160–86. São Paulo: Editora Perspectiva, 1972.

Silva Lisboa, José da. *Contestação da Historia e Censura de Mr De Pradt Sobre Successos do Brasil.* Rio de Janeiro, 1825.

———. Speech of October 21, 1823, in *Annaes do Parlamento Brazileiro: Assembléa Constituinte 1823.* Rio de Janeiro, 1879.

Silva Passos, José da, and Manuel da Silva Passos. *Parecer de Dous Advogados da Caza do Porto.* Paris, 1832.

Sims, Harold. *Descolonización en México: El conflicto entre mexicanos y españoles (1821–1831).* Mexico City: FCE, 1982.

———. *The Expulsion of Mexico's Spaniards, 1821–1836.* Pittsburgh: University of Pittsburgh Press, 1990.

Sintierra, Juan. "Carta VI: Sobre un artículo de la Nueva Constitución de España." In *Cartas de Juan Sintierra (Crítica de las Cortes de Cádiz),* edited by Manuel Moreno Alonso. Seville: Universidad de Sevilla, 1990.

Slemian, Andréa. "Instituciones, legitimidad y [des]orden: Crisis de la monarquía portuguesa y construcción del Imperio de Brasil (1808–1841)." In *De las independencias iberoamericanas a los estados nacionales (1810–1850),* edited by Ivana Frasquet and Andréa Slemian. Madrid and Frankfurt: Iberoamericana, 2009.

Smith, Joseph. "New World Diplomacy: A Reappraisal of British Policy Toward Latin America, 1823–1850." *Inter-American Economic Affairs* (1978): 3–24.

Sobrevilla Perea, Natalia. *The Caudillo of the Andes: Andrés de Santa Cruz.* Cambridge: Cambridge University Press, 2010.

———. "From Europe to the Andes and Back: Becoming 'Los Ayacuchos.'" *European History Quarterly* 41, no. 3 (2011): 472–88.

Souza, Paulo César. *A Sabinada: A revolta separatista da Bahia, 1837.* São Paulo: Editora Brasiliense, 1987.

Spieler, Miranda Frances. "The Legal Structure of Colonial Rule during the French Revolution." *William and Mary Quarterly* (3rd series) 66 (2009): 365–408.

Stapleton, E. J., ed. *Some Official Correspondence of George Canning.* London, 1887.

Starzinger, Vincent. *The Politics of the Center: The* Juste Milieu *in Theory and Prac-*

tice, France and England, 1815–1848. New Brunswick, NJ: Transaction Publishers, 1991.

Stein, Barbara H., and Stanley J. Stein. *Edge of Crisis: War and Trade in the Spanish Atlantic, 1789–1808.* Baltimore: Johns Hopkins University Press, 2009.

Stein, Stanley J. *Vassouras: A Brazilian Coffee County, 1850–1900.* Cambridge, MA: Harvard University Press, 1957.

Stein, Stanley J., and Barbara H. Stein. *Apogee of Empire: Spain and New Spain in the Age of Charles III, 1759–1789.* Baltimore: Johns Hopkins University Press, 2003.

———. *The Colonial Heritage of Latin America: Essays on Economic Dependence in Perspective.* New York: Oxford University Press, 1970.

Stokes, Eric. *The English Utilitarians and India.* Oxford: Clarendon Press, 1959.

Stoler, Ann Laura, ed. *Haunted by Empire: Geographies of Intimacy in North American History.* Chapel Hill, NC: Duke University Press, 2005.

———. "On Degrees of Imperial Sovereignty." *Public Culture* 18, no. 1 (2006): 126–46.

Straka, Tomás. *Las alas de Icaro: Indagación sobre ética y ciudadanía en Venezuela (1800–1830).* Caracas: Universidad Católica Andrés Bello, 2005.

Street, John. *Gran Bretaña y la independencia del Rio de la Plata.* Buenos Aires: Paidos, 1967.

Strong, Rowan. *Anglicanism and the British Empire c. 1700–1850.* Oxford: Oxford University Press, 2007.

Stuardo Ortiz, Carlos. "El Liceo de Chile: Antecedentes para su historia." *Revista Chilena de Historia y Geografía,* no. 114 (1949).

Sturtevant, David. *Popular Uprisings in the Philippines, 1840–1940.* Ithaca, NY: Cornell University Press, 1976.

Suárez, Federico. *Las Cortes de Cádiz.* Madrid: Rialp, 1982.

Sucre, Antonio José de. *De mi propia mano.* Mexico City: FCE, 1995.

Tandeter, Enrique. *Coacción y mercado: La minería de la plata en el Potosí colonial, 1692–1826.* Buenos Aires: Editorial Sudamericana, 1992.

Tella, Torquato Di. *National Popular Politics in Early Independent Mexico, 1820–1847.* Alburquerque: University of New Mexico Press, 1995.

Temperley, Harold. *The Foreign Policy of Canning, 1822–1827.* London: Frank Cass, 1966.

Tenenbaum, Barbara A. "Mexico's Money Market and the Internal Debt, 1821–1855." In *La deuda pública en América Latina en perspectiva histórica,* edited by Reinhard Liehr. Madrid: Iberoamericana, 1989.

———. *The Politics of Penury: Debt and Taxes in Mexico, 1821–1858.* Albuquerque: University of New Mexico Press, 1986.

Ternavasio, Marcela. *La revolución del voto. Política y elecciones: Buenos Aires, 1810–1852*. Buenos Aires: Siglo XXI, 2002.

Thibaud, Clément. *Repúblicas en Armas: Los Ejércitos Bolivarianos en la Guerra de la Independencia en Colombia y Venezuela*. Bogotá: Editorial Planeta, 2003.

Thibaud, Clément, and María Teresa Calderón. *La majestad de los pueblos en la Nueva Granada y Venezuela, 1780–1832*. Bogotá: Taurus, 2010.

Thibaud, Clément, Alejandro Gómez, and Genevieve Verdo, eds. *Les empires atlantiques entre Lumières et libéralisme (1763–1865)*. Rennes: Presses Universitaires de Rennes, 2009.

Thompson, Andrew. *The Empire Strikes Back: The Impact of Imperialism on Britain from the Mid-nineteenth Century*. London: Pearson, 2005.

———. "Informal Empire: Past, Present, and Future." In *Informal Empire in Latin America,* edited by M. Brown, 229–41.

Thomson, Guy P. C. "Popular Aspects of Liberalism in Mexico, 1848–1888." *Bulletin of Latin American Research* 10, no. 3 (1991): 265–92.

———. "Traditional and Modern Manufacturing in Mexico, 1821–1850." In *América Latina en la época de Simón Bolívar,* edited by Liehr, 55–85.

Thomson, Guy P. C., with David LaFrance. *Patriotism, Politics, and Popular Liberalism in Nineteenth-Century Mexico: Juan Francisco Lucas and the Puebla Sierra*. Wilmington, DE: Scholarly Resources, 1999.

Thurner, Mark. *From Two Republics to One Divided: Contradictions of Postcolonial Nation-Making in Andean Perú*. Durham, NC: Duke University Press, 1997.

Thurner, Mark, and Andrés Guerrero, eds. *After Spanish Rule: Postcolonial Predicaments of the Americas*. Durham, NC: Duke University Press, 2003.

Todd, David. "A French Imperial Meridian, 1814–1870." *Past & Present* 210 (2011): 155–86.

———. "John Bowring and the Global Dissemination of Free Trade." *Historical Journal* 51 (2008): 373–97.

Tomás y Valiente, Francisco. "Génesis de la Constitución de 1812." *Anuario de Historia del derecho Español* 65 (1995): 13–125.

Tomich, Dale. *Through the Prism of Slavery: Labor, Capital, and World Economy*. Lanham, MD: Rowan and Littlefield, 2004.

Tomich, Dale, and Michael Zeuske. "Introduction: The Second Slavery: Mass Slavery, World-Economy, and Comparative Microhistories." *Review: A Journal of the Fernand Braudel Center* 31 (2008): 91–100.

Tornel, José María. *Manifiesto del origen, causas, progresos y estado de la revolución del imperio mexicano, con relación a la antigua España*. Puebla and Mexico City: Imp. de Ontíveros, 1821.

Torre, Ernesto de. *La independencia de México*. Madrid: Mapfre, 1992.

Tosta, Virgilio. "Extranjeros en la Ciudad de Nutrias y en el Puerto." *Boletín de la Academia Nacional de la Historia (Venezuela)* 76, no. 303 (1993).

Trouillot, Michel-Rolph. *Silencing the Past: Power and the Production of History*. Boston, MA: Beacon Press, 1995.

Urcullu, José de. *Catecismo de geografía elemental*. London, 1823.

———. *Catecismo de historia natural*. London, 1826.

Uribe de Hincapié, María Teresa, and Liliana María López Lopera. *Las palabras de la guerra: Un estudio sobre las memorias de las guerras civiles en Colombia*. Medellín: La Carreta Histórica, 2006.

Utrera, Fray C. *Diario de la Reconquista*. Santo Domingo: Ciudad Trujillo, 1957.

Vale, Brian. *The Audacious Admiral Cochrane: The True Life of a Naval Legend*. London: I. B. Tauris, 2004.

———. *A War Betwixt Englishmen: Brazil against Argentina on the River Plate, 1825–1830*. London and New York: I. B. Tauris, 2000.

Valencia Avaria, Luis. *Bernardo O'Higgins: El "Buen Genio" de América*. Santiago de Chile: Editorial Universitaria, 1980.

Van Aken, Mark. *King of the Night: Juan José Flores and Ecuador, 1824–1864*. Berkeley: University of California Press, 1989.

Van Young, Eric. "Of Tempests and Teapots: Imperial Crisis and Local Conflict in Mexico at the Beginning of the Nineteenth Century." In *Cycles of Conflict, Centuries of Change: Crisis, Reform, and Revolution in Mexico*, edited by Elisa Servín, Leticia Reina, and John Tutino. Durham, NC, and London: Duke University Press, 2007.

———. *The Other Rebellion: Popular Violence, Ideology, and the Mexican Struggle for Independence, 1810–1821*. Stanford: Stanford University Press, 2001.

Varela Suanzes-Carpegna, Joaquín, ed. *Álvaro Flórez Estrada (1766–1853): Política, economía y sociedad*. Llanera: Junta General del Principado de Asturias, 2005.

Vázquez, Josefina Zoraida. "El modelo del pronunciamiento mexicano, 1820–1823." *Ulúa* 7 (2006): 31–52.

Verna, Paul. *Petión y Bolívar: Cuarenta años (1790–1830) de relaciones haitiano-venezolanas y su aporte a la emancipación de Hispanoamérica*. Caracas: Oficina Central de Información, 1969.

Viana Lyra, Maria Lourdes. *A Utopia do Poderoso Império: Portugal e Brasil, Bastidores da Política, 1798–1822*. Rio de Janeiro: Sette Letras, 1994.

Vianna, António. *Apontamentos para a Historia Diplomática Contemporânea*. Vol. 3: *A Carta e a Reacção*. Lisbon: Gráfico Santelmo, 1958.

Vickers, Daniel. "Nantucket Whalemen in the Deep-Sea Fishery: The Changing Anatomy of an Early American Labor Force." *Journal of American History* 72, no. 2 (1985): 277–96.

Vicuña Mackenna, Benjamín. *Vida del Capitán General Don Bernardo O'Higgins.* Santiago de Chile: Editorial del Pacífico, 1976.

Villalobos, Sergio. *El proceso de la emancipación: Historia de Chile.* Santiago de Chile: Editorial Universitaria, 1977.

Villanueva, Joaquín Lorenzo. *Catecismo de los literatos.* London: Ackermann, 1828.

Villegas Revueltas, Silvestre. *Deuda y diplomacia: La relación México-Gran Bretaña, 1824–1884.* Mexico City: Universidad Autonoma, 2005.

Vincent, Theodore G. *The Legacy of Vicente Guerrero, Mexico's First Black Indian President.* Gainesville: University of Florida Press, 2001.

Vivero, Domingo de, ed. *Galerías de Retratos de los Gobernantes del Perú Independiente (1821–1870).* Lima, 1893.

Voekel, Pamela. *Alone before God: The Religious Origins of Modernity in Mexico.* Durham, NC: Duke University Press, 2002.

Vogel, Hans. "New Citizens for a New Nation: Naturalization in Early Independent Argentina." *Hispanic American Historical Review* 71, no. 1 (1991): 107–31.

Von Grafenstein, Johanna. *Nueva España en el circuncaribe, 1779–1808: Revolución, competencia imperial y vínculos intercoloniales.* Mexico City, D.F: Universidad Nacional Autónoma de México, 1997.

Von Humboldt, Alexander. *The Island of Cuba: A Political Essay (1826).* Princeton: Markus Wiener, 2001.

Waddell, D. A. G. "International Politics and Latin American Independence." In *Cambridge History of Latin America,* edited by Leslie Bethell. Cambridge: Cambridge University Press, 1985.

Walker, Charles F. *Smouldering Ashes: Cuzco and the Creation of Republican Perú, 1780–1840.* Durham, NC, and London: Duke University Press, 1999.

Walker Howe, Daniel. *What Hath God Wrought: The Transformation of America, 1815–1848.* New York: Oxford University Press, 2007.

Walter, Rolf. *Los Alemanes en Venezuela: Desde Colón Hasta Guzmán Blanco.* Caracas: Asociación Cultural Humboldt, 1985.

Weber, David. *Bárbaros: Spaniards and Their Savages in the Age of Enlightenment.* New Haven: Yale University Press, 2005.

Webster, C. K., ed. *Britain and the Independence of Latin America, 1812–1830: Selected Documents from the Foreign Office Archives.* 2 vols. London and New York: Oxford University Press, 1938.

Wellington, Duke of. *Despatches, Correspondence, and Memoranda of Field Marshall Arthur Duke of Wellington, K. G.* 15 vols. London, 1868.

Wilberforce, Edward. *Brazil Viewed Through a Naval Glass*. London: Longman, Brown, Green, and Longmans, 1856.

Will, Robert M. "The Introduction of Classical Economics into Chile." *Hispanic American Historical Review* 44, no. 1 (1964): 1–21.

Willard, Emma. "Female College at Bogotá." In *Lady's Book*. N.p., 1937.

Williams, Caroline A., ed. *Bridging the Early Modern Atlantic World: People, Products, and Practices on the Move*. Aldershot: Ashgate, 2009.

Williams, Judith Blow. "The Establishment of British Commerce with Argentina." *Hispanic American Historical Review* 1 (1935): 46–49.

Williford, Miriam. *Jeremy Bentham in Spanish America: An Account of His Letters and Proposals to the New World*. Baton Rouge and London: Louisiana State University Press, 1980.

Winch, Donald. *Classical Political Economy and Colonies*. London: L.S.E. Press, 1965.

Winn, Peter. "British Informal Empire in Uruguay in the Nineteenth Century." *Past & Present* 73 (1976): 100–126.

Zago, Manrique, ed. *José de San Martín, Libertador de América*. Buenos Aires: Instituto Sanmartiniano, 1995.

Zahler, Reuben. "Complaining like a Liberal: Redefining Law, Justice, and Official Misconduct in Venezuela, 1790–1850." *The Americas* 65, no. 3 (2009): 351–74.

———. "Liberal Justice: Judicial Reform in Venezuela's Courts, 1786–1850." *Hispanic American Historical Review* 90, no. 3 (2010): 489–522.

Websites

http://www.genderlatam.org.uk, accessed March 31, 2012.
http://arts.st-andrews.ac.uk/pronunciamientos/, accessed March 31, 2012.
http://www.eroj.org/fonoteca/Riego.htm, accessed March 31, 2012.

Contributors

MATTHEW BROWN is a reader in Latin American studies at the University of Bristol. He is writing a short history of Latin America's relationship with global empires since independence.

WILL FOWLER is a professor of Latin American studies at the University of Saint Andrews. He is the author of *Mexico in the Age of Proposals, 1821–1853* (1998), *Tornel and Santa Anna, the Writer and the Caudillo* (2000), *Latin America since 1780* (2008), and *Santa Anna of Mexico* (2007).

JOSEP M. FRADERA is a professor of modern history at the Universitat Pompeu Fabra (Barcelona). He is the author of many books and articles, including *Colonias para después de un imperio* (2005), a detailed consideration of the transition from the greater Spanish Empire to the three remaining insular colonies after 1824.

CARRIE GIBSON completed her doctoral thesis at the University of Cambridge in 2010.

BRIAN HAMNETT is a research professor at the University of Essex. He is the author of many books, including *A Concise History of Mexico* (2007).

MAURIZIO ISABELLA is a senior lecturer in history at Queen Mary College, University of London. He has been a research fellow at Birkbeck College, London, and a Stanley J. Seeger fellow at Princeton University. He is the author of *Risorgimento in Exile* (2009).

IONA MACINTYRE is a lecturer in Hispanic studies at the University of Edinburgh and the author of *Women and Print Culture in Post-independence Buenos Aires* (2010).

SCARLETT O'PHELAN GODOY is a professor of history at the Pontifica Universidad Católica del Perú and in 2008 and 2009 held the Simón Bolívar Chair of Latin American Studies at the University of Cambridge. She is the author of many books and articles on Peruvian history.

GABRIEL PAQUETTE is an assistant professor of history at Johns Hopkins University. He was previously a junior research fellow in history at Trinity College, Cambridge, and a lecturer at Harvard University. He is the author of *Enlightenment, Governance, and Reform in Spain and Its Empire, 1759–1808* (2008) and the editor of *Enlightened Reform in Southern Europe and Its Atlantic Colonies, c. 1750–1830* (2009).

DAVID ROCK graduated from Cambridge University in 1967 and received a PhD in 1971. He has worked in the Department of History, University of California, Santa Barbara, since 1977, teaching the history of Latin America and specializing in Argentina. He is the author of four books on Argentina, including *Argentina, 1516–1982*. He is currently completing a book on the British community and British influence in Argentina from 1806.

CHRISTOPHER SCHMIDT-NOWARA is a professor of history and Prince of Asturias Chair in Spanish Culture and Civilization at Tufts University. His most recent book is *Slavery, Freedom, and Abolition in Latin America and the Atlantic World* (2011).

JAY SEXTON is a university lecturer in American history at Oxford University. He is the author of *Debtor Diplomacy: Finance and Foreign Relations in the Civil War Era, 1837– 1873* (2005) and *The Monroe Doctrine* (2010).

REUBEN ZAHLER teaches Latin American history at Robert D. Clark Honors College at the University of Oregon. He is the author of *Honor, Law, and Corruption: Liberal Projects in Venezuela, 1780–1850*, forthcoming from the University of Arizona Press.

Index